American Cinema of the 1990s

SCREEN
▪▪▪▪▪▪▪▪▪ AMERICAN CULTURE / AMERICAN CINEMA
DECADES

Each volume in the Screen Decades: American Culture/American Cinema series presents a group of original essays analyzing the impact of cultural issues on the cinema and the impact of the cinema in American society. Because every chapter explores a spectrum of particularly significant motion pictures and the broad range of historical events in one year, readers will gain a continuing sense of the decade as it came to be depicted on movie screens across the continent. The integration of historical and cultural events with the sprawling progression of American cinema illuminates the pervasive themes and the essential movies that define an era. Our series represents one among many possible ways of confronting the past; we hope that these books will offer a better understanding of the connections between American culture and film history.

LESTER D. FRIEDMAN AND MURRAY POMERANCE
SERIES EDITORS

Ina Rae Hark, editor, *American Cinema of the 1930s: Themes and Variations*

Wheeler Winston Dixon, editor, *American Cinema of the 1940s: Themes and Variations*

Murray Pomerance, editor, *American Cinema of the 1950s: Themes and Variations*

Barry Keith Grant, editor, *American Cinema of the 1960s: Themes and Variations*

Lester D. Friedman, editor, *American Cinema of the 1970s: Themes and Variations*

Stephen Prince, editor, *American Cinema of the 1980s: Themes and Variations*

Chris Holmlund, editor, *American Cinema of the 1990s: Themes and Variations*

American Cinema of the
1990s

Themes and Variations

EDITED BY
CHRIS HOLMLUND

RUTGERS UNIVERSITY PRESS
NEW BRUNSWICK, NEW JERSEY, AND LONDON

For my dearest dad

LIBRARY OF CONGRESS CATALOGING-IN-PUBLICATION DATA

American cinema of the 1990s : themes and variations / edited by Chris Holmlund.
    p.   cm.
  Includes bibliographical references and index.
  ISBN 978-0-8135-4365-9 (hardcover : alk. paper)—ISBN 978-0-8135-4366-6
(pbk. : alk. paper)
   1. Motion pictures—United States—History. 2. Motion pictures—United States—Plots,
themes, etc. I. Holmlund, Chris.
  PN1993.5.U6A8579 2008
  791.430973'09049—dc22

                                        2007051728

A British Cataloging-in-Publication record for this book is available from the British
Library.

Visit our Web site: http://rutgerspress.rutgers.edu

Manufactured in the United States of America

CONTENTS

ACKNOWLEDGMENTS

From start to finish this anthology has been a collective endeavor, even though I have held primary responsibility as editor. Together the essayists and I have discussed how best to showcase key films among the many from the 1990s we find intriguing. We have tried to make our individual essays dovetail with each other, in order to provide a more complex picture of the cultural, political, and technological shifts that affected both Hollywood and U.S. independent films during this decade. We have also tried to highlight how and why the U.S. film industry was connected to other film industries and multinational corporations. And we have made a point of mentioning other films and authors we think you will appreciate in our essays as well as in the bibliography.

In these acknowledgments, therefore, I want first and foremost to thank my ten co-authors for their great insights, good humor, and warm support over the several years it has taken to finish this project. I'm so pleased to count you as friends! Many thanks, too—and on behalf of my colleagues as well—to our students. You may not always realize it, but we learn a lot from you. Every essay included here draws on our teaching experiences, not just on our research. My work on the volume has benefited immensely from testing my ideas and those of others in this collection in classes on U.S. cinema of the 1990s and American independent film. Profound thanks to my students in these classes in particular for your feedback and suggestions.

Working with Rutgers University Press has been great: special thanks to Leslie Mitchner and Rachel Friedman for their help, as well as to Marilyn Campbell and Eric Schramm. Thanks, too, to series editors Les Friedman and Murray Pomerance. I really appreciate how readily and cheerfully you pitched in each time I needed you! I also want to thank the skilled staff at the University of Tennessee library and the Motion Picture Academy of Arts and Sciences Margaret Herrick library for help with archival sources. And I thank the Department of Modern Foreign Languages and Literatures, the Office of Research, and the Humanities Initiative at the University of Tennessee for funding the cost of the cover image and indexing.

Last and not least, warm thanks to my friends and family in the United States, Sweden, and elsewhere. Special hugs to Diane Waldman for many wonderful hikes and discussions over the years; "tack så mycket" to Karin

Bark, my oldest friend; "tack också" to my beloved aunt Gunnel Källgren. And Dad: "tusen tack" for being such a terrific father and role model, and for becoming one of my very best friends.

T I M E L I N E

The 1990s

1990

10 JANUARY   Time Inc. and Warner Communications Inc. merge to form TimeWarner.

11 FEBRUARY   Anti-apartheid activist and African National Congress (ANC) leader Nelson Mandela is released from prison in South Africa after being incarcerated for more than twenty-seven years on charges of "terrorism."

15 APRIL   Glamorous, beautiful, and reclusive Swedish screen star Greta Garbo (*Grand Hotel* [1932], *Queen Christina* [1933]) dies.

2 AUGUST   Iraq invades and conquers Kuwait.

7 AUGUST   Operation Desert Shield begins, and the first U.S. forces—F-16 Eagle fighters from Langley Air Force Base, Virginia—arrive in Saudi Arabia.

3 OCTOBER   Germany is reunited for the first time since the end of World War II, less than a year after the fall of the Berlin Wall.

13 NOVEMBER   The first known web page is written.

1991

16 JANUARY   The U.S. government authorizes the use of military force to liberate Kuwait from Iraqi president Saddam Hussein's invasion. Operation Desert Storm and the first Persian Gulf War begin on 17 January with air attacks on Iraq.

3 MARCH   Amateur video captures the beating of taxi driver Rodney King by four Los Angeles police officers after King is stopped for a traffic violation.

13 AUGUST   The Super Nintendo entertainment system is released in the United States.

3 SEPTEMBER   Beloved American director Frank Capra (*Mr. Smith Goes to Washington* [1939], *Meet John Doe* [1941], *It's a Wonderful Life* [1946]) dies.

15 OCTOBER   Clarence Thomas's nomination to the Supreme Court is confirmed after bitter Senate Judiciary Committee hearings in which former employee Anita Hill accuses Thomas of sexual harassment.

25 DECEMBER   Soviet president Mikhail S. Gorbachev resigns, ending seventy-four years of communist reign. On 31 December the Soviet Union officially ceases to exist.

1992

16 JANUARY   El Salvador officials and rebel leaders sign a pact in Mexico City, ending a twelve-year civil war that killed at least 75,000.

29 APRIL   Violence and looting erupt in Los Angeles after four white police officers are acquitted in the beating of Rodney King. Fifty-eight people are killed with nearly $1 billion in damages within five days.

22 MAY   Johnny Carson retires from "The Tonight Show" after thirty years as its host.

24–28 AUGUST   Called the costliest storm ever in the United States, Hurricane Andrew devastates south Florida, Louisiana, and Mississippi.

3 NOVEMBER   Arkansas governor Bill Clinton defeats incumbent President George H.W. Bush and independent H. Ross Perot in the U.S. presidential election.

1993

26 FEBRUARY   Terrorists connected to Osama bin Laden park a van containing a bomb below the North Tower of the World Trade Center. Six people are killed and more than a thousand are injured in the blast.

27 FEBRUARY   Screen legend Lillian Gish (*Birth of a Nation* [1915], *Broken Blossoms* [1919], *Night of the Hunter* [1955], *Whales of August* [1987]) dies.

28 FEBRUARY   The Bureau of Alcohol, Tobacco and Firearms raids the compound of the Branch Davidian religious sect near Waco, Texas, with arrest warrants for cult leader David Koresh on federal firearms violations. An exchange of gunfire results in the deaths of four agents and six Branch Davidians. A fifty-one-day siege by the Federal Bureau of Investigation follows. Attorney General Janet Reno orders a final FBI assault on 19 April. A fire set by sect members destroys the complex, and seventy-six people, including women and children, perish.

25 MARCH   The final episode of the popular television show "Cheers" airs.

30 APRIL   The World Wide Web is born in Geneva at the Organisation européenne pour la recherche nucléaire (CERN).

9 SEPTEMBER   Viacom acquires Paramount Communications for $10 billion.

17 NOVEMBER   After a bruising political battle, the United States ratifies the North American Free Trade Agreement (NAFTA), allowing for free trade between Canada, the United States, and Mexico, thereby forming the largest free-trade area in the world.

1994

7 MARCH   The Supreme Court rules in *Campbell v. Acuff-Rose Music* that parodies of an original work are generally covered by the doctrine of fair use.

7 APRIL   Rwanda erupts in genocidal ethnic strife. In the next 100 days, between 500,000 and 1,000,000 Tutsis are killed by Hutu militants.

12 JUNE   Nicole Brown Simpson and her friend Ronald Goldman are murdered outside O. J. Simpson's home in Los Angeles.

1 SEPTEMBER   The Independent Film Channel (IFC) begins broadcasting unedited, uncensored, and commercial-free independent films to an initial audience of one million satellite and cable viewers.

14 OCTOBER   *Pulp Fiction* is released by Miramax. Aided by the studio's skillful marketing campaign, Quentin Tarantino's provocative writing and directing, and a talented cast, the $8 million movie grosses over $200 million worldwide.

8 NOVEMBER   Led by Georgia congressman Newt Gingrich, soon to become Speaker of the House, the Republicans win control of both houses of Congress for the first time in forty years.

19 DECEMBER   An investigation into the real estate dealings of Bill and Hillary Clinton and their associates in the Whitewater Development Agency in the 1970s and 1980s begins.

1995

19 APRIL   Former U.S. Army veteran Timothy McVeigh and fellow militia member and friend Terry Nichols bomb the Alfred P. Murrah Federal Building in Oklahoma City, killing 168.

15 JULY   Amazon.com is launched.

16 OCTOBER   The Million Man March, led by Nation of Islam leader Louis Farrakhan, brings hundreds of thousands to Washington, D.C. The event is designed to increase black participation in voting and to support welfare, Medicaid, housing programs, student aid programs, and education programs.

4 NOVEMBER   After attending a peace rally, Israeli prime minister Yitzhak Rabin is mortally wounded by a right-wing Israeli fanatic.

21 NOVEMBER   *Toy Story*, the first feature-length film created entirely using computer-generated imagery, is released.

1996

29 FEBRUARY   The Sundance television channel is launched. A film that had opened the 1995 Sundance Festival, Richard Linklater's *Before Sunrise*, is its first major feature.

3 APRIL   The target of the most expensive manhunt in the FBI's history, "Unabomber" suspect Theodore Kaczynski, is arrested for killing three people and injuring twenty-three others in sixteen bombings beginning in the 1970s.

5 JULY   Dolly the sheep is the first mammal to be successfully cloned.

27 JULY   A bomb explodes in Centennial Olympic Park during the Olympic Games in Atlanta. Two people are killed and over one hundred are wounded.

27 SEPTEMBER   Moslem fundamentalist Taliban militia capture Afghanistan's capital, Kabul, and begin imposing Islamic law.

5 NOVEMBER   Bill Clinton and Al Gore are reelected as president and vice-president. The Republicans retain control of Congress.

26 DECEMBER   Six-year-old beauty queen JonBenét Ramsey is found murdered in her family's basement in Boulder, Colorado.

1997

1 JANUARY   U.S. television networks adopt ratings systems for their programming similar to those used for motion pictures.

19 MARCH   The first DVD titles are released in the United States.

1 MAY   Led by Tony Blair, the Labour Party routs the Tories in the British election, ending eighteen years of conservative rule.

30 JUNE   The first book in the *Harry Potter* series by J. K. Rowling is published.

4 JULY   The *Pathfinder* space probe explores the surface of Mars. A webcast of the event is seen by over one million viewers.

31 AUGUST   Diana, Princess of Wales, is killed in a Paris car crash together with her companion and lover Dodi Al-Fayed and their driver Henri Paul. Diana's funeral on 6 September is viewed by over one billion people worldwide.

19 DECEMBER   James Cameron's *Titanic* is released, starring Leonardo di Caprio and Kate Winslet as star-crossed lovers. The film will set all-time box office records, raking in $7 billion in the U.S. and Canada alone.

1998

27 MARCH The first drug treatment for male impotence, Viagra, is approved by the Food and Drug Administration.

14 APRIL The online DVD rental company Netflix begins U.S. operations.

7 AUGUST U.S. embassies in Dar es Salaam, Tanzania, and Nairobi, Kenya, are bombed by terrorists with links to Osama bin Laden, killing 224 people and wounding over 4,500.

7 SEPTEMBER Google is founded as a privately held corporation by two Stanford University Ph.D. students.

19 DECEMBER President Clinton is impeached in the House of Representatives for misleading the American public regarding his relationship with former White House intern Monica Lewinsky.

1999

1 JANUARY A common European currency, the euro, is introduced.

20 FEBRUARY Influential film critic Gene Siskel dies from complications during brain surgery.

20 APRIL Dylan Klebold and Eric Harris kill thirteen and wound two dozen before committing suicide at Colorado's Columbine High School.

7 SEPTEMBER Viacom Inc. announces plans to acquire CBS Corporation for $36 billion in the largest media merger ever.

12 OCTOBER The world population reaches six billion.

20 DECEMBER The Vermont Supreme Court legalizes same-sex unions.

31 DECEMBER Millennium celebrations begin worldwide (although technically the millennium starts in 2001, not 2000). Concerns of serious Y2K computer system failures are rife but little of note happens.

American Cinema of the 1990s

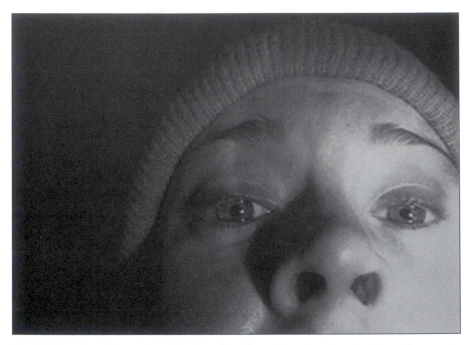

Terrified student filmmaker Heather Donahue (Heather Donahue) confronts the unknown in the woods in *The Blair Witch Project* (Daniel Myrick and Eduardo Sánchez, Artisan Entertainment, 1999). Digital frame enlargement.

INTRODUCTION

Movies and the 1990s

CHRIS HOLMLUND

On the Verge of a New Millennium

The World Wide Web. The Internet. Cell phones. Palm pilots. Chat rooms. Spam. Computer viruses. Netscape. E-Bay. Amazon.com. Google. Yahoo. E-mail. Blogs. Webcasts. CD-Rs. Digital cameras. DVDs. Netflix. Zip drives. Cyber space. iFilm. "See you online." "The server's down." A flood of words and concepts linked to digital technologies changed our lives in the 1990s. A new communications revolution was under way that continues to alter daily life in both developed and developing countries. By 1994, three million people were online; by 1998, one hundred million. At the end of the decade, the number had leapt to almost one billion. Nonetheless, as the 1990s ended, a marked digital divide partitioned the world into those with access to computers and those without. Even in the United States, the richest country in the world, rural areas and the urban poor were underserved.

How to assess a decade most of us remember? The movies and the moods of the 1990s depict a period that most Americans experienced as both peaceful and prosperous. Previously unimaginable technological advances in connectivity were promised everywhere we turned. But new dangers also threatened. The mosquito-borne West Nile virus reached American shores. AIDS and tuberculosis became global health threats. Domestic terrorism appeared more widespread, more frequent, and more deadly than ever before. Periodically there were foreign terrorist attacks on buildings and airplanes. Spam clogged our e-mail programs; computer viruses damaged desktop and laptop computers. On the verge of a new millennium, governments, banks, and businesses spent billions backing up the computer systems that now controlled electricity, water delivery, banking, and more—all for fear of a "Y2K" meltdown that never came.

Scores of big- and small-budget U.S. films testified to our fascination with, and fear of, these digital revolutions. Who can forget *Total Recall*

(1990), *Terminator 2: Judgment Day* (1991), *You've Got Mail* (1998), or *Being John Malkovich* (1999)? Would digital technology replace live actors by resurrecting dead stars? A 1991 Coke ad promised as much: it featured a party that included Louis Armstrong, Humphrey Bogart, Jimmy Cagney, Cary Grant, and Groucho Marx. Would digital technology bring about "the end of cinema as we know it," as the title of Jon Lewis's 2000 anthology provocatively suggested? Was cinema—that is, celluloid—dying, as George Lucas famously suggested in 1999 when he declaimed, "I love film, but it's a 19th century invention" (Romano 37)?

▰▰▰▰▰▰ The American Movie Industry and Production: From Merger Mania to Online Alternatives

The media industries that produce, promote, exhibit, transmit, and showcase movies were profoundly affected by the decade's technological, political, and economic transformations. This is hardly surprising. After all, the conglomerates they all belonged to had helped to create and promote these changes. Film after film announced media breakthroughs and became marketing milestones. *Dick Tracy* (1990) was the first 35 mm feature film with a digital sound track. That same year, testifying to the longevity of hit movies, *Top Gun* (1986) became the first VHS title to ship more than one million copies. *Batman Returns* (1992) introduced the six-channel stereo sound system that is now industry standard: Dolby Digital. With computer graphics used for the first time to create "real" animals, *Jurassic Park* (1993) savored colossal box office success: thanks to global interest and product tie-ins, it grossed $1 *billion* worldwide. George Lucas's digitally shot prequel, *Star Wars: Episode I—The Phantom Menace* (1999) inaugurated digital theatrical screenings on four U.S. screens. On a completely different scale, yet also a portent of things to come, was Eduardo Sanchez and Daniel Myrick's low-budget independent horror film *The Blair Witch Project* (1999). With no stars and no big special effects, but with savvy online promotion and marketing, *Blair Witch* was the most profitable (in terms of percentage gross) film of all time, reeling in $248 million on a budget of $35,000.[1]

What's behind these signposts? Although *Blair Witch* and other "indie" success stories testify to the increasing importance of economies of scale within the film industry, they were exceptions. The Big Six—Disney, Warner Bros., Sony, Twentieth Century Fox, Universal, and Paramount—continued to dominate moviemaking, consolidating and extending their influence both horizontally and vertically throughout the decade. By 1999 all were part of bigger conglomerates, each possessing connections to some combination of broadcast television, cable networks, the recording industry, video and DVD rentals and sales, and more. Several also exerted control over television news coverage.[2] What would this centralization mean for freedom of information and expression? The Big Six were oligopolies, controlling and channeling from a huge number of buyers. Although independent films, documentaries, and fiction shorts offered alternatives, how many people saw them?

Topping the list of Big Six companies in 1999 was Walt Disney, headquartered in Burbank, California. Everyone knows the Disney brand: it's stamped all over theme parks, merchandise, and movies. By the end of the decade, Disney owned several film- and television-related divisions, among them Hollywood Pictures, Buena Vista Pictures Distribution and Home Video, and Walt Disney TV. (It closed Touchstone Pictures in 1998.) Add to this empire the lucrative lifelong loyalty of Disney viewers. Like all Big Six studios, Disney expanded during the 1990s. In 1993, the company acquired Miramax. In 1996 it bought ABC television and radio. And by decade's end Disney also owned and operated several ABC stations, the ESPN sports networks, the Arts & Entertainment (A&E) television network, the History Channel (partially), the Disney Channel, and Lifetime. It also had music holdings (Hollywood Records). And that's just a partial list.

A second Big Six company, Warner Bros., had become part of New York–based TimeWarner in 1993. In 1996 TimeWarner bought Turner Broadcasting and New Line, thereby ensuring it would have cable "downstream" channels and advertising venues. (Turner Broadcasting housed CNN and TNT.) Add to that HBO, Cinemax, Turner Classic Movies, Warner Home Video, music, magazine and other publishing holdings, the Six Flags theme parks, D.C. Comics, the Atlanta Hawks basketball team, and the Atlanta Braves baseball team. Talk about diversifying with an eye to what interested the nation!

Sony Pictures, allied with Columbia Pictures, Tri-Star, and other film and television companies, and owned by Tokyo-based electronics giant Sony Corporation, constituted a third Big Six company. Sony also owned Epic Records, Sony Music International, and other music companies, and a vast array of electronic and electrical equipment manufacturing firms. Thinking globally, Sony was a partner in the Hispanic Telemundo broadcast group. Within the United States, Sony controlled broadcast TV stations in various cities. In 1997, the corporation made trade headlines when, with Seagram, it merged the Sony Loews Theaters into Loews. As a result, Sony and Seagram could ensure exhibition for their various film and TV production companies when the 1990s ended. Only Paramount's owner, Viacom, could do the same.

By 1999 a fourth Big Six company, Twentieth Century Fox, owned Fox television, certain stations, Fox Video, Sky Channel satellite in Europe, STAR TV in Asia, the Los Angeles Dodgers, and many widely read newspapers. News Corporation was Twentieth Century Fox's parent company, with Rupert Murdoch at the helm managing all this (and more) from Sydney, Australia. For Murdoch and News Corp., TV and print journalism were more important than film. All over North America we tuned in each week to Fox TV's "The Simpsons," "The X-Files," and NFL football programming.

The Seagram Company owned a fifth Big Six studio, Universal Pictures, with headquarters in Montreal. Seagram had part ownership in the Home Shopping Network and was in the process of creating the USA cable network. In addition to substantial liquor and beverage companies, Seagram boasted big music holdings, owning MCA, Decca, Motown, and others. It also owned the Sony Cineplex movie theater chain (in partnership with Sony Entertainment) and the Universal Studios theme park. And in 1997 Seagram bought independent film production company October Films.

Last: Paramount Pictures. New York–based Viacom bought Paramount in 1993. By 1999, Viacom owned several popular cable TV shows, including MTV, Nickelodeon, Showtime, the Movie Channel, and Comedy Central. In 1999 it bought CBS. It also owned and operated broadcast TV stations in several larger cities, smaller movie theater chains at home and abroad, video production and distribution companies, Blockbuster Music and Famous Music, and publishing houses like Simon & Schuster, Prentice-Hall, and Macmillan. Crucially, it owned the world's largest video retail and rental chain, Blockbuster Entertainment (Allen 37). Like Disney and Warner Bros., moreover, Viacom operated a chain of amusement parks.

Every Big Six company employed a different strategy as the decade proceeded. All these economic tactics represented attempts to negotiate rising costs (Gomery, "Film Industry" 366). Star salaries were rising, thanks to powerful agents. Top talent like Sylvester Stallone, Tom Cruise, Arnold Schwarzenegger, Mel Gibson, and Julia Roberts earned $15–$20 million per picture. Increasingly, they also garnered a share of the profits.[3] Similarly, top directors like James Cameron and Steven Spielberg also commanded hefty fees and a share of the profits. Writers were typically paid much less, but a few bankrolled $1 million or more per film. Two of the highest paid were Joe Eszterhas, who earned $3 million for *Basic Instinct* (1992), and Shane Black, who received $4 million for *The Long Kiss Goodnight* (1996). More than any other budget item, however, it was the ballooning cost of special effects that sent 1990s budgets spiraling upward. By 1999, the average cost of a movie had reached $60 million for the first negative and $80 million once marketing and publicity were included (Gomery, "Film Industry" 267, 361). Blockbusters like *Armageddon* (1998) and *Titanic* (1997) had much higher price tags.[4] By the end of the decade, a $100 million film needed to earn $250 worldwide just to break even (Bordwell and Thompson 683).

So why would anyone sink their money into a movie when they have always been notoriously risky investments? Thanks to their global connections, the Big Six could reduce risk by guaranteeing that their films would be distributed in theaters around the world and seen in downstream markets that they also controlled.[5] Wherever you looked, Hollywood ruled. It's no coincidence that the prime organization representing Big Six interests, the Motion Picture Association of America (the MPAA), with Jack Valenti at its head, boasted branches in sixty nations. It's also no coincidence that international co-productions increasingly shared the costs of moviemaking. By decade's close, France's Canal + and Australia's Village Roadshow regularly helped the Big Six co-produce films. Films were also frequently shot abroad to save money and sidestep laws governing stunt safety. Among the most popular locations for these "runaway productions" were Canada, Russia, Eastern Europe, Australia, and New Zealand. And the studios found other ways to make a buck as well. In 1996, Disney signed a ten-year contract with McDonald's: the company knew from experience that offering product tie-ins (e.g., bundling movie action figures with burgers) could offer substantial profits. Scripts were routinely vetted as companies looked for sequences that could be the source of new theme park rides: *Backdraft* (1991), *Terminator 2*, and *Jurassic Park* all proved highly successful. Music scores and songs could net studios and their parent companies additional income, too. Presold properties based on popular novels, comic strips, and Broadway hits provided other safety nets. Some films, *Mortal Kombat* (1995) among them, were based on popular video games.

But the Big Six were not the only Hollywood players. In 1994, for the first time in decades, a brand new Hollywood studio emerged: DreamWorks SKG. Created by industry insiders director-producer Steven Spielberg, ex-Disney executive producer Jeffrey Katzenberg, and film producer/music industry mogul David Geffen, DreamWorks produced several big hits, among them *Deep Impact, Saving Private Ryan, Antz* (all 1998), and *American Beauty* (1999). By the end of the decade DreamWorks was so successful that it competed with studio stalwart MGM/UA for seventh place.[6]

At the beginning of the 1990s, powerful "mini-majors" like Castle Rock, Morgan Creek, Imagine Entertainment, New Line, and Miramax also competed with the majors. But they were at best second-tier players. By mid-decade all found themselves affiliated with a Big Six studio. Other mini-majors disappeared in the 1990s: Orion filed for bankruptcy in 1991, and although Carolco, partnered with Tri-Star, had three big hits with *Total Recall*, *Terminator 2*, and *Basic Instinct*, it too, went under when the expensive swashbuckler *Cutthroat Island* (1995) tanked at the box office.

Most influential among the mini-majors were New Line and Miramax. Begun in the late 1960s as a nontheatrical distributor catering to art and exploitation-oriented college audiences, New Line skillfully added sexploitation, gay films, rock documentaries, and "midnight specials" to reach niche markets the majors ignored. In the 1990s, the company struck gold with the wildly successful *Ninja Turtles* series and franchise: the first film grossed a whopping $135 million domestically in 1990 alone. That same year, New Line created its own "indie arm," Fine Line, which became responsible for offbeat art films like *My Own Private Idaho* (1991) and *The Player* (1992) (Holmlund, "Introduction" 6–7; Wyatt, "Formation" 76–78). New Line's success captured Ted Turner's attention: he bought it in 1993. When Turner Broadcasting Corporation merged with TimeWarner, New Line and Fine Line joined the Warner Bros. family.

The Weinstein brothers' company, Miramax, also moved mainstream with a vengeance in the 1990s. In 1993, Miramax launched a genre-film oriented subdivision, Dimension Pictures. That same year the company became the first mini-major to be purchased by a major, Disney. Known for aggressive marketing around controversy—recall the company's skillful promotion to U.S. audiences of *The Crying Game* (1992) as a film more about sexual mystery than politics—Miramax captured everyone's attention with the phenomenal success of Quentin Tarantino's *Pulp Fiction* (1994). Winning the *Palme d'Or* at Cannes and nominated for seven Academy Awards, including Best Picture and Best Director, *Pulp Fiction* grossed more than $100 million in U.S. theaters and more than $200 million worldwide. No wonder Tarantino imitators sprang up everywhere. During the decade, Miramax could brag about lots of other success stories, too, among them *Sling Blade* (1996), *Good Will Hunting* (1997), *The Talented Mr. Ripley* (1999), and foreign imports such as *Like Water for Chocolate* (1993), *The Piano* (1993), *Il Postino* (1995), and *Life Is Beautiful* (1997) (Holmlund, "Introduction" 7; Wyatt, "Formation" 79–84).

From the point of view of the majors—"production/distribution companies with access to extensive financing, usually from abroad" (Bordwell and Thompson 680)—control of these "mini-majors" made sense. The Big Six also appreciated the fact that in the 1990s these companies operated more efficiently than earlier mini-majors had done. Typically they employed skeletal staffs. They concentrated on film and didn't branch out to TV. They fielded a few high-quality productions per year. They raised financing with an eye to foreign markets. And they typically distributed their films through the majors (Balio, "Major Presence" 64). As a result, by decade's end every Big Six studio had its own "classics" or art division to produce and market (quasi-) independent films. Besides ex-mini-majors like New Line and Miramax, there were also Fox Searchlight, Sony Picture Classics, and Paramount Classics. All were part of larger studios.

Yet although the majors and (for a time also certain mini-majors) dominated the industry, a few stand-alone independent production/distribution companies remained. Chief for the future among hybrid companies, count Artisan and Lion's Gate. Both functioned mainly as distributors in the 1990s: Artisan brought us *Glengarry Glen Ross* and *Bob Roberts* (both 1992), *Breaking the Waves* and *Trees Lounge* (both 1996), *π* (1998), *The Blair Witch Project*, and more, while Lion's Gate made it possible to see *Kids* (1995), *Affliction,* and *Eve's Bayou* (both 1997) in theaters. Originally a distribution company founded in 1991, Good Machine had so many hits that in 1997 it engineered a first-look deal with Twentieth Century Fox. Killer Films, with Christine Vachon at its head, produced and sold several important independent films during the 1990s as well, among them Todd Haynes's *Poison* (1991) and *Safe* (1995) and Mary Harron's *I Shot Andy Warhol* (1996).[7] And there were lots of smaller independent production companies: of the roughly 460 theatrical releases each year, half were made by independents.

On the outer margins of independent production, there lay companies that proved harbingers of how media would function in the near future. These companies often mocked notions of propriety and ran circles around the MPAA censors. Consider Atom Films.com, launched online in 1999. It featured individually produced short films, many of which parodied Hollywood hits like The *Phantom Menace* and *The Blair Witch Project*. Downloads from Atom Films and other online companies were made possible by faster computers and by streaming video players like QuickTime, Real Video, and Windows Media Player (Klinger 195–96). A few feature-length films premiered simultaneously on iFilm and in theaters: Ed Vilga's film noir *Dead Broke* (1999) is an example. But production and marketing are always just one part of the film industry puzzle. You also have to think about distribution and exhibition. The 1990s brought new answers here, too.

The American Movie Industry, Distribution and Exhibition: From the Multiplex to the Art House to Your House

The big studios typically distributed their blockbuster films in wide release, using saturation booking. Megapics opened everywhere, showing on 2,000 to 3,000 screens at a time. Summers became the hot time to release a movie, with roughly half of all yearly box office monies coming in from films that reached theaters from June to August. In contrast, the brass ring for independently produced films involved pickup by a big or mid-size distributor that could provide national (often art-house) release on maybe 200 screens at a time. (This was also the kind of release accorded most foreign films shown in the United States.)

For the Big Six, downstream viewing was partially assured by their network and cable TV holdings. Cognizant of cable TV penetration (74 percent of U.S. homes subscribed to cable at the end of the decade ["American Cultural History"]), the Big Six and their parent companies regularly cut deals with cable and satellite companies they did not own. Release typically followed a preset, sequential pattern. First came theatrical distribution, then VHS release, pay-per-view television, premium cable TV, and, last, basic cable and broadcast TV. Smaller distributors like Good Machine or Strand Releasing (the latter specializing in gay films) instead booked their films into city art theaters that specialized in showing independent and foreign films to niche audiences. They hoped that "buzz" would build, thanks to critical praise and word of mouth, so that they could subsequently distribute their films in smaller cities.

Censorship was a major concern to producers and distributors of all sizes, but it was especially troubling for independents. A new MPAA category, NC-17, replaced the earlier X rating in 1991, prompted by controversy over *Henry & June* (1990). Because NC-17 prevented any mall screenings, all newspaper advertising, and all video pickups by the powerful Blockbuster video rental chain, smaller companies like Killer Films usually preferred to cut questionable material to avoid the rating. They had to be sure their films would be seen.

Everyone jockeyed for Oscar nominations, for which fall and winter releases were especially important. Success on festival circuits was crucial, with Sundance and Toronto the most important places for getting an independent film picked up for distribution.[8] Smaller independent films benefited enormously from two new cable TV channels devoted to independent film: the Independent Film Channel (launched in 1994) and the Sundance

Channel (1996). Both premiered independent films that had been shown at festivals yet had limited or no theatrical release. Both also offered original programming and presented short films, documentaries, and the occasional classic (Eberwein 270).

The combination of all these markets meant that, if a distributor was lucky, profits could be huge. Paramount's *Titanic* set new records, ultimately earning $7 billion in the United States and Canada alone (Gomery, "Film Industry" 360). Each year the top ten films routinely grossed between $135 and $220 million each at the U.S. box office (Bordwell and Thompson 683). (Total box office often spans more than a single year, however, especially for Academy Award winners or films released late in the season.) The 1990s also saw salient shifts in where profits originated. From 1994 on, the majors consistently earned more in rental income overseas than they did at home. By the mid-1990s, domestic and foreign video sales and rentals matched domestic box office (Gomery, "Film Industry" 360).

But the majority of films never saw theatrical release in the 1990s; instead they played festival circuits, were screened on cable, or went straight to video. Some companies, such as New Yorker Films, Women Make Movies, Frameline, California Newsreel, and Third World Newsreel, specialized in distributing art films, gay/lesbian/queer films, films by women, and films by "Third World" makers to festivals and universities. Other distributors, among them Canyon Film, Video Data Bank, and Electronic Arts Intermix, specialized in avant-garde and experimental film and video. The popularity of bootleg copies worried everyone, although the bigger studios clearly had more to lose by failing to control downstream markets. They introduced and won legislation to prevent illegal duplication of VHS tapes, and they coded their video releases so that copying would be difficult. Digital piracy loomed as a hot-button issue for the future. In the 1990s, however, the majors' failure to agree on digital sound and image systems explained in large part why digital rollout in theaters didn't happen.

Such issues take us straight into a discussion of 1990s exhibition. Independent chains dominated U.S. theatrical exhibition throughout the decade. Figures for 1998 showed Regal Cinema Companies leading the field, with nearly twice as many screens (5,347) as its closest rivals: Carmike (2,720), Cineplex (2,600), and AMC Entertainment (2,117) (Gomery, "Film Industry" 399). Lagging further behind were the studio-affiliated Loews Cineplex and National Amusements chains. To attract audiences, many of these exhibition chains built megaplexes that housed multiple screens under a single roof. Offering new creature comforts like stadium seating, soft-drink holders, and digital sound, megaplexes became immensely popular both in the United States and abroad. Thanks in no small part to their success, the global market skyrocketed in the 1990s, reaching over $5 billion in worldwide rentals by mid-decade, even after sharing profits with exhibitors (Gomery, "Film Industry" 376).

Some "art-house miniplexes," such as the Angelika Film Centers in Houston, Dallas, and New York, specialized in showing art, foreign, and independent films "in conditions of previously undreamt-of comfort" (Negra, "Queen" 76). At the beginning of the decade, cities and certain smaller communities also housed independent art cinemas with one, two, or three screens. Unfortunately, many of these had disappeared by 1999. Rising rents and competition from the megaplexes were only partially responsible.

Despite the setbacks for foreign, art, and/or independent films, however, by the end of the decade theatrical exhibition was doing so well that the United States housed a staggering 38,000 screens (Bordwell and Thompson 687). Domestic attendance climbed: U.S. admissions rose from $5.02 billion in 1990 to $7.45 billion in 1999.[9] Teenagers were the most avid moviegoers, but college-educated attendees also figured significantly at the box office.

This isn't to say that we usually saw movies in theaters. On the contrary, movies were rapidly becoming things we watched at home using our videocassette recorders (VCRs). By the end of the decade, VCRs were so popular that nine out of ten U.S. households owned at least one, making VCR penetration second only to that of TV (Gomery, "Film Industry" 411). Most households could afford both: televisions cost $200–$750, while VCRs cost $150–$550.

Introduced in 1997 at $300–$500 apiece, DVD players quickly grew in popularity as well (Oxoby 237). They offered better-quality images, often included commentary and other extras, and took up less space than VHS tapes.[10] A final 1990s breakthrough came in 1999 when TiVo introduced a personal video recorder that stored programs and movies digitally. Home theaters featuring large screens grew in popularity, making it easy to see movies again and again. Small wonder, then, that top stars, key directors, blockbusters, and cult hits were discussed everywhere, at dinner tables, at work, in chat rooms, on blogs. We grew used to seeing our favorites repeatedly, in between daily doses of sports, weather, and—for younger viewers especially—video games.

More occasionally we were aware of political events and cultural, economic, and demographic trends. Yet because all these affect the media industry in general and sometimes directly influence individual films and their marketing and reception, too, let's turn to our next topic.

American Politics and Culture: Of Peace and War, Sex and Violence

A series of earth-shaking political transformations accompanied these corporate shifts and technological tidal waves. The decade began auspiciously on the world stage. In 1990, following the fall of the Berlin Wall the year before and a tumbling of Soviet bloc dominoes thereafter, East and West Germany were officially reunited. The same year white minority rule ended in South Africa, and Chile elected a civilian to the presidency, ending nearly two decades of a U.S.-backed military dictatorship. The following year the U.S.S.R. formally dissolved, leaving the United States as the world's only superpower. By the end of the decade, Eastern Europe had undergone a radical makeover that was both good and bad. On the good side, Poland held its first free parliamentary elections in decades in 1991. Former Soviet republics gained independence. Czechoslovakia divided in 1993 without problem. But—the bad side—Yugoslavia slid into civil war, and from 1996 onward ethnic strife and genocide pervaded Bosnia to the point where in 1999 NATO finally intervened with air strikes in an effort to halt the killing. Ominously, the Middle East also continued to be a hot spot. Iraq invaded Kuwait and, notwithstanding baby steps toward peace, Israelis and Palestinians could not resolve their conflict.

Mercifully for Americans, the United States engaged in no big foreign wars over the course of the decade. But confident of the U.S.'s "democratic" mission and, as always, eager to protect its economic and strategic interests, both of the decade's presidents at various points exercised America's military muscle. One-term Republican president George H. W. Bush intervened in Panama, Iraq and Kuwait, and Somalia. Two-term Democratic president Bill Clinton sent troops to Haiti and Bosnia. But the United States looked away as extremist Hutu groups in Rwanda massacred anywhere from 500,000 to 1,000,000 Tutsis in 1994. This led many to charge that U.S. foreign policy was fundamentally racist.

Clinton, the man from Hope (Arkansas), defeated Bush in the 1992 election in large part because of a recession and the president's agreement to a tax increase despite his 1988 "Read my lips, no new taxes!" campaign promise. "It's the economy, stupid" was the Clinton campaign's mantra to remind everyone what the election was supposed to be about. Running a distant third in the November election, Texas billionaire H. Ross Perot nevertheless far exceeded the vote share of every third-party candidate since Teddy Roosevelt by tapping into America's exasperation with politics as usual. The desire to avoid "Beltway insiders" was—and would continue to be—strong.

As the decade wore on, Americans divided bitterly once again. Race was often responsible, with Los Angeles erupting in riots in 1992 over the acquittal of four white policemen who had viciously beaten a black motorist, Rodney King, for speeding and running a red light. Unbeknownst to the cops, a bystander had captured the incident on videotape. Soon afterward, the media began airing the assault endlessly, and Americans watched in shock. But when the officers were acquitted and nearly a week of rioting resulted, it was King himself who asked in heartfelt horror, "People, I just want to say, you know, can we all get along?" With thousands in the streets, as many as 2,000 injured, and between $800 million and $1 billion in damages, the L.A. riots became the largest racial protest of the century.

The Republican-led "culture wars" fueled national divisions. In 1994 Newt Gingrich, the House Republican whip, stoked frustration with the failures of the Clinton administration's first two years by appealing to hot-button conservative issues such as gay rights, gun control, multiculturalism, and a host of Religious Right favorites such as obscenity in the media and, as always, abortion. With a national campaign touting its "Contract with America," the Gingrich-led Republicans gained control of both the House and the Senate for the first time in forty years. But Republican control of Congress did not resolve the nation's ills, let alone end gridlock in Washington. With the Congress and White House unable to agree on a budget, the government was forced to shut down twice in 1995, to the wide disapproval of Americans. To secure a second term, Clinton moved toward the center, abandoning a proposed plan for universal health care and backpedaling on his earlier support for gay rights.

As the decade drew to a close, things got nastier. A wide-ranging, five-year investigation into the first couple's financial dealings in Arkansas regarding an obscure land deal eventually focused on Bill Clinton's sexual peccadilloes. Although Clinton at first denied having had "sexual relations with that woman," it became obvious that he had indeed engaged in an extramarital affair with White House intern Monica Lewinsky. Pouncing upon a special prosecutor's finding that Clinton had evidently lied under oath regarding the affair, Republicans in the House gleefully turned up the heat into full-scale impeachment proceedings. Even after their party lost seats in the midterm election of 1998, largely due to voter disapproval of congressional priorities, House Republicans voted to impeach Clinton, though his acquittal in the Senate was never in doubt. Meanwhile, Europeans wondered why we fussed so much about a political leader's private life. By the end of the decade, Americans had to admit that the personal seemed to have become political with a vengeance.

Violence, sex, and disasters drove the media, with emphasis increasingly on personalities rather than policies. Ghoulish amounts of television and print coverage were accorded serial killers Aileen Wuornos, John Wayne Gacy, and Jeffrey Dahmer. The unexpected deaths of John F. Kennedy Jr. (in a small plane crash) and Princess Diana (in a car crash) floored millions around the world. For hours, journalists in helicopters tracked O. J. Simpson's white Ford Bronco as the former football star fled from police to avoid arrest for the murder of wife Nicole Simpson and her friend Ronald Goldman. CNN dominated news coverage throughout the first Gulf War. Charges of pop singer Michael Jackson molesting children, Olympic figure skater Tonya Harding's hammer attack on competitor Nancy Kerrigan's knee, the Clarence Thomas–Anita Hill hearings, and the unsolved murder of six-year-old beauty queen JonBenét Ramsey all received far more than the fifteen seconds of fame Andy Warhol had predicted everyone would enjoy.

Tragedies involving U.S. citizens at home or abroad were the focus of month-long media investigations and intense political debates. Seventy-six people died in the 1993 FBI siege of the Branch Davidian complex near Waco, Texas; six other sect members and four ATF agents died earlier in an ATF raid. In 1995 former Army soldier and security guard Timothy McVeigh and friend Terry Nichols bombed the Oklahoma City federal courthouse: 168 died and more than 800 others were wounded. Thirty-eight members of the Heaven's Gate cult committed suicide in California in 1997. Even today, the 1999 school shootings near Littleton, Colorado, count as the fourth worst school disaster in history: twelve students and one faculty member were killed and twenty-four other students wounded before the two teenage assailants killed themselves. Natural disasters also made news, among them 1992's Hurricane Andrew and 1998's Hurricane Mitch. Andrew trashed Florida and Louisiana and was the second costliest natural disaster in U.S. history to that time. Mitch ravaged Central America and caused nearly 11,000 deaths.

But most Americans are more interested in sports and entertainment than politics and current events. Baseball fans like my brother hated the strike that forced the cancellation of the World Series in 1994, and home runs proliferated as never before. Tiger Woods emerged as the world's leading golfer, Michael Jordan dominated the NBA, NASCAR sped to unprecedented popularity, the Dallas Cowboys won three Super Bowls, and the Kentucky Wildcats and Tennessee Volunteers were the decade's most successful teams in men and women's college basketball. On television, actors came to seem part of our families: we fell in love with the cast and characters of "Cheers," "Seinfeld," "E.R.," "Friends," "The Simpsons," and "Frasier." For those who wanted investigative, if "soft," journalism there was still "60 Minutes." Audiences interested in "reality TV" flocked to "Cops" and MTV's "The Real World." A TV milestone—and a point both of gay pride and of anti-gay protest—occurred when Ellen DeGeneres's character on "Ellen" came out on network TV. The success of "Will and Grace" proved that 1990s audiences were gradually warming to out gay characters. And the decade also brought us "Buffy the Vampire Slayer" and "South Park": both had enormous followings. Yet on the TV downside, how about all those infomercials on cable TV? And—ugh!—just as we were sitting down to watch TV and/or eat dinner: all those obnoxious telemarketing calls! By the end of the decade there were nearly four million people working for roughly one thousand telemarketing companies. Annual sales reached $650 billion (Oxoby 51).

Many (older) Americans still read books and daily newspapers, although several smaller newspapers disappeared and larger newspapers merged with media conglomerates. Amazon.com and chain bookstores like Borders and Barnes and Noble drove smaller bookstores out of business. Top-selling novels included the first three titles in the *Harry Potter* series, and mysteries by Tony Hillerman, Sara Paretsky, and Sue Grafton (books G through O of Grafton's alphabetical series were published this decade). Other best sellers included Stephen King's *Dolores Claiborne* and *Insomnia*; Danielle Steel's *Mirror Image, The Long Road Home,* and *Five Days in Paris*; Robert Ludlum's *The Bourne Ultimatum*; Anne Rice's *The Witching Hour*; John Grisham's *The Client, The Rainmaker,* and *The Pelican Brief*; Michael Crichton's *The Lost World: Jurassic Park* and *Timeline*; Terry McMillan's *Waiting to Exhale*; and Robert James Waller's *The Bridges of Madison County*. (Note how many became hit movies.) Nonfiction fans relished Madonna's controversial coffee table book, *Sex,* and lapped up radio conservative Rush Limbaugh and shock jock's Howard Stern's vituperative rants. Testifying to how hard it was to begin and maintain a relationship at the end of the century, John Gray's *Men Are from Mars, Women Are from Venus* topped nonfiction bestseller lists three years in a row.

Hit Broadway shows like *Angels in America, Oleanna,* and *The Vagina Monologues* took America's cultural pulse, while musicals like *Rent* and *The*

Lion King garnered huge audiences. (The latter inaugurated a new trend, becoming a stage play *after* being a successful movie.) The Cirque du Soleil's inventive act moved to Las Vegas. Radio increasingly targeted niche audiences. Country music garnered new fans thanks to singers like Garth Brooks, Dwight Yoakum, and the Dixie Chicks. Hip-hop and rap spoke to global audiences and influenced fashion, too. By the end of the 1990s, few could ignore Latin pop: Ricky Martin and Selena rocked. And while Brazil's macarena dance craze was sweeping the United States, even Vice President Al Gore tried to prove he wasn't so humorless by offering his own version at the 1996 Democratic National Convention in which he stood completely still.

As globalization proceeded apace under President Clinton, the economy boomed. Fads like Beanie Babies, Tickle Me Elmo dolls, body piercing, tattoos, and Pokemon testified to the amount of disposal income available. Superstores shot up, with Wal-Mart in the lead. Designers like Liz Claiborne, DKNY, and Tommy Hilfiger enjoyed enormous success. New fabrics like tencel and other microfibers appeared. In 1991 the Dow Jones average surpassed 3,000 for the first time. By 1999, it had topped 10,000. Despite opposition from labor and other groups, in 1994 Clinton signed the North American Free Trade Agreement (NAFTA), establishing a free-trade bloc among the United States, Mexico, and Canada, and the General Agreement on Tariffs and Trade (GATT). (Later GATT would evolve into the World Trade Organization.)

The U.S. population increased by thirty million thanks to a surge in the birth rate and to a rise in the number of immigrants, now coming primarily from Latin America. By the end of the decade, roughly 12 percent of the total population was foreign-born; in 1990, the figure had been more like 9 percent. But did 1990s movies recognize these new audiences? Which genres, stars, and directors were popular with audiences and critics? What aesthetic impact did digital shooting and composition have?

The Movies: Genres, Stars, and Auteurs

Action—broadly defined to include cop films, spy movies, certain epic science fiction films, gangster extravaganzas, martial arts movies, and more—was without question the most popular 1990s genre. Increasing numbers of female viewers joined male viewers, delighting in the explosions, the special effects, the stunts, the buff male and female bodies. Zany comedian Mike Myers imitated and broke action rules in *Austin Powers: International Man of Mystery* (1997) and *Austin Powers: The Spy Who*

Edward Lewis (Richard Gere) finds beautiful prostitute Vivian Ward (Julia Roberts) to be the perfect escort in *Pretty Woman* (Garry Marshall, Buena Vista Pictures, 1990). Digital frame enlargement.

Shagged Me (1999). (In the latter, in one fell swoop, he gleefully sends up both blaxploitation movies and spy/caper films.) Thanks to the success of their action films, producers like Joel Silver, Jon Peter, Don Simpson, and Jerry Bruckheimer became immensely powerful in Hollywood.

Other popular genres included horror films, romantic comedies, and neo-noirs. Relatively inexpensive slasher films like *I Know What You Did Last Summer* (1997) and the *Scream* franchise (1996 and 1997) ripped records. *Blair Witch*, of course, had even greater success. Predictably, there were new entries in the endless *Nightmare on Elm Street* series starring the oh-so-creepy Freddy Krueger (Robert Englund). Toward the end of the decade supernatural horror pictures made a comeback. Millions of Americans gleefully got goose bumps as a terrified Haley Joel Osment admitted, "I see dead people" to kindly psychiatrist Bruce Willis in *The Sixth Sense*, number two at the 1999 box office.

The decade's biggest female star, Julia Roberts, had smash hits with romantic comedies like *Pretty Woman* (1990), *My Best Friend's Wedding* (1997), and *Runaway Bride* (1999). The box office success of Whoopi Goldberg in *Ghost* (1990), Meg Ryan and Tom Hanks in *You've Got Mail*, and Jack Nicholson and Helen Hunt in *As Good As It Gets* (1997) testified to renewed interest in romance. Raunchy sex farces like *There's Something about Mary* (1998) and *American Pie* (1999) raked in profits, too. At the opposite end of the spectrum were odder couples. Jodie Foster, as detective Clarice Starling, sidled up to Anthony Hopkins's threatening-even-when-caged cannibal, Hannibal Lecter, in *The Silence of the Lambs* (1991). Gina Gershon and Jennifer Tilly played deadly lesbian lovers in independent favorite *Bound* (1996). Those who relished tracking serial killers thrilled to David Fincher's *Se7en* (1995). There were several intriguing neo-noirs, among them John Dahl's *Red Rock West* (1992) and Bryan Singer's *The Usual Suspects* (1995). And who can forget Tim Burton's edgy independent, *Ed Wood* (1994), starring Johnny Depp as the cross-dressing director of *Plan 9 from Outer Space*?

Westerns and musicals languished as endless sequels and multiple remakes in other genres proliferated. Studios tried to cash in on bankable stars and familiar titles as the decade progressed. We got *Sister Act* (1990) and *Sister Act II* (1992), both featuring Whoopi Goldberg as an irreverent singing nun. There were three *Home Alone* films (1990, 1992, 1997), all showcasing child star Macaulay Culkin. *Wayne's World* (1992) and *Wayne's World 2* (1993) had us all repeating, with Mike Myers and Dana Carvey, "Party on, dude!" Older viewers guffawed at Jack Lemmon and Walter Matthau's lines, delivery, and antics in *Grumpy Old Men* (1993) and *Grumpier Old Men* (1995). Action franchises were ubiquitous. Building on 1980s hits were *Lethal Weapon 3* (1992) and *Lethal Weapon 4* (1998), *Die Hard 2* (1990) and *Die Hard with a Vengeance* (1995), *Terminator 2* (1992), *Beverly Hills Cop III* (1994), and more. Live action and animated children's films lived on eternally, it seemed, as well. There were no fewer than three *Free Willy*'s (1993, 1995, 1997), two *Toy Story*'s (1995 and 1999), and three *Teenage Mutant Ninja Turtle*'s (1990, 1991, 1993). Fueled by right-wing trumpeting of "family values" and our newfound love of CGI (computer generated imagery) effects, family friendly films did very well in the 1990s. Disney had several hits, including *Beauty and the Beast* (1991), *Aladdin* (1992), and *The Lion King* (1994). From 1995 on, CGI features like *Toy Story* became tremendously popular.

Tom Cruise was the decade's biggest box office draw, scoring in *A Few Good Men* (1992), *The Firm* (1993), *Mission: Impossible*, and *Jerry Maguire* (both 1996). Together with Tom Hanks (whose variations on the boy-next-door many found adorable), Cruise was one of the decade's most dependable male stars. Many of today's superstars made their first $100 million movie in the 1990s, among them Sean Connery, Bruce Willis, Matt Damon, Nicolas Cage, and Leonardo DiCaprio. Comedians Jim Carrey and Robin Williams were consistently popular. Both Cruise and Mel Gibson launched their own highly lucrative production companies. For *Mission Impossible,* for example, Cruise earned $20 million for his performance and, as producer, received 25 percent of the gross (Allen 124).

Every popular 1990s male star figured in one or more action films. Tellingly, however, with the exception of Will Smith in *Independence Day* (1996), all the biggest 1990s action stars were—as usual—white.[11] Among them, Arnold Schwarzenegger shone biggest, brightest, and bulkiest. Also memorable were Sylvester Stallone in *Cliffhanger* and Harrison Ford in *The Fugitive* (both 1993), Sean Connery in *The Hunt for Red October* (1990) and—with Nicolas Cage—*The Rock* (1996), and Mel Gibson in *Braveheart* (1995) and *Payback* (1999). By decade's end, the aging Schwarzenegger and Stallone looked ragged, yet they continued to make films despite box office and critical flops. In their stead, offering a less beefy look and a blank performance style, laconic newcomer Keanu Reeves emerged to captivate audiences with *Speed* (1994) and *The Matrix* (1999).

By the mid-1990s, most white male stars were, in effect, like Reeves—slimmer and slighter. The ability to wear clothes well—something George Clooney did with panache—replaced full or partial male nudity. At the same time, few women climbed to the top of the box office charts. Besides Julia Roberts and Meg Ryan, the only woman to rank as a megastar was Sandra Bullock. Female action stars like Linda Hamilton and Jamie Lee (aka "the body") Curtis briefly carried on the 1980s' emphasis on "musculinity." But although Demi Moore pumped iron and even executed one-armed push-ups in Ridley Scott's 1997 *G. I. Jane,* a lipstick lesbian–inflected "femme-ininity" was more prominent than "musculinity" in most late-1990s female action vehicles. There, action "babes" like Jennifer Lopez, Geena Davis, Salma Hayek, and Bridget Fonda ran around in cut-out and/or clinging costumes that emphasized their naturally endowed, pushed up and padded, even surgically enhanced curves.

Many 1990s stars moved back and forth between big- and small-budget films. Superstars in particular looked for more diverse roles than studio pictures offered. Some jump-started flagging careers by acting in independent films: witness John Travolta's return to stardom as a result of *Pulp Fiction*. Other stars were primarily known for their work in independent films. Harvey Keitel's name alone was enough to guarantee an independent film's production. Parker Posey stamped many a 1990s indie film with her street-wise chic (see Negra "Queen"). Like the older Keitel, Steve Buscemi seemed omnipresent. Noteworthy, too, is the fact that other actors, among them Robert De Niro, Billy Bob Thornton, Vincent Gallo, and Buscemi, directed their first films as independents.

Early in the decade, two groups of independent film directors stood out as particularly innovative. For the first time since the mid-1970s and blax-ploitation, a handful of African American directors (Spike Lee, Mario Van Peebles, Matty Rich, Ernest Dickerson, John Singleton, and the Hughes brothers) wowed critics and audiences with films like *Malcolm X* (1992), *New Jack City* (1992), *Straight Out of Brooklyn* (1991), *Juice* (1992), *Boyz n the Hood* (1991), and *Menace II Society* (1993). And by 1992 there were so many fascinating films by gay directors—among them Gregg Araki, Todd Haynes, and Gus Van Sant—that B. Ruby Rich proudly announced the birth of the "new queer cinema" ("New Queer Wave").

Both groups of identity-oriented independent films moved mainstream as the decade wore on. *Set It Off* (1996) was a riveting all-female action caper starring the divine Queen Latifah, and in the latter half of the decade the studios jumped on the black bandwagon to serve up "buppy" films (about black urban professionals) like *Waiting to Exhale* (1995), *How Stella Got Her Groove Back* (1998), and *The Wood* (1999). By decade's end Rich was already lamenting the death of a boldly experimental, politically engaged New Queer Cinema ("Queer and Present Danger"). For her, the most recent "queer" films primarily used "queer" as a brand designed to reach audiences without promoting reflection or action.

Yet whether or not, like Rich, one regrets the movement of many in-dependents from the margins to the mainstream, there's no arguing with the fact that the 1990s were *the* decade when independent directors, virtu-ally all of them white men, moved into the spotlight. Younger talent joined established independent filmmakers, among them John Sayles, John Waters, Hal Hartley, the Coen brothers, Steven Soderbergh, and Abel Fer-rara. At Sundance and elsewhere, Kevin Smith, David O. Russell, Richard Linklater, Wes Anderson, Robert Rodriguez, P. T. Anderson, Alexander Payne, Todd Solondz, Alexandre Rockwell, and Spike Jonze dominated scenes. A few women, among them Allison Anders and Kimberly Peirce, also earned acclaim and enjoyed decent box office scores.[12] Their films tack-led topics that the studios wouldn't touch with a ten-foot pole. To cite just a few examples: *Bad Lieutenant* (1992) follows an incredibly corrupt Catholic cop and offers a full-frontal view of actor Harvey Keitel; *Citizen Ruth* (1996) features Laura Dern as a pregnant, chemical-sniffing, homeless woman around whom pro-life vs. pro-choice debates swirl; *Boogie Nights* (1997) pokes fun at a ring of low-budget pornographers; *Happiness* (1998) follows characters who are telephone stalkers, masturbators, and pederasts; and *Boys Don't Cry* (1999) re-creates the real-life hate-crime murder of a transgendered person.

By the twenty-first century, indie mavericks were poised to take over Hollywood. Quentin Tarantino towered over everyone, thanks to his box office and his blarney. Like David Lynch, Jim Jarmusch, Wayne Wang, Ang Lee, Gus Van Sant, and Steven Soderbergh, Tarantino excelled at cutting deals with the studios. Other 1990s independents, such as Bryan Singer, would soon cross over to become studio directors. As a result, some critics increasingly complained that independent filmmaking was becoming more risk-adverse and less creative. They pejoratively labeled the more mainstream independents "dependies." They also spoke sneeringly of "Indiewood."

But not all independent directors sold out even when they joined forces with the major studios. And moving to the majors meant that more stars were available for casting. Tom Cruise, for example, after an exhausting two years of shooting *Eyes Wide Shut*, and with a divorce from wife and co-star Nicole Kidman in the offing, readily agreed to star in P. T. Anderson's bruising investigation of wounded hyper-masculinity, *Magnolia* (1999). Alexander Payne's clever second film, *Election* (1999), featuring Reese Witherspoon and Matthew Broderick, earned the first Independent Spirit Award ever accorded a studio release. Having begun with the fiercely independent *Spanking the Monkey* (1994) and *Flirting with Disaster* (1996), David O. Russell also moved mainstream for his first studio release, in this case to Warner Bros., for *Three Kings* (1999), with a cast that included George Clooney, Ice Cube, and Mark Wahlberg. The film tackles a sensitive political topic: the blitzkrieg 1991 Gulf War and President Bush's subsequent abandonment of the Kurds to Saddam Hussein. Russell and his interracial cast and crew deliver a devastatingly prescient political satire disguised as a surrealist comedy/action/caper film. Sadly, Private Conrad Vig (Spike Jonze)'s comment, "You all think America is Satan, right?" rings chillingly familiar today.

Documentaries did extremely well throughout the decade, demonstrating to distributors and exhibitors alike that nonfiction films could make money. Errol Morris's *A Brief History of Time* (1991) poetically investigates the life and work of cosmologist Stephen Hawking, who despite near total paralysis, remained one of the great minds of all time. Those interested in political campaigns flocked to *The War Room* (1993), a gripping behind-the-scenes coverage of Bill Clinton's first presidential campaign. Terry Zwigoff's *Crumb* (1994) adroitly interviews quirky countercultural cartoonist R. Crumb and his exasperated family. Twenty-two years in the making, *When We Were Kings* (1997) includes riveting footage of George Foreman's historic 1974 "Rumble in the Jungle" fight with, and unexpected loss to, the charismatic Muhammad Ali in Zaire. Other independent documentaries delved into the lives of the not-so-rich and famous. *Hoop Dreams* (1994) chronicles what happens to two young black athletes from the Chicago ghettos who try to win basketball scholarships to colleges. *Slam* (1998) charts the passionate rhymes and rhythms of slam poetry contests. Shot with a small, handheld camcorder, *Silverlake Life: The View from Here* (1993) makes viewers feel part of the private lives and love of a devoted gay couple, both dying of AIDS-related illnesses before their film was completed. Heartwarming and wrenching at the same time, *Silverlake Life* remains an unforgettable viewing experience.

There were, of course, any number of talented directors with long careers behind them working for the studios, the major independents, and/or as independents. Key 1970s auteurs like Terrence Malick, Stanley Kubrick, and George Lucas managed just one film each in the 1990s, but *The Thin Red Line* (1998), *Eyes Wide Shut* (1999), and *The Phantom Menace* were all remarkable achievements. Steven Spielberg made several striking films over the course of the decade, among them *Schindler's List* and *Jurassic Park* (both 1993), *The Lost World: Jurassic Park* and *Amistad* (both 1997), and *Saving Private Ryan* (1998). Although Martin Scorsese's films earned less at the box office, the 1990s were highly productive for him as well. In 1990 he finished *Goodfellas,* in 1991 *Cape Fear,* in 1993 *The Age of Innocence,* in 1995 *Casino,* in 1997 *Kundun,* and in 1999 *Bringing Out the Dead*. Like Scorsese a dyed-in-the-wool New Yorker, Woody Allen also directed several films during the decade, though he, too, did not enjoy the box office success of the 1970s and 1980s. For the chance to see actors like John Cusack, Dianne Wiest, Jennifer Tilly, Edward Norton, Drew Barrymore, Billy Crystal, Sean Penn, and Uma Thurman, however, *Bullets over Broadway* (1994), *Everyone Says I Love You* (1996), *Deconstructing Harry* (1997), and *Sweet and Lowdown* (1999) are all worth renting.

Working as always with stellar casts, staunch independent Robert Altman released no fewer than eight films during the decade. Best among these are *The Player* (1992), a snide but playful examination of the Hollywood industry under the guise of solving a murder, *Short Cuts* (1993), Altman's omnibus film, and *Cookie's Fortune* (1999)—tag line: "Welcome to Holly Springs, home of murder, mayhem, and catfish enchiladas."

Among long-lived directors, last and by no means least is Clint Eastwood. In the 1990s, Eastwood finally came into his own. That he received an Irving G. Thalberg Award at the Academy Awards in 1993 and an AFI Life Achievement Award in 1995 speaks volumes. In 1992 Eastwood was lauded around the world for his direction of *Unforgiven*. The same film also finds him giving a brilliant performance opposite Gene Hackman and

Will Munny (Clint Eastwood) gets dirty trying to save his dying hogs in *Unforgiven* (Clint Eastwood, Warner Bros., 1992). Digital frame enlargement.

Morgan Freeman as an aging cowboy who tries to keep his family together at (almost) whatever cost. *The Bridges of Madison County* (1995), also directed by Eastwood and casting him opposite Method actress extraordinaire Meryl Streep, brought fresh kudos, especially because it revealed just how well Eastwood could play a romantic hero. Eastwood directed and acted in several other popular—and always money-making—films during the decade, too. *A Perfect World* (1993), with Kevin Costner, and *In the Line of Fire,* opposite John Malkovich, are especially intriguing to anyone interested in studying Eastwood's acting and directorial range.

Stylistically, of course, 1990s films were quite varied, assisted by the digital revolution. Thanks to their starts in music videos and advertising, directors such as Russell Mulcahy, Michael Bay, David Fincher, and Spike Jonze increasingly added a pop, promo visual style into their features (Allen 112; see also Bordwell *Way*). Not for nothing was Jonze called "the Orson Welles of rock video" (Mottram, *Sundance* 161). With digital cameras and editing software, directors routinely used computers to clean up shots or generate imagery. With downstream markets so essential, such tools allowed makers to preview how a movie would look on TV; consequently, there were more close-ups and fewer long shots. Prompted by the success of MTV, cutting grew faster and more furious. Steadicams and stand-and-deliver staging meant that the camera could easily swoop in for a key line or arc around the actors (Bordwell and Thompson 689). Were digital aesthetics really more "painterly" than film could be? Did they "bear the imprint and signature of the creator" to a greater extent? (Elsaesser in Allen 205–06).

You be the judge. In the essays that follow, we discuss a variety of the decade's most significant and intriguing offerings. In addition, we underscore the trends and highlights of a decade during which the digital revolution promised to change the film industry as dramatically as the introduction of sound had. The richness of special effects and the ease of shooting and editing that put serious moviemaking within the reach of even unschooled amateurs has been one of the greatest legacies of the 1990s, one that will surely continue to have an impact on the twenty-first century.

NOTES

1. For other media events of note, see Schauer and Bordwell 225–38, "Film History of the 1990s," and "Media History Timeline: 1990s."

2. By 1999, primetime TV was controlled by a handful of companies: the Big Six plus NBC (owned by General Electric).

3. Most movies with high returns don't have big stars, however, but instead are made on tiny budgets (De Vany 84), increasing the net profit. The presence of stars can, however, help guarantee that a given film opens widely, and may also ensure its longevity in theaters, on TV, and elsewhere.

4. *Armageddon*'s estimated costs were $150 million, *Titanic*'s more than $200 million.

5. MPAA releases were relatively stable from 1995 on, ranging from 212 to 221 films a year (Schauer and Bordwell 231–35).

6. In 1990, the Italian-owned communications company Pathé bought MGM/UA. In 1992, Pathé lost control to the Crédit Lyonnais. Crédit Lyonnais renamed the studio Metro-Goldwyn-Mayer (Allen 38).

7. For an engaging and informative read about how a low-budget movie gets produced, see Vachon and Edelman.

8. Although no one knows exactly how many festivals there were by the end of the decade, "it's possible that an outlandish-sounding *New York Times* estimate of more than a thousand fests around the world might not be as wild as it seems" (Turan, *Sundance* 2).

9. Factor in, however, the rise in average ticket price: from $4.22 in 1990 to $5.06 in 1999 (Schauer and Bordwell 226, 235).

10. Not until the next decade however, would DVD rentals and sales surpass VHS rentals and sales.

11. Ranked fourteenth in a "Star Power" survey by *Hollywood Reporter*, Will Smith was an exemplar of a black crossover star who was nonthreatening to 1990s white audiences, in part because he hopped between making films and functioning as a chart-topping rap performer who avoided explicit lyrics (King, "Stardom" 62).

12. Women directors were also rare in the major studios, the noteworthy exceptions being Mimi Leder, Penelope Spheeris, and Kathryn Bigelow.

1990

Movies and the Off-White Gangster

LINDA MIZEJEWSKI

In *Goodfellas,* one of the year's most critically acclaimed films, the main character says of a fellow mobster, "Jimmy was the kind of guy that rooted for bad guys in the movies." In the first year of the new decade, Americans sometimes found it difficult to tell the good guys from the bad guys. With the Berlin Wall and the Soviet bloc newly dismantled, Cold War political anxieties were suddenly replaced by fears of a reunited Germany and nationalist conflicts in Eastern Europe. Mikhail Gorbachev was elected as the first executive president of the Soviet Union and received the Nobel Peace Prize. Closer to home, U.S. troops were still in Panama at the start of the year following an invasion the previous month that President George H. W. Bush had justified by characterizing Panama dictator Manuel Noriega as a drug-dealing gangster and thug. But in putting a million-dollar bounty on Noriega's head, Bush himself was criticized in some quarters for gangster behavior. The matter was all the murkier given that Noriega had previously been on the payroll of the CIA, which Bush had directed in the 1970s.

In the first week of the year, a sensationalized national news story further confused the good guys with the bad guys. On 4 January, a well-to-do young white Boston widower named Charles Stuart jumped to his death from Tobin Bridge into Boston Harbor. A few months before, Stuart claimed that a black man had hijacked his car and fatally shot his pregnant wife. While civil rights advocates protested, young black men all over Boston were seized and searched, and eventually one was picked up and identified by Stuart in a lineup. But before the suspect could be formally charged, Stuart's friends and family members came forward with evidence that the black hijacker story was a hoax and that Stuart himself was the murderer. His motives were the stuff of pulp fiction—a three-figure insurance policy and a blonde female associate at the office. It was the decade's first national "melodrama of black and white," to use the term Linda Williams assigns to a larger American racial narrative that often entails the black man "in melodramatic configuration with the body of the white woman, and the white man" (300). The white couple in this particular story fit the popular category of "yuppies"—educated, urban, ambitious Anglo Americans not often caught in the wrong part of town.

Yuppies were prominent figures in the national imagination because tax cuts for the wealthiest Americans allowed the income share of the wealthiest fifth to rise to a record 46 percent this year. But even this top tier was experiencing an economic slowdown that was openly being labeled a recession. Meanwhile, investigations revealed that thousands had been defrauded in junk bond scandals, in which Michael Milken—who pleaded guilty to securities fraud and was imprisoned and fined $600 million—became an icon of thirtysomethings' corruption. At the same time, the working classes suffered from a stagnated minimum wage and the increasing move of manufacturing jobs to overseas sites (Borger 51; Samuelson 22–23). The widening gap between rich and poor was widely blamed for the rising crime rates, as increased drug use and drug trafficking made crime profitable.

Charles Stuart's story was credible because the face of urban crime at this moment was "colored." Black and Hispanic gang warfare, escalating through the previous decade, reached critical proportions in urban areas nationwide. The Crips and the Bloods, the most notorious of the Los Angeles–based gangs, showed up in other American cities and in the common American vocabulary as shorthand for urban violence.[1] The eminence of gang warfare raised the stakes on the threatening poses of rap music, which had edged from the margins to the mainstream of popular culture. As a fashion, an attitude, and a music style, rap was cool instead of cult, appealing to both white and black youth. "Yo! MTV Raps!" was MTV's highest-rated show, and journalists noted that teens tuned in "and hit the malls to put together the new styles by Saturday night" (Darnton 78). Some rap groups had socially conscious agendas, but others glamorized transgressive behavior and street violence, often with sexually explicit language. Censorship efforts frequently backfired, with groups such as 2 Live Crew instead playing up a menacing, in-your-face, bad boy masculinity.

Homosexuality made headlines, too. Although gay activism was more than two decades old, the AIDS crisis launched gay visibility to another level, galvanizing gay fights for civil rights, domestic partner benefits, and child custody. A Gallup poll showed Americans were still divided about recognizing the legitimacy of gay sexuality, though far more tolerant about equal rights for homosexuals than in previous years (Baker, "Future" 21). Nevertheless, gays were increasingly targeted for hate crimes, illustrating that sexual identity was a contentious and often dangerous issue. Given the increasing visibility of homosexuals and bad boy rappers, masculinity itself was an object of debate this year. The corporate macho warrior was undergoing reconstruction at the level of talk-show chat and self-help movements. John Bradshaw's *Homecoming: Reclaiming and Championing Your Inner Child* was a best seller, while poet Robert Bly led men into retreats in the woods to reconnect with their lost feminine selves. However, gender anxieties also fueled a backlash reaction. "The new macho is everywhere," proclaimed a *Time* essay reporting on the current mixed messages for men: make a fortune, go to Lamaze class, build those triceps (Allis 80).

The real-life international hero of the year was Nelson Mandela, jailed for twenty-seven years in South Africa because of his militancy against that country's apartheid policies. His release in February marked the beginning of a new era for South Africa and the triumph of Mandela's endurance; he had repeatedly refused conditional releases that would have limited his political clout. Most Americans had found apartheid repugnant because of its clear demarcations of racial privilege. More difficult to acknowledge was racial privilege closer to home, as the Charles Stuart case illustrated. George Lipsitz has termed this system of privilege "the possessive investment in whiteness," the cultural systems and choices that maintain racial whiteness as an ideal, an asset, and a means of exclusion (vii–viii).

The major box office draws this year demonstrated how popular culture stakes this investment. Three of the four top-grossing films featured beleaguered white males in need of redemption. In *Dances with Wolves,* an army lieutenant (Kevin Costner) is recovered by frontier Native Americans; in *Pretty Woman,* a businessman (Richard Gere) is rescued by a prostitute; and in *Ghost,* a Wall Street accountant (Patrick Swayze) is transfigured into a guardian angel.[2] In the latter film, the casting of a dark-skinned Puerto Rican hit man (Rick Avila) played to the same racist imagination that pictured Stuart's phantom hijacker as black. As the African American psychic who communicates with and eventually embodies the murdered white hero, Whoopi Goldberg plays a controversial role described variously as a "mammy" and a white fantasy of African American spirituality (Jones, "Defiant Ones" 69; Mayne 142–56; Merck 21–37). *Dances with Wolves* was similarly criticized for making "the Sioux like genial versions of us" (Kael 115).

Given national anxieties about crime, it is not surprising that *Home Alone* was also one of the year's major hits. At the heart of the film lurks a disturbing narrative—the suburban home turned into a fortress under attack. Similarly, the Arnold Schwarzenegger comedy *Kindergarten Cop* ends with a bloody shoot-out in an elementary school. In his other film this year, the blockbuster science fiction flick *Total Recall,* the Schwarzenegger hero faces a riddle of identity: he may or may not be who he thinks he is. Fittingly, the last Cold War film, *The Hunt for Red October,* was also about transformed identity, featuring Sean Connery as a Russian defector who ends a nuclear threat to the United States.

The independent film *Longtime Companion* was the first cinematic representation of AIDS to gain fairly wide release, thanks to its prominence in the annual major awards. Its success signaled the new salience of small studios, including Miramax, which was also the U.S. distributor for *The Grifters,* a crime film that was nominated for four Academy Awards and tallied a domestic gross of $13 million. The indie company Morgan Creek distributed *Pacific Heights,* which placed in the top fifty box office draws of the year, and the new company Propaganda Films released David Lynch's eagerly awaited *Wild at Heart* in the wake of Lynch's popular television series "Twin Peaks" (1990–91).

One of the most significant trends was the comeback of the white gangster at the very moment when the black and Hispanic gangster had seized the headlines and rap songs often rooted for the bad guy. Like Charles Stuart's phantasmic criminal, the black gangster hovers at the perimeters of these films, suggesting—often by his absence—their investments in whiteness. Women likewise hover on this perimeter, necessary outsiders in a genre built around the bad guy with a gun.

Off-White Gangsters

The highest-profile gangster films were the long-awaited Corleone family finale, Francis Ford Coppola's *The Godfather: Part III* from Paramount and Zoetrope (grossing $67 million domestically), Martin Scorsese's critically celebrated *Goodfellas* from Warner Bros. ($47 million), and Joel and Ethan Coen's *Miller's Crossing* from Twentieth Century Fox and Circle Films (a paltry $5 million). All three films portrayed gangsters of earlier eras, from the 1920s up to 1980, when black and Hispanic gangs began to be prominent. Meanwhile, the contemporary gangster scene was represented in two films set in New York City. Sean Penn starred in Phil Joanou's *State of Grace* from Cinehaus and Orion (domestic gross $2 million), and Christopher Walken starred in Abel Ferrara's *King of New York* (also $2 million), produced by Caminito, Reteitalia, and Scena International. Of all these gangster offerings, only *King of New York* represents black and Hispanic gangsters, although a white actor—Walken—plays their idolized gang boss.

Critic Richard Corliss, noting the comeback of the gangster genre this year, explained it as cinema's effort "to confront, in code, the awful ethnic schisms of American life: Italian vs. Wasp stands in for Black vs. white" ("Married" 83). What Corliss does not take into account is that these gangster films actually focus on what Diane Negra calls "off-white" America— the marginalized ethnic groups among which whiteness itself is an issue. The fictional gangster has always been about legitimacy and access to power. As the Stuart case indicated, those qualities are racially weighted. The "off-white" nature of the traditional gangster film further exposes the instabilities of these weights and identities in the ethnic mix of American cities. Tracing the genre's early history as a history of race in America, Giorgio Bertellini describes the gangster hero's conflicts rooted in his exclusion from whiteness: "His very American ambition clashed against the marginalizing reality of social origin and racial identity" (229).

The idea that gangster films are *implicitly* about race is borne out by analysis of the racial dynamics in this year's gangster films. *State of Grace* is about an Irish gang struggling with an Italian gang in the Hell's Kitchen neighborhood of Manhattan. Both gangs are facing the sudden gentrification of this neighborhood, which is being bought up by Yuppies and turned into a neighborhood of condominiums and upscale restaurants. That is, the off-white ethnic neighborhood is being dismantled by investments in white culture. The Irish gang leader, seeing the trend, has already moved out and bought a house in the suburbs. *The Godfather: Part III* is about the aging Michael Corleone (Al Pacino) attempting to legitimate his business dealings through corporations associated with the Vatican. This enterprise takes him and his family to Italy, where his son Anthony (Franc D'Ambrosio), an aspiring opera singer, debuts in a spectacular production of Mascagni's *Cavalleria Rusticana*. At the opera house, in the film's grand finale, an underworld shooting goes wrong and ends in the death of Corleone's young daughter. Pre-release film publicity emphasized director Coppola's decision to end Michael Corleone's story as a retelling of *King Lear*, with Corleone destined to pay for his past mistakes through this terrible loss (Kroll 58–61; Rohter 1).

These films illustrate the slippery identifications and struggles for legitimacy in two ways. First, the Italian or the Irish gangsters represent the tiers of marginalization around a core mythical whiteness. As Lipsitz points out, "Race relations in the United States have always involved more than one outcast group at a time acting in an atomized fashion against a homogenous 'white' center" (210). The "white" center in these films is the ideal of the suburb or opera or Shakespeare—external markers of legitimacy. Second, the stardom of key actors in *State of Grace* and *The Godfather: Part III* suggests the high stakes of white masculinity in these films and also the unstable nature of that whiteness.

In *State of Grace*, the Irish gangs had always dominated the neighborhood, defending the territory from the competing Mafia drug trade. For the Irish, the Italians are the "greasers" who would "sell you out for a piece of pizza," as one Irish gangster puts it. When the two gangs are headed for a major showdown, Jackie Flannery (Gary Oldman) salivates at the idea of a "dumpster full of dead guineas."[3] But the Flannery gang must forge alliances with their despised rivals in order to ensure survival in the new economic order where, as Jackie puts it, "Yuppies are thicker than the rats and the roaches." He then douses one of the reconstruction projects with gasoline and sets it afire—"It sends a message," he says.

Yet the film does not pit the Irish against the Italians or the yuppies against the combined ethnic groups. Instead, *State of Grace* foregrounds the conflicts within the Irish gang as their self-identity unravels under the pressures of neighborhood transition. Gang leader Frankie (Ed Harris) believes the neighborhood is already lost to the yuppies and that the Mafia can be used as a "ticket" for the Flannerys so they can "retire to Phoenix." We see him at his home in the New Jersey suburbs, directing gang warfare from a parallel universe of multi-car garages and rolling lawns. Like his planned retirement home in the Southwest, these are his investments in whiteness.

The Flannery gang performs masculinity as ruthless throat slitting and bravado that verges on insanity. Jackie lights his arson fires while he's still in the building, so he can dance through the flames. But the hero of *State of Grace* is Terry Noonan (Sean Penn), a brooding, hard-drinking roughneck who is also the film's sexual dynamo. Noonan has been away from the Kitchen for ten years and returns as an undercover cop, infiltrating his previous gang so he can help the police clean up the neighborhood for the higher-priced tenants. As this suggests, his loyalties are split between the law, which represents the interests of the yuppies, and his childhood Irish American friends. Noonan sports a James Dean pompadour and sulk, and he wears a necklace cross, a clue to the film's lingering nostalgia for a traditional ethnic masculinity. The casting of Penn as sexy gangster tapped his current reputation as a Hollywood bad boy (he did jail time in 1987 for assault) and heartthrob (he had just ended his tumultuous four-year marriage to Madonna). Penn as Noonan is Hollywood's white version of the sexy bad boy of rap, seductive and dangerous, wearing a cross instead of a flashy gold chain.

The cross he wears, like the theological title of the film, emphasizes this film's explicit identification of the gangster as off-white—specifically, as Irish Catholic. Given Ireland's bloody twentieth-century history, this specific ethnic identity illustrates the gangster film's "opposing ideologies," in the words of Fran Mason, of both "order, hierarchy, and discipline" and "the excess and chaos of modernity" (5). As both cop and former gang member, Noonan embodies this opposition himself. *State of Grace* punctuates the dynamic with its final sequence, cross-cut between the St. Patrick's Day parade and Noonan's suicidal shoot-out with the gang several blocks away. While the bodies of Noonan and the Flannery gang explode in slow motion to a barrage of bullets and gunshot, we see the traditional pipers and baton-twirling redheaded girls marching past St. Patrick's Cathedral.

Only one black face appears in *State of Grace*, a background figure at a cop's funeral, so the film carves out an ethnic space that can be pictured as "white" despite the narrative conflict that complicates definitions of whiteness. Writing about the lack of black representation in the gangster film, Mark Winokur observes that Hollywood's most typical response to racial anxiety is "to submerge as fully as possible all controversial discussion," with the result that racial tensions are registered in other ways (10). For Winokur, the cinematic elision of black and Hispanic gangsters in favor of the Irish, Jews, and Italians creates nostalgia for the 1920s and 1930s, when Catholics and Jews were the targets of discrimination. In contemporary ethnic gangster films, he argues, "the audience is made to feel sympathy for a group that is no longer threatening, whereas those groups that would show how America still discriminates are not represented" (11).

Ethnic nostalgia and the erasure of obvious racial difference similarly characterize *The Godfather: Part III*. The first half of the film takes place in Manhattan's Little Italy, the second half in Rome and Sicily, imagined as sites where black and Hispanic faces would be unlikely to appear, though even the scenes in Atlantic City are—visually at least—lily-white. As in *State of Grace*, one of the major scenes of violence takes place in the context of an ethnic parade full of Italian regalia and religious icons, specifying the cultural and religious ties of the warring families.

Vera Dika interprets *The Godfather: Part III* as a retreat from the glamorizing mythology of the Mafia. Michael Corleone's decision to move his investments to Vatican businesses is ironic because the latter turn out to be as corrupt as anything Corleone had run in Atlantic City. However, the financial legitimacy that Corleone craves in the plot is eerily mimicked in the film's aspirations to cultural legitimacy. The move to Italy culminates in the opera sequence, in which the theater performance is intercut with shots of political assassinations and mob traps, leading to the accidental death of the daughter that echoes the ending of *King Lear*. Considering how contemporary black and Hispanic gangs were rendered through staccato rap dialogue and hip-hop music, we can read a racial distancing from this popular figuration in Coppola's decision to render *The Godfather: Part III* through Shakespeare and opera—traditionally considered "white" and "elitist" culture. Film scholars had long spoken of the *Godfather* saga as "operatic," praising Coppola's ability to convey "the sense that we are witnessing a titanic struggle between good and evil rather than a mere battle or skirmish between rival gangs or Mafia families" (Greene 143; see as well Browne; Hess; Knapp; and Lewis *Whom*). Given the privileged relationship of legitimacy to WASP culture, Jonathan Munby points out that the ethnicity of gangsters has always posed "awkward questions about the line that separated legitimate from illegitimate Americans" (2).

Nevertheless, the racial difference so carefully excised from this film is startlingly reestablished in the casting of Andy Garcia as the illegitimate nephew and godfather-to-be, a choice that made one reviewer ruminate that "Hispanics seem to be taking over the Brotherhood" (Simon, "Mob" 65). A rising star, Garcia played Hispanic roles in two other films this year, *Internal Affairs* and *Show of Force*. In light of this star context and the high-profile status of the black and Hispanic gangster, Garcia's casting as a flashy, highly sexualized thug in *The Godfather: Part III* resonates with ethnic/racial difference. Garcia plays Vincent, the bastard son of Michael's brother Sonny. His illegitimacy is an allusion to the Edmund character in *King Lear*, but legitimacy/illegitimacy is obviously the hot button of this film, not only in the narrative about making the family business respectable but in the film's larger ambition to produce the Corleones as the *real* American gangsters, the ones deserving Shakespearean tragedy and operatic status.

Garcia's evocation of racial difference underscores the racial tensions around the off-white gangster. Like Sean Penn's character in *State of Grace*, Vincent is sexually and criminally volatile. Early in the film, he proves himself by trying to bite off the ear of a mobster who is harassing Michael. But his difference from the other Corleones is signified as intense sexuality. He shows up in a snug leather jacket for a reception where everyone else is in a suit. Fighting would-be assassins in the middle of the night, he wears a lush, silky red bathrobe. He is also physically different, the one with the sensuous widow's peak. And in a bedroom scene, the camera lingers on his thick, ample chest hair.

Vincent Mancini-Corleone (Andy Garcia), the illegitimate, highly sexualized nephew in *The Godfather: Part III* (Francis Ford Coppola, Paramount). Courtesy Photofest New York.

Predictably, the focus is the illicit nature of Vincent's sexuality, for he gets involved with his first cousin, Michael's daughter, despite multiple warnings of "dangers"—an allusion to the misfortunes of other women who tangle with powerful Corleone men, but also to the incestuousness of this relationship. In *The Godfather: Part III,* the anxieties over Vincent's incest embody anxieties about his borderline outlaw identity in this family. Vincent is a Corleone because of his father's tempestuous coupling with a bridesmaid at his sister's wedding in *The Godfather*. Vincent's illicit sexuality thus points to the instabilities of family identity and the lapses that produce "other" Corleones.

Garcia's casting suggests the specifically racial component of this anxiety. As one critic has noted, "The *Godfather* films have thrived on meaningful casting" (Hoberman, "Like Godfather" 73). The doomed daughter in *The Godfather: Part III* is played by the director's own daughter, Sofia Coppola, implying a strong investment of family identification in this saga. In the tragic third act of the Corleone epic, family power slips to its exoticized dark Other, played by a star who can "pass" as Italian but who also represents the ambiguous racial history of Italian Americans. The Vincent character is an implosive force, embodying both the arbitrary definitions of race and the racial weight of the legitimacy issues surrounding the gangster.

■ Real Men, Black Phantasms

The year's gangster film that most blatantly sets up the racial question in relation to sexuality and masculinity is *Goodfellas,* a film that "brings the gangster down to the level of ordinary greed-is-good suburban America," as reviewer Gilberto Perez put it (190). *Goodfellas* is based on the real-life story of Henry Hill, the small-time New York gangster who ratted on his pals when he realized they would soon have him "whacked." The film's complicated narrative structure spirals around questions of violence and identity. It opens with a grotesquely bloody and botched gangland execution, the meanings and consequences of which become apparent only later in the film's narrative, which is composed of a series of flashbacks spanning three decades.

The gory opening is seen from the perspective of Henry (Ray Liotta), whose comment on this nightmarish scene is a deadpan riff on the American success story: "As far back as I can remember, I always wanted to be a gangster," he says in voiceover. The film's speeding camera movements, rapid editing, and hurtling zoom shots suggest that Henry's childhood dream rushes him to this gruesome scene with swift, dizzying inevitability. In an interview, Scorsese described the film as both "anthropology" and tragedy (Smith, "Interview" 28–29). But the inevitability of tragedy in *Goodfellas* is tempered by the anthropological details of class, ethnicity, and consumerism that shape Henry's dreams and choices. The film sometimes pauses around these details with a freeze frame or lingers on them with a long take, such as the celebrated four-minute shot of Henry leading his future wife Karen (Lorraine Bracco) down the back hallways of the Copacabana, revealing an entire economy and entertainment system bending to his desires. The irony of Henry's opening remark is replayed with varying resonances as *Goodfellas* documents the alligator shoes, the shootings and executions, and the specific ethnic codes of masculinity and authority in the mob.

Hill takes us through his boyhood apprenticeship in the mob and his attachment to his mentor, Jimmy (Robert De Niro)—the one who roots for bad guys in the movies. As a kid, Henry (Christopher Serrone) makes his first juvenile court appearance—in front of a paid-off judge—for unloading stolen cigarettes. The guys in the gang greet him with a hearty cry outside the courtroom: "You broke your cherry!" As this makes clear, gangster life is a specific male sexuality, its wives and girlfriends mere accoutrements to the more important bonding and pleasures of the gang.

The whiteness of this masculinity is made clear in a later scene showing "girlfriend night" (as opposed to wife night) at the Copacabana, when one of the "girls" idly comments that she could "see how a white girl can fall" for Sammy Davis Jr. Her date, the hot-tempered Tommy de Vito (Joe Pesci), reacts with near panic, and the other wiseguys at the table look uneasy. Tellingly, the scene of "girlfriend night"—the enactment of male sexual privilege—is the scene that specifies the racial stakes of that sexuality. For Tommy in particular, whose small stature goads him into hyper-aggressive masculinity, the comment about black sex appeal touches a raw nerve. As Iain Colley reminds us, "Tommy's childish wish for stature and importance—for manliness—are [sic] finally summed up in the idea of being a 'made man'—i.e. a fully accredited Mafioso" (34). In *Goodfellas*, the ultimate measure of the "made man" is ethnic purity; Henry himself is ineligible for this status, he tells us in voiceover, because he is half Irish (see Ruberto on the ethnic dimensions of this film, and also Colley; Nicholls; Kolker; and Nyce).

The girlfriend's casual remark about interracial desire conjures up the spectral black criminal who is the elusive rival of the "goodfellas" in this film. Early in the movie, we learn about this rival realm of crime when, in an otherwise unmotivated and unrelated bit of business, a white man runs into a diner exclaiming, "Two niggers just stole my truck!" We never see the truck or the criminals, nor do we even see the speaker again, nor is this bit in any way incorporated into the narrative. But the phantasmic black criminal, like the one conjured by Charles Stuart, is invoked again when Henry explains to his frightened wife why "goodfellas" don't go to jail: "You know who goes to jail? Nigger stick-up men, that's who." The scene takes place in their bedroom. The implication is that real men—white men—don't get caught. Ironically, Henry and his pals end up in prison a short time later, but the "nigger stick-up men" are nowhere to be seen there. Instead, we see the gangsters in privileged domestic bliss, cooking elaborate pasta dinners and shaving garlic bulbs with razor blades. Prison as a site of male rape has been replaced with another kind of homosocial scene, the all-male family, with gang member Billy Batts (Frank Vincent) in an apron, stirring the meat sauce. Far from being feminized by this activity, gang members can claim the kitchen work as ethnic masculinity. (Later in the movie, Henry worries about his tomato sauce simmering on the stove on a frantic day when he is selling guns and cocaine.) The prison as a scene of homosocial feeding instead of homosexuality illustrates the dependence of gangster masculinity on specific ethnic and racial claims.

The only black character in *Goodfellas* shows up in the final quarter of the movie, when Henry's narration introduces us to the men who have been lined up for the $6 million Lufthansa heist. "Even Stacks Edwards got

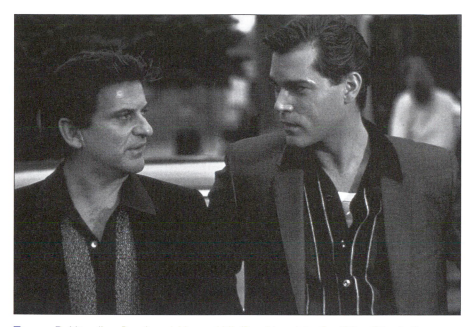

Tommy DeVito (Joe Pesci) and Henry Hill (Ray Liotta) in *Goodfellas* (Martin Scorsese, Warner Bros.). Courtesy Photofest New York.

in on it. He used to hang around the lounge and play guitar. Everybody loved Stacks," Henry says. The heist goes smoothly, but Stacks (Samuel L. Jackson) gets stoned and doesn't show up to do his part. Vengeance is swift. Tommy—the one so shaken by the appeal of Sammy Davis Jr.—is the one dispatched for the execution. He bursts into Stacks's bedroom, demands if any "bitches" are in there, and briefly leafs through a porno magazine before putting a gun to Stacks's head. Stacks dies in his underwear, curled beside an unmade bed, and the murder scene is replayed later, in slow motion, with Tommy pumping more bullets into the inert body. Writing about the representation of race in this film, Stephanie Hull and Maurizio Viano have pointed out that of all the executions following the heist, this is the only one depicted onscreen, "an aestheticized portrayal of violence by an Italian American against a black man" (193). Throughout the film, Tommy does some psychotic killing, but the specific sexualization of this one caps the film's dramatization of the black sexual threat to the wiseguys.

The racism of the gangsters in *Goodfellas* is complicated by their own skewed relationship to "whiteness." Both the Italians and the Irish, the groups foregrounded in this year's gangster films, have complicated histories as "white" Americans. In the past, both groups were associated with African Americans because they lived in or near black neighborhoods and took on jobs coded as "black." Historians have documented how both groups were considered "intermediate" races and were often linked to blacks as criminal populations (Bertellini 210–14; Guglielmo 10–11; Jacobson 48–62). This relationship is startlingly implied in a comic scene involving Karen, whose prominence in *Goodfellas* is exceptional for the genre. For a portion of the film showing Henry's courtship and marriage, Karen actually assumes the voiceover narration, describing the mob and Italian American culture from a middle-class Jewish perspective that is fascinated by the guns in kitchen cabinets and the wives in polyester. In one scene, she calmly watches television while federal agents search the house—an event that has become a commonplace activity for her. She's watching *The Jazz Singer* (1927), a film about a man who gives up his Jewish identity to become a blackface performer.[4] As Michael Rogin has forcefully argued in his scholarship on this film, *The Jazz Singer* documents the losses of assimilation, specifically the loss of Jewish identity through the fetishization of Blackness (*Blackface* 79–80). In *Goodfellas,* the implication is that Karen has likewise used another nonwhite identity—the Italian mob—to achieve status and a version of American success.

Boys' Night Out

The strong homosocial bonds of the gangster film and the casual sidelining of its women have always suggested the genre's homoerotic undertones of "masculinity and the intersection of violence, pain, sexuality, and male bonding" (Studlar 123). With homosexuality in the United States far more visible than it had been in other eras of the gangster film, the meaning of male-bonded masculinity was particularly at stake in these films (for more on masculinity and the gangster film, see Sonnet and Stanfield 117). In *King of New York,* an ambiguous homoerotic subtext flavors the film's racial dynamics. In *Miller's Crossing,* homosexuality is actually included in the plot and is part of the Coen brothers' ironic homage to the gangster genre and its male-bonding nuances. In both films, a nervous homophobia keeps the male bonding in check. Gaylyn Studlar, drawing on Eve Kosofky Sedgwick, describes the "dialectic between homophobia and homoeroticism" as a strategy in "Hollywood's fragile negotiation of homoeroticism within gangster-derived depictions of masculinity" (121–23). This is the dialectic found in two gangster films that blatantly acknowledges the genre's reliance on intense emotional bonds among men.

The independent film *King of New York* was the only gangster picture that actually represented the black and Hispanic gangs dominating the headlines, crime statistics, and city streets. However, as reviewer Stuart Klawans put it, the racial scenario was a "fantasy that a white man— Christopher Walken—can be tough enough to lead a gang of jiving, rapping Blacks and Latinos" ("Films" 539). Director Abel Ferrara pursued shock value, exploiting both news headlines about gangs and rap culture's obsession with sex and violence. As a result, *King of New York* delivers the visual slickness and self-conscious stylization of MTV. The name of the Christopher Walken character is Frank White, implying a sly or campy mockery of race in this film, even though the racial dynamics more often seem stereotyped than parodied. The lieutenant of White's multiracial gang is Jimmy Jump (Laurence Fishburne), a jive-talking gangster straight out of hip-hop culture, and this pair is pitted against a white and black cop team, Dennis Gilley (David Caruso) and Thomas Flanigan (Wesley Snipes). The film is casually littered with glamorous, sexually available women, but the two interracial male couples are the locus of the film's sexual energy, suggesting anxieties about what masculinity entails for the eroticized, MTV-style gangster.

The white-black cop team has become a staple of the buddy-formula action film, as Sharon Willis points out. Willis claims that this pairing inevitably works to assuage anxieties surrounding white heterosexual masculinity, and the legally sanctioned cop status of the buddies serves to disavow "homosexuality as well as interracial desire" (Willis 31). In *King of New York,* the questions of legitimacy and emotional bonding are even sharper, because the outlaw couple matches the lawman couple, and the film's sympathies are strongly with the latter. In this sexually charged scenario, homosexuality is anxiously posited as real but elsewhere. Newly released from jail, White is taunted by the cops about whether he had picked up AIDS there; later, when Flanigan threatens Jimmy Jump with jail time, he puts it in sexual terms: "You're gonna be somebody's bitch!" Yet the most erotic scene in the movie is the death struggle between the latter two on a dark, rainy street, when they fall into each other's arms, each firing a gun point blank into the other's chest. Their extended fatal embrace is strikingly similar to the famous death embrace between Barbara Stanwyck and Fred MacMurray at the end of *Double Indemnity* (1944). Gilley enters the scene too late and discovers his dying partner; a close-up shows him covering Flanigan's bloody lips with his own as he attempts resuscitation—all of this in the gorgeous noir shadows of black and blue.

The white cop's embrace of his black partner stands in for Frank White's own racial desire—his obsession with black masculinity, the homoerotic

Multiple races and ethnicities: Frank White (Christopher Walken) threatens a racist Mafia boss (Frank Gio) while Jimmy Jump (Laurence Fishburne) looks on in *King of New York* (Abel Ferrara, Seven Arts Entertainment). Courtesy Photofest New York.

dimensions of which are both disavowed and teased out through inference. An Italian mob leader (Frank Gio) who refuses to deal with White because he's a "nigger-lover" is shot to death for his opinion. The scene presents itself as an ironic retort to racism, but the more literal reading of the scene prompts the question of who, exactly, are White's "lovers." His sexual partner is a female white lawyer (Janet Julian), but the film most emphatically eroticizes him in the shoot-outs, in which homoerotic desire is diffused through the bloody openings and merging of bodies. In White's final "big bang" orgy, we see him as an honorary black man, dancing to rap music in an otherworldly blue light until the cops break in—significantly, disguised as rival gang members—and the violence is choreographed into a bloody dance. The fetishization of the black gang members recalls Willis's description of black masculinity as cultural cachet: "Through white men's identifications with them, black men become icons, gestural repertoires, and cultural artifacts . . . the white subject wants to be in the other's place, without leaving its own" (210).

Indeed, *King of New York* insists on White's whiteness and sets up a disturbing racial hierarchy in which White's "royalty" entails not only racial and class privilege but ethical purity. The visual establishment of these racialized values occurs early in the film, when the camera cuts from his gang's bloody shoot-out in a ratty hotel to White in a shower at the Plaza Hotel, being washed clean by gilded plumbing. In the film's curious Robin Hood thematic, White directs part of his drug fortune to the building of an inner-city hospital for the poor. He also wipes out rival mobs that do business he considers immoral—slumlord real estate and child prostitution. So while his black and Hispanic gang members do the dirty work in the streets, White dabbles in philanthropy and Upper West Side culture.

As a result, despite the film's multicultural casting, a racist dynamic develops around Frank White as idol/king/celebrity who can not only participate in this macho nonwhite culture but give it meaning and tragic stature. We see him, in fact, at the Lunt-Fontanne Theatre watching a highly stylized production of *The Emperor Jones,* staged in the same deathly blue lighting later used in the drug-den shoot-out scene. The inclusion of the O'Neill play parallels the use of Shakespeare in *The Godfather: Part III*— it blatantly pushes an understanding of the gangster as a tragic figure familiar from "elite" white culture. However, the troubling racial politics of *The Emperor Jones*—a white playwright's rendition of black tragedy—mirrors that of *King of New York,* in which tragic stature is reserved for Frank White. The film's primary black gangster, Jimmy Jump, goes to his death in a hideous spectacle: on a rainy night in a parking lot, he flops, screams, and laughs hysterically in his death throes after he's been shot to death by the white cop. The dignified tragedy, as delivered by the film's aesthetics, is Frank White's. He too is eventually shot by a white cop, but he manages to walk stoically away from the shooting—bullet in his gut—and make it to the crowds of Times Square, where he dies in the privacy of a taxicab while the cops spread out in a dragnet from which he could not possibly escape.

Robert Warshow, describing the gangster's tragedy, emphasizes his stoic singularity: "The gangster's whole life is an effort to assert himself as an individual, to draw himself out of the crowd, and he always dies *because* he is an individual. . . . What has been brought low is not the undifferentiated *man,* but the individual with a name" (133). In this case, the tragic individualism of Frank White—the King of New York—is the payoff of the film's investment in whiteness and in his unique racial position among the multiracial gangsters, which at the same time gives him access to the cultural cachet of black masculinity.

Like *King of New York, Miller's Crossing* is a highly stylized film but not a flashy one, its earthy, muted colors and dark mise-en-scène reinforcing the film's moral darkness (for analyses of this film in the context of the

Coen brothers' work, see Mottram; Palmer; and Körte and Seeslen). The visual austerity is also part of the film's tribute to the gangster genre and film noir, a tribute that is primarily ironic. The film's mixed tone is described by John Richardson: "*Miller's Crossing* is a post-modern *Godfather* that rollicks in the silliness of the genre but still somehow plumbs the depths of emotion" (94). This combination of parody and emotional appeal results in a disturbing ambiguity about the film's stereotypes, misogyny, and homoerotics. Unlike the other gangster offerings of the year, *Miller's Crossing* actually includes homosexual gangster characters, boldly playing out the logic of intense male loyalties in this genre. The gangster genre's attitude toward women is summed up by one of the gay characters, the scary henchman known as the Dane (J. E. Freeman), who shouts after a woman he's been assigned to kill: "Go ahead and run, sweetie! I'll track down all you whores." A profoundly cynical film, *Miller's Crossing* glamorizes none of the gangsters, but the gay characters include the one who is most vicious—the Dane—and the two who are most cowardly. As reviewer Gary Giddens put it, "Everyone in this movie is reprehensible, but three characters are conspicuously worse than the rest, and they are all homosexuals" (62).

A sexual rivalry is at work among these three, with the killer Dane vying with the treacherous Bernie (John Turturro) for the favors of the effeminate Mink (Steve Buscemi). But this happens offscreen; we only hear about the consequences in conversations. Instead, we see in great detail the *other* sexual rivalry of the narrative: the older gang boss Leo (Albert Finney) and his brilliant, taciturn advisor Tom (Gabriel Byrne), both involved with *femme fatale* Verna (Marcia Gay Harden). The link between these two triangles is Verna, Bernie's sister, who tries to save Bernie from the consequences of his crooked bookmaking. As a favor to Verna, Leo and then Tom each tries to protect the shifty brother, but Bernie's own greed dooms him. Eventually, Tom is the one who kills him, and Verna's revenge on Tom is to marry Leo. However, this is a triangle with a decidedly homoerotic twist. Tom and Leo seem to be rivals for Verna, but it would be just as easy to read Tom and Verna as rivals for Leo. As film reviewer John Simon noted: "Though he enjoys sex with Verna, Tom seems to care more about Leo, albeit in some twisted, tormented way, which appears to make him enjoy being beaten up by Leo when he confesses to being Verna's lover" ("Difficult Crossings" 54). Later film scholars were more likely to interpret the Tom-Leo relationship as a postmodern outing of the homoerotic bonds that previous gangster films had suppressed (Levine 79–80; Robson 84).

Despite this bold disruption of the traditional gangster mystique, the homoeroticism works with and against more hostile positionings of homosexuality. As Giddens points out, the three openly gay characters are truly the least sympathetic, and all three are dead by the end of the film, while Leo, Tom, and Verna survive. Also, traditional masculinity is asserted through a subtle racial and ethnic social order. The characters in *Miller's Crossing* are a cross-section of "off-white" America: Leo and Tom are Irish, Verna and Bernie are Jewish, and the rival gang is Italian. The Dane is plucked from a different set of stereotypes, the bloodless Nordic psychopath. Critic Richard McKim speculates that this "polyglot ethnic menagerie" serves to "spoof the blood-mysticism of Coppola's Sicilians" (46). The casting of British and Irish actors (Byrne and Finney) as American gangsters sharpens this satirical edge. But even as a spoof of the gangster genre's macho characterizations, *Miller's Crossing* constructs a hierarchy of masculinity for this ethnic mix, with the Irish Tom and Leo at the top and the Jewish Bernie at the bottom. While the Dane is portrayed as insanely homicidal, Leo's brief transition into a killing machine is celebrated in the film's most tour de force sequence. Surprised by assassins in his own home, Leo springs from his bed and into action, single-handedly killing half a dozen men half his age, including one ill-fated mobster whose dead body is suspended in a macabre dance as it's sprayed with bullets. All this happens as "Danny Boy" plays on Leo's gramophone and is amplified as the scene's musical theme, carefully scored to "tailor the cadences of the song to the mounting body count," as one behind-the-scene report explains (Levy, "Shot by Shot" 68).

Unlike the Irish piper music in the finale of *State of Grace,* "Danny Boy" is a joke; clearly this is the Coens' send-up of the shoot-'em-up ethnic gangster flick. But the sequence ends with a shot of the grinning, self-satisfied Leo, puffing on his cigar and cooling off his Tommy gun while the surviving assassins speed away. Both Leo and the gangster genre are pictured as larger than life, larger than the effect of the satire, and the dimensions are clearly phallic—the cigar, the smoking gun. Leo emerges as the film's most charming and likable character—the enduring old-world patriarch who ends up with the girl. At the opposite end of this spectrum is the whining Bernie, whose cunning and greed can be interpreted as a nasty ethnic stereotype and who ends up with a bullet in his head. The closing scene, in fact, is Bernie's funeral, where Leo shyly announces to Tom that Verna has agreed to marry him. Verna's Jewishness is never an issue. For the traditional gangster genre, masculinity is what's most invested in routes of privilege and power—that is, in whiteness.

■■■■■■■■ Siding with the Good Old Boys

The year's sudden resurgence of the gangster film needs to be read within the cultural contexts of race relations in the United States, the prominence of black and Hispanic gang activity, the glamorization of that gang activity in hip-hop culture, and anxieties about masculinity exacerbated by the new visibility of homosexuality. These were the cultural issues present during the planning and production of these films, and they were the contexts within which audiences saw them. The poststructural perspective is that black and Hispanic gangsters, as well as the bad boys of rap music, functioned as the structuring absence of these gangster films, simultaneously positing binary racial terms (Italians and Irish as not-Black) and the slippage of those terms (the indeterminacy of blackness and whiteness). The cultural perspective is that the gangster genre, always motivated by its off-white origins, was under particular pressure to reinvest not only in whiteness but in white masculinity, specifically through white tough guys played by prestigious actors Al Pacino, Robert De Niro, and Albert Finney, as well as by sexy new stars Sean Penn, Christopher Walken, and Andy Garcia.

At work here are genre theory and theories of stardom, both of which position films as porous texts that interact with other media, historical conditions, and contemporary discourses. Al Pacino and Robert De Niro, for instance, bring to these films associations with their previous hard-edged criminal roles, which in turn connote authenticity. Here are the *real* American gangsters (as opposed to the Crips and Bloods). In a parallel usage of stardom, Sean Penn and Andy Garcia serve as attractive alternatives for a younger generation attuned to the hypnotic rhythms and aggressive masculinities of rap music. We can see here the function of stars as ways to imagine not just masculine identity and versions of sexiness, but national, racial, and ethnic identities as well.

My primary method has been genre theory, which concerns textual formulas but—like star theories—is also dependent on cultural contexts and responses. The gangster genre is a social history. Its repeated stories about outlaw heroes remain popular because they play to the American history of urban violence and frustrations with the exclusionary nature of WASP power structures. The codes that relay those stories—the narratives, characterizations, and mise-en-scène—cue us to this larger social narrative, so that Frank White's death scene in *King of New York,* or the manic characterization of Jackie Flannery in *State of Grace,* or the silky men's suits in *Goodfellas*—resonate as part of a recognizable, meaningful history of the urban renegade up against larger, indifferent forces.

Yet even while we recognize these motifs and characters as formulaic, recent work on the gangster genre has emphasized its complexity, diversity, and uneven historical productions. As one group of critics argues, it would be more accurate to think of the gangster genre not as a formula, but as series of production cycles attuned to current "discourses about crime, inflected in specific ways in relation to class, gender, and race" (Grieveson et al. 4). The films discussed here exemplify one such cycle, responding to widespread "colored" gangland violence by reclaiming the off-white gangster hero. As Diane Negra remarks in her study of white ethnicities in Hollywood, "off white" groups have been "useful in defusing social tensions by activating assimilation myths" (3), assuring us of a "real" America where differences are essentially among white Europeans.

Although these films share these themes, they also illustrate the divergences within the gangster genre in terms of style and tone. *The Godfather: Part III* and *State of Grace* engage in theology, history, and melodrama in order to cast their gangsters as doomed and heroic. These narratives cite the violent history of Ireland, the secrets of the Vatican, and even Catholic theological treatises on "grace" as recited by Terry Noonan in his goodbye speech to his girlfriend in *State of Grace*. The two ethnic parades in these films and the operatic and Shakespearean references in *The Godfather: Part III* situate the gangster's story within formidable power structures of the state, family, and religion, and within discourses of theology and destiny. The sexual relationships in these films are rendered through melodrama—scenes of high emotion, the presence of family pressures, and an emphasis on the doomed nature of the relationship. The shoot-outs take on epic resonance, and the heroes realize too late that their efforts to do good are condemned to failure.

In contrast, the protagonists of *Goodfellas* and *Miller's Crossing* are treated like hoods, not heroes, and the tone of both films could be described as black comedy or absurdist drama. *Goodfellas* documents mob life as a seductive parallel universe to suburbia and legitimate business. *Miller's Crossing* plays across the gangster film genre itself, parodying its excesses and exposing its ironies. *King of New York* shares the cynicism of these films, though it retains the figure of the gangster as epic hero. But *King of New York* also engages in the conventions of MTV, its violence choreographed and aestheticized. In all three films, sex and violence are about money and power, and there is no easy recourse to meta-narratives that would give them meaning. Meaning, indeed, is often altogether absent. The mysterious hat that flies through the air during the main title of *Miller's Crossing* is described in a dream that Tom relates to Verna. Verna guesses that the hat changed into something else—that is, that it had meaning. Tom tells her, "No, it stayed a hat."

The stakes of the racial anxieties in these films are broader and deeper than the icons of popular culture or the evolution of a cinematic genre. The phantasmic black gangster in these films exemplifies Ralph Ellison's description of how white Americans find an identity through "the presence of black Americans . . . as a marker, a symbol of limits, a metaphor for the 'outsider'" (165–66). In the year when apartheid ended halfway around the globe, these films mapped out the ghostly boundaries that continued to haunt American concepts of race and continued to produce figures of a dangerous outsider navigating the system's underworld.

NOTES

1. For example, there were 690 gang-related homicides in Los Angeles County, where membership in 450 gangs and crews topped 50,000. The L.A. police staged well-publicized sweeps of "bad" neighborhoods, but gang members outnumbered the police four to one (Sullivan and Silverstein 15). For more on gang activity during this time, see Sanders.

2. The top box-office film, *Home Alone*, grossed $285.7 million. It was followed by *Ghost* ($217.6 million), *Dances with Wolves* ($184.2 million), and *Pretty Woman* ($178.4 million).

3. The derogatory word "guinea" illustrates the racial root of anti-Italian prejudice; it was a term originally used to describe the inferior status of African slaves and their descendants (Guglielmo 11).

4. She is watching the scene in which Al Jolson sings "Toot, Toot, Tootsie, Goodbye" to his showbiz girlfriend. Colley points out how the song wittily foreshadows the frantic scene late in the movie when, with federal agents at the door in a more serious situation, Karen flushes her husband's entire stash of cocaine down the toilet (50).

1991

Movies and Wayward Images

SHARON WILLIS

The Gulf War came to us as a seamless flow of eerily simu-
lacral images, remarkably consistent grainy black-and-white computer pictures from the point of view of unmanned missiles, producing an entirely
abstract landscape cut to the measure of the TV screen that we watched
every day. Images provided by a disembodied agency as abstract as a video
game occupied the whole picture, pushing concrete locations and real
bleeding and dying bodies out of the frame.

But Gulf War imagery produced only one of a series of weird inversions
between fiction and reality that played out across our mediascape. Many of
these inversions cast politics, history, and material events as spectacles, but
conversely treated fictional entertainment cinema as a potentially dangerous social agent that could provoke violent imitation by its audience. Race
and gender frequently anchored public debates about the effects of images,
though often these categories became confused. During the confirmation
hearings of Supreme Court nominee Clarence Thomas, in which African
American legal scholar Anita Hill testified that Thomas had sexually
harassed her years earlier, the race and gender of these antagonists worked
to transform congressional proceedings into national theater. The drama
played out such that Thomas became the representative of blackness as victim and Hill was cast as the delegate of white feminism (see Morrison).
Cynically calling the hearings a "high-tech lynching," and with the collusion of Congress and the press, Thomas became a racially inflected icon of
suffering while Hill became de-racialized, abstracted as a representative of a
feminism coded only as white. The hearings thereby staged the inadequacy
of official and popular rhetorics of representation, or image repertoires, to
handle race and gender simultaneously.

But while Thomas strategically evoked the image of lynching—the historical act of racial terrorism that centrally depends on the effects of public
spectacle—what of Rodney King's real-life beating, captured on videotape
in March? Wasn't this arguably a lynching under the auspices of civil
authority? Although the legal standing of the videotape as evidence was

only evaluated the following year, its long circulation in the popular media surely affected the Simi Valley verdict. The eminent black scholar Houston Baker characterized the tape of the King beating as reproducing a classic "scene of violence" in U.S. cultural and narrative history, one dating back to the slave narrative. As the tape replayed endlessly on TV screens across the United States, Baker concluded, "King is still silent and manifestly invisible, in proper person. It is as though he is sickeningly caught forever in the graceless heaviness of his attempts—crudely videotaped—to escape the next crushing blow from the LAPD" (43). Hamid Naficy emphasizes the importance of silence and repetition. He argues that "the repeated screening of dissected images"—as in sports replays, for example—far from yielding a hidden truth behind the moving images, instead "turns them into abstractions, into images without referent, into simulacrum" (301). Significantly, for Baker, too, to restore a sound track to this image is to give voice to history, to interrupt the visual spectacle of the black body. In Baker's estimation, the proper sound track to destabilize this image is rap. And rap, of course, provides the sound track for the year's most successful and attention-grabbing black-authored films.

N.W.A., the West Coast hip-hop group, released its final album, *Efil4zaggin* (Niggaz41ife), before breaking up for good, just as Ice Cube began his movie career in *Boyz n the Hood* and Naughty by Nature's rap single "O.P.P." crossed over to climb the pop music charts and MTV broadcast its video. Musical boundaries continued to shift. Nirvana, one of the bands most closely associated with grunge, released its album *Nevermind,* which featured its breakthrough song, "Smells Like Teen Spirit." Also reflecting the grunge aesthetic, Douglas Coupland's *Generation X: Tales for an Accelerated Culture* provided a name for the generation coming of age in the late 1980s. This book sought to capture the cultural landscape of twentysomething slackers, and it shaped a new lexicon, crafting terms like "McJob," that would enter into broader circulation. Elsewhere on the literary front, Bret Easton Ellis's *American Psycho* sparked heated controversy with its over-the-top depictions of violence, mainly against women. When Simon and Schuster ceremoniously dropped the novel from its publication list, the new media-savvy director of Vintage, Sonny Mehta, picked it up and allowed the controversy to advertise the book and propel sales.

Beyond the Gulf War on the international front, borders crumbled and gave way to conflict-ridden reorganizations of territories: the Soviet Union collapsed and Yugoslavia broke apart into nationalist ethnic war. Indian prime minister Rajiv Gandhi was assassinated; the failure of the Bank of Credit and Commerce International represented the most costly case of banking fraud to date; American hostage Terry Anderson was released after six years in captivity in Lebanon; and sanctions against South Africa were lifted. Inside the United States, Magic Johnson courageously announced his HIV-positive status in an effort to combat public stigmatization of people with HIV/AIDS. The year also saw the "launch" of Biosphere 2, a self-enclosed synthetic environment that was meant as a prototype for space colonization missions. Revelations of massive and systematic sexual abuse at a convention of naval aviators (the Tailhook scandal) helped to open the military to serious investigations of such charges. Jeffrey Dahmer's arrest brought to national attention his shocking case: the Wisconsin serial killer chose as his victims young men of color whom he lured to his home, murdered, and sometimes cannibalized. These revelations also raised questions about policing practices in Milwaukee, given the lack of attention to these young men's disappearances.

On the movie screen Hollywood auteurs produced a diverse range of projects. Steven Spielberg brought us the fantasy of a grown-up Peter Pan in *Hook*. Martin Scorsese remade *Cape Fear*, in a graphically overwrought style that only highlighted the more compelling creepiness of J. Lee Thompson's 1962 original. Terry Gilliam offered the whimsical *Fisher King*, while Jim Jarmusch made *Night on Earth*, a cosmopolitan exploration of globalism in intimate local sites. Disney released *Beauty and the Beast*, the first animated feature to be nominated for Best Picture. Using the studio's proprietary CAPS (Computer Assisted Production System), this film succeeded in revivifying animation practices and paved the way for future animation features.

As "Roseanne" became the second most popular show on TV, movies began to offer somewhat more flexibility and access to white women, just as they did—somewhat provisionally—to black men. In Alan Rudolph's *Mortal Thoughts* and Joseph Ruben's *Sleeping with the Enemy*, abused women took control and fought back against monstrous husbands. Alek Keshishian's *Madonna: Truth or Dare* took as its very subject feminine control; this film is about, by, and for dominant female agency. Rapper icons also circulated in the year's films. Ice-T appeared in Russell Mulcahy's *Ricochet*, where he played the head of a crack ring, a reversal of his role in *New Jack City*. Significantly, video technology drove *Ricochet*'s plot. In the most perverse of the year's dialogues between big and small screens, movies and news, this film obliquely referenced the King beating video (see also Torres).

Of course, white men—traumatized, enraged, or hapless—occupied the lion's share of screen time. Bruce Willis failed as a husband twice, as the drunken, abusive boor in *Mortal Thoughts* and also in a comic subplot to *The*

Last Boy Scout, directed by Tony Scott. The latter film also contributes to one of the year's most marked tendencies, as movies repeated the black-white buddy trope. While *The Last Boy Scout* derived much of its humor, and all of its erotic energy, from the wisecracking between Damon Wayans and Willis, Lawrence Kasdan's *Grand Canyon* organized its plot around the oafishly earnest efforts of Mack (Kevin Kline), an immigration lawyer, to bond with Simon (Danny Glover), the tow-truck driver who has rescued him from a gang. Most spectacular of all, however, the interracial buddy device emerged in Kevin Reynold's *Robin Hood: Prince of Thieves,* as Robin (Kevin Costner) returns from crusading in Turkey with a "Moorish" sidekick, Azeem (Morgan Freeman).

Gays and lesbians flickered intermittently onscreen, occasionally centrally, more often as ghostly effects or sites of unresolved ambiguity. While Gus Van Sant's *My Own Private Idaho* explored the complexities of gay desire, Oliver Stone's sublimely paranoid *JFK* imagined a lurid gay sub-conspiracy in the assassination. Tropes of secrecy abounded. In *Prince of Tides,* the affair between the psychiatrist (Barbra Streisand) and patient (Nick Nolte) revealed the tormented origins of his dysfunction in a scene of male gang rape. Meanwhile, *Fried Green Tomatoes,* a film centrally organized by secrets— and not just the one in the sauce, it turned out—foregrounded "friend-ships" that it couldn't fully account for narratively. "Friendship" magically produced astonishing racial harmony as its black characters allied with the two central white women, Idgie (Mary Stuart Masterson) and Ruth (Mary-Louise Parker), whose lesbian relationship likewise remained cloaked in euphemism. Stunningly enough, this cross-racial bonding cohered around the cannibalistic feast that disposes of the body of Ruth's wife-abusing, racist ex-husband (see Berglund; Holmlund "Cruisin'"). Differences resolved through a ritual of incorporation, as this unthreatening oral management united a "community." Significantly, as gay and lesbian audiences consolidated to speak critically to the industry, they challenged the frames of these "ambiguously gay" representations.

A few black male directors were given cultural authority as ethnographic native informants, as if an experiential frame guaranteed the "authenticity" of their representations of black community. This representational authority, as we will see, largely rendered black women invisible.

Incendiary Images

This year saw the release of three features by first-time directors: Mario Van Peebles's *New Jack City* (Warner Bros.; grossing $47.6

million), John Singleton's *Boyz n the Hood* (Columbia; $57.5 million), and Matty Rich's *Straight Out of Brooklyn* (premiered at Sundance, then distributed by MGM; $2.7 million). In the wake of their success, popular discourse reflected contemporary anxieties about the connections between media images and real-world violence, about a crisis of the frame. Perhaps these debates around representations of young black men, which dovetailed with those concerning angry white women, demonstrate that, by becoming news themselves, movies *do* exercise a kind of social agency, though not of the sort these discussions imagined. Within these interdependent representational frames of cinematic fiction and news formats, popular discourse took cinematic figures for representatives of social groups and focused on identification as structuring both audience formation and spectator response. But these discussions tend to collapse identification with identity, and representativeness with representation, thus imposing what Kobena Mercer has called "the burden of representation" on African American productions (21).

The *New York Times Magazine* of 17 July carried a cover story on "Hollywood's Black Directors" by Karen Grigsby Bates. Recounting Hollywood's "discovery" of this group of cultural producers along with an audience for them, the story also highlighted the fragility of the cinematic frame, since its "black product" opened onto the arena of rap musical culture *and* onto an imagined continuity with the daily life of black urban youth. In this context, audience became central. Concerns emerged immediately after *New Jack City* opened when a few theaters reported violent skirmishes. The *Times* article also registered industry anxiety about stories that treated black urban experiences. One director interviewed for the story, Mario Van Peebles, was quick to reply to such fears by citing a murder at a screening of *The Godfather: Part III* (1990), which led to no such anxiety about the film's impact (40) (see, for further analysis, Smith-Shomade; Baker "Screening"). Still, in marketing its newly [re]discovered product, Hollywood anchored a film's "realist" claims to a director's life, taking his work as a direct expression of personal experience. Valerie Smith characterized that effect as the "documentary impulse," as "most reviews of or feature articles on these films assure us that the directors are in positions of authority relative to their material" (58).

The very marketability of these films was tellingly symptomatic, as African American women critics have forcefully registered, since it both depended upon and perpetuated the representational marginalization of black women. Jacquie Jones argues that Van Peebles's and Singleton's films produced a certain mass appeal (something for *almost* "everyone") at the same time that they offered narratives familiar to us from television news. She contends that, as "the news became a factory for black mass media imagery in cautious, conservative times," serious consequences for gender ensued (96). These films shared with the media a tendency to push black girls and women to the margins, and to pathologize that marginal space. For Jones, "these girls seemed . . . to exist in the space of the accused," since "it was those teen-age, female-headed households that produced these boys" (96). Girls and women were not just marginalized within the frame, but they were constructed as the symptomatic cause underlying the narrative.

For different reasons but with a similar critique, Paul Gilroy criticizes the focus on "authenticity" that anchored critical reception of these films. "This authenticity," he argues, "is inseparable from talk about the conduct of bitter gender-based conflicts, which is now recognized as essential to familial, racial, and communal health. Each of these—the familial, the racial, the communal—leads seamlessly into the next" (306). If we insist on reducing the complexity of community through an analogy with the family, we foreclose the conflicts and contradictions within communities. Likewise, we obscure their political struggles in and with the dominant culture. If familial and oedipal (father-son) narrative tropes worked to elide complexities within the films, critical responses from divergent perspectives conflated realism with reality or truth. In so doing they constructed African American cultural producers as the voice of "reality" for the mainstream, but they also foreclosed the complexities of audience response, and the questions of fantasy, artifice, and the aesthetics specific to film.

Rather than bypass the aesthetic for the sociological, as many critical accounts have tended to do, we may better understand *New Jack City* and *Boyz* if we pay close attention to their representational means, and especially to the ways that they continually play with the cinematic frame, but not in order to substitute documentary for fiction. Extra-textual framing also comes into play in particular ways as both films launched a number of important careers besides Singleton's and Van Peebles's: Cuba Gooding Jr. made his debut, and Ice Cube and Ice-T crossed over from rap music into acting. Both rappers emerged from the West Coast "gangsta" rap world; Ice-T had released *O.G.: Original Gangster* (Sire) and Ice Cube his solo record *AmeriKKKa's Most Wanted* the previous year, before his bitter split from N.W.A. The aggressive political content, and especially the critique of the police, in both rappers' work contributes to ongoing public controversy about the power of this music to evoke or promote violence in its audience. In his person, then, each actor imports the resonance of his music into the film medium.

New Jack City constantly works with boundaries, both diegetically and meta-cinematically. Placing itself within the American gangster film genre, it tells the story of Nino Brown (Wesley Snipes), a slick, glamorous, and ruthless dealer who builds an empire for himself by monopolizing the sale of newly introduced crack cocaine in Harlem. Soon Brown becomes the object of an undercover police operation. Directing that operation is Van Peebles's own character, Detective Stone, who has recruited the "renegade" cop, Ice-T's Scotty Appleton, to go undercover. Ice-T imports rap culture into the film in his very person, doubling his fictional character through his iconic status as a rapper well known for his consistent critique of the Los Angeles police. So, when he embodies a policeman in *New Jack City,* ironies proliferate, especially when he spins violently out of control.

Several other performers circulate through the film, as musical numbers punctuate the narrative, taking on equal standing with the violent eruptions that propel the plot. Throughout, the sound track provides a sharp critical counterpoint to the narrative. Van Peebles's anti-drug morality play sustained frequent criticism that it glamorized precisely what it clearly intends to criticize. To maintain this position, however, one would need to ignore the sound track—the voice—that troubles the visual frame, by constantly challenging the satisfactions of the spectacle. *New Jack City* frequently comes off as a tug-of-war between the pointed anti-drug message that frames it and its power as visual spectacle. The film's rhythm replicates the volatile back and forth between the gangsters and the black community they have invaded. Significantly, that community, embodied by crowds of extras, is given voice through one character, the "Old Man" (Bill Cobbs), the community's righteous avenger who becomes the incarnation of justice: he assassinates Brown. Once again, we encounter the fantasy that only the responsible black father can save the community.

Although it seems intent on depicting the catastrophic effects of the crack epidemic, the film's spectacle sometimes pulls away from its narrative as it plays with the frame. In a sharply ironic scene, Nino and his lieutenant, Gee Money (Allen Payne), watch Brian De Palma's *Scarface* (1983) with their girlfriends. As they watch, Gee Money's girlfriend, Uniqua (Tracy Camilla Johns), dances seductively before the screen. At this point, the images have shifted to the last sequences of Melvin Van Peebles's groundbreaking 1971 film, *Sweet Sweetback's Baadasssss Song*. So Van Peebles's real-life father, along with his family film history, appears in cameo within the internal frame. Yet *New Jack City* insistently zooms in on the abject underside of the glamour, violence, and maniacal power that define Nino's position. In the repeated image of someone "sucking on the glass dick" of the crack pipe, the film hammers out its social message. Despite its explicit analysis of the external forces that profit the most from the drug's incursion into the community, the film's most haunting figure is that of the addict desperately consuming the smoke that, in turn, consumes his body in a perversely morbid image of self-consumption.

Significantly, *Straight Out of Brooklyn*, a much less widely circulated independent film (whose name echoes N.W.A.'s 1988 album *Straight Outta Compton*), is also organized by relentless oral obsession and haunted by paternal failure. In this film's bare, almost Brechtian world, where characters perform themselves as types, the father stands out as most volatile. The film's verbal center, he subsists entirely through oral transactions: he drinks in alcohol and spews out rage, resentment, and insult.

Perhaps the most striking common ground that *Boyz n the Hood* shares with *New Jack City* is its depiction of the brutally rigid partitioning of the urban spaces its characters inhabit. Set in South Central Los Angeles, *Boyz n the Hood* follows the struggles of three young friends—and their families— to navigate the pressures of the streets: the temptations of drugs and crime, the black-on-black violence that proliferates violence, and oppressive policing. Even as the sounds of helicopters overhead repeatedly signal their surveillance, the police regularly provide harassment instead of protection. Again and again, the film emphasizes the dramatic rigidity of boundaries, both the territorial ones that mark the neighborhood and the fragile ones that attempt to isolate domestic space from the menacing street. That is, the fortress-prison structure of the housing project turned crack factory in *New Jack City*, heavily blockaded against the chaos of the street, returns in *Boyz n the Hood* (for significant readings see Dyson; Farred; Massood).

This film's establishing shots consistently linger outside the houses, framing the doorway as characters enter and exit the house or wait in the entryway, focusing on the door's metal bars. The camera's anxious surveillance of the threshold emphasizes the continued vulnerability of domestic spaces to violent invasion from the outside. Alongside its visual obsession with doorways, barriers, and boundaries—both visible and invisible—this film inscribes the liminal position of its adolescent male protagonists in their oral obsessions. An oral talisman marks most of these young men. Mad Dog (Lexie Bigham) sucks on a white pacifier; Darin/Doughboy (Ice Cube) favors quarts of malt liquor, while his brother Ricky (Morris Chestnut) prefers quart cartons of milk, their beverages encoding the good son/bad son structure. Only Tre (Cuba Gooding Jr.) seems immune to oral pleasure. These oral signs remain quite striking in a fictional universe where the mothers are variously cast as distant, unreliable, or incompetent.

Sons are tied to mothers, or to a mother surrogate, in a world where strong fathers, like Furious Styles (Laurence Fishburne), fail to interrupt the connection.

But the vulnerability of the home space in *Boyz* registers as a limitation on the visual field. The film opens on a black screen while the sound track registers what is unmistakably a drive-by shooting, followed by the sounds of sirens and a helicopter. These last two sounds will regularly puncture the visual field, suggesting either an urgency elsewhere, just off frame and inaccessible to our sight, or a menace from above. At night, sweeping searchlights redouble the invasive sound effects, reinforcing the impression that the houses are actually porous. As the overhead menace grows atmospheric because its appearance is so frequent and so pronounced, one realizes that this film unfolds through a strongly horizontal drive. This effect echoes the movement of the automobiles that are so central to the characters' world. But the strong horizontal also emerges in the characteristic tracking shots that follow the protagonists along the street, and it even recurs in the preference for horizontal pans to capture characters in conversation. Visually, this is a world where the horizon line coincides with the rooflines of the one-story bungalows that make up the neighborhood, or with the top of a car's windshield or side window. Don't look up, the film seems to enjoin us, as it shows the characters' resolute focus at street level.

But if the helicopter and sirens constitute an intrusion of the outside into the fragile domestic or neighborhood space, so too does music, though more ambiguously. Rap music frequently emanates from an unseen source, and it encodes a threat, the approach of a possibly menacing car. Yet this same music can code as the reassurance of "home," enfolding the inhabitants of a given car. Rap music thus serves multiple functions: it connects and divides spaces, it menaces and reassures, and it marks definitively the ambivalent status of the car as a semi-private, semi-public space.

When Tre and Ricky drive Tre's VW Beetle to the regular hangout site on Crenshaw, the sound track suggests diegetic music. It seems that the music the men are playing comes from multiple automobiles, and by the time they park to greet their friends, the music has swelled to envelop them all in the environment of community. But this automotive community is abruptly disrupted by the arrival of outsiders who precipitate a shooting incident that sends all the cars careening away. In the temporary quiet of Tre's car, the two friends discuss their increasing sense of urgency about leaving the 'hood. This vehicle has functioned throughout as a site of intimacy, where the friends discuss their relationships and their aspirations.

The "boys" of *Boyz n the Hood*: Darin "Doughboy" Baker (Ice Cube) in the driver's seat, with Ricky Baker (Morris Chestnut) alongside and Mad Dog (Lexie Bingham) enjoying his pacifier (John Singleton, Columbia Pictures). Courtesy Photofest New York.

But on this occasion, the car becomes a site of exposure, as a siren interrupts their reflections and they are arrested by sadistically menacing cops.

Native Informants?

Continuing with the autobiographical focus that led critical discussion of films about young black men to cast their directors as "native informants," cultural authorities of the sort that ethnographers seek to interview, *Newsweek*'s cover image of 10 June posed Wesley Snipes and Annabella Sciorra in a highly theatrical embrace. The magazine used *Jungle Fever*'s box office draw—the film grossed some $32.5 million, a testimony to its volatile appeal—to open a discussion of interracial love and sex in articles entitled "Tackling a Taboo: Spike Lee's Take on Interracial Romance" and "Mixed Couples on Love and Prejudice." Lee's film focused on a troubled love affair between Snipes's character, a married architect, and his Italian American secretary, played by Sciorra. Even as it tracked the conflicts that eventually drive the couple apart, the film remains equally attentive to the responses, ranging from critical and contemptuous to phobic and violent, from the lovers' respective families and communities.

But if the subject of race was figured as an issue through discussions of, and polls about, interracial love, desire, and sex surrounding the film, all this happened within a representational field now more obsessed with consuming "race" than representing it (see Paulin; Guerrero). As they had done with Spike Lee's *Do the Right Thing* (1989), the mainstream white press sought to acclaim or reject *Jungle Fever* in terms of the correctness of its "argument." This impulse collapsed its cinematic "real effects" with social reality, and constructed Lee as a privileged interlocutor who spoke for a whole population. However, organized as it was by collisions among competing characters' views, Lee's film resisted resolution as a clear statement. David Denby was representative of critics who responded negatively to the film: "The movie is words, words, words. . . . *Jungle Fever* is raucous, tendentious, shallow, self-canceling. . . . Lee carefully sets up an interracial love affair and then buries it in the predictably enraged opinions everyone has about it" (76). A corollary of this criticism was the widely shared complaint that the characters we expected to act as protagonists came off as ciphers, lacking psychological depth or interiority. But this film played as pointedly with the question of how people *look*—in both senses of this verb—as it did with the meanings of race and of interracial coupling.

Denby criticized the film for its failure to provide us access to the inside of the love affair, highlighting instead the "outside" by concentrating on the reactions to it. "*Jungle Fever,* it turns out," he argued, "is not about adultery, or marriage, or sex, or even sex and race together, that most explosive of combinations . . . it's really about what interests Lee the most, race hatred and color. . . . But is Lee perhaps a bit . . . overwrought? I know a few interracial couples, and I see more walking around the city. They don't seem pursued by howling furies every minute of the day" (76). In response to the film's refusal to supply a confessional interiority as the "truth" of the relationship, Denby produced his own "native informants." Not surprisingly, the film's TV reception paraded native informants on talk shows reporting from a newly visible social territory. If, like Denby, the dominant media kept trying to read *Jungle Fever* as a failed ethnography of interracial relationships, it overlooked the possibility that the film might perform *another* ethnography, examining the dominant *white* gaze. Flipper (Snipes) and Angie (Sciorra) do function visually as ciphers. More looked at than looking, their individual points of view are gradually submerged in the figure they make, as the object of others' looks. Holding them together in two-shot, where the obvious artifice of lens filters and lighting effects heightens or subdues the contrast in skin tones, the editing deprives them of point of view. As visual strategies evacuate their interiority, they also place the

Flipper (Wesley Snipes) and Angie (Annabella Sciorra) on their first real date, in *Jungle Fever* (Spike Lee, Forty Acres & A Mule Filmworks). Courtesy Photofest New York.

spectator in a position to observe how they operate as signs that the other characters continually interpret. We see them as the figure of difference fetishized in contrasting skin.

Visually restless, *Jungle Fever*'s camera remains obtrusive, interfering with effects of naturalism or "reality" through canted angles and filtered lenses. No scene escapes the intervention of a situated gaze. This film forces us to acknowledge the camera's agency, as in its use of "double" tracking shots, with the camera on a track following characters rolling along on a track as well, so that they glide off in an impossible space, moving both too quickly and too smoothly for any verisimilitude. Equally obtrusive visually is the mise-en-scène. Take the self-consciously stagy environment of the stock room in the women's clothing department where Flipper's wife, Drew (Lonette McKee), works. As husband and wife engage in an intense dispute about Flipper's affair, the characters are framed as if on stage by fabric that drapes across the top and down the sides of the frame. They move to stand between curtains of yellow fabric, just at the moment when Drew is running through the litany of epithets that have characterized her as "high yellow."

At the level of editing, the film forces us to struggle over meaning, much as its characters do. A single example should suffice here: the sequence of Flipper's and Angie's dinner at his parents' house, and the subsequent scene of the couple's return to their downtown apartment. These sequences explore the gaze as a social phenomenon, examining the construction of racialized meaning based on visibility, and emphasizing the couple's obliviousness to "how they look." Flipper's father, the Good Reverend Doctor (Ossie Davis), presents a didactic speech that far exceeds the boundaries of the moment to reverberate through the film, making Angie's whiteness emerge as a sign whose meanings are produced in a densely saturated historical nexus. His father sees Angie as an emblem of historical "white Southern womanhood": "her husband ran down to the slave quarters . . . the white ladies felt abandoned . . . late at night and alone on the hot bed of lust, they must have thought what it would be like to have one of them . . . thought about the big black bucks their husbands were so afraid of."

In this context, Angie's ethnicity and her working-class position disappear beneath her white femininity. Indeed, it is her femininity that makes her whiteness visible and meaningful in the context of her relationship with Flipper. At the same time, however, the Good Reverend Doctor sets the couple's image in a historical frame, recalling the history, sustained by eroticized racist fantasy, of white men's rape of black women and lynching of black men. That it is Ossie Davis, known for decades of activism and key roles in black productions, who delivers these lines adds another dimension.

As the Good Reverend Doctor's affective pitch escalates to near hysteria—"alone on the hot bed of lust, they must have thought . . . about the big black bucks their husbands were so afraid of"—his speech takes on the intensity that characters bring to bear on the juncture of racialized sex within the film. This affective intensity is crucial, for it reminds us of the force of repression and of historical pressures that relegated white men's interracial couplings to invisibility, while speaking obsessively about black men's, rendering them hyper-visible. Here the film establishes a striking parallel through paternal rebuke: the Good Reverend Doctor's recourse to rigid sanctimoniousness echoes Angie's father (Frank Vincent), who reacts in his turn to the news of her relationship by beating her and casting her out. Paternity is a central organizing principle. This is a world in which all the fathers are "bad."

These fathers' hysterical gazes on their children's interracial desire doubles the authority of the police on the domestic front. In the next sequence, as the couple play outside their parked car, mock-boxing while calling out the names of Italian American and African American boxers, they are brutally interrupted by two white cops. Structurally, this scene functions to make Flipper aware of the futility of this relationship, because he breaks it off shortly thereafter. If Flipper's position paradoxically coincides with the cops,' this sequence would suggest, it is because he has finally realized how he looks together with Angie for anonymous surveying gazes. The arrival of the police brutally literalizes one of the meanings of the Good Reverend Doctor's story, that the culture polices racialized borders all the more strenuously for their being imaginary, while those borders take on a certain hyper-visibility when a sexual pairing calls attention to the ways they are always already intensely eroticized.

Some of the complexity surrounding racialized sexuality emerges explicitly, however, in *Jungle Fever*'s famous women's "war council" scene, where Drew has gathered a group of her woman friends to discuss how she might respond to her husband's infidelity. The matter of infidelity, however, is immediately displaced by the issue of his choosing a white woman as a partner. Naturalistic lighting and the spontaneous feel of the camera work, panning from speaker to speaker, and introducing actors who don't appear elsewhere in the film, all work to produce a visual texture entirely foreign to the rest of the film, interrupting the narrative. This scene's characters all offer articulated positions that don't reduce easily to sound bites, and none is privileged over the others. Rehearsing a series of positions and emotions, this sequence invests not so much in knowledge or truth as in the ways that affect and the imaginary are mobilized around racial and ethnic boundaries. Refusing to reduce the question of interracial relations, or of race, to simple binary opposition, these speakers complicate the issues by recognizing that any "racial" field is intertwined with ethnicities, class, and sexuality. But we are asked to see this scene as a parenthesis and to put it aside. Because the documenter's position is not inscribed in the scene, the spectator is placed as eavesdropping on native informants privately speaking about the publicly unspeakable.

If *Jungle Fever* momentarily assigns to the African American women in this sequence the power to know more and to speak more truthfully, it also runs the risk of setting them up in the role of judges. If women are supposed to be the "ones who know" the truth of the matter, then that leaves the men free from responsibility to do their homework. This effect echoes forcefully in Queen Latifah's cameo appearance as a waitress in the Harlem restaurant to which Flipper takes Angie. She aggressively scolds Flipper as much for a childish flaunting of his erotic choice as for the choice itself. The real rapper, imported into the film for this one scene, breaks the fictional frame as another figure of black female judgment comes down on the man who seems to have gone out of his way to encounter it. In this connection, the parenthetical status of the women's "war council" scene becomes symptomatic because it foregrounds the social specificity of African American women's position as one that does not allow the fantasy that racial and gender identity could be separated, or that one could override the other. But *Jungle Fever* doesn't seem to follow out the critical challenge the scene posed, and instead chooses to frame it parenthetically. While, by and large, *Jungle Fever* skillfully refuses the burden of authentic testimony with which the dominant culture wishes to saddle it by structurally posing the women's discourse here as a "moment of truth," it risks passing this burden on to African American women. And because, as many critics have pointed out, most of the women who appear in this scene appear in cameo, so to speak, since they are not characters anywhere else in the film, the film risks offering them as mere "figures" of the truth, an all-too-common gesture in contemporary discussions.

Fighting Feminists

If race displaced gender in films about black communities, gender thoroughly trumped race in films that celebrated violent women. This effect comes into relief when we consider that in both *Thelma & Louise* and *Terminator 2: Judgment Day* a black male character emerges but is quickly reduced to a mere trace, in order to function as a prop that highlights the steadfast whiteness that underwrites this feminine agency.

As cinematic fantasies this year invested heavily in feminism as a cultural sign, *Thelma & Louise* ($45.4 million) claimed a sizable share of intense media attention alongside the most expensive film to date, *T2* ($516.8 million). But the smaller film sparked intense debate in the popular press because it intersected with fantasies about women and aggression that plugged into cultural anxieties about sexual difference, and about men's and women's places in a newly reshaped "battle of the sexes." *Thelma & Louise* follows its increasingly aggressive pair of female buddies as they take flight from a husband, a boyfriend, and the police, after Louise (Susan Sarandon) has murdered the man who has attempted to rape Thelma (Geena Davis). No doubt the film drew some of its disruptive force from its ending: rather than allow themselves to be caught, the protagonists drive their Thunderbird off the edge of the Grand Canyon. Ending as it does on a freeze-frame of the car suspended against the sky, the film resolutely refuses closure.

Regularly citing this "battle of the sexes," critics insistently read *Thelma & Louise* as a political statement. In a crudely inverted feminist vocabulary that focused on the film's women as negative and dangerous models of feminist assertiveness, some critics accused the film of male bashing. From a

feminist perspective, Margaret Carlson read the film as coming to a political dead-end: "*Thelma & Louise* sends the message that little ground has been
won. . . . They become free but only wildly, self-destructively so—free to
drive off the ends of the earth" (57). Widely shared anxieties about feminine aggression and self-destructiveness depended on a distinct overesti-
mation of the film's few moments of violence and on a conviction that its
characters are representative of and for feminism (see Sturken; Griggers;
and Hart). Such energetic responses to the film's "violence" understood the
image as shaping spectator consciousness through the identifications to
which they imagined female spectators and audiences to be especially sus-
ceptible. As films worked to shape images that would attract a feminine
audience by speaking women's anxieties and desires, feminist and nonfem-
inist popular discourse alike ended up figuring this audience itself as out of
control, like Thelma and Louise.

Women critics, whether they defended or attacked the film, always
seemed compelled to address the crude question of role models, and always
at some point fell back on their private temptations to identify with spectacular images of feminine rage. What allowed so many women critics to
take this film so personally? Why did popular media discussion sympto-
matically participate in the very "crisis" it sought to diagnose, reproducing
a "battle of the sexes" despite itself? The answer must lie in the film's openness to the fantasmatic scenarios one can bring to it. Thus, critics would find
destabilizing fantasies coming to them in an exaggerated form from the
"outside," in representation. Such a scenario would of course pertain
equally to masculine anxieties about women's violence directed toward
men and to feminine anxieties about a "bad object" within feminism. The
critical drive to regulate the film's meanings had to shut down its irony, and
to repress the difference between fantasy and agency. This drive depends on
forgetting that the film's spectacle is made of the play between plausibility
and fantasy. While that play is certainly organized around a female body,
this body in motion cannot be dissociated from the drive forward into loss.

Emphatically fantasmatic, the film reminds us that one of the effects of
driving is to render landscape as image, as cinematic flow, across the frame
of a windshield. Saturated with unreal color, this landscape is marked as a
screen for special effects. Frequently veiled by uninterrupted sheets of too
even rain, this geography recalls the deliberately whimsical atmospherics of
commercials, as the film seems to revel in its own artifice. At every turn,
the film displaces its energy from narrative justification and explanation to
other seductions: the road, the speed of motion, and the image. Its fantasmatic machinery produces displacements that overthrow resolutions and

explanations that might support a stable political meaning. For example, the much-discussed violence that turned a simple weekend vacation into a journey of no return comes when Louise murders a man (Timothy Carhart) who attempts to rape Thelma. But discussion "forgot" that Louise shoots him, not in the heat of rage when she intervenes to prevent the rape, but rather in a calm pause afterward, when he insists upon having the last word with the verbal challenge, "Suck my cock!" She kills him, then, not for what he does, but for what he *says*, a far thinner pretext.

In this context, arguments that remained riveted on this film's "violence" radically reduced the complexity of the film as a social text. Significantly, however, the urgency with which critical responses sought to bolster Louise's fragile pretext by providing it with the justification of a previous sexual victimization betrays other anxieties: about feminism, about femininity, or about sexual difference itself. Any spectator might experience the identificatory relays that open around this act of violent "revenge" as an invitation, or a demand, to take up a gendered position aligned anywhere on the victim-aggressor axis. Remaining an ambivalent object, *Thelma & Louise* continually highlighted the shakiness of this excuse for a headlong flight with no destination. Equally ambivalent is the plot turn that definitively precipitates Thelma and Louise over the edge of no return. Thelma becomes an armed robber because J.D. (Brad Pitt), a hitchhiker with whom she has had her first good sex, has stolen all their money. Here is another incident of victimization: seduction and abandonment compounded by theft. But Thelma reads the event as a fortunate one, and subsequently she incorporates J.D.'s theatrically scripted robbery routine: we watch her perform the way J.D. did, through a store's video surveillance camera. Thelma has become an image before our eyes, and through the explicit theft of a man's posture.

This film's most compelling fantasies keep emerging through cross-gender identifications that escape a narrative logic of cause and effect. Its wandering story mimics the detour that becomes the whole trip, and it invites the spectator to reproduce Thelma's lusty appreciation of J.D. as he walks away: "I luuuuve watchin' him go." *Thelma & Louise* wants us to love watching it go, not watching it get somewhere. *Thelma & Louise*'s women raid exhausted images and worn-out stories drawn from westerns, road movies, and buddy films, occupying the tired clichés of Hollywood masculinity and male bonding. But this occupation foregrounds the posturing involved, which mobilizes for women viewers the pleasures of fantasmatic identifications with embodied agents of travel, speed, force, and aggression, pleasures that we have historically enjoyed in a cross-gender framework, but this time offering room for a different mix of desire with that identification. At the same time, the spectacle of women acting like men works to disrupt the apparent naturalness of certain postures when performed by a male body.

Ending with a frozen image of its heroines impossibly suspended hanging over the abyss, monumentalized in their last kiss, the film stresses its demand to be read as fantasy. But it also recalls another suspended image, one that hints at the broader cultural terrain. This is the black bicyclist (Noel L. Walcott III) who comes out of nowhere. We might see him as fetishized: he recalls the obtrusiveness of social difference in the wider cultural field, but he also arrests our gaze, stops us looking further. This figure can only operate as an *effect* here, a sort of shadow cast against the desert landscape, the whiteness of the universe in which the film performs its interrogations of gender construction. Strangely enough, a similarly unaccountable racial trace emerges in *T2* as well.

As this year's cinema seemed unusually fascinated by destabilizing gender play, *Thelma & Louise* intersected with *Terminator 2* in the figure of the female hard body. Part of this fascination arose, no doubt, from the same mix of desire and identification that kept *Thelma & Louise* steadfastly available to lesbian readings and viewing positions, even before the final kiss. Yet most critical discussions repressed its lesbian eroticism. Since the film refused an image or narrative structure that would allow a clear alignment of gender, sexuality, and posture—butch or femme—any obsession with the film's contribution to a "battle of the sexes" seemed to reclaim the film's sexual differences as heterosexual difference, and not as a difference, unstable though it might be, between hetero- and homosexuality.

Thelma & Louise's dramatic and exhilarating transformation of women's body language did not read as a revelation of the "natural" body underneath the feminine masquerade of the housewife or service worker. Rather, the prominence of this bodily transformation sets the film in a network of recent images of women clearly "reconstructed" on or for the screen. Of these, this year's most spectacularly retooled female body appeared in *Terminator 2*'s Sarah Connor (Linda Hamilton). In stark contrast to their male hardbody precursors, these muscled female bodies presented a "masculinity" that aggressively displayed its difference from an anatomical base. They thus paraded an interruption. We saw the body itself as costume.

Significantly, *T2* seemed as fascinated with the spectacle of its female hard body as with her over-the-top aggression, and critical reception seemed unfazed by her violent rage. *T2*'s murderous female action hero remained securely within the frame of the science fiction serial, which was supported by the much-hyped special effects pioneered for the film. These digital compositing effects reshape the ontology of the film image itself. Industrial Light and Magic's technology enhanced this film's market value not only by the sheer excess of expense but also by the new technique of "morphing," which merges digital and film images so seamlessly that they threaten to render the material body of the actor superfluous to the production of his/her filmed image (for more on the morphing effects in this film, see Alcalay; Arthur).

The kinder, gentler *Terminator 2* offered a parade of astonishing images that body forth what it thematizes: transformations. Its very material format emphasizes feats of technological wizardry at the same time that Sarah Connor's dramatic reconstruction as a female hard body emerges as a spectacle that interrupts or suspends the narrative of heroic maternity. A nonlethal, negotiating Terminator joined forces with a heroine whose muscular physique visibly inscribed her psychic and emotional hardness. As she hardens, her surface closed like a shell, her eyes concealed by aviator sunglasses, her body draped with weapons, he softens, becoming increasingly obsessed with the human emotions that he lacks. We might almost say that—to take an extreme angle on this odd couple—as she becomes increasingly "butch," the Terminator (Arnold Schwarzenegger) is "femme-inized."

But *T2* maintains competing logics around this couple. Its oedipalizing plot reinforces the economy of the human-cyborg couple, claiming it for a determinedly heterosexual universe of gender difference. And the film struggles to make those developments perfectly coincident with its newly central "humanist" discourse, which is crucial to the narrative resolution. If Sarah Connor has a future, it is a function of that humanism, as her voiceover makes explicit at the end of the film: "If a machine, a terminator, can learn the value of human life, then maybe we can too." With its distinctly "pro-life" resonance, her speech recalls the competing ideological lures that run through this film, as it produces an ironic swerve that transfers the oedipal dream of being one's own father to the Terminator. Since the film discloses that Skynet has originated from the debris the Terminator left behind on his first visit, it reveals the "good" Terminator to be a literal "chip off the old block," sent back in time to expiate the father's crimes. Consequently, *T2* bypasses the mother once again.

If we read it through these irreconcilable images and its uncontainable residues, *T2* appears more and more as an ideologically incoherent text. Residual effects continually interrupt the already ironic reconstitution of a nuclear family. *T2* works to redeem the psychotically combative "bad mother," but does this within a filmic universe that is shakily and ironically secured by the shifting poles of "good" object and "bad" object. The "original"

Sarah Connor (Linda Hamilton) prepares to do battle in *Terminator 2: Judgment Day* (James Cameron, Carolco Pictures). Courtesy Photofest New York.

Terminator returns to us as the good one, but also as a piece of junk in comparison to the new model, the T1000 (Robert Patrick)—more a replicator than a cyborg—that threatens to become indistinguishable from its objects. And the T1000 highlights the film's preoccupation with radical visibility, as it spectacularly morphs into copies of its victims. In this universe, the Terminator qualifies as the best possible father: "In an insane world, it was the sanest choice." But while it seems to trumpet the privilege of the nuclear family unit headed by some version of a heterosexual couple, producing this image within a speech whose key word is "choice," the film also undercuts paternal privilege. The best father speaks only in the fixed phrases he learns from the son, like "no problemo."

As Sarah Connor's resemblance to the Terminator suggests a brutal incarnation of women's reproductive autonomy, her mastery of destructive technologies may operate as a metaphor for women's continued, if increasingly limited, access to technologies necessary to maintain choice about reproduction—technologies of "termination." And this is why the film takes pains to bind her ferocity to maternity. In wanting to have it both ways, *T2* may have represented the culture's most powerful wishes and fears concerning women's reproductive rights. But it also raises a parallel anxiety about medical technology's capacity to penetrate and modify bodily interiority, and to prolong life. *T2*'s last scene confirms this underlying preoccupation as the Terminator reveals what may be the most powerful difference between this cyborg and his human companions: he is constitutionally unable to end his own life. Thus, specific issues of women's autonomy are subsumed into more general anxieties concerning technology's impact on self-determination and the very status of the body.

T2's "bitch," then, operates at the nexus of the film's ambivalences. One of its most violent spectacles occurs when the heavily armed Connor terrorizes scientist Miles Dyson (Joe Morton) and his family. This moment is crucially pivotal to the plot, since it is only through Dyson that Connor and the Terminator gain access to Cyberdyne headquarters to destroy the increasingly autonomous computer network and thus to change the future. Dyson, the African American scientist, turns out to be the central architect of this menacing system, and his sacrifice is required to destroy it.

Connor begins lecturing Dyson about his responsibilities, constructing him as the embodiment of scientific arrogance: "Men like you . . . you don't know what it's like to really create something, to feel it growing inside you. All you know how to create is death and destruction." The phrase, "men like you," ironically highlights Dyson's exceptional position: at the racial level, there *are* no men like him in this film. At this point, the film elides racial difference under a global gender conflict that it forcefully attributes to Connor's crude feminism. But while it constructs this "feminist" moment in a speech we can easily find laughable, it cannot so easily write off the meanings of racial difference.

This scene condenses several fantasies. The combative force of the woman warrior is directed at an African American male professional, who is, just by the way, ultimately responsible for the destruction of the world. Moving from the spectacle of the black man cowering in abject terror before his white female assailant to align these two with Connor's son (Edward Furlong) and the Terminator, this scene's utopian fantasy imagines an alliance between two iconic and greatly simplified figures for contemporary identity politics: the white feminist and the black man. At the same time, however, Miles Dyson winds up as a conventionally sacrificial black helper, blowing himself up along with Cyberdyne, while allowing the bio-engineered "white" nuclear family to escape intact. But *T2* quickly outruns this scenario, leaves it behind as a subplot, just as Connor and company leave Dyson behind at Cyberdyne headquarters. So while Dyson emerges as a centrally necessary component of the future threat that both guarantees and generates the narrative, the moment of his generative centrality is also the moment of his elimination. But racial difference mattered little to the film's reception. *T2* could evacuate racial significance because its science fiction frame seemed to secure it as a fantasy, which internally determined the meanings of bodies. Likewise, framed by its market position as a blockbuster, a category that has increasingly defined itself through its address to "everyone," *T2* seemed to generate no concerns about impressionable spectators. Why did critics worry about *Thelma & Louise*'s audience but not about *T2*'s, despite its unprecedented volume of female spectators? This must be because *Thelma & Louise*'s audience was specified, linked to an image of feminism that remained a source of anxiety.

But we might continue to question another form of representational violence common to both films. What does it mean that autonomous white women's hard bodies seemed to be propped on "ghostly" black men? And why was this so hard to register in critical response? This kind of propping depends on a film's ability to evaporate social and historical referentiality in the displacement of one difference onto another, which is structurally cast as the "central" difference. In the mixed and ambiguous political effects of this year's cinematic representations, figures of social and sexual ambivalence, mixing or indifferentiation, unstable or "undecidable" identity, are all sites of eroticized intensity. As the culture continued to understand "race" as its greatest conditioning social divide, it may be reassuring to cast some of the aggressive intensity that charges this divide onto sexual difference, spectacularly figured in white female bodies.

Skin Deep?

In its strange and even tormented negotiations around embodied identity and the status of images, this year's cinema seemed as preoccupied with boundary problems as with identity. Perhaps it is no accident that Jonathan Demme's *Silence of the Lambs* turned on the grotesque fantasy of a gender dysphoric male literally "trying on" the female body. This film focuses on an FBI trainee (Jodie Foster) who seeks the help of an imprisoned psychiatrist, himself a serial killer, in order to develop a profile that will help her track down Buffalo Bill, a killer who, horrifyingly, skins his female victims. In a year when the cinematic frame frequently came into question, *The Silence of the Lambs* also stands out for its emphatic framing. Agent Clarice Starling's interviews with Hannibal Lecter (Anthony Hopkins) provide most of the film's central drama, and they develop through intense and amplified close-ups, unfolding through nuanced shifts of the subject's placement in the frame. At the film's climax, Starling's confrontation with Buffalo Bill (Ted Levine) comes in a searingly anxious sequence during which he observes her through night vision goggles. She is cast in sickening greenish light, groping blindly. We watch her with Bill through the claustrophobic frame formed by the goggles he wears, as his menacing hand reaches into the space between them. This sequence traps its viewer in suffocating proximity to this voyeur who desires to get inside women's skin.

This film is obsessed with boundaries and their violation. Beside the horrific image of a man skinning women in order to stitch their hides into a "woman suit," Lecter himself charges the screen, like the plot, with electrifying anxiety about penetration. His famous cannibalistic drives produce images—photographic or mental—that haunt everyone around him. Among the film's most powerful images is Lecter trussed up for transport, his mouth sealed into a leather mask. But equally powerfully, he is displayed under glass in his cell. This image may put us in mind of medical quarantine: his total visibility, hermetically sealed, highlights his quality as a specimen, but it also codes him as contagious. And infectious he surely is at the psychic level. Clarice is enjoined not to let him "get into her head," and Buffalo Bill, we remember, was once Lecter's patient. Isn't the image of the shrink as literal cannibal as well as psychic invader among the most compelling that this film deploys?

The Silence of the Lambs refreshingly eschews the seductions of conventional heterosexual romance, but at the cost of some weighty trade-offs. Clarice remains remarkably impervious both to the casual suggestiveness of the creepy prison psychiatrist and to the hostile or baffled gazes of the groups of young law officers by whom she frequently finds herself uncomfortably surrounded. At the same time, her resistance to the heterosexual gender theater gives way to the film's lugubrious reveling in oedipal twists. Lecter's countertransference pierces her calm façade as he challenges her through the class semiotics of fashion, citing the telling contradiction between her "good bag" and her "cheap shoes." Clarice's delicately calibrated and desperate longing for recognition from her paternalistic FBI supervisor (Scott Glenn) is exquisitely unease-making. But this film produces an environment haunted by ghostly traces of homosexuality, alternately over- and under-invested. Establishing an interpretive vacuum around Clarice's sexuality, it overloads Buffalo Bill. While Judith Halberstam read this figure as refusing identity, as a kind of post-gender identity, in her essay "Skin-Flick: Posthuman Gender Identity in Jonathan Demme's *Silence of the Lambs*," gay protest steadfastly framed him as homosexual and as marking the film's homophobia (see Robbins; Young). Perhaps most destabilizing is the film's assault on skin as framing both body and identity. This challenge becomes all the more striking in the year when critics repeated the phrase "skin deep" in criticizing *Jungle Fever* for its superficiality (both David Denby and Terrence Rafferty used it to title their reviews of the film), as cinematic representations came under increasing pressure from the media to produce appropriate images of black communities. Appropriate, of course, meant both authentic—enlightening—and nonthreatening for the dominant white audience.

In a year that produced an unprecedented preoccupation with volatile images, the play between surface and depth, screen and reality, extended across fiction films and their reception, and across the media in general. As TV news images rendered the Gulf War ghostly and endlessly replayed a private image maker's capture of the shocking King beating, the movies produced images that themselves made news themselves by igniting public discussions. *Jungle Fever* shared with *New Jack City* and *Boyz n the Hood* a curious pseudo-ethnographic treatment, as the media sought testimony from real interracial couples. Likewise, popular critical reception for the new black filmmakers focused on sociological concerns that film violence might spark real-life violence in debates concerning the efficacy of images in the material world.

Lastly, these debates produced another striking effect: a new visibility for the spectator. Or, rather, for specific spectator groups. *Thelma & Louise* sparked heated debate on feminine violence, and along with *Terminator 2*, it promoted ambivalent media fascination with female hard bodies and their masculine posturing. Angry white feminists joined aggressive young black men at the center of anxious speculation and cultural fantasy. Yet movies that seemed obsessed with non-dominant identities consistently represented race and gender as jostling for centrality and squeezing each other out of the frame. This year's films presented us with our most utopian egalitarian fantasies and with the disappointing consequences of the enormous social anxieties that intertwined with them.

1992

Movies and the
Politics of Authorship

AMY VILLAREJO

This was the year President George H. W. Bush lost to Bill Clinton in the presidential election. At stake in this election, which marked a cataclysmic shift to the liberal/left after more than a decade of Republican leadership, was the question of who would embody the values and political responsibilities of the American people. The election makes visible a number of themes, foremost among them the condensation of male authority in the face of a shifting social landscape. And authority embeds within it the idea of authorship. Who scripts the story of the nation and its future? Which voices are legitimate and legitimated in the public sphere? The events of this election year congeal importantly, then, around individuals and the need to shape stories around monumental male figures in public life. Through new digital circuits, ideas about the world became tied tightly to individuals and the images they sought to present.

Clinton represented more than a shift from the right to the left. The first President Bush memorably vomited onto the plate of the Japanese prime minister while on a diplomatic visit. Many Americans viewed this moment as demonstrating Bush's infirmity, less in his personal health than in terms of his administration's intellectual exhaustion. In the months before the November election, Clinton increasingly appeared as the vigorous, youthful, and "with it" alternative to both the Republican incumbent and the attention-grabbing third-party candidate, Texas billionaire H. Ross Perot. Responsibility didn't need to look stodgy. Wielding a saxophone rather than a sword, Clinton brought a message of hope that had wide appeal to the Baby Boom generation. Like Clinton himself, baby boomers had experienced shifts in the possibilities of social and political change from the 1960s to the 1990s. With his Rhodes scholar erudition, JFK-channeling vigor, and combination of cosmopolitanism and down-home southern pedigree, Clinton appeared to embody a smooth synthesis of 1960s radicalism and 1990s caution. He represented a solution to a number of crises of the moment.

Some were created by his predecessor—like the escalating federal deficit, increasing inequalities between rich and poor, the effects of deregulation and privatization—and some merely molded by them—like the devastations wrought by HIV/AIDS. A tempered optimism, a level-headed reckoning, a clear confrontation with the sins of the past, including American racism and imperialism: Clinton's personal style promised a return to the dreams of many Americans that had been deferred for too long by a Republican White House and its wealthy white supporters.

In international developments, Bush and Boris Yeltsin, the Russian president, proclaimed a new world order by jointly declaring an end to the Cold War. Easing tensions allowed the new Russia to emerge from the wreckage of Eastern European communism, right into the flotsam of capitalism American-style: one could now watch "Dallas," dubbed, on Russian television. Similarly, the Yugoslav Federation was broken and the new republics that emerged in its wake, primarily Serbia, initiated genocidal war against the Bosnian and Croatian Muslim population. In a show of force abroad, U.S. military forces invaded Somalia in an ill-fated attempt to bring humanitarian relief to a starving region dominated by warring factions. The United States also lifted trade sanctions against China, and the North American Free Trade Agreement (NAFTA) was signed. This controversial trilateral agreement among the United States, Mexico, and Canada was designed to remove substantive tariffs on trade among North American nations and to stimulate economic convergence.

On the domestic scene, Bush pardoned Reagan administration officials who had been indicted in the Iran-Contra scandal.[1] In a visit to a New Jersey elementary school, Vice President Dan Quayle lived down to his bumbling reputation by suggesting that a student's spelling of "potato" should have an "e" at the end. Minnesota's Mall of America opened, cementing America's super-sized approach to consumption. Amy Fisher, the "Long Island Lolita," shot her lover's wife and stayed in the headlines for months. Racial tensions were high: in Los Angeles, four white police officers on trial for their use of excessive force in the beating of black motorist Rodney King were found not guilty. The verdict resulted in several days of riots in L.A. and smaller riots around the country. Meanwhile, in Detroit, two policemen beat another black motorist, Malice Green, to death during a struggle (though these officers were later convicted and imprisoned).

In technology, cassette tapes gave way to compact discs, and a text-based web browser was made available to the public for the first time, paving the way for millions to use the World Wide Web. The Michelangelo virus infected computers worldwide. In popular culture, figures long associated with the entertainment industry left the stage: Johnny Carson hosted "The Tonight Show" for the last time; Lawrence Welk (the king of champagne music) and Bert Parks (longtime host of the Miss America pageant) died. The last episode of "The Cosby Show" aired after an extremely successful seven-year run. "Barney and Friends" and "Melrose Place" premiered. After the cultural boycott of South Africa ended in celebration of the end of apartheid, Paul Simon became the first major artist to tour there. Sue Grafton published *I Is for Innocent* in her series of mystery novels featuring detective Kinsey Milhone. Bobby Fischer sat for a rematch with Boris Spassky in the former Yugoslavia that was billed as the "World Chess Championship." Nirvana and Pearl Jam dominated MTV. Madonna's coffee-table book *Sex* overshadowed her musical ambitions. And heavyweight boxer Mike Tyson was convicted of raping a Miss Black America pageant contestant named Desiree Washington and was sentenced to a six-year jail term.

In the midst of these events, dominated by the elections' emphasis on male power and leadership, the issues of personal responsibility and authority loomed large in popular culture as well. Understood here in the broadest sense of creating a bounded work of art, authorship is likewise everywhere thematized, proposed, contested, rejected, and exploited in the films of this year, across genres and even across national borders, linked to an ongoing project of securing particularly male authority. In this year, questions of film authorship arise especially at the crossroads of studio-produced cinema and a flourishing independent sector of film production. In this year, too, the shifts in male authority brought with them the overwhelming marginalization of women along with heightened registers of queer sexuality in film, bursting onto the scene as it had never before with an array of queer voices and queer voicings in the year's movies. The year's biggest biopic, Spike Lee's *Malcolm X*, weaves footage taken straight from current events into its fabric, beginning as it does with the beating of Rodney King. Lee's film on the monumental civil rights figure self-reflexively thematizes the struggle of the black auteur to bring his vision to the screen. The other big biopic of the year, *Chaplin*, weds two star images together by similarly following the theme of the great man and his contemporary symbolic function: the legendary Charlie Chaplin with his latest embodiment, Robert Downey Jr. Like Lee's film, *Chaplin* also thematizes the struggle of a director to author his own filmic visions within an industry modeled upon the assembly line—with Chaplin's independent venture United Artists (established with Mary Pickford, Douglas Fairbanks Sr., and D. W. Griffith) standing as an early rebuke to the mass production or standardization of an American sensibility by profiteers. Clint Eastwood's revisionist western,

Unforgiven, put the man who had become a star in Sergio Leone's "spaghetti westerns" back at the center (as star and director) of a film that exposes a genre built on the violence of expansion and the genocide of native peoples while simultaneously excluding women. *Unforgiven* sought to be a western literally to end all westerns, a triumph that can't be disconnected from the name Clint Eastwood.

Several films also reveal complex relations to authorship. American director James Ivory's *Howards End,* based on the E. M. Forster novel, is arguably more forcefully tied to the names and transnational production and distribution circuits of its director/producer team of Ivory and Ismail Merchant (as well as German-born writing partner Ruth Prawer Jhabvala) than to its literary originator. The film is generally considered the team's most impressive transnational success. Woody Allen's films are usually tied closely to New York and to Allen's specifically neurotic New Yorker auto-biography. *Husbands and Wives* could be seen, in the genre of recent reality TV, as a chronicle of the very public dissolution of Allen's marriage to Mia Farrow, his co-star and wife in the film. Here authorship extends to the social and intellectual circle Allen inhabits in life and in his movies. *Glengarry Glen Ross* trades upon its literary heritage as a Broadway play set in Chicago. Playwright and screenwriter David Mamet's violent and angst-ridden men reveal a darker side to the city. *A River Runs Through It,* based upon the fly-fishing memoir by Norman McLean, proposes a more tranquil portrait of masculinity, while *The Player,* a satire by the legendary Robert Altman, pokes fun at Hollywood ruthlessness, offering a loving, insider look at the industry from the perspective of a studio mogul being blackmailed by a writer.

Male bonding and rituals are at the heart of several films tied more powerfully to their stars' signatures than their sources, screenwriters, or directors. *A Few Good Men,* the Tom Cruise star vehicle and courtroom thriller (and an adaptation from Aaron Sorkin's Broadway play), immerses itself in the betrayals and behaviors of men at war, while Al Pacino's tri-umph *Scent of a Woman* remains literally blind to all but the core relation-ship between his character, Lieutenant Colonel Frank Slade, and his young helper, Charlie Simms (Chris O'Donnell). Both films police the boundaries between individuals and institutions, revealing permissible levels of mascu-line softness as well as the limits of tolerance. Male bonding and male strug-gles are also at the core of several of this year's documentary films, such as *Liberators: Fighting on Two Fronts in WWII,* a film about black soldiers fighting racism in combat in segregated forces and on the home front, and *Fires of Kuwait,* an IMAX film that documents the physical struggles to tame the massive fires Saddam Hussein lit in the oil fields of Kuwait. Even Mark Achbar and Peter Wintonick's film about linguist and political dissident Noam Chomsky, *Manufacturing Consent: Noam Chomsky and the Media,* is built around the heroic male figure battling unyielding institutions on the path to a new vision of freedom and justice. Only *Passion Fish,* a female melodrama from longtime independent American filmmaker John Sayles, stands as an exception to the cardinal rule of this year: sign your film "by, for, and about men." And the idea of a signature is not just a metaphor. It took *Basic Instinct* to dramatize how authorship can function at the level of character, centered as it is on the story of a woman writer who wants to control the story of her own murderous inclinations.

Basic Instinct: Mimicking Female Authorship

The first instance of troubled authorship in this year's films involves conflicts between a female character who is an author and male authorities, as also between audience agency and studio control of Hollywood stories. Because *Basic Instinct* emerges from the context of HIV/AIDS devastation and activism, it concentrates upon the realm of sexual politics as the node for exploring its central character's conflict; this context shaped reception as well. Dutch director Paul Verhoeven's film, written by the notoriously provocative Joe Eszterhas (the Hungarian-born Hollywood bad boy who received a whopping $3 million for his screenplay), created enormous commotion for its portrayal of bisexual character Catherine Trammell (Sharon Stone). The film also did phenomenally well at the box office, grossing nearly $118 million domestically and $353 million worldwide. Gay and lesbian activists, who had nabbed the script early on, protested the film while it was shooting on location in San Francisco for its potent blend of homophobia and misogyny. At stake was the issue of representation. In a world of movies in which very few gay or lesbian characters make it to the final cut, what are the consequences of typecasting homosexuals as evil and perverted, of depicting a lesbian as an ice-pick wielding killer?

This question cannot be isolated from the climate of activism and social transformation effected by the AIDS epidemic. The incidence of HIV/AIDS began to peak in this year, according to the Centers for Disease Control, and the disease occupied a prominent position in public discourse. The public face of AIDS was articulated, on the one hand, in terms of pragmatic activist demands for effective and reasonably priced treatment and research toward a cure and, on the other hand, in terms of larger public debates around sexual practices, scientific knowledge and information, communities affected by HIV infection, and issues of privacy and control associated with testing, treatment, and insurance. These issues are knotted together in intricate ways that hinge on the sometimes paradoxical association between homosexuality and HIV/AIDS. In identifying AIDS early on as a "gay disease," for example, scientists had unwittingly identified a community—gay men—as previously, by definition, "healthy." The attribution of health to gay men was a significant leap from previous ways they had been pathologized.

But the discourse (i.e., the social complex of ideas and languages through which meaning is socially produced and circulated) of HIV/AIDS also reconsolidates illness in the body of the person with AIDS. Scholar and activist Cindy Patton explains how medical diagnosis frames this person:

> Diagnostic medicine abstracts the symptoms from the body to produce a totalizing explanation with a single or primary cause, a pathology. Because the immune system, understood metaphorically, transcends the place of the body, the abstraction "AIDS" folds back to correspond exactly to the space of the body. The virus is lost and, metaphorically speaking, the homosexual/prostitute/African/injecting-drug-user/hemophiliac body becomes AIDS. (55)

As Patton argues, the paradigmatic representation or embodiment of AIDS is the gay man, to whose body is returned the stigma of disease he was thought to have escaped when the American Psychiatric Association removed homosexuality from its list of pathologies in the mid-seventies in its *Diagnostic and Statistical Manual* (*DSM*). These loops by which disease or pathology and sexuality are intertwined illustrate why the representation and circulation of images of lesbian and gay people in (especially) the mainstream media of this year become such fraught and important issues. The very life of a community was at stake. Surrounded by death, gay men and lesbians came together to build paths for survival. Vocally and openly, as the motto of the AIDS activist group ACT UP has it, SILENCE = DEATH.

One can, then, read *Basic Instinct* allegorically. Sharon Stone's character, a classic femme fatale, embraces those fatalistic truisms around which the plot is threaded. Catherine Trammell, a fiction writer, is in the process of writing the core of the film's own action. In her novel, as presumably in the film, a detective will fall for the wrong girl, and she will kill him. "Somebody has to die," she says to Nick Curran (Michael Douglas). When he asks why, she responds with apparent common sense, "Somebody always does." Her response operates on a number of levels. It gestures toward genre, toward those patterns and repetitions that congeal and define what counts as a thriller or a murder/detective novel or film. Catherine, the writer, knows the rules of genre fiction, and Catherine, the murderer, knows the consequences of her agency, even if her murder of Nick lies offscreen, beyond the film's final frame (which famously shows the ice pick murder weapon lying on the floor next to the bed in which she and Nick are having sex). Audiences share knowledge of the rules, too, and they expect a murder in the first several frames just as they demand a car chase, a dark alley, a blonde, a gun, all of which Verhoeven offers through the lens of brilliant Dutch cinematographer Jan de Bont's careening, craning, and pursuing camera.

Catherine's answer also gestures toward the fatal logic of HIV/AIDS. With the disease, as in the film, death is intimate, linked to sex, pleasure, and attraction. The *petit mort,* the "little death" of orgasm, is visually associated with murder, as Stone wields the ice pick in the midst of climax when she kills Johnny Boz (Bill Cable) in the first few moments of the film. Verhoeven builds a world in which sexuality and violence more generally are inextricably bound together, just in the way that the characters are built, as Chris Holmlund has observed, through and as mirrors. She summarizes the charges of misogyny leveled against the film:

> Those who called the film misogynist did so primarily because they felt the female characters were bruised. Some women articulated contemporary feminist concerns, charging that the sex scene between Nick and Beth was a date rape. Others felt the entire film implied women liked violence, a decades-old feminist critique. The president of LA-NOW, for example, indicted the film because for her "the message [was] that women like violence, women want to be used, women want to be raped." ("Cruisin'" 35)

Basic Instinct is provocative, however, because it treads a particularly fine line between female agency and control, and masculine domination and containment. Catherine proposes herself as the author of the film's action, the master puppeteer who pulls the strings of the characters around her. Everything about her appears to be active: she manipulates, she seduces, she aggresses, and she even reproduces or clones herself in the character of Lisa Hoberman/Beth Garner (Jeanne Tripplehorn). Her self-possession and defiant streak are further highlighted through her frank sexuality: she enjoys sex, and she enjoys it with women as well as with men (Lisa/Beth and Roxy/Rocky [Leilani Sarelle]). And her enormous wealth (the $10 million she inherits after presumably killing off her parents) adds the details of bourgeois allure to her independence: a fast car, an ocean view, a warmly lit fire, a maid, and a Picasso. Stone's star image, beautifully toned thin body, and immense sex appeal round out the character as an alluring vixen. In sum, Catherine represents an ideal woman in perfect alignment with the antifeminism Susan Faludi describes in her book *Backlash: The Undeclared War against American Women,* which appeared as a paperback best seller this year. According to the "backlash thesis," "American women were unhappy because they were too free; their liberation had denied them marriage and motherhood" (113). In backlash periods, such as the years leading up to the release of *Basic Instinct*, "efforts to hush the female voice in American films" have been prominent means to quell dissent and enforce the antifeminist analysis (114).

While Catherine thus represents a contained version of American female agency and sexual control, her character's actual control is undermined in the film in three significant ways, all three products of dominant Hollywood ideologies and filmmaking practices. First, she is immediately pathologized. Any element of her independence or allure is tempered by the recognition by the film's team of psychologists that Catherine is "very dangerous, very ill." Her own stories are caught in loops of blame and alibi, premeditation and repetition, so much that it would appear that female fictions of any sort are, according to the film's logic, suspect and dangerous. Second, her character is associated not only with violence but with excess, with the vices of cocaine and openly confessed kinky sex, as well as with smoking and drinking. In this association, too, Catherine becomes linked to gay subcultures, overtly in the scene in her murdered former lover Johnny Boz's disco. When Nick then succumbs to his old habits of drinking and smoking, he is drawn into Catherine's clutches, lured into the shadows of addiction and repetition, such that he cannot resist her stories or her seduction. The film's equation of liquor, smoking, and drugs with degradation and murderous pathology exposes its moralism and endeavor to contain Catherine as character and image.[2] Finally, de Bont's camera itself resists Catherine's agency. It is almost aggressively aligned with the investigating, pursuing, voyeuristic, excited men, whether revealing Catherine's lack of underwear or surveying her from above.[3]

By simultaneously displaying and containing the potential powers of female desire, *Basic Instinct* may therefore be read as a brazen example of the way in which Hollywood uses homosexuality as a platform for titillation and misogyny. It shows, furthermore, how indebted Hollywood remains to crafting portraits of defiance and alluring sexuality that carry with them wealth (a house on Stinson Beach) and beauty (Sharon Stone's chiseled face). When Catherine Trammell tells the investigating cops to charge her with a crime or "fuck off," one is aware that immense privilege licenses her defiance, but one may also take great pleasure in her sexy and saucy retort to the law. In this sense, *Basic Instinct* raised the possibility that protesting organizations such as the Gay and Lesbian Alliance Against Defamation (GLAAD) failed to address fundamental issues of pleasure and

Sharon Stone as Catherine Trammell with titillating crossed legs in *Basic Instinct* (Paul Verhoeven, TriStar). Courtesy Photofest New York.

desire in the context of a raging epidemic: gay men and lesbians wanted more than sagas of loss and instructions about safe sex practices. Like the election of this year, then, *Basic Instinct* serves as an arena for struggle over whose stories are understood as legitimate, whose stories generate profit, and whose stories shape larger understandings of social issues such as HIV/AIDS. The power or authority to shape those stories became a political issue of its own.

The Crying Game: Remarketing Sexual Secrets

In the case of the extraordinarily successful ($62.5 million) American release of Neil Jordan's *The Crying Game*, the conundrum of authorship comes from the studio's rewriting of the film in its marketing campaign for an American audience that received the film quite differently than its initial audiences did. In the context of HIV/AIDS discourse, U.S. film scholars have frequently argued that the version of *The Crying Game* seen in the United States was actually a different film than that seen by audiences elsewhere. The film's distributor in the United States is of course none other than the Oscar-chasing Miramax, an independent "mini-major." In order to understand the contours of authorship at this moment, it is helpful to see how industrial structures mutate to accommodate diverse production, distribution, exhibition, marketing, and advertising methods that determine the marketplace for independent film. As scholar Janet Wasko notes, "The big news in the late 1980s was co-production" (235). By the 1990s these were truly cooperative relationships across national borders, not simply deals made post-production for distribution: "Distributors and sales agencies were increasingly originating or participating at the very early stages in the development, preparation and assembly of the film package. Often complete funding was provided, through a combination of pre-sales and a domestic US distribution agreement" (Wasko 235).

In order to develop movies able to break out of niche or art house markets, both New Line Cinema and Miramax, the two largest independent film companies at this moment, conceived of the film package in different ways. Justin Wyatt suggests that while "New Line has continually favored gradual expansion and diversification only following breakthrough successes, Miramax's presence is based much more on marketing and targeting audiences beyond a narrow art house niche" ("Formation" 76). Such was the strategy for *The Crying Game*.

A romantic thriller, *The Crying Game* centers on a man's search for his identity. In the first half of the film, Fergus (Stephen Rea), a member of the

Irish Republican Army, kidnaps Jody, a British soldier (Forest Whitaker), with the help of seductress Jude (Miranda Richardson) while Jody is on leave at a carnival outside Belfast. Kept in captivity by a group of IRA operatives, Jody looks to Fergus for friendship and sympathy. Fergus is increasingly drawn to his prisoner and learns through their interchange of Jody's "special friend" Dil (Jaye Davidson) at home in London. Fergus is given the order to shoot Jody, but the plan is botched when Jody runs and Fergus is unable to shoot him in the back; at the same moment, the British army invades the IRA hideout. In the second half of the film, Fergus escapes to London, loses himself in an alias ("Jimmy" from Scotland), seeks out Dil, and strikes up a relationship with her, only to be found out by his former IRA associates who enlist him in an assassination scheme. By the end of the film, Dil has shot Jude, and Fergus pays for her crime in jail.

This summary, of course, omits the very detail around which the film's advertising campaign in the United States was built, the fact that Dil is transgendered. "This major secret," Wyatt observes, "was responsible for the film's cross-over success; due to the barrage of publicity and press coverage growing from the secret, an amazing $62.5 million was grossed by this film which would seem to be firmly within the boundaries of the art cinema" ("Formation" 81). In their book *The Film Experience*, Timothy Corrigan and Patricia White use the film as a case study to examine precisely shifting contexts of promotion and the ways in which a film's promotion shape audience responses:

> Especially in the United States, word of mouth functioned as the most powerful strategy in the promotion of *The Crying Game*. Viewers, including most movie reviewers, were urged to keep the secret of Dil's sexuality as a way of baiting new audiences to see the film. A widely announced word-of-mouth promotion—'Don't tell the secret!'—drew a continuous stream of audiences wanting to participate in this game of secrets. Word of mouth became part of a strategy to entice American audiences who, anticipating a sexual drama of surprises and reversals, would in most instances overlook the political tensions that complicated the film for British audiences. (29)

By way of corroborating evidence, Corrigan and White cite the poster campaigns in Britain and the United States. In the United Kingdom, Stephen Rea's portrait is combined with a smoking gun to promote the film's political violence, and tag lines emphasize Jordan's authorial legacy ("daring film," "brilliant," "Jordan's best work to date"). In the United States, the poster features Miranda Richardson with a smoking gun and three key words: "sex, murder, betrayal." The phrase "play at your own risk" follows the film title, and no mention is made of Jordan's directorial reputation;

Jaye Davidson (as Dil) and Stephen Rea (as Fergus) in *The Crying Game* (Neil Jordan, Miramax). Courtesy Photofest New York.

instead the film's genre, the thriller, is emphasized: "Nothing is what it seems to be."

In other words, distributor Miramax functions as auteur, sidestepping the film's political references and instead enlisting audiences to take up the generic elements of intrigue. What is useful about Wyatt's and Corrigan and White's emphasis on promotion is that it alerts us to the importance of weighing how films circulate in cultural and economic contexts, rather than merely producing hermetic textual analyses. British and Irish audiences were aware of escalating IRA activities and the fact that an IRA bomb had exploded in the Baltic Exchange in the City of London, killing several and injuring almost one hundred people. American audiences were more familiar with the sexual and identity politics of HIV/AIDS activism, the direct actions of the group Queer Nation, and public demands for visibility for and by gay and lesbian peoples. American readings thus emphasize a dialectic of hiding and revelation that resonates with queer identities.

The task, however, remains to understand how this movie in fact fuses sexual and national dissidence, and how it does so to shore up a version of male power that is exportable and that might exert transnational pressure and appeal. Miramax's marketing campaign heightens the film's own work in placing overt politics in the background. For the central perspective of

The Crying Game belongs not to Dil, or to any among her bar-based, marginalized community of drag queens and tranny performers, nor to Jude or to any among her group of committed Republicans, but to Fergus, a reluctant participant in both Dil's world and in the IRA cell's activities. His character, in other words, is neither queer nor entirely dedicated to the cause of Irish freedom. Fergus is affably resistant and noncommittal, paternal and gentle, class-bound and happily masculine. He is, in short, a more genial version of the kind of containment we saw in *Basic Instinct*: a man with whom the majority can cast its lot, while toying with what is forbidden and what is rendered criminal, terrorist, beyond the pale.

The Crying Game revises those traditional and stereotypical representations of Irish masculinity that are staples of the cinema (Landy 22). Neither the comedic "paddy" nor the fanatic "terrorist" occupies much screen time; instead, Jordan's portrait of Fergus exploits actor Stephen Rea's capacity for sensitivity, ambiguity, longing, and humor. While Jordan paints his female character Jude as a deadly force who subordinates her personal/sexual life to the nationalist cause, he reserves more care in his representation of Dil, who, after all, is a woman for much of the film. The pattern of homosocial bonding observed by Eve Kosofsky Sedgwick, in which a female figure functions as triangular glue for dyadic male bonding such as that elaborated in the first part of the film between Fergus and Jody, is frustrated by Dil's role as Fergus's fully delineated companion, partner, and lover. Furthermore, the racism directed at Fergus at the construction site where he finds "honest" work in London parallels the homophobia and misogyny Dil encounters in the queer world in Spitalfields (a working-class London neighborhood that gained its reputation as a refuge for migrants, including Irish, Jewish, and Bangladeshi immigrant groups). Longstanding racism and conflict between the British and the Irish are thus reconfigured through sexual politics, emergent in the postcolonial context of contemporary London and in a new imaginary devoted to emergent political alliances.

The representation of ur-Britishness in *The Crying Game* is, of course and paradoxically, Jody, played by an African American actor (with an American accent), whose character is obsessed with the most British of sports, cricket. In addition to redrawing portraits of Irish masculinity, then, Jordan's film realigns antagonisms between Britain and Ireland, and Britain and America, in cinematic terms. The film draws upon tropes of British cinema, particularly the British white flannel genre film,[4] in order to highlight the changing nature of domination from colonialism to post-colonialism, from direct domination to forms of indirect domination. Jody's appearance in fantasized flashback sequences, motivated by Fergus's memory of and guilt over Jody's death, combines romantic cinematography and iconography (soft focus, slow motion) with a sort of mimicry of the kind of white flannel mise-en-scène in which the desire of men to bond with one another are garbed through effete class depictions like cricket games. (Jody wears cricket whites and wields a bat as he runs toward the camera, but Jody is no effete Englishman, no lithe public schoolboy. That the character is played by an athletic African American man who began his college career on a football scholarship is emphasized when Dil disappears within Jody's cricket sweater when she is compelled to inhabit the gender codings of maleness late in the film.) Jody's image challenges the ways in which Britishness is associated with colonialism and whiteness, suggesting both that nostalgia can easily accommodate a black British soldier and that forms of domination are changing, becoming mobile and implicating America as much as Britain. American audiences who could recognize Whitaker as their own could find in Jody's character a condensed set of references to the history of slavery, with a black man in captivity and thus an indictment of brutality. Because the film launched Whitaker's career, moreover, *The Crying Game* is in fact often understood by American audiences as his "American" debut.

The sexual politics of *The Crying Game* are thus dependent upon the frank acknowledgment of cinema's international production and circulation, since the film builds its scaffold of identification and desire upon the flows of nations and their exertions of power. Moving from place to place is something characters do, but it's also something films and queers do, forging bonds and communities and love where they might seem improbable. This is not uncritically to laud a film that trades on its capacity to withhold secrets and to shock by full frontal revelation of Dil's penis, or to praise a film that seems anxious to dispense with complicated understandings of femininity in order to get (back) to men and their quests. It may be, as Shantanu Dutta Ahmed argues, that this climactic exposure of what is presumed to be Dil's authentic identity (that is, he is seen by the camera to be a "biological man" and thus understood in sexual terms to be gay) actually and "ultimately undercuts the proposed egalitarianism of [Jordan's] project," which would be to celebrate sexual diversity (61). But it is to acknowledge *The Crying Game* as American, insofar as what is seen by American audiences is crafted by American distributors in their framing campaigns just as candidates are framed in elections; and to see it in continuity with coeval popular treatments of sexual politics, made with big money for the big screen. For in the films of this year, there is a surprising convergence of the authorship of queer lives in mainstream films such as *Basic Instinct* and *The Crying Game*, and independent cinema. If the film companies could turn titillating bisexuals and marginal art house pictures into box office gold, independent directors could author stunning new portraits of gay lives, revising stories and genres toward new, living, ends.

New Men, Negative Images, and the New Queer Cinema

Reporting on independent films on display in Toronto, at Sundance, and in Amsterdam, B. Ruby Rich found herself stunned by the movies that begin to circulate widely in film festivals in this moment: "There, suddenly, was a flock of films that were doing something new, renegotiating subjectivities, annexing whole genres, revising histories in their image" ("New Queer Cinema" 15). People similar to those who had disrupted the shooting of *Basic Instinct*, or who critiqued *The Crying Game* for shaming and disciplining the character of Dil, were now also making their own films, authoring their own stories of queer lives. Increasingly, these queer makers and queer audiences made their presences felt via special festivals, video rentals, and video sales. Queer films garnered critical attention and audience acclaim at all the major festivals Rich attended. For her, Tom Kalin's *Swoon* and Gregg Araki's *The Living End* were among the most prominent, but others included Todd Haynes's *Poison* (1991), Marlon Riggs's *Tongues Untied* (1990), Jennie Livingston's *Paris Is Burning* (1991), and Christopher Münch's *The Hours and Times* (1991). Mostly made by gay white men, the films in large measure respond to the ravages of the HIV/AIDS epidemic. The New Queer Cinema, says film scholar Monica Pearl, is "how AIDS makes movies" (23).

In dubbing this group of films with a tag, Rich risks rendering them homogeneous or flattening their differences. The spirit of her essay runs to the contrary:

> Of course, the new queer films and videos aren't all the same, and don't share a single aesthetic vocabulary or strategy or concern. Yet they are nonetheless united by a common style. Call it "Homo Pomo": there are traces in all of them of appropriation and pastiche, irony, as well as a reworking of history with social constructionism very much in mind. Definitively breaking with older humanist approaches and the films and tapes that accompanied identity politics, these works are irreverent, energetic, alternately minimalist and excessive. Above all, they're full of pleasure. They're here, they're queer, get hip to them. ("New Queer Cinema" 16)

Both stylistically innovative and politically demanding, the films of the New Queer Cinema tread on some dangerous ground.

Swoon is as much a story about murder as *Basic Instinct* is, and it would be hard to call the images of gay men in *The Living End* "positive." What these films do that mainstream Hollywood films don't is tell the stories of queer lives from a queer point of view. These queer auteurs respond to the stereotypes of gays and lesbians circulated through Hollywood with counter-stories of their own. In an article on these two independent films, Roy Grundmann contrasts Hollywood's production of stereotypes with those that emerge from gay film culture:

> Guided by the principle of the lowest common denominator, West Coast cor-
> porate film-making creates stereotypes partly out of ignorance, yet primarily
> out of economic compulsion. Under the delusion it still represents the mass
> culture, Hollywood hands each minority only one spot on the canvas, a pol-
> icy inadequate to achieve actual diversity. . . . Stereotypes emerging from
> within our own film culture may be no less reductive but at least we can con-
> trol their production and make sure they will always be only a few of the
> multiple ways in which we see ourselves. (25–26)

They are great films, as Rich acknowledges, precisely because of the way in which they are gay, and they draw their aesthetic, generic, and ideological force from their queer associations.

Authored by men, films such as *Swoon* and *The Living End* foreground the very question of authorship, too, insofar as they rely heavily on the revision (the rewriting) of forms and stories that precede them. Drawing upon legendary topics (diabolical murderers in *Swoon*), legendary films (writer and queer convict Jean Genet in *Poison*), legendary genres (the road movie in *The Living End*), or legends-in-the-making (the drag balls in *Paris Is Burning*), these films are preoccupied with writing, rewriting, and revising the past in the service of a vibrant queer future. Unlike their counter-parts in mainstream cinema, they do not presuppose the prerogatives of authorial status; they fight for it, they earn it. They also claim it. *Swoon* showcases text at every turn, listing its literary queer predecessors (Wilde, Proust, Forster), citing its textual assemblages (in performance artist/theo-rist Richard Schechner's cameo), and acknowledging its writing contribu-tions (Hilton Als helped with the screenplay). *The Living End* is an ode to film authorship and criticism. One of its protagonists is a film critic, with posters of queer predecessor auteur Andy Warhol and French New Wave director Jean-Luc Godard prominently plastered to his house's walls. To whatever extent they reference or rely on the past, however, both of these postmodern stories urgently address the queer present.

Swoon reworks a biopic, using materials from previous stories and films. The film retells the notorious 1920s Leopold and Loeb case about the murder of a young boy and the subsequent trial that also serves as the primary material for Hitchcock's *Rope* (1948) and Richard Fleischer's *Compulsion* (1959). The $250,000 film did unusually well, grossing $340,000 at the domestic box office. Kalin researched the film meticulously, drawing upon court transcripts, Leopold's autobiography, and even a scrapbook Kalin's grandmother had kept on the case (Grundmann 28). In *Swoon,* the events of history are not treated as sacrosanct or as demanding fidelity, but rather as capable of shedding light on the present through the act of reprocessing and retelling. Making plain the story's gayness and Jewishness, Kalin also investigates the mechanisms by which such a story might be told—by whom and to whom—in the first place. Using the device of voiceover narrations reading fake dated diary entries by "genius" students Nathan ("Babe") Leopold (Craig Chester) and Richard ("Dickie") Loeb (Daniel Schlachet), Kalin splits narrative point of view and conjoins the sense of authenticity usually associated with diaries and confession to a theatricalized view of history understood through artificial tableaux and staged readings. Layering together Brechtian theatricality, formal readings, archival footage (authentic and recreated), and reenactments, Kalin fractures the generic conventions and assumptions of both period pieces and adaptations.

While a relationship between two young men is at the heart of *Swoon,* it would be a misreading of the film to declare its interests to be merely or decidedly anthropocentric, even if women are literally banished at one point in the narrative: roughly halfway through the film, the judge commands that the women present leave the courtroom where Leopold and Loeb are being tried for the grisly murder of Bobby Franks. The material presented by the defendant's expert witness, he suggests, will be unfit for women to hear. While the women in the gallery reluctantly file out, the camera settles on the African American stenographer (cast against realist likelihood), who also slowly lifts herself to her feet and, in a reverse shot above the gallery, follows the white women from the courtroom.

This improbable character has companions: props and presences whose function is more to alert *Swoon*'s viewers to the undoing of realist conventions than to provide any secure footing for generating a reading. A touch-tone phone, a remote control, a head shot of queer art historian and critic Douglas Crimp that "passes" as a mug shot all contribute to the generalized aesthetic and epistemology of what Kalin has called the graphic quality in *Swoon.* By that term he means to summon the architectural feel of the film, its preoccupation with line and angle as well as its minimalist mise-en-scène (Beene et al. 17). It also references the surface of the black-and-white

Daniel Schlachet and Craig Chester in the stylish *Swoon* (Tom Kalin, Fine Line Features). Courtesy Photofest New York.

film, described by Kalin as an aftereffect of production but functioning as a signature of independent production:

> There is actually an accidental origination of the black-and-white film technique in *Swoon*. We shot *Swoon* in 16mm film, and when it became obvious that we were going to release it theatrically, I had to blow it up to 35mm, and suddenly there was this enormous contrast in the image. The grain was multiplied, and the most curious thing was that the blacks all took on a kind of inky outline, as if it were a photograph that had been copied on a copier again and again. (Beene et al. 13)

What better way to describe a story told and retold, magnified and amplified for its graphic—that is to say, its overt, explicit—combination of brilliance, violence, perversion, and desire? Leopold and Loeb were two wealthy students at the University of Chicago who murdered a fourteen-year-old boy under the supposition that their superior intellects would allow them to commit the perfect crime.

If one of the tasks of *Swoon* is to restore an overtly queer component to the story of Leopold and Loeb's murder through queer authorship, another is to see how desire, including but not limited to queer or murderous desire, operates. The film anatomizes desire in much the same fashion as it anatomizes the 1920s era in which the action is set: loosely, operating more by feel than by science, more in the broad strokes of sensibility than in fidelity to details that can be taxonomized. Kalin paints Loeb as a psychopath whose talent lies in his capacity to seduce Leopold. Once they have joined, however, Loeb's murderous desires leak onto Leopold and they become one in coercion, provocation, seduction, and betrayal. If the fact that they blame one another after they are arrested for the murder attests to the balance with which Kalin treats his pair (they are not romanticized), it is just as significant that the pain Leopold experiences when Loeb is murdered in jail comes, through an emphasis on sound effects, screeching off the screen (their emotional bonds are not dismissed). What Kalin ultimately offers is the strongest possible case against pathologizing and marginalizing rhetoric. *Swoon* is, as Rich observes, a film of its time but one that "demonstrates how easily mainstream society of the 1920s could unite discrete communities of outsiders (Jews, queers, Blacks, murderers) into a commonality of perversion" ("New Queer Cinema" 21). While the film sides with the outsider-queer-murderers, it refuses to solicit our identification with them, so that the audience is forced to watch a horrible murder and its aftermath without the comfort of either pathologizing the villains or delighting unproblematically in their forbidden fantasies.

Produced by Gregg Araki himself, *The Living End* similarly processes what Grundmann calls "negative stereotypes and exploitation fare," redefining sickness and health, sexuality and violence, desire and pathology (25). In Araki's case, however, authorship becomes a mishmash of rewriting what has come before, both in terms of predecessors and in terms of genre.[5] Araki's road film is about two HIV-positive gay men on the lam. Jon (Craig Gilmore), a film critic and writer, learns of his sero-status the moment the film begins, and he picks up the drifter Luke (Mike Dytri) after Luke has apparently killed a cop. The two take off to San Francisco, fall in love, kill some more, have steamy sex, lie on their backs a lot, talk in the car, and ultimately perhaps chart some direction for living on, although the film's ending, of the two on a Pacific beach, suggests an ambiguous closure that is indebted to the French New Wave. And *The Living End* wears its film history more generally on its sleeve. Its author delights in cheesy, knowing allusions to visual and pop culture at every turn. A quick list would add to Warhol and Godard Dead Can Dance, Jack Kerouac, k.d. lang, Michelle Shocked, Derek Jarman, Jack Daniels, Barbie cereal, Clint Eastwood, and an Araki favorite, Doritos.

If *Swoon* takes a view of the world we might call "disturbing," Araki's film declares its sensibility in its promotion: *"The Living End*, An Irresponsible Film by Gregg Araki."* It may be irresponsible insofar as the film celebrates antisocial rampages by its lead characters, Jon and Luke: cop-killing, shooting up ATMs, self-injury, drinking, and sex. But that celebration touches important chords in youth culture. As Robin Wood observes in an essay on Araki's later film *The Doom Generation* (1995):

> The most interesting among our young men and women are those who, in various ways, set up varying degrees of resistance to their incorporation into the contemporary norms of capitalist culture, the world of alienated labor and the nuclear family; they seem to know, instinctively, the cost of such incorporation. Their situation is appalling, and every allowance should be made for their antisocial behavior, even though it can only prove, in the long run, both destructive and self-destructive. (336–37)

Some of the forms of resistance to incorporation on offer in *The Living End* seem naive. Luke's "take" on social repression, even if mocked by Jon, is blanket paranoia about the "neo-Nazi Republican final solution." Likewise, his political intervention would be to go to Washington, D.C., either to "blow [the first President] Bush's brains out" or to inject him with a syringe of HIV-positive blood ("What do you bet they'd have the magic cure tomorrow?"). Despite his status as a writer, Jon is rendered almost bereft of language in his response to his diagnosis, typing "fuck" over and over on his computer, and that word is the most prominent in the film's dialogue, some of which is comically banal California-ese ("This is not a vacation, we're supposed to be on the run, dude"), some knowingly melodramatic and citational ("You'll never find anyone who cares about you as much as I do"), and some merely pretentious in its existential ambitions toward being HIV-positive ("We've got nothing to lose. Fuck work. Fuck the system. Fuck everything. We're totally free; we can do whatever we want to do").

Other elements of *The Living End*'s energy are irresistible. Araki finds a visual style and vocabulary that transforms genre. As Rich notes:

> Cinematically, it restages the celluloid of the sixties and seventies: early Godard, *Bonnie and Clyde*, *Badlands*, *Butch Cassidy and the Sundance Kid*, every pair-on-the-run movie that ever penetrated Araki's consciousness. Here, though, the guys are HIV positive, one bored and one full of rage, both of them with nothing to lose. They could be characters out of a porn flick, the stud and the john, in a renegotiated terrain. Early Araki films are often too garage-hand, too boychick, too far into visual noise, but this one is different. Camera style and palette update the New Wave. Araki's stylistic end runs have paid off, and this time he's got a queer-on-the-lam portrait that deserves a place in movie history—an existential film for a post-porn age, one that puts queers on the map as legitimate genre subjects. ("New Queer Cinema" 21)

The Los Angeles that Araki seeks out is dusky and sprawling: the viaduct, a fluorescent-lit parking lot, household interiors, fast-food joints, Ralph's supermarket, an AM/PM Minimarket. When the California sky is blue, it lies suspended above the lolling heads of Jon and Luke, vast but not conquering, hinting at possibility and bathing beautiful faces in light. Araki exploits the intimacy of the car, too, contrasting the sexually charged front seat and a normalized, unknowing exterior.

The sense of being in a world of one's own, open to anything, free from constraint, is the fantasy this movie enlists and reproduces, and it is, of course, bound to fail or ultimately disintegrate. The fact that *The Living End* builds this fantasy upon caricatures or wholesale exclusions of women opens it to feminist critique, repeating the marginalization of women in most of the films of this year: the murderous lesbians Fern (Johanna Went) and Daisy (played by Warhol alumna Mary Woronov) and Jon's painter/best friend Darcy (Darcy Marta) barely figure in the film's central identification with the character of Jon. Like *Swoon*, however, *The Living End* announces new possibilities for queer filmmakers authoring their own portraits to redress those scripted by corporate Hollywood. This year, the dialogue between the studio (or the still-independent "mini-major," such as Miramax) and the independent filmmaker expressed itself as an authorial quest for the nation's attention and direction, much as that on which candidate Bill Clinton embarked in his own pursuit of a new, youthful spirit. In his campaign, Clinton's hometown almost mythically stood in for his vision: he hailed, improbably enough, from a town called Hope. In the quest of independent filmmakers to make new voices heard also lay hope, perhaps of more modest proportions.

NOTES

1. The Iran-Contra affair was a scandal in which members of the Reagan administration were caught selling arms to Iran (in violation of the president's public position of not trading arms for hostages) and using the proceeds to fund the Contras, an anticommunist guerrilla organization in Nicaragua (in violation of a congressional ban against doing just that).

2. In a knowing gesture, the film also casts Dorothy Malone, an icon of fifties excess for her role in Douglas Sirk's film *Written on the Wind* (1956), as the murderous housewife Hazel Dobkins.

3. Other critics point out that the gaze is also reversed, with Catherine's aggressive look directed at her interrogators as objects. See Wood "Somebody" and Cohan.

4. White flannel films are typically nostalgic. They frequently center on adolescence or young adulthood and are set in British public schools.

5. Katie Mills ("Revitalizing") discusses the film in terms of the genre of the road movie.

1993

Movies and the New Economics of Blockbusters and Indies

CHUCK KLEINHANS

In the year the Clinton presidency began, New York's World Trade Center was attacked by Islamic fundamentalists exploding a truck bomb in the parking garage, and Michael Jackson was accused of pedophilic assault, making famous the "wacko Jacko" personality to which the tabloids had alluded for years. But these were surface phenomena compared to the surge of neoliberal economics as the driving force in international and national affairs and the increasingly globalized cinema industry.[1] Having beaten his predecessor by hammering at George H. W. Bush's stressed economy, Bill Clinton pressed for federal spending cuts combined with new taxes to reduce the massive deficit inherited from the Reagan-Bush era. Clinton's style of neoliberalism encouraged global trade while shortchanging traditional Democrat constituencies. With an eye on the official creation of the European Union as a rival trading bloc and on the phenomenal growth of East Asian "tiger" economies, the White House aggressively pushed the North American Free Trade Agreement (NAFTA), most favored nation status for China, and neoliberalized positions in the General Agreement on Tariffs and Trade (GATT). France pushed back on GATT, gathering support for a "cultural exception" that resisted "free trade" in movies, to the supreme irritation of the Motion Picture Association of America (MPAA), which represents the six major studios. After aerospace, entertainment supplied the second largest U.S. export, at $3.7 billion for the year. Add an aggressive financial and business environment that forced out executives who couldn't produce high returns in the short term (CEOs of IBM, Westinghouse, American Express, Apple, and Eastman Kodak quit), and the stage was set for an extended period of mergers, acquisitions, takeovers, and a bullish stock market, particularly in new technologies. Meanwhile, traditional manufacturing declined with outsourcing of production abroad. The Clinton administration promised that new high tech and service sector jobs would make up for job loss, but the actual policy was clearly set: the economic gap between rich and poor, owners and workers, would grow at an unprecedented pace while the social safety net would be shredded.

In the wake of the Gulf War, Iraq agreed to United Nations weapons inspections, yet Clinton's initial foreign policy decisions were timid at best. Faced with Russian president Boris Yeltsin's increasing consolidation of power, the U.S. position seemed to be that it was better to have dictatorial stability than true democracy in the former USSR. Some modest material aid was sent to Bosnia, but no direct involvement in the former Yugoslavia was envisioned, particularly in the wake of the vicious slaughter of UN troops by Somalia's warlords, documented on TV. In a much publicized but historically meaningless photo op, Israel's prime minister Yitzhak Rabin and the Palestine Liberation Organization's Yasir Arafat shook hands on the White House lawn promising to work for progress, little of which was to occur in the subsequent fifteen years.

On the domestic front, the Clinton administration's plans were countered by an increasingly vocal and well organized opposition of Republican conservatives and the Christian Right. Their messages were amplified by an effective presence on talk radio, exemplified by opinion monger Rush Limbaugh and evangelist Dr. James Dobson. The growth of tabloid journalism on Fox television as well as the presence of influential cable TV ministers such as Jerry Falwell and Pat Robertson furthered right-wing propaganda (Lesage and Kintz). Trailing longstanding rumors and accusations about sexual philandering, Clinton became a personalized focal point for those discrediting his policies. The most virulent issue erupted around an early executive order on gays in the military, articulating a "don't pursue, don't ask, don't tell" policy. Personal vituperation also focused on Hillary Rodham Clinton, particularly when she became the lead advocate for the administration's central domestic issue: expanding universal health care. An effective coalition of conservatives, insurance companies, physicians, the pharmaceutical industry, and big healthcare providers quickly made the proposal dead on arrival at Congress. A major police misstep led to the FBI killing more than seventy religious cult members in a stand-off near Waco, Texas.

In other news, the United States experienced a natural disaster with the Flood of 1993 inundating nine midwestern states. With the first cloning of human embryos, a new wave of contention began between science, ethics, and religion. The Nobel Prize in Literature went to Toni Morrison, while Broadway celebrated the appearance of Tony Kushner's *Angels in America*, examining the AIDS epidemic in the Reagan years. In popular music, country singer Garth Brooks became the top-selling artist of all time, while rap hailed the major achievement of Dr. Dre's album *The Chronic* and grunge celebrated Nirvana's *In Utero* album. "Seinfeld" finally caught on and enjoyed extreme popularity on TV. In sports, the Chicago Bulls achieved an enviable third consecutive basketball championship, after which star Michael Jordan retired.

Understanding the cinema year demands accounting for the new mixed landscape for feature-length dramatic films: this was the first year that foreign theatrical gross exceeded domestic receipts, and pay-per-view, cablecast, and video rentals and sales became a very significant part of a film's gross. While first-week theatrical gross and total sales became news items, the actual income distribution for the MPAA studios reveals a variety of sources. About 16 percent of total income came from domestic (North American) theatrical receipts and the same amount came from international theatrical receipts. Domestic home video accounted for about 25 percent of income and international home video for about 19 percent. Domestic TV produced about 11 percent and licensing and merchandising produced about the same. The successive windows of release for the major studios became, in order, theatrical, home video, pay-per-view, pay cable, and broadcast and basic cable.

The film industry was going through major changes in its own efforts to tap into both global and expanded local trade.[2] Disney's acquisition of Miramax, the highly successful independent or "Sundance" distribution company, stood for the solidification of two distinct strata of theatrical film: the global mega-blockbuster (represented by the high-tech *Jurassic Park*) and the low-budget "indie" (*El Mariachi*). Concurrently, middle-budget films such as Martin Scorsese's adaptation of the Edith Wharton novel *The Age of Innocence* tended to founder, grossing only $32 million domestically on a $34 million production budget. These trends were compounded by rising revenues, due to higher ticket prices, the expansion of domestic screens,[3] and increased revenue streams from overseas box office and video rental. The need for more "product" for expanding cable TV and direct-to-video (DTV) films opened opportunities for new, modest-budget "content providers."

For Hollywood, it was a boom year. The most important season, summer, brought in the highest box office ever: $2.1 billion. Although theatrical receipts amounted to only 25 percent of revenue (compared to 80 percent in 1980), downstream revenue floated all boats to record highs. In the year after which five majors (Disney, TimeWarner, News Corp./Fox, Sony [Columbia/Tri-Star], and Paramount) saw annual profit increases of 60 percent, the last straggler, Matsushita/MCA/Universal, caught up due to the unprecedented success of *Jurassic Park*. Each of the studios was part of a much larger media conglomerate, with Paramount acquired by Viacom this year. As opposed to the older model of entrepreneurial studios, film was now a small section of a vast corporation that expected steady and predictable profits matching other sections of the conglomerate. Increasing rationalization of the creative process and expansion of studio marketing efforts followed.

The summer dynamic was astonishing. Sylvester Stallone's action film *Cliffhanger* opened Memorial Day and grossed $84 million as summer rolled on ($255 million worldwide). The romantic Tom Hanks/Meg Ryan vehicle *Sleepless in Seattle* followed, making $126.6 million ($227.9 million worldwide) from a modest $21 million budget and later picking up domestic video rentals of $64.9 million. The 11 June opening of *Jurassic Park* swept away the season, with North American grosses of $357 million ($920.1 million worldwide). *In the Line of Fire*, a Clint Eastwood action film, followed on 9 July, racking up $102.2 million domestically and $85 million overseas, with rentals of an additional $49 million. The next week, the kids/family film *Free Willy* opened, grossing $77.7 million, eventually picking up rentals of $36 million. Then the Harrison Ford action vehicle *The Fugitive* opened in August, making $183.8 million ($368.9 million worldwide) from a $44 million budget and later taking in $97 million in video rentals. Some films intended as summer blockbusters stumbled out of the gate, however: the Arnold Schwarzenegger *Last Action Hero*, made on a budget of $85 million, grossed only $50 million domestically, but later pulled in $26.8 million in video rentals; *Super Mario Brothers*, with a budget of $42 million, grossed only $20.9 million in theatrical release. Top-grossing films of the year included the Robin Williams farce *Mrs. Doubtfire* ($219.1 million; $423.2 million worldwide), two John Grisham adaptations—*The Firm* ($158.3 million; $262.3 million worldwide), starring Tom Cruise in a tale of corporate law corruption, and another legal thriller, *The Pelican Brief* ($100.6 million; $195.3 million worldwide), with Julia Roberts and Denzel Washington—as well as the morality fantasy tale *Indecent Proposal* ($106.6 million; $266.6 million worldwide), headlined by Robert Redford and Demi Moore, and Spielberg's second hit of the year, *Schindler's List* ($96 million; $317.1 million worldwide).

A larger picture is useful here. During the year there were 450 theatrical releases and 19 reissues: 156 were from the majors (the six MPAA studios) and 275 were independent films; all these figures were up from the previous year. The MPAA actually rated 605 films (including foreign films and films that were rated but not shown theatrically). Of those the category totals were as follows: G, 22; PG, 98; PG-13, 111; R, 370; NC-17/X, 4. This demonstrates the paucity of family-friendly films compared to the heavy output of sex and violence for teens and young adults. The major chain exhibitors do not show NC-17, nor do the chain video stores rent them, and thus the studio films *Kalifornia* (Brad Pitt as a sociopath killer in a road film) and John Woo's U.S. debut *Hard Target* (Jean-Claude Van Damme hunted and running for his life) were cut to get the R rating. Indie auteur Abel Ferrara kept the NC-17 for his *Bad Lieutenant,* with Harvey Keitel playing out the last days of a violent, drug-addicted cop.

The average cost of a studio feature was $29.9 million, and the marketing average (prints and advertising) was $14 million (a 4.5 percent increase over the year before; marketing had risen 224.9 percent in the previous ten years). Understanding this, one can see that a film that initially appears to be profitable, such as *Poetic Justice* starring Janet Jackson, which cost $14 million to produce and returned a theatrical gross of $27.5 million, actually just came close to breaking even when marketing is included.

On the other hand, very clever release and smart low-cost marketing could make a film profitable, as with Miramax's distribution of the 1992 Mexican film *Como Agua para Chocolate* (Like Water for Chocolate), which Harvey "Scissorhands" Weinstein recut for North America and released in February. It grossed $21.6 million, a new record for a foreign film.[4] Respectable profits also came to Miramax for the Australian comedy *Strictly Ballroom* (1992, released 1993; $11.2 million), and this kind of savvy made the distributor attractive to Disney, which acquired Miramax in the spring. Miramax, in turn, got an infusion of capital and the deep pockets to steamroll over other independent distributors in subsequent bidding wars.[5]

In terms of exhibition, admissions grossed $5.15 billion for the year. The National Association of Theater Owners marked admissions at $1.24 billion (the MPAA computed ticket sales at $1 billion) and reported the average ticket price at $4.14 (MPAA quoted $5.45), but New York City saw a spike from $7.50 to $8.00. The number of exhibition sites was slowly trending downward, at about 7,000 for the year, while the number of screens due to multiplexing was moving upward to 25,626.

The evolving media landscape heavily favored sheer entertainment films, but some serious message works were successful. *Schindler's List* came in tenth in gross receipts and topped almost all reviewers' best-of-year lists. Certainly Spielberg's Holocaust film is a sentimental favorite, but it has its legitimate critics ("White Male"), and, like the year's Tom Hanks vehicle directed by Jonathan Demme, *Philadelphia* ($201.3 million theatrical worldwide), about a gay man with AIDS fighting for rights and dignity, in retrospect it seems very much a film of its time, and evidence of the director's motivation to produce a serious statement against the backdrop of an extremely successful entertainment career.[6]

Within this economic framework, racial/ethnic representation also changed. Trailing the box office success of Spike Lee and "New Jack Cinema" earlier in the decade, black-directed and/or -themed films found a still uncertain but slightly more stable niche, complementing the rise and crossover of rap/hip-hop/gangster musical culture. The studios released the Hughes brothers' violent inner-city film *Menace II Society,* Mario Van Peebles's black western *Posse,* Tamra Davis's rap music mockumentary *CB4* with comedian Chris Rock, and John Singleton's romantic *Poetic Justice,* while on the indie side Miramax distributed first-timer Leslie Harris's neorealist *Just Another Girl on the I.R.T.* and Haile Gerima self-distributed his Afrocentric *Sankofa.* In a parallel vein, Anglo auteur Allison Anders finished her drama of East L.A. Chicano girl-gang members, *Mi Vida Loca* (My Crazy Life). Some parts of the cinema scene seemed to follow the theme song of the successful Clinton-Gore campaign of the previous year: Fleetwood Mac's "Don't Stop Thinking about Tomorrow."

The Dialectics of Blockbusters and Independents

The Hollywood system functionally connects blockbusters and indies. We can see the infrastructure at work in considering *Jurassic Park* and *El Mariachi* along with a "middle" film, *Falling Down.* On its June arrival, *Jurassic Park* was widely recognized as representing a new stage in U.S. cinema. It was certainly the quintessential summer blockbuster, quickly meeting and then exceeding all commercial expectations. The film fused two increasingly antagonistic commercial aspects: marketability and playability (Lewis "Following"). The studios hold a vested interest in marketing, promoting the film, and opening as widely as possible to maximize initial receipts (of which they typically get 90 percent), making it an event that will be remembered when later exhibition windows open. Exhibitors want films with a long play because they get a larger share of the gate with every passing week. Increasingly, theater owners complain that many event films don't maintain a good draw after the opening weekend. Meanwhile, studio insiders often admit that for many films the theatrical opening run serves just as a trailer for later sales. Spielberg's blockbuster bridged the gap.

The film used new technology, particularly in its mix of computer generated images (CGI) and advanced animatronics (modeling and puppetry). It continued and developed the pattern of the high-concept film (Wyatt

High Concept), a creative and marketing fusion that fueled the blockbuster direction of Hollywood since the mid-1970s. The creative team followed an established pattern, drawing on a best seller by Michael Crichton that recycled the theme park-gone-deadly from his earlier *Westworld* (1973) and added a hot new sci-fi topic: cloning. Director Spielberg had declared an interest before the book was completed. (His commitment probably helped shape the presold novel.) The narrative (monstrous nature threatens mankind) was one he exploited before in *Jaws* (1975), and it included his familiar theme of establishing/saving the nuclear family. George Lucas's effects house, Industrial Light and Magic, delivered an impressive new look. Thus the marketing team worked with preestablished material (perennial kids' interest in dinosaurs), a best-selling novel, and multiple opportunities for product tie-ins (toys, kids' fast-food meals, etc.).

With the previous decade's system of advance saturation advertising in place and a newer pattern of multi-screen cineplex premieres, the film had a spectacular opening weekend (earning back $50.2 million of its $63 million production cost in three days on 3,500 screens in 2,404 theaters). It quickly became the highest grossing film to date ($882.1 million worldwide by the following March, with $1 billion in licensed merchandise sales), a position it held until *Titanic* created a new benchmark five years later. Many critics noted the irony of a film that was ostensibly critical of capitalist exploitation of nature for profit producing extensive ancillary merchandise (the T-shirts and school lunch boxes sold at the Jurassic theme park being a sad marker of failure at the end of the film, with raptors raging in the welcome center). The merchandizing machine rolled on with logo-branded items flooding the kid market and product placement tie-in synergy such as the Ford Explorer SUVs incorporated into the film. (With crude oil prices a record low $15 a barrel, what better way to protect your family from raging dinosaurs?) A few years later a Jurassic Park ride was incorporated into the Universal Studios theme park.

Jurassic Park fits the general constellation of attributes that industry analyst Edward Jay Epstein calls "The Midas Formula" of money-making megahit films.[7] The storyline centers on a childhood fantasy (here humans interacting with dinosaurs) with (some) child/adolescent central characters. The plot moves protagonists from weakness to purpose, the cast has chaste sexual relations, and the film shows eccentric supporting characters. There is physical conflict but not so violent as to miss out on a PG-13 rating.[8] Good triumphs over evil, allowing a happy ending and reconstituting the nuclear family. Digital effects and animatronics enhance the spectacle, and the actors are not expensive top-list stars.

Raptors destroy the welcome center in *Jurassic Park* (Steven Spielberg, Universal), marking the triumph of nature over human attempts to control and merchandise it. Digital frame enlargement.

The formula's existence and development merit explanation. With vertical integration gone (formerly studios had controlled not only finance and production but also distribution and exhibition by owning theaters), studios had to exploit intellectual properties in different markets and platforms over the long term. Disney had been the most successful model, rolling films into print comics, toys and tie-ins, and finally in the 1950s television and theme parks. For studios, the cash cow became TV, both made-for-TV movies and syndicated shows, not theatrical movies. Increasingly films were made with an eye to eventual release on other platforms: cable, video/DVD, broadcast TV, and then a new cycle abroad, contributing to the increasing conglomeration of the entertainment and media industry through the decade. Thus *Jurassic Park*, the theatrical movie, justified its financial investment through its popularity and box office receipts, but it also served as a starting point for a successful theme ride at Universal Studios theme park, a sequel, the branding of dinosaur-themed toys, and an arcade game (shoot the raging raptors with a "tranquilizer" gun), among other properties. It became the studio ideal: a "tent-pole franchise"—a center for sequels, computer games, and a surfeit of merchandise around the world.

The film presents an interesting amalgam that emerges most fundamentally from the commercial imperative Hollywood has always followed of producing works that are legible and satisfying to the largest audience.

We can spot at least three different authorial intentions in the finished product. For Universal executives, *Jurassic Park* exploits the Midas formula for maximum international commercial advantage. Becoming *the* summer event film in North America ensures global marketing success and sale in future downstream windows, as well as opening the possibilities for a sequel and a theme park attraction. For novelist and screenwriter Michael Crichton, the film is a platform for a critical skepticism to corporate capitalist enterprise: messing with nature through sci-fi biotechnology. And for Spielberg, it uses thrills aplenty to return to his familiar theme of validating the nuclear family.

Jurassic Park trades on the well-worn Frankenstein story of human hubris—driven here by entrepreneurial capitalist showmanship—defying God's plan and creating monsters. Motivated by compensation that will allow them to continue their fieldwork dig for another three years, a visiting paleontologist and paleobotanist, Alan Grant (Sam Neill) and Ellie Sattler (Laura Dern), arrive at the island park for one three-day weekend, ostensibly to verify its safety for prospective customers. After the initial science setup, explaining that the park contains live dinosaurs cloned from ancient DNA, things go awry and the desperate chase is on. Along the way Dr. Grant learns to shed his aversion to children and actually becomes a model parent. As Lester Friedman describes it:

> Grant and the children take refuge in a giant tree for the night. Climbing astride a large tree branch jutting out between his legs, an apt if exaggerated symbol of his assumption of patriarchal control, Grant mimics the "singing" of the vegetarian brachiosaurs, as the soundtrack breaks into a gentle lullaby. "They're not monsters," he patiently explains to the frightened Lex. "Just animals. They do what they do." He climbs off the branch and sinks back into the trunk, exhausted. The children lean against him and, for a moment, Grant seems uneasy with their need for affection, reassurance, and protection. He expresses a bit of pain, uncomfortably shifts his weight, reaches into his back pocket, and extracts the raptor claw he used to scare the boy in Montana, silently contemplating the artifact. "What are you and Ellie going to do now if you don't have to pick up dinosaur bones anymore?" asks Lex. "I don't know," responds Grant. "Guess we'll just have to evolve too." . . . Grant takes one last look at the claw, a symbol of his hostility toward children, and throws it to the ground, sifting his focus from past enmities to present obligations. Spielberg restates this exact father/children configuration in the last scene, when the characters flee from the island, as Sattler smiles approvingly, and Grant, also with a shy smile, accepts his evolution to fatherhood. (139)

In a wide-ranging article on the film, Constance Balides deals with its fusion of a display of magical bioengineering and a critique of neoliberal practices while itself becoming a marketing phenomenon: *"Jurassic Park's* project is hypervisible, not hidden—its own economics out there, on the surface and celebrating commercial success. . . . The film points to a present marked by the imbrication of economic and cultural realms and by pervasive identifications with economic rationales, and to the way the lustre of capital itself is an attraction in a post-Fordist economy" (160).[9]

At the opposite end from studio blockbuster status, filmmaker Robert Rodriguez, fresh from film school, intended to make an inexpensive feature for the Spanish-language home video market for under $10,000. A clever and resourceful Texan, he knew that video stores throughout the Southwest and in urban areas with Chicano populations had a flourishing trade in low-budget action adventure features, commonly produced in Mexico. So becoming a "cockroach capitalist," he worked in the neglected interstices of the market, building up his skills and credits before trying the mainstream. By lucky accident, he was in the right place at the right time—U.S. producers who spotted his work on *El Mariachi* found it similar to the movies of newly discovered Hong Kong director John Woo, who had influenced Quentin Tarantino and others—and he subsequently parlayed this success into a major directing career. An early version of *El Mariachi* was shown at the 1992 Toronto Film Festival and a considerably upgraded version played at Sundance in January, winning the audience award and gaining sensational press and widespread attention.

El Mariachi introduces the title character as an itinerant musician (Carlos Gallardo) who enters a small, dry, dusty Mexican town looking for employment. Mistaken for a notorious gunman who also travels with a guitar case holding his weapons, the guitarist becomes embroiled in a criminal feud, emerging at the end, having lost his fingers and thus livelihood, as El Mariachi, the musician transformed into an avenging killer. The raw story has the simplicity of a folktale, the creation of a legend told in story and ballad. Multiplying fast action sequences, a romance plot, and both menacing and comic secondary characters, the film quickly covers its technical limitations with inventive short cuts and improvisations. By shooting just one take of each shot and working fast with a small crew, Rodriguez was able to transfer the film to video and rough-edit it on two VCRs. Full of energetic action, the film moves quickly while utilizing existing locations to clever effect and casting nonprofessionals whose unusual look is more important than their acting ability. The result is a satisfying, even intriguing, kinetic film experience, which shows that much of effective cinema depends on core elements of dramatic narrative and visual style that even a poverty-level budget can achieve given imaginative direction.

One much-hyped aspect of independent features—working on bare-bones budgets—is extremely misleading to the uninformed. It makes good copy to say someone shot their first feature on $100,000 or $25,000 or even $7,000, but the realities are very different. Rodriguez gained a lot of attention for the claim that he made this first feature for $7,000 in out-of-pocket expenses (Rodriguez). But this disguises numerous details. First of all, that figure covered only the initial outlay for film stock and processing. Rodriguez was "discovered" while in the editing stage of his film (actually while making a videotape rough version), and then signed to a deal that allowed him to finish editing and pay for the blow-up to 35 mm, the cost of optical effects (such as fades and dissolves), the remixing of all sound including extensive Foley (sound stage) work, payment for music rights, and other matters needed to bring the film to completion. Beyond that was the distributor's cost of prints, advertising, negotiating distribution and exhibition deals, and residual sales abroad, as well as cable TV and videocassette sales. The actual cost of the film was hundreds of thousands, perhaps several million, not a few thousand dollars. The myth of *El Mariachi* also omits that Rodriguez borrowed rather than rented his equipment, that he shot a type of film that did not require skilled physical acting or dialogue delivery or synch sound recording, and that he had made and edited little videotape "movies" at home as a teenager. So he actually had ten years of background and thousands of hours of shooting and editing experience with narratives before starting on this feature project. With a minuscule cast and crew, by editing his rough cut at cable access on video, and by living and working at home and thus having no office or overhead expenses, Rodriguez carried out the production and post-production with remarkable efficiency.

While *Jurassic Park* and *El Mariachi* represent the industrial extremes of the action film, both present an attractive masculinity: the preoccupied professional who learns the proper pleasures of fatherhood and family, and the itinerant artist who becomes the romantic loner and avenger. A "middle" film in budget also appeared as a contemporary allegory on white middle-class American masculinity. Perhaps the year's most historically located film, Joel Schumacher's *Falling Down* features Michael Douglas as a white-collar defense industry worker who violently rampages across Los Angeles, the leading popular image-location of urban violence. Known only as D-FENS to the police (from the vanity license of his abandoned auto), the Douglas character, under a restraining order to stay away from his divorced wife and children, has lost his aerospace engineering job (that year Boeing released 32,000 workers) and finally his grip on himself. The film encapsulates widespread social tensions of the time: high unemployment, loss of

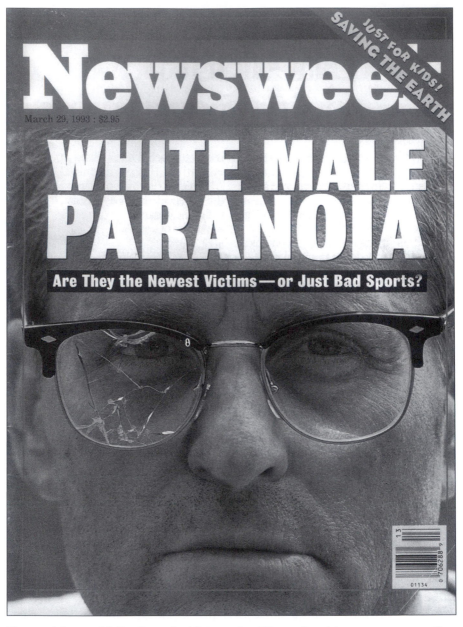

Newsweek featured *Falling Down* (Joel Schumacher, Warner Bros.) in a cover story to illustrate changes in white masculinity. Digital frame enlargement.

the familial corporation that respected age and experience, large immigrant presence in urban areas, fear of feminism, escalating lawlessness from police and gangs. *Newsweek* featured the film on its cover with the headline: "White Male Paranoia: Are They the Newest Victims—or Just Bad Sports?"

While some read the film as an expression of white male anxieties, the film also underlines the paltriness of D-FENS's grasp of the world. He scapegoats minorities and is unwilling to understand the specific impact of the global neoliberal agenda on his own life. There is no release for him or the audience in his rampage. Arriving at a fast food restaurant minutes after the breakfast menu has ended, he uses a gun to get his morning food (providing a comic and audience-pleasing retort to retail bureaucracy), but while this confrontation overcomes the corporate rules of Taylorized food service, the payoff is only crappy fast food.

The Douglas character contrasts with that of Robert Duvall, who plays a methodical and dutiful police detective pursuing the enraged D-FENS. Due to retirement, it is the cop's last day on the job, and the film carefully matches the two to show a rampaging and resentful male anger contrasted to a mature, responsible, and socially sensitive masculinity. Against the recent historical backdrop of the O. J. Simpson murder trial, the Rodney King beating, and the urban rioting following the LAPD verdict the year before, *Falling Down* encapsulates social anxieties fresh in the national imagination. At the same time, industrial analysis reveals other aspects. Although a bankable star, Douglas found it hard to develop this pet project's finances, since it wasn't a generic action vehicle but a thoughtful allegory containing a cautionary message. The film produced a respectable domestic theatrical gross of $40.9 million (37th highest for the year) followed by video rentals of $18.1 million.

Family Dramas

While the high drama of global capitalism's public face often appears in the heroic action film with the lone protagonist or small team determined to fight transnational corporate corruption, international terrorism, or gangster plots, the daily small-scale symptoms often can be found in domestic melodrama. Two films present contrasting allegories of the effects of neoliberalism on personal life. *Laurel Avenue*—made by Carl Franklin and originally broadcast in the summer as a two-part series on HBO, then released on video as a film—realistically dramatizes an extended working-class, midwestern family facing the effects of social disintegration in the post-Vietnam, post-Reagan-Bush era. *The Wedding Banquet* [*Xiyan*]—directed by Taiwanese-born, U.S. film school-educated Ang Lee, co-produced in Taiwan and the United States—comically resolves the contradictory expectations of old and new ways in a Chinese (and) American family.

In its structure, *Laurel Avenue* bears traces of having been conceived as a mini-series that could run in six half-hour segments on pay cable, or three hour-long segments, or (as in its original screening) as two hour-and-a-half shows. This flexibility also indicates that it could have been thought of as pilot for an annual series like other HBO dramas. Such malleability is a plus in programming and marketing. Running against the grain of expectation, *Laurel Avenue* is notable as a family melodrama centered on a midwestern African American family. While the family melodrama has been declining in appeal as a film genre form, it has continued on television. Why it has declined in theatrical film form can be explained most obviously by box office demographics dominated by the young and by males, but that also points toward the logic of its continuation in domestic exhibition on TV.

The film can be read as an allegory of the change to a post-Fordist economy. Set in St. Paul, Minnesota, the narrative unfolds in a multigenerational working-class family that is undergoing the primary and secondary effects of a drastically changing economy. Institutional context aside, *Laurel Avenue* shows the remarkable potential of the family drama precisely in showing the unexpectedly typical. A midwestern black family with a range of types, tensions, and traumas has to cope with a weekend of coalescing crises. Patriarch Jake Arnett (Mel Winkler) is a factory worker in a time of layoffs as production is outsourced abroad. His unionized employment was generous and stable, and its long tenure is evidenced by the large two-story frame house on an ample lot that serves as the magnet for diverse activities through a weekend. Matriarch Maggie (Mary Alice) tries to stage-manage the events. Her twin thirtysomething daughters from her first marriage face their own milestones: Yolanda (Juanita Jennings) is a cop being promoted to sergeant, while Rolanda (Rhonda Stubbins White) is a recovering drug addict who reverts to using and has to go back to rehab.[10]

Meanwhile, Woody (Dan Martin), Jake's son from his first marriage, a Vietnam vet who went through his own postwar addiction, tries to start up a career in music while Kathleen (Gay Thomas), his 3M corporate executive wife, wants him to take over her father's funeral home business so they can start having kids. Maggie and Jake's firstborn son, Marcus (Monté Russell), finds himself caught between working in a Mafia-owned clothing store and the schemes of an old army buddy who is trying to make a fast-buck deal on contraband steroids. Other plotlines involve the Arnett's sixteen-year-old daughter, Sheila (Malinda Williams), on the cusp of sexual activity (she carries condoms in her purse but hasn't used them) that leads to a moment of parental drama Saturday night and the instigation of Maggie's determined discussion with the preacher Sunday morning on the church steps. Son Keith (Scott Lawrence) lives at home and serves as a high school basketball coach where his nephew Rushan (Vonte Sweet), Rolanda's son, is a basketball player and a petty dealer. A somewhat testy old uncle (Jay Brooks) lives in the Arnett home along with Rolanda's five-year-old daughter (Ondrea Shalbetter). The complex web of a large cast marks the film's origins in serial drama, but it also contributes to the story reflecting on the strengths of a black family faced with external pressures in changing times.

Much of the story progresses with low-key exposition. Jake and the uncle duck out of going to Sunday services and wager on the day's NFL football game. Keith has to pull Fletcher (Ulysses Zachary), Sheila's boyfriend, from a game when the boy's on-court performance is erratic in front of college scouts. Sheila is attracted to the boy (though not to his furtive drinking), but she is not willing to go as far as he wants on a date. Maggie frets about her cop daughter not taking a police desk job but staying on the street, and also notices, with disdain, that Woody brings store-bought potato salad—instead of Kathleen providing homemade—for the Sunday promotion party. We see one reason for the culinary *faux pas* when we find Woody going down on Kathleen before Sunday breakfast. This interweaving of the mundane and everyday with a few moments of high tension drama (the basketball game, the steroids deal) marks an unusual pace and a realistic attention to the dynamics of personal and family life that is so noticeable precisely because the dominant depiction of African American families on television and in film is based on sit-com simplicities or gang-banger stereotypes. The film chronicles hopes and disappointments, none of which are earthshaking, but which gradually reveal the strength of a family bound by responsibility and love. Keith hopes he can get Fletcher a basketball scholarship, but the kid fails. Sheila prepares for sexual activity, but realizes she's not ready. Yolanda faces the frustration of her junkie sibling, but finds strength from her white husband's support. Rolanda stumbles again, but her parents take her back to rehab one more time. Following a realist tone and low-key resolution, the film displays endurance as a social value in a time of large and small traumas.

Ang Lee's *The Wedding Banquet* (*Xiyan*) was a low-budget ($1 million) indie success in the United States ($6 million) and also in the Asian market (where it brought in a spectacular $30 million). The film presents a series of mistaken identities built out of gay yuppie New York real estate developer Wai-tung's (Winston Chao) need to arrange a marriage of convenience to Wei-wei (May Chin), a mainland Chinese painter whose student visa is expiring. With his parents (Sihung Lung and Ah-Leh Gua) arriving from

Wedding guests force the couple into bed in *The Wedding Banquet* (Ang Lee, Good Machine). Digital frame enlargement.

Taiwan, Wai-tung's white boyfriend Simon (Mitchell Lichtenstein) suggests the sham relation as a piece of theater for the parents. Once begun, things get out of hand when a former family servant, now a Chinatown restaurateur, insists on throwing a grand wedding banquet. The set piece dinner ends with two complications. Dad has a stroke and must stay on to recover, while Wei-wei is found to be pregnant from unplanned post-banquet intercourse.[11] In the final resolution the son comes out to his mother as gay, and the father reveals to Simon he knows his son is queer but is glad there will be a grandchild. Wei-wei gets a green card and the chance to stay on in a not-very-traditional family.

As a comedy of manners built out of the confused complexities of the characters' identities, the film highlights dynamic changes pointing to the future. Thus, distinctions such as PRC/Taiwan, Chinese/American, gay/straight, traditional/contemporary, core/periphery, aspiring artist/real estate businessman are all in dynamic play. Gina Marchetti argues that the film's commercial success stems from

> a fundamental contradiction concerning its classification. . . . [It] fits easily into several categories, and therefore can be marketed to a variety of audiences as an Asian film, a Chinese film, a Taiwanese film, an Asian American film, a Chinese American film, a New York Chinatown film, a "green-card" story, a popular comedy, a melodrama, an "art" film, a gay film, an "ethnic" family film, or a "multi-cultural" feature designed to raise the consciousness of viewers. (276)

Chris Berry provides a further consideration, arguing that the comic film presents a Chinese family melodrama, depicting a collectivity in crisis, rather than individual character drama centered on psychology character- istic of the West. For Berry, audience empathy and identification focus less on any individual and more on the Confucian family unit embedded in social and kinship relations as it negotiates the interface with globally hege- monic American culture. In the Chinese framework, homosexuality is less a moral or sexual dilemma than an ethical one for the son who is expected to produce a grandson to continue the family line. This is set within a film in which the audience has access to the feelings of all the central characters and thus enables knowledge exceeding the perspective of any one charac- ter. Berry concludes:

> The film's ambivalence is itself an ideological move appropriate to the suste- nance of globalized liberal capitalism, for it enables that system by finding a way to maintain simultaneously two otherwise incompatible value systems that it brings into proximity. In this way it produces a new melodramatic hybrid appropriate to the negotiation of the "moral occult" of globalism. (189)

The Woman's Film

While being a staple form and thematic of feature dramatic narrative film, the newer woman's film undergoes significant changes evi- denced in three different films this year. The large studio film *What's Love Got to Do with It* is a musical biopic about singer Tina Turner, detailing her rise to stardom and escape from the battering of her husband, Ike Turner. It alternates musical performance as expressive self-achievement with har- rowing depictions of verbal, psychological, and physical abuse. A low- budget neorealist indie auteur film, *Ruby in Paradise,* shows a young woman coming to maturity and self-respecting independence. And the direct-to- video (DTV) narrative *Indecent Behavior* updates the gothic novel heroine to a sexually active post-feminist scenario in which erotic thrills are produced by the fear and lure of sexuality.

What's Love Got to Do with It entered the market on 9 June with high public consciousness of its story. Based on the tell-all autobiography *I, Tina* (1986), produced by Disney, and with logical tie-ins to CD music sales and live concert tours, the film was well positioned in the summer season, eventually grossing a respectable $39.1 million. Its two leads, Angela Bassett and Laurence Fishburne, were subsequently nominated for Oscars. As with any well-known life story, the audience's principal pleasure is in seeing a dramatic reenactment of "actual" (behind the scenes) events, and the basic story is predictable. On the basis of raw talent, a naive young woman begins a performing career. She blossoms professionally and is initially attracted to her driven and worldly mentor. But as time goes on, she comes to overshadow him professionally and in public acclaim, and he becomes jealous of her success. As he slides downward, his abuse gets more severe and meaner, while she reacts with denial and then terror to his violent outbursts. This naturally melodramatic narrative reaches its high point with Tina's escape, a tense and explosive sequence. Throughout, musical performance showcases Tina's expressive body and voice and provides the showcase for her talent and will. In contrast, Ike is driven to control her, but in performance she exceeds his grasp.

The film alternates public performance with domestic details, and the hard work of professional singing is matched by the hard work of trying to maintain the domestic sphere in a time of family disintegration. It opens with a rural black church choir rehearsing. Little Tina (Rae'Van Larrymore Kelly) has too much vocal and body energy for the gospel director, and she is ushered out to go home where she discovers that her mother is leaving her marriage and abandoning the kid to Grandma. Cut to 1958 and teenage Tina arrives in St. Louis to live with Mom and older sister while starting nursing school. But following her sister to the club where the older one works as a bartender, the country girl observes Ike Turner's band and the next night sings, immediately wowing the audience. The film displays the common trope of artist bio films, that all concerned immediately recognize her raw talent. Seen as a rival by Ike's common-law wife who threatens the singer with a gun but then shoots herself, Tina drops into the middle of another dysfunctional family. She is quickly seduced by Ike's pathetic admission of his fears that others always hurt him, don't believe in him, and will abandon him. She comforts him. This leads to her sexual initiation and (it is implied) to a new level of performance onstage when she sings "Rock Me Baby." Thus the pattern is set.

On tour the band has growing success, but Tina faces a punishing schedule. Even when she is ill, Ike puts her to work, and when she has a baby and is ordered to rest by the doctor, Ike carries Tina out of the hospital along with the infant so they can continue the tour schedule. Repeatedly, he torments her: following a rush marriage across the border in Mexico, he teasingly drives away while she tearfully runs to catch him. At their New York City premiere a sullen Tina resists by standing silent on stage. Ike approaches her from behind, kisses her cheek, and with tears streaming down her face, she performs a spectacular version of "A Fool in

Love." The framing and cutting emphasize (for the first time) her famous legs and strut. This scene can be read in two ways. In terms very familiar in the popular imagination, thanks to several decades of feminist interventions on spousal abuse, we see the familiar pattern of male abuse, female shock and intimidation, then male "apology," and the apparent (but unstable) resolution. But on another level, we see Tina actually resist the sadism by transmuting the humiliation into a higher level of performative expression. Pain advances her art.

While her attempts to run away from the abuse are frustrated (escaping on a bus, she is betrayed by her mother), Ike's humiliations are increasingly public, sadistic, and violent. He abuses drugs, and as Tina's star continues to rise he punishes her with a horrifying, violent rape, after which Tina overdoses on prescription drugs. Returned from the hospital, she bonds with a girlfriend. For the first time, she has someone she can trust. Tina is then introduced to Buddhism, which gives her calmness and self-assurance. She finally escapes Ike (her hysteria is visualized in shots of her running through dense street traffic) and sues for divorce. Her career blossoms as a solo act and his disintegrates. While the subject of battered women was firmly in the public consciousness by this time, the film can offer only an individual way out. It depicts no way to control or change violent masculine misogyny but simply dramatizes the need for the victim to get her act together, and then, if she is a talented international recording star, to take that act on the road. Surviving abuse is a solo act in the domestic sphere of neoliberal social policy. Thus this biopic validates individual solutions, matching the celebrity stardom of the performer.[12]

Another coming-to-self-awareness narrative, *Ruby in Paradise,* tells a white Appalachian woman's tale. Ruby (Ashley Judd, in her first major role) leaves her rural Tennessee home and drives to Panama City, Florida, on the "Redneck Riviera"—the low-rent Gulf Coast resort area at the end of the summer vacation season. She gets a retail job at Chambers, a souvenir and resort wear store, and starts a journal of her progress. Reflecting on her past, she confides to her co-worker girlfriend (Allison Dean) that she "got out without getting pregnant or beat up." From this minimal milestone, Ruby begins her new life. Admirably low-key in its approach, the film depicts the gradual awakening of her own consciousness and her expanding horizons as she encounters a caddish handsome guy (Bentley Mitchum), the store owner's son; finds a respectful Nice Guy (Todd Field), tender and romantic but with his own cynical negative energy; and begins to make her way as a self-respecting young single woman. Throughout this first year of being on her own, Ruby experiences novelties such as oysters, a stylishly furnished high-rise apartment overlooking the ocean, and a Jane Austen novel, all with a sensible judgment. She makes up her own mind, measuring everything, and remains especially wary of the easy way out: depending on a man. When the bad-boy son tries to rekindle their brief affair by forcing himself on her, she resists and he fires her, precipitating a crisis of unemployment, a despairing job search, and finally hard physical labor in a commercial laundry service. Even in this phase she learns about herself and the world. Entering a topless strip bar at a low point in the job search in response to a "now hiring" sign, she sees a dancer working for the first time, realizes it isn't something she could do, and yet remains curious about the stripper so freely manipulating men with her physicality. And in the laundry she bonds with two women co-workers, appreciating their humor and quiet strength.

The film is especially remarkable in representing through cinematography and script writer-director Victor Nunez's ability to use place in an expressive way, matching the undramatic banality of a coastal resort town in its off season with the coming to consciousness of the protagonist. For Ruby, Panama City, a place her family visited when she was ten, and the only place she knew outside of Tennessee, did seem like Paradise in her dreams. Experiencing it as an adult, the romantic edge comes off, but her quiet optimism remains, strengthened when the boss takes her to Tampa for a trade show where she can see a wider world with new possibilities, including a young woman in a business suit with a briefcase who might be Ruby herself in the near future. Later, finding that her son lied about Ruby quitting, Mildred Chambers (Dorothy Lyman) rehires Ruby, getting her back on track. The neorealist drama ends affirmatively, recognizing that the economic and career possibilities of working-class women are often tied to their region.

Ruby in Paradise won the Grand Prize at the Sundance Festival and represents the best spirit of that institution: prizing the small, independent, character-driven psychological drama created by a writer-director-cinematographer auteur with an expressive cinematography, a sensitivity to regional locale, to class and gender politics, and to the gradual time of everyday personal change. At the same time, despite its award-winning status and high critical acclaim (Roger Ebert included it on his ten-best list for the year), the film could not turn the corner in distribution (handled by October Films, an art house niche specialist outfit), recouping only $1.1 million, just a shade over its $800,000 production cost. Nunez remains a remarkably talented auteur who is not well served by the dominant system, completing each successive film only after years of self-sacrifice.

Indecent Behavior represents a different take on the lone contemporary woman. In the noir tradition, the film depicts a detective investigating a murder and starting a sexual relation with a prime suspect; also in the noir pattern, it is heavily stylized with interiors infused with Venetian-blind shadows, even when there is no apparent light source. It is also indebted to the new sexiness of neo-noirs like *Body Heat* (1981) and borrows obviously from the box office success *Basic Instinct* (1992). Yet it is not a big-budget, mega star vehicle. Rather it is a competent but low-budget, direct-to-video production with small-scale stars: Shannon Tweed, a 1981 *Playboy* Playmate who often plays a sex therapist; Jan-Michael Vincent, remarkably stiff here, an aging has-been whose name appears on the video box but who trails the rest of the cast in the initial credits; and Gary Hudson as the cop, a dependable, handsome supporting actor with a long TV career. In short, the film is a soft-core erotic thriller, filling a reliable market niche. It's estimated that Tweed has enough of a following that her name will support sell-through of over 20,000 units and support late-night pay-cable viewing. While it's often assumed that these films target a voyeuristic male audience looking only for "T&A," in fact erotic thrillers have a substantial female audience, reflecting several decades of the sexual revolution and feminism making sexual/sexy dramas more socially acceptable.[13] Yet these films typically not only show the lure but also spell out the danger, seeming in some ways like extensions of the Gothic novel, showing a caretaking woman alone and facing the tension of sexual fear.

Tweed plays Dr. Rebecca Mathis, a sex therapist who uses surrogates to help patients. Her marriage to Vincent is on the rocks, and her niece, a student training to be a therapist, is sleeping with hubby. Considerable time is spent with Rebecca and the niece observing the surrogates at work in (heterosexual and lesbian) sessions on the other side of a one-way mirror. The drug-induced death of a client following therapy provokes an investigation by detective Nick Sharkey, and then, after dinner in a nice romantic restaurant and her confession that "I'm fascinated by the edge," a warmly lit, long, conventionally tasteful lovemaking scene. Yet the peculiar characteristics of the soft-core thriller form don't provide the frisson of the detective being duped by a femme fatale, since we know from Tweed's star image that Rebecca is not a bad girl, but she can be stalked and framed for murder (by the surrogate who turns out to be a nut-case avenger). She willingly "proves" her innocence to Sharkey by taking the sex-enhancing drug and then having sex with him a second time (in a new location, however). As a genre, low-budget DTV erotic thriller movies mix mystery and sex with danger in a time when women, especially the educated professional women who are the central characters, are supposed to have ready access to sex. The films are titillating but also modern-day Gothic tales, cautionary narratives indicating that for women pleasure and danger are always linked, in both the public and private spheres. Even a former Playmate, and even a sex therapist with a Ph.D., can find erotic pleasures a dangerous terrain in postmodernity. The erotic thriller (and this example is not outstanding cinematically or narratively, but is rather typical) exists at the intersection of industrial economics (the space and financing for modest-budget competent adult content) and a new audience segment (adult women open to decorous and tasteful soft-core porn).

Conclusion

What do we learn from taking a one-year cross-section of the dramatic feature film market in an age of global "free" markets? For the major studios, the industrial/financial logic of the blockbuster is overwhelming. Although film production is a high-risk affair, more like wildcat oil drilling than competitive industrial manufacturing, it is also clear that the majors, through oligopoly and lobbying for direct government intervention, particularly on tariffs, trade, and copyright, try to moderate those variables overall. The post–Cold War opening of new global markets provided new opportunities and smoothed out the big picture. The need, domestic and international, for more "content" seemed, particularly with vastly overhyped media attention, to offer low-budget indie auteurs a window of opportunity. Everyone could be the next Quentin Tarantino, Robert Rodriguez, or Ang Lee. But most aspirants didn't want to consider the institutional and industrial constraints through the entire chain. In the brave new world of neoliberal filmmaking, new openings appeared, like an HBO realistic serial drama on a midwestern African American family, but the result was an interesting pilot, not a sustained series. A regional realist auteur like Victor Nunez could receive critical recognition, but his films were not marketable within the existing free-market system. In the era of neoliberalism, art must bow to commerce. Where there was an opening was in highly generic niche markets like erotic thrillers, which combine glossy (but low-cost) production values, "bankable" stars like Tweed who can turn a predictable sell-through, and a steady audience interest in a domestic viewing space. The year as a whole was witness to gradual but fundamental changes in high-tech production as well as theatrical and domestic exhibition, marketing, and overseas distribution. The entertainment business was profitable and would ride the rollercoaster along with the bullish stock market. Cinema as art, expression, and social statement filled in the margins.

NOTES

1. Neoliberalism is the economic doctrine of unregulated "free" trade and markets, accompanied by downsizing the state and privatization of government services. With the end of the Cold War the doctrine has spread globally, espousing the view that unrestricted capital flows produce progress and abundance for all. Critics argue that neoliberalism is a new form of imperialism and that reduced government spending, taxation, and regulation results in greater inequality.

2. Wasko provides an excellent overview and analysis of the early 1990s situation. Authoritative data is found in Monush *Almanac 1994* and *Almanac 1995*. Detailed industry economic analysis appears in Acland; Corliss "There's Gold"; De Vany; Epstein; Gomery "Economic," "Hollywood Blockbuster," and "Hollywood Film Industry"; Hayes and Bing; Kleinhans "Independent"; Lewis "Following"; Menand; Miller et al.; "The Monster"; Perren; and Sanjek.

3. The number of screens soared due to a real estate development boom fueled by lower interest rates and mall developers who built new, smaller theater multiplexes to anchor their retail operations.

4. Hollywood considers all of North America a "domestic" market; a very profitable Canadian film such as *Porky's* (1982) is not foreign by this measure. *Like Water for Chocolate* was surpassed that year by *The Crying Game*, which opened in fall 1992 but had a long slow build (a Miramax strategy that opened it wide after Academy nominations), finally recouping $62.5 million; *The Piano* opened in the United States late this year and quickly totaled $40.1 million theatrical in North America. Of course with foreign films the distributor is not concerned with production cost and only bids on regional distribution rights.

5. Peter Biskind's *Down and Dirty Pictures* provides the essential (gossipy) story.

6. For a distinctly contrary political analysis, Richard Lippe reads *Philadelphia* as an impressive mass circulation political melodrama—the most progressive commercial film statement possible at the historical moment.

7. Epstein, "The Midas Formula" 236–41. Epstein's sure-fire characteristics are based on an analysis of 1999–2004 blockbusters, but the general outline applies to earlier works, most obviously the *Star Wars* franchise and most of Disney's major films.

8. The children end up the pursued in the most threatening sequence. Adults who weren't attentive to the PG-13 rating sometimes had unexpected experiences. For example, my Aunt Alice took her seven-year-old grandson Nicholas, a kid with a huge dinosaur fascination, to see the film. When Nick became terrified at the first T-Rex attack, they had to flee to the lobby, leaving behind brother Danny, age ten. When the film ended Danny emerged, saying he had wanted to leave the movie also but was too scared to get out of his seat. On the way out, Nick turned to Alice and plaintively asked, "Grandma, why did you take me to such a scary movie?"

9. Post-Fordism identifies the currently dominant mode of production exploiting new technologies, the globalizing of financial markets, the increase in the service and white-collar workforce at home, and the outsourcing of industrial production to the low-wage developing world. For an introduction, see Bourdieu; Harvey.

Reading *Jurassic Park* as visually complex character drama, Warren Buckland argues, in contrast, that "these set pieces are not autonomous action sequences (spectacles) but are narratologically motivated, serving to transform the main protagonist, enabling him to overcome his dislike of children" (185). See also Roger Beebe, who suggests that, like certain

other 1990s films, *Jurassic Park* initiates "a new model of narrative with a radically transformed role for digital effects. . . . The lack of a strong central (human) star . . . results in a
. . . multiplication of narrative centers," for Beebe characteristic of "postmodern cinema"
(171).

10. Although the point is not explicit in the film, Yolanda's success can remind us that
the police, penal, and private security sectors are growth areas of the economy paralleling
the decline in industrial employment and social welfare. And Rolanda's struggles fit the
surging national drug problem in the wake of covert government protection for opium production in Southeast Asia during Vietnam, in Afghanistan during the fight against Soviet
occupation, and in Central America with regard to the CIA's transportation and protection
of drugs and dealers to pay for arms deals and support for the Contras, as well as failed
attempts to prop up repressive Andean regimes against insurgents in coca regions.

11. Underlining the plot development's social foundation, following the banquet the
wedding guests invade the bridal suite and insist not only that the couple drinks, but forces
them under the bed covers and to remove their clothes before the party makers will depart.
Thus the community gets the couple drunk and naked together. Intercourse follows from
the guests' agenda.

12. For a contrasting musical bio film in which family and community form the essential basis of stardom, see my analysis of *Selena* (1997) (Kleinhans "Siempre").

13. For a full context of women consuming porn at home, see Juffer. Three excellent
recent studies examine erotic thrillers in depth: Andrews; Martin *Encountering;* and Williams
Erotic.

1994

Movies and Partisan Politics

DIANE WALDMAN

Two political cartoons by Mike Peters help to illustrate the year's zeitgeist: in the first, a man in a voting booth stands poised before a ballot offering a choice between "Thief," "Liar," "Crook," "Adulterer," and "Psycho," and in the second, labeled "Foreign Gump," a Bill Clinton/ Forrest Gump composite sitting on a park bench proclaims to an onlooker, "My Haiti policy is like a box of chocolates, you never know what you're going to get" ("1994 Perspectives," 65, 70). Together they articulate something fundamental about the year's mood: hostility toward politicians and politics as usual, and the use of popular movie figures for partisan political purposes.

President Bill Clinton began the year with a radio address that spoke to his goals. The passage of legislation to guarantee health insurance for all Americans would be, he said, his number-one priority, but the plan stalled as critics decried administration proposals as "socialized medicine." Although another Clinton goal, economic expansion, was achieved according to various measures—the gross domestic product grew modestly, inflation remained relatively low, and the unemployment rate fell—such successes masked other economic realities, such as increased reliance on part-time and temporary workers and a decline in real wages for many Americans (McDermott). In part, contending with two major scandals distracted the Clinton administration from its professed goals. The first became known as the Whitewater affair, which involved a series of financial and real estate deals made by Bill and Hillary Clinton in Arkansas in the 1980s. The second was a sexual harassment lawsuit filed against Clinton by Paula Corbin Jones, a former Arkansas state employee, the first civil suit ever brought against a sitting president.

In November, Democrats suffered a crushing defeat in the midterm elections. Riding on voters' concerns over crime, taxes, and a general anti-incumbent sentiment, Republicans won control of both the House and the Senate for the first time in forty years. Led by Georgia congressman Newt Gingrich, the GOP promised increases in defense spending, cuts in taxes and welfare benefits, and attacks on affirmative action and public funding of the arts, all enumerated in its preelection "Contract with America."

Both major parties focused on crime, leading to harsh new legislation passed in August. The issue was legitimated in part through extensive coverage of sensational criminal trials that mobilized fears around gender, sexuality, race, and class. Lorena Bobbitt was found not guilty by reason of temporary insanity for cutting off her husband's penis. Lyle and Erik Menendez were accused of killing their parents (this court action first ended in a mistrial). Following a widely televised flight from police, actor and former football star O. J. Simpson was arrested for the murder of his ex-wife, Nicole Brown Simpson, and her friend Ron Goldman. Susan Smith told the nation her missing children had been kidnapped at gunpoint "by a black man" only to confess several days later that she had drowned them herself. Xenophobia was evident in California's passage of Proposition 187, an initiative denying undocumented immigrants most public benefits and ultimately blocked by a federal judge's temporary restraining order. Fears of foreigners were also fueled by the trial and conviction of three Palestinians and one Egyptian national for their roles in the previous year's bombing of the World Trade Center.

Outside the United States, civil war and genocide raged in Rwanda, and Russia invaded Chechnya. After a threatened U.S. invasion, President Jean-Bertrand Aristide returned to power in Haiti. There were hopeful signs: South Africa held its first fully multiracial elections, and Nelson Mandela was inaugurated as president. Bosnian Serb forces withdrew heavy weapons from Sarajevo and signed a "cessation of hostilities" agreement. British officials and Sinn Fein representatives began formal peace negotiations in December. Although talks on Palestinian self-rule stalled after a Jewish settler shot twenty-nine Muslim worshipers inside the Tomb of the Patriarchs in February, Israel withdrew forces from the Gaza Strip and the West Bank town of Jericho in May, raising hopes for a resolution to this bloody conflict. Palestinian leader Yasir Arafat, Israeli prime minister Yitzhak Rabin, and Israeli foreign minister Shimon Peres were jointly awarded the Nobel Peace Prize, and Israel and Jordan formally ended the state of war that had existed between their countries since 1948.

The deaths of former president Richard M. Nixon and former First Lady Jacqueline Kennedy Onassis prompted recollections (and revisions) of their actions and the eras with which they were most closely associated. The Smithsonian Institution's National Air and Space Museum's exhibit "The Last Act: The Atomic Bomb and the End of World War II" and a postage stamp depicting this event with the caption "Atomic bombs hasten war's end, August 1945" set off fierce arguments about the reasons and effects of that crucial historical moment.[1] Former East German leader Erich Honecker, former Speaker of the House Thomas "Tip" O'Neill, former secretary of state Dean Rusk, and activist Jerry Rubin also passed away, as did writer Ralph Ellison, playwright Eugene Ionesco, composer Henry Mancini, band leader Cab Calloway, Nirvana's lead singer Kurt Cobain, and film stars Burt Lancaster, Jessica Tandy, John Candy, and Raúl Julia. Independent film lost a major talent with the death of director Marlon Riggs.

Among the biggest sports stories of the year was the participation in the Winter Olympics of American figure skater Tonya Harding, despite her involvement in an attack on rival Nancy Kerrigan (who also competed and won a silver medal). In baseball, a protracted strike by the player's union led to the unprecedented cancellation of the end of the regular season and, with it, the World Series.

"Friends" debuted on NBC, and the Independent Film Channel began transmission via satellite and cable. Mergers reached their highest level since the 1980s, among them Viacom's acquisition of Paramount Communications, continuing the "tight diversification" and "synergy" movements in the entertainment industry of the late 1980s and early 1990s (Schatz 199). The foreign market surpassed the domestic in film rentals for the first time (Balio 60). The majors scored huge hits with big-budget, technically sophisticated summer blockbusters, but there was still room for low-budget, low-tech indies like *Go Fish* and *Clerks* with queer or "slacker" sensibilities. The biggest film story of the year, however, was the stupendous critical and commercial success of Quentin Tarantino's *Pulp Fiction*, which won the *Palme d'Or* at Cannes and, with the financial clout of Disney-backed Miramax, became the first independent film to earn over $100 million.

Debates over the interpretation of U.S. history were prominent this year (Sobchack 3–4), and a rhetorical raiding of the past for purposes of the present was a prominent feature of many of its films as well. Robert Redford's *Quiz Show*, for example, returned to the scandals of the 1950s to comment on "a set of issues that continue to bedevil television and American culture: the borders between reality and entertainment, the notion of the airwaves as a public trust, and the lengths to which ordinary Americans will go to gain fame, money" (Doherty "Quiz Show"). Tim Burton's *Ed Wood* went back to the same period for a loving tribute to the low-budget auteur and his "entourage of weirdos, misfits and dope fiends" (Klawans, "Ed Wood" 434). Gillian Armstrong adapted Louisa May Alcott's nineteenth-century *Little Women* from the perspective of 1990s feminism, crafting a female-centered version of "family values" and validating female authorship

Sylvia's take on the year's films' gender politics. Courtesy Nicole Hollander.

and feminine genres in a year when testosterone reigned and even main-stream publications bemoaned the lack of decent roles for women.[2]

Many of the year's films were linked to partisan politics in even more explicit fashion. Former U.S. drug czar and secretary of education William Bennett conjoined "the phenomenal increase in social pathologies—crime, broken families and so on" with "a culture that's becoming increasingly trashy" ("Conversation"). Some constructed the 67th Academy Awards held in March as a race between the hip, violent, postmodern ironic sensibility of *Pulp Fiction* and the old-fashioned sincerity of *Forrest Gump,* with the triumph of the latter over the former regarded as the validation of conservative values (see Cassells 8–11 and Leitch "Know-Nothing").

Two months later, Senate Minority Leader (and future GOP presidential nominee) Bob Dole attacked the entertainment industry in general, and media conglomerate TimeWarner in particular, for "mainstreaming deviancy" and for undermining the moral fabric of the nation through rap music and popular movies. Concentrating principally on the year's films, Dole distinguished between "nightmares of depravity" such as *Natural Born Killers* and "friendly to the family" films such as *Forrest Gump* and *True Lies.*[3] Implicit in Dole's harangue and in the response to it by his critics is the invocation of the same historical events for different political agendas: Dole said approvingly, "We will name names and shame them as they deserve to be shamed," to which Oliver Stone, director of *Natural Born Killers,* responded by denouncing the senator's remarks as "a nineties form of McCarthyism" (qtd. in King "Attacking"). Whatever its merits or faults, Dole's speech provides a way to write about some of the most popular films of the year and to forge connections between those he highlighted and the events enumerated above, both thematically and in the realm of reception. It also provides a lens through which to view other films—*Blue Sky, Hoop*

Dreams, Complaints of a Dutiful Daughter, The Smell of Burning Ants—that Dole neglected to mention. Examining how these films represent the past, the family, and the causes and consequences of violence challenges his notion of family and prompts questions about just whose nightmare those other films are presenting.

Back to the Future

Forrest Gump and *Blue Sky* illustrate what is most at stake in the year's cinematic representations of the past. One of the year's most popular films, earning $330 million at the box office for a major studio, Paramount, *Forrest Gump* was also widely discussed. In contrast, *Blue Sky* was only a modest success commercially (from "mini-major" Orion, earning $3.4 million), and, correspondingly, it received less critical attention. Both films are partially set in early 1960s Alabama, and both earned awards and kudos for their respective stars, Tom Hanks and Jessica Lange. But where *Forrest Gump* returns to the past in order to validate a static masculine hero whose virtue derives from his distance from political engagement and the social movements of the 1960s and 1970s, *Blue Sky* focuses on a female protagonist whose redemption depends upon acting deliberately in ways that connect the personal and the political.

Narrating his life story to a series of progressively more sympathetic and more engaged listeners, the mentally retarded Forrest Gump (Tom Hanks) serves as a highly selective tour guide through the decades of his childhood and young adulthood, namely the 1950s through the early 1980s. Beginning as a crippled boy taunted by bullies in rural Alabama, Forrest miraculously loses his leg braces and becomes a football star, Vietnam war hero, successful entrepreneur, and semi-religious cult figure all the while meeting, separating from, and eventually reuniting with his childhood sweetheart, Jenny Curran (Robin Wright Penn). His personal story is interwoven with numerous nonfictional/historical events, principally through the digital compositing of Hanks into documentary archival footage.

As has been noted (see in particular Cassells and Wang), Winston Groom's satirical 1986 novel has been shaped and adapted by screenwriter Eric Roth and director Robert Zemeckis to emphasize the relationship between Forrest and Jenny and to reassign the character traits associated with each, thus rendering (the masculine) Forrest the repository of all that is valued by the film and (the feminine) Jenny the storehouse of what it sees as countercultural hedonism and self-destruction. Certain additions, such as a scene in which a good-ol'-boy doctor assesses Forrest's legs to be fine but his back to be "as crooked as a politician," mesh neatly with the year's political cynicism and its anti-incumbent mood.

But it is principally through an inconsistent use of structural irony that the film's political perspective emerges.[4] At times, the movie depends upon the *difference* between the way Forrest understands the events described and the way the filmmaker seems to: thus, for example, when Forrest describes Jenny's father as a "lovin' man, always kissing and hugging her and her sisters," the spectator is encouraged to read him as a violent abuser, both through stereotypical signs marking him as "white trash" (ramshackle house, overalls, half-empty liquor bottle) and subsequent narrative events (Jenny is afraid of him, runs from him, and is eventually taken away by the police to live with her grandmother). Yet at other times, and as the film progresses, no such gap opens up between Forrest's perspective and the one we are encouraged to take up. When Forrest tells us that "some of America's best young men served in that war [Vietnam]" or that he "knows what love is," subsequent events affirm rather than contradict his perspective: the soldiers exhibit courage and compassion, whereas male antiwar protestors and Black Panthers are depicted as verbally and physically abusive and vicious (Byers; Burgoyne; Cassells; Pfeil; Wang). Even Jenny eventually admits that she was "messed up" and returns to Alabama to live (and die) with Forrest. Forrest's disclaimers that precede these statements ("I don't know much of anything, but . . . ," "I'm not a smart man but . . .") mark the film as profoundly anti-intellectual, implying that it is his mental incapacity that somehow gives him access to these personal and historical truths.

Thus, while some vestiges of the satirical elements of Groom's novel remain (for example, in the sequences that suggest Forrest's mental limitations and literal-mindedness make him especially suited for dominant American institutions such as college football or the military), the film lends itself rather to a sentimental reading that simply valorizes Forrest's perspective, easily appropriated by conservative mid-1990s politicians. As Jennifer Hyland Wang argues, *Forrest Gump* was readily enlisted into an already existing ideological project that blamed 1960s political movements for current social ills. Not coincidentally, Newt Gingrich and Pat Buchanan invoked it quite explicitly and self-consciously in the midterm congressional election campaign.[5] Such conservative readings may in fact make more sense, as Thomas Byers maintains, than the filmmakers' later attempts to depoliticize the film and to disarticulate it from this conservative appropriation (Byers; Cassells; Wang).

Blue Sky also returns to the past for purposes of the present. Cultural and political allusions such as Brook Benton and Dinah Washington singing

"Baby, you've got what it takes," a *Life* magazine cover with Elizabeth Taylor and the caption "An Oscar At Last," an officer saying he didn't risk his life in Guam so "some damn Harvard boy could run this country into the toilet," and a discussion of the pending banning of atmospheric nuclear testing all place the film in 1961 or 1962, on the brink of two 1963 events that signaled the beginning of the breakdown of Cold War consensus: the signing of the Nuclear Test-Ban Treaty and the publication of Betty Friedan's *The Feminine Mystique*. Based on the memoirs of screenwriter Rama Laurie Stegner, and directed by Tony Richardson, *Blue Sky* tells the story of a military family coping with and contesting postwar conformity.

In direct contrast to *Forrest Gump, Blue Sky* deals sympathetically with those chafing against or actively resisting political and sexual conformity. Where *Forrest Gump* only strays occasionally from the narrative perspective of its title character, *Blue Sky* distributes points of view among three personae, Hank (Tommy Lee Jones), an army scientist in charge of evaluating radiation hazards to U.S. army personnel; Carly (Jessica Lange), his highly sensual and theatrical wife; and Alex (Amy Locane), the teenage daughter trying to make sense of her parents' marriage and her own emerging sexuality. From the start of the film, it is clear that Hank's whistle-blowing activities and nonconformist ideas (he is an advocate of underground, as opposed to atmospheric, testing) and Carly's sexuality are perceived as threats to postwar "containment culture."[6] After Carly sunbathes topless and Hank's defense of her is described as "close to insubordination," he is transferred from Hawaii to a base in Alabama, a move the film portrays as a punishment for her exhibitionism and his filing of reports with the Atomic Energy Commission. Their move is first presented aurally through Hank's voiceover (he has a "good feeling about Fort Matthews"), but it is subsequently depicted visually from Carly and Alex's points of view, alternating between progressively more dilapidated surroundings and their despair over the transfer.

The film interweaves two narrative strands. As Hank gets involved in his job on the base, Carly gets involved with an amateur theatrical production put on by the officers' wives. The two plots come together when Hank's superior officer, Vince Johnson (Powers Boothe), viewing Carly's dirty dancing with him as promise of things to come, sends Hank off to a Nevada test site. Hank unsuccessfully attempts to stop a test that endangers several civilians. Meanwhile, Carly gets involved with the officer back at the base. When Hank returns and confronts Johnson, we are positioned to think the issue is the affair rather than the military cover-up. The two plots are further entwined as Johnson convinces Carly that temporarily committing

Hank to a mental hospital is the only way to save his military career. When Carly actually sees her husband, drugged beyond recognition, she realizes the depth of Johnson's treachery and exposes the nuclear test accident in order to save Hank.

Where Alex has a peace sign in her room, thinks most of her father's colleagues are "cretins . . . dedicated to armed nuclear destruction," and threatens to start a "Teens for Test Ban" club, Hank is a "containment" man par excellence. Just as he is opposed to atmospheric testing but supports underground nuclear testing, he tries to "handle" his wife's explosions of rage and sensuous public displays by comforting her gently or by channeling that sexuality within their marriage. The "Blue Sky" program for underground testing becomes an explicit metaphor for trying to keep those forces potentially threatening to the status quo below the surface. But ultimately such containment is shown to be both risky and futile, especially where nuclear power is concerned. When Hank sees the depths to which the army will go to suppress the dangers of radiation, he quits, turning to university teaching rather than continuing to "contribute to nuclear warfare."

The film handles the domestic plot more ambiguously. Carly is particularly complex. On the one hand, the film admires her sexual energy and dismisses the forces arrayed against it as hypocritical and/or repressive. On the other, however, it demonstrates that her sexuality hurts and embarrasses her husband and two children, as well as separating her from other women who have befriended her. Ultimately, it solves the "problem" of her sexuality by doing what Hank tries to do, having her take responsibility for the affair and using her exhibitionism to save her husband. (She "borrows" a horse and rides out onto the proposed nuclear test site, getting arrested and prompting embarrassing publicity.) Joseph Natoli describes Lange's role as "a part . . . contained in an old-fashioned moral fable—monogamy is led to the abyss by a distracted woman who falls and then rises magnificently to redeem monogamy" (81), and Carly as a woman who "submits in the end to loyalty to her husband and responsibility for her children" and "once again agrees to play act within the realities that his choices create" (82). Indeed, one can read the film as a narrative about the channeling of sexuality and passion within a traditional marriage, culminating in the restoration of patriarchy. The last line of the film—"C'mon, Daddy, you drive"—is particularly telling, as we simultaneously see Carly relinquish her seat behind the wheel in her new convertible.

But such a reading is only part of the story. As Natoli signals, Lange's performance mitigates against it, because what remains "is the frenetic desperation . . .—the outbursts of revolt, the wild blows against house arrest,

the bitter and angry declarations of rebellion" (82). Neither amateur theatrical productions nor children nor even a passionate, sexy marriage can
compensate for her dissatisfactions, and we know it. The character of Alex,
too, works against a reductive reading of the film as uncritically endorsing
a containment narrative; smart and politically engaged, she does not want
to end up like her mother. If, as Thomas Byers posits, it is the baby boomer
white male who is "the subject of *Forrest Gump*'s version of history, and it is
on his (our) behalf that the past is repressed and rewritten" (425), then it
is the baby boomer white female who is the subject of *Blue Sky*'s. And if *Forrest Gump* offers an opportunity for men of that generation to "reinven[t]
themselves by identifying with the dutiful sons of that era . . . and disow[n]
the difficult or oppositional ones" (Byers 425), then *Blue Sky* offers the
opportunity for identification with those (women *and* men) who chose an
oppositional path.

  Blue Sky was completed in 1991 but not released until this year, due to
Orion's financial problems. Perhaps this was fortunate, in that concerns
over nuclear weapons and atomic power would ultimately shape its reception. Not only was *Blue Sky* released, as mentioned, during debates over
how to represent the decision to use the atomic bomb against Japan, but it
also came out in a year of related public disclosures: that the government
had performed experiments on U.S. citizens to test the effects of atomic
radiation in the 1940s and 1950s, and the Atomic Energy Commission had
exposed millions of people to radioactivity during a nuclear accident in
1965. Meanwhile, other films directly articulated threats posed by nuclear
weaponry (and to the nuclear family) in the present. I now turn to one of
these, the studio release *True Lies,* and to two independent documentaries,
Hoop Dreams and *Complaints of a Dutiful Daughter,* that challenge the vision of
family and nation *True Lies* offers.

The Family That Plays, Prays, or Slays Together

  Since Dole designated certain films "friendly to the family,"
the question logically arises as to what sort of family he had in mind. As
might be expected, especially since the presidential hopeful was attempting
to curry favor with the Religious Right/"family values" wing of his party,
the family he referenced in the films was patriarchal and nuclear, indeed,
obsessed with paternity at a time in which, as one end-of-year essay put it,
"American families are now in uncharted territory—economic and cultural
pressures have seen to that. Divorce, single parenthood and the rise of
working women—. . . have changed the ways in which we can respond to

the world outside" (Elliott 133). Several of the films Dole mentioned take as part of their project the restoration of the (threatened) father's authority, either by naturalizing it, as in *The Lion King* (Buhler; Lang; Roth), or by replacing an absent or abusive father with a kinder, gentler one, as in *Forrest Gump* (Byers; Burgoyne). Several films link this restoration to the welfare of the nation, none more explicitly than James Cameron's and Fox's $110 million action blockbuster *True Lies*. Here, threats to the father's authority are linked to threats to the nation through interlocking domestic comedy and international terrorist plots. The solution to domestic woes and uppity wives and daughters proves to be—no surprise—a father-led united front against national and ethnic others.

Most observers of action cinema in the 1990s point to the way that threats to the family influence the genre (Jeffords; Schneider; Tasker "Family"), and *True Lies,* as both Yvonne Tasker and Mark Gallagher note, is a particularly cogent example. Although some reviewers were bothered by the screen time accorded domestic diversions in an action plot involving terrorists threatening to detonate stolen nuclear warheads,[7] their clever imbrication is precisely the point. From the outset of the film, the domestic world intrudes into the terrorist plot and vice versa. As both Gallagher and Tasker note, Harry Tasker's (Arnold Schwarzenegger) first words in the film, "Honey, I'm home!" are spoken not to his wife, Helen (Jamie Lee Curtis), but to his national security agency partner Gib (Tom Arnold) (Gallagher 216; Tasker, "Family" 263). The latest spy equipment catches Harry's daughter Dana (Eliza Dushku) stealing money from his wallet. (Later it will be used to monitor Helen's meetings with the pseudo-spy, Simon [Bill Paxton].) Although this domestic material is played for laughs, the point is clear: from the father's perspective, the family needs to be policed. A subsequent sequence further delineates the nature of some of these patriarchal fears, as partner Gib queries Harry about his adolescent daughter's sexuality (asking whether she's still a virgin, joking that she probably needed the money to get an abortion) and proclaims the negative influence of popular culture ("Her parents are Axl Rose and Madonna"), all while the two drive to and pass through an elaborate, high-tech security clearance at work. Further sequences develop masculine anxieties around wives as well as daughters. For example, Harry shows up at Helen's office and overhears her setting up a lunch date with Simon and a cover story with a co-worker. Although most commentators have emphasized Helen's association with the domestic world (she is referred to disparagingly by the villainess as "Suzy Homemaker"), she works outside the home as well and the film thereby also taps into (heterosexual) masculine anxieties over the opportunities working women might have to meet other men and to forge alliances with other women.

But *True Lies* is not only about masculine anxieties; it is also about feminine dissatisfaction with traditional domesticity and boring white-collar jobs. The only reason why Harry's ruse (international spy pretending to be traveling computer salesman) works in the first place is because of the existence of the garden-variety, absentee, workaholic husband and father. The film, then, could be seen as a critique of such arrangements. Even the otherwise misogynistic Gib ("Women—can't live with 'em; can't kill 'em") comes to Helen's defense when Harry confides his suspicions that Helen is having an affair: "What do you expect, Harry? Helen's a flesh and blood woman and you're never there." And in the much-discussed interrogation sequence so disturbing to many reviewers,[8] where Harry, a powerful unknown force hiding behind a voice modulator and one-way glass, grills Helen tied to a chair in a huge padded room, she voices her longing for action and adventure: "I just wanted to feel alive. To do something outrageous. It felt good to be needed and trusted and to feel special."

In articulating these fears and desires, then, *True Lies* is most interesting. The solutions it posits are, however, disturbing. The answer the film presents to Helen's problems is to allow her to join Harry's adventure, but it is enacted by eroticizing her for Harry (and the heterosexual male viewer) in pretty conventional terms: he and Gib convince her that she must pose as a prostitute, perform an erotic dance, and strip for a mysterious agent (actually Harry in disguise). She remains in her sexy outfit, "boobs bobbling," as one reviewer put it, for the rest of the film (Travers "*True Lies*"). In response to Harry's dilemma, Gib prescribes that he do what he (Gib) always does when his life "turns to dog shit"—concentrate on work: "We're going to catch some terrorists, we're going to beat the crap out of them and we're going to feel a whole lot better." Jokingly, then, the film connects imperial foreign policy and aggression with masculine anxiety over loss of control in the domestic scene, just one of the many comic, parodic, or self-conscious generic references the film makes throughout. But there is nothing in the film's trajectory that implies a real critique of the position the joke references. Just at the moment Harry is called upon to explain his presence to Helen the terrorists burst into the room, and that subplot takes over for the remainder of the film. As to the terrorists, they embody the worst racist and Orientalist stereotypes, which prompted several Arab American organizations to demonstrate on the film's opening day ("Arab-Americans Protest").

Many critics comment on the way the film trivializes terrorism by depicting its "Crimson Jihad" as a group of "raving psychotics" (Harry's phrase for them). Actually, it's a bit more complicated. *True Lies* allows its villains an explanation of sorts only to dismiss it. Aziz (Art Malik), the group's leader, addresses an imagined American public by saying, "You have killed our women and children. Bombed our cities from afar. And you dare to call us terrorists!" In response, he demands a withdrawal of forces from the Persian Gulf or he threatens to bomb one major American city each week. Here the film flirts with the notion that American foreign policy may not be very "family friendly" if one is on the receiving end. Yet this speech is succeeded by a bit of business wherein Aziz goes ballistic at the incompetence of his accomplice's use of a video camera with a low battery, thus placing more emphasis on the rage of his reaction than on the content of his speech. This attitude toward so-called "collateral damage" is bolstered by one of the film's running jokes, clumsy Harry's constant apologies as he wreaks havoc and hapless bystanders attempt to leap out of his way.

But it is not enough that Harry joins with Helen to kill hundreds of Arabs, or that he spectacularly rescues her, dangling from a helicopter over the Florida Keys Causeway, or that they embrace with one of the nuclear devices "safely" detonating in the background of the shot. In order to address the anxieties articulated in the opening sequences, to link those anxieties to external threats to the nation, and to restore the daughter's respect for her father, *True Lies* introduces a further complication where the villain, still in control of a nuclear device, kidnaps Dana. Harry alone must come to her rescue, in a tour de force sequence where he steals and pilots a hover-jet high above a downtown office building under construction.[9]

Tasker points to the ways *True Lies* and similar films use familial metaphors to describe other types of relationships, and she sees in these films "other allegiances, alternative families and, crucially, the community of work" ("Family" 263). As she argues of these feature fiction films, "the ideological persistence of a particular familial norm in political rhetoric should not obscure the diversity of kinship and community structures in both social life and in popular culture" (264). I couldn't agree more. But where Tasker's examples are limited to the fictional action film, I would like to turn to another genre, documentary, and two quite different examples of the "diversity with which popular culture imagines families" (265), Steve James's *Hoop Dreams* and Deborah Hoffmann's *Complaints of a Dutiful Daughter*.

At first glance, *Hoop Dreams* might appear to be just the sort of "family friendly" film that Dole extols. Tracing the quest of two inner-city African American teenagers (Arthur Agee and William Gates) to become professional basketball players, it presents kids who appreciate their parents' sacrifices. The film also offers a religious conversion narrative wherein one of the boys' fathers, after a stint in jail for burglary and drug-dealing, vows to return to the fold. Several critics (Baker "Hoop Dreams"; Cole and King; hooks) maintain that *Hoop Dreams,* with its absent or drug-dealing fathers, plays into neoconservative arguments about the supposed pathology of black families. Indeed, bell hooks finds that "ultimately, *Hoop Dreams* offers a conservative vision of the conditions for 'making it' in the United States. It clearly argues that the context in which one 'makes it' is within a nuclear family that prays together, works hard and completely and uncritically believes in the American dream" (23). But *Hoop Dreams* is simultaneously too bleak a film and the positive vision of family and community it offers diverges too strongly from the white patriarchal fantasy ever to get Dole's seal of approval.

Nobody really "makes it" in the film, unless one counts ending up as Arthur does, at a junior college in southern Missouri with only seven black students, six of whom are basketball players, as "making it." William, who fares better academically, ends up thoroughly disillusioned with the notion of a professional basketball career. Although Agee's father Bo's religious professions are treated respectfully, they are tempered by cutaways to Arthur staring out a church window and by a sequence in which Bo describes his son's wariness about his return to the family. In effect, *Hoop Dreams* documents the struggles of the poor, who in spite of "working hard" barely scrape by on minimum-wage jobs and descend into poverty (or opt for criminality) when corporate layoffs or health problems cause unemployment.

Yet at the same time that *Hoop Dreams* paints this bleak picture, it also offers an alternative vision of family and community that demonstrates the strength of mothers, proffers an extended notion of family, and shows how families ensure survival in a hostile dominant culture. Strapped as they are, Arthur's family takes in his best friend when he is experiencing difficulties at home, and countless sequences demonstrate extended family support not only at athletic events but when dealing with academic and other institutions as well. There's a painful scene where, as John Edgar Wideman puts it, Arthur's family must "bow and scrape" in order to get Arthur's transcripts released, and a sequence where Sheila, his mother, goes to talk with his teachers about problems in school. Contrary to some critics, therefore, I would maintain that the boys' view that sports is the only "ticket out of the ghetto, the only way he's going to get to college," as William at one point puts it, is not necessarily the film's, not only because James demonstrates the willingness of high school and college athletic programs to exploit black athletes and dump them when they don't perform but also because he offers sequences where several of the women present alternatives. William's girlfriend Catherine, for example, insists that *she* is going to college and doesn't play ball, and the film includes a lengthy sequence where Arthur's mother graduates from a nurse's aide program. Shot mainly to emphasize Sheila's joy at her accomplishment (she has received the highest grade point average in the class) and Arthur and his brother's support of her in the audience, the sequence ends with a shot from the rear of the hall, showing rows of empty chairs. Not many are celebrating this woman's achievements, yet we are told in the voiceover accompanying the next image that "the gym is packed" for Arthur's next game. Such juxtapositions emphasize the warped priorities of a U.S. culture obsessed with sports and sports celebrities.

Hoop Dreams is a rare example of a documentary film that was not only a mainstream critical success but also a commercial one, winning the Audience Award at Sundance, making (and often topping) many "year's best" lists, and earning more money ($7.8 million) than any other documentary to that date. But in their zeal to get the film nominated for an Academy Award in the Best Picture category, and in their criticism of the documentary committee's failure to select it for Best Documentary Feature,[10] critics such as Gene Siskel and Roger Ebert wound up unfairly trashing the year's other nominees by implication, among them Deborah Hoffmann's *Complaints of a Dutiful Daughter*.

Like *Hoop Dreams*, at first glance *Complaints* seems "family friendly." It was described, when shown on PBS's "P.O.V." series, as a film about Alzheimer's disease and caring for aging parents, a topic made even more timely by the release in November of a letter by former president Ronald Reagan announcing that he suffered from the same condition. Yet through a highly personal style very different from the filmmaker-effacing aesthetics (Arthur and Cutler; Nichols 158) of *Hoop Dreams*, *Complaints* also ends up expanding and critiquing the traditional ideal of family far beyond Dole's narrow notion.

Complaints, moreover, departs from so many of the year's films' focus on fathers to explore a relationship between mother and daughter, documenting the filmmaker's gradual acceptance of her own mother's diagnosis and both humorously and seriously tracing the progression of the illness and the stages of her response. The precredit sequence presents an older woman on the image track, and we hear the questions of a younger woman inquiring about whether she was closer to her mother or her father. "My mother," she replies, after some confusion, and reciprocates by asking the interviewer if she had been close to her own parents. "I was closer to my

Filmmaker Deborah Hoffmann with her mother, Doris, in *Complaints of a Dutiful Daughter* (Deborah Hoffman, Women Make Movies). Courtesy Tom Erikson.

mother," the interviewer answers and probes further: "And do you know who my mother is? You." The interviewee responds with surprise, and the opening credits are displayed. This shocking and poignant opening sequence establishes many of the film's concerns—Alzheimer's, motherly love, and the effect of the mother's loss of memory on the filmmaker's own sense of identity.

Much of the film consists of Hoffmann speaking to the camera and of her interactions with her mother, Doris. These are intercut with images of artifacts that represent the stages of the illness and Hoffmann's attempts to deny, manage, or contain it, and family photographs and home videos that testify to the nature of the relationship the mother can no longer access through memory. At first it appears as if the question of who is filming these confessions and interactions will not be at issue, but Doris keeps looking at the camera and referring to someone named "Frances," acknowledging the camera operator and hinting at a relationship she has with this person. About midway through the film an outing is planned, and Doris tells her daughter, "You're going to be here . . . and Frances." The film fades up to Doris at an outdoor café, we hear someone refer to getting "a picture of Deborah and me together," and suddenly we see things from Doris's point of view and through her (more amateurish) camerawork: Hoffmann and another woman smiling and laughing. The outing has become a different sort of outing. By visually acknowledging Hoffmann's domestic partner, filmmaker Frances Reid, the film recognizes Hoffmann's lesbian family of choice as well as her heterosexual family of origin. At this point Hoffmann discusses the way her mother struggled with her daughter's gay identity for many years, but "once she had this disease, she was down to basics . . . and the basics were, I had a friend Frances . . . this person was very nice to me . . . made me happy . . . that was a good thing . . . this person was very nice to her . . . made her happy . . . that was a good thing . . . it was simple." Queer spectators are implicitly recognized, and straight viewers who may have empathized with struggles around Alzheimer's perhaps confront their own heterosexist assumptions or homophobic prejudices. In a different way than *Hoop Dreams,* then, *Complaints* also testifies to the "diversity of kinship and community structures" that Tasker applauds, and contests the narrow notion of "family friendly" films Dole put forward.

For both the documentary filmmakers and the critics of these two works, ethical issues around the filmmakers' relationships to and responsibilities toward their *subjects* loom large. To what extent should they acknowledge their relationships to the people they represent? To what extent should they acknowledge the effects of the filmmaking process itself on those subjects? For the filmmakers and critics of the films in the next section, *Natural Born Killers* and *The Smell of Burning Ants,* filmmakers' responsibilities toward their *audiences,* especially around issues of the causes and consequences of violence, loomed even larger.

Natural Born Killers: Born or Made?

Many pundits were mystified by or amused at Dole's inclusion of the violent and raunchy R-rated *True Lies* as family-friendly, while *Natural Born Killers,* a critique of media romance with murderers, was designated a "nightmare of depravity," a film that "revel[s] in mindless violence and loveless sex." Was it simply that Dole hadn't actually seen these films, as many suggested? Was it Schwarzenegger's connections with the GOP? Or, as Michael Tomasky suggested, since the films Dole cited as "family friendly" were the year's top box office hits, was it a hopeless attempt to reconcile free-market economic policy with "family values" conservatism, "proof that movies can be family-friendly and profitable at the same time" (21)?

Double standards often inform denunciations of cinematic violence, however. As Christopher Sharrett writes, "Cultural representations of violence and genocide . . . that explicitly replicate dominant ideology . . . rarely meet with very much moralizing from state power, organized religion, or the private sector" (67). Rather, "films and other media singled out for cen-

"Children's Hour? Schwarzenegger cocks his trigger in *True Lies*, the 1994 killfest that Dole mysteriously counted as family friendly," ran the caption in *Time* to a similar still from the film (James Cameron, Twentieth Century Fox) (Lacayo 27). Digital frame enlargement.

sorship or various forms of public assault are most often works that offer a critique of violence and its role in history and current civilization" (71). Writing about the positive role given to violence as a way to suture the fractured family unit in some action films of the 1990s, Karen Schneider notes that "it is not violence per se that most people object to; it is the breaking of the Father's law, in this case the dismemberment of the family unit that embodies and reproduces that law" (11). I find it instructive, for example, that when former National Endowment for the Humanities Chair and American Enterprise Institute fellow Lynne Cheney supported Dole's denunciation of *Natural Born Killers,* she focused on a sequence she describes as one in which "the hero drowns his girlfriend's father in a fish tank and kills her mother by tying her down on her bed, pouring gasoline on her and burning her alive. Meanwhile a raucous, laugh-filled sound track tells the audience to regard this slaughter as the funniest thing in the world" ("Tough Talk" 32). This literal reading ignores not only the intent of the grotesque stylization of the sequence, but also the paternal incest and abuse that preceded and motivated these acts of rage and revenge.

Natural Born Killers chronicles the murderous exploits of Mickey (Woody Harrelson) and Mallory (Juliette Lewis) Knox, two serial killers who gain international celebrity largely due to the efforts of tabloid schlockmeister Wayne Gale (Robert Downey Jr.) and his show "American Maniacs." Through both its subject matter and its frenzied, fragmented, anti-illusionist style, the film attempts simultaneously to be a ruthless satire of the media's (particularly television's) romance with killers and a serious exploration of the etiology of violence in contemporary postmodern life. Unlike *True Lies*, which simultaneously mocks and endorses its hero's sur- veillance and terrorizing of the patriarchal family in the name of its sur- vival, *Natural Born Killers* clearly indicts both domestic abuse and the patriarchal family as at least in part responsible for the kinds of "mindless violence" Dole, Cheney, and others decried. Before two of the murders, director Oliver Stone intersperses black-and-white images representing Mallory's abuse at the hands of her father and Mickey's abuse by his par- ents. By setting the broadcasting of Gale's prison interview with Mickey right after the Super Bowl ("These guys want to tear their wives' heads off," Gale argues), Stone further connects the cult of violence to domestic abuse and now to sports ritual, too.

Nevertheless, Stone's efforts to provide explanations for his protago- nists' violence got him in trouble with many critics. They felt the accounts made Mickey and Mallory too sympathetic and attractive (and their victims too unsympathetic and repulsive), undermining the satiric thrust of the original Quentin Tarantino screenplay and the aim of denouncing media glorification of their exploits (Caputi 150–55; Natoli 160; Prince 243–48). These critics also argued that Stone's use of animal predator/prey or demonic imagery throughout the film undercut his attempts to root vio- lence in childhood abuse or saturation in brutal media imagery. For some, such imagery lent credence to then-circulating biologically deterministic explanations for criminality and reinforced ideas about the supposedly inherent intellectual inferiority of the poor, as advanced in Richard J. Herrnstein and Charles Murray's controversial current best seller, *The Bell Curve*.[11]

Nowhere is the film's stance on the causes of violence more problem- atic than in its conclusion. After Mickey and Mallory make Gale their final victim, Stone attempts to link the film's fictional story with actual events, cutting from a fictional anchorwoman to documentary footage of the Menendez brothers, Tonya Harding, Lorena Bobbitt, O. J. Simpson, and Rodney King. As Stephen Prince says, "It is a bewildering series of images. During the 1990s, these people all became media stars as the result of mas- sively publicized crimes and trials, but beyond this general connection, the film can offer no account of the range of disparate issues that emerged in these cases" (247). Sylvia Chong continues:

> In blurring the line between fiction and fact, Stone ends up making the real seem fake rather than making the fictional seem true; for example, he juxta- poses Bobbitt's retaliation against domestic violence and King's suffering of police brutality against Simpson's infliction of domestic violence and the FBI's

use of unreasonable force at Waco, Texas, thereby flattening the context of each of these events under the signifier "violence." By erasing the differences between acts of violence, Stone promotes a sense that all violence is literally *meaningless*—that is, violence resides in a symbolic system where there no longer exist any distinctions between violent acts. (264)

This rhetoric of the "meaninglessness" of acts of violence was, Chong argues, a central feature of the discourse around violence and it obstructs our understanding of its disparate causes and disproportionate effects. Yet in spite of its problems and contradictions, I would still defend *Natural Born Killers* as a serious attempt to analyze contemporary phenomena against the efforts to censor, condemn, or litigate against it.[12]

In his description of the opening of *Natural Born Killers,* Steven Pizzello wrote at the time that Mallory turns on one of the men who comes on to her "with the fury of a scorpion that's been poked once too often with a stick" (143). This is also a central metaphor in another of the year's serious cinematic explorations of the causes and consequences of violence, Jay Rosenblatt's *The Smell of Burning Ants,* where a threatened scorpion that poisons itself with its own venom stands in for a destructive and self-destructive masculinity. But as opposed to Stone's big-budget, full-length extravaganza, funded by Warner Bros., a major studio, Rosenblatt's film is a low-budget, twenty-minute experimental documentary, the kind of film made possible by the support of the public money for the arts that conservative Republicans were trying to eradicate.[13]

Using found footage from educational films of the 1950s and 1960s and a third-person autobiographical voiceover narration, the film chronicles the construction of masculinity from infancy through young adulthood as violent and sadistic. Harsh childrearing practices, especially for boys, the suppression of emotions other than anger, the definition of masculinity as the negation of the feminine, the encouragement of competition rather than cooperation, the deployment of homophobia to enforce conformity to masculine norm are all indicted as responsible for male aggression toward and domination over insects and other animals, smaller and weaker boys, and finally adult women. Like *Natural Born Killers, The Smell of Burning Ants* sees domestic violence as a causal factor in other types of violence: "His parents fight all the time . . . his father can't control his temper . . . the father also has no idea why he is angry . . . and the boy never knows when the father will decide . . . he is angry because of him," the male narrator intones over footage of a small boy and an angry couple. But unlike Stone's film, *The Smell of Burning Ants* is less vulnerable to charges that it attributes violence solely to the aberrations of a white-trash underclass (Rafferty "Helter

Skelter"; Sweeney), both because the found footage represents children and fathers from a range of social classes and because Rosenblatt posits violence as central in the construction of a hegemonic (not abnormal or demonic) masculinity.

The use of third- rather than first-person narration for a discourse nevertheless understood as autobiographical, and the juxtaposition of this narration with found footage that obliquely relates to the events being described rather than literally illustrating them, means that the personal and the social, individual, and collective intersect in compelling and interesting ways. For example, in one incident "the boy" of the narration participates in a mob that taunts and beats a weaker classmate. The scene is described in such detail ("In 5th grade they pick on this weak kid . . . Alan Dubrow . . . Doofus, spastic, retard, faggot . . .") that it seems to stem from personal memory.[14] Yet the use of accompanying found footage of a group of boys running, jumping on cars, and breaking ice or glass allows the film also to evoke other instances of bullying and violence and the sense of menace and shame that may attend them. Such sequences and the closing dedication ("for all my brothers") allow the filmmaker to connect his own personal memory and experience to those of other men of his generation.

Compare the statement that appears at the beginning of the director's cut version of *Natural Born Killers,* where Stone defends his film against critics' claims "that the film glorified violence and was part of the problem and not the solution. . . . By saying that, you are trying to kill the messenger because it's not the filmmaker's fault that society is where it is. The filmmaker does his best to reflect society the way he sees it. And our society is culturally in a very violent and bankrupt mode" (qtd. in Caputi, 155). But then remember Stone's inclusion of footage from his own *Midnight Express* (1978) and *Scarface* (1983) (he wrote the screenplays) in the barrage of violent imagery that shapes the consciousness of the protagonists. This suggests, contrary to his extradiegetic statement, that filmmakers do more than merely "reflect."

Rosenblatt clearly goes further in exploring the (male) filmmaker's complicity in perpetuating oppressive hegemonic norms. He repeatedly includes an image of a boy (not yet the man) with a movie camera. Here narration and found footage combine to link the filmmaker with the collaborator. "He is not a bully . . . he is not a victim," the narrator intones as a camera pans a row of schoolchildren. "There he is at the end of the line." Cut to a closer shot and then another of a boy with a camera on a tripod. "He is an observer." This is immediately followed by found footage of a group of boys punching another. "There he is again." There's a freeze frame, then a cut in to a detail of the footage showing yet another boy punching the victim. "A collaborator." Yet through his appropriation and manipulation of found footage—slowing it down, isolating details, obsessively looping and repeating them—and through his recontexualization of that footage through narration, Rosenblatt shows that the filmmaker does more than simply observe. He can contribute, or he can comment and critique.

Conclusion

Willingly or not, then, the films of this year became weapons in the ongoing culture wars of the decade, and in the struggle to interpret the past, analyze the problems of the present, and direct the nation's future. Natoli refers to a campaign such as Dole's as a "discourse of distraction" (98), a diversion from the consequences of an increasingly rapacious global economy with its sharply distinguished winners and losers. Yet it's also important, he maintains, because without such discourse other more blatantly political efforts to sustain such injustice "would be vulnerable to counter-discourses" (98). Such counter-discourses were present, both in some of the year's independent films and in the debates that swirled around the more popular ones. Dole's denunciations allowed critics such as Wideman, Britt, and Pollitt to point to the long history of censorship and condemnation of black art forms ("Tough Talk" 33), to indict Dole's hypocrisy in "blasting movies in which fictional characters use the same assault weapons he supports in real life,"[15] and to signal the contradictions in his trashing what the marketplace delivers while trying to cut off public funds that enabled alternatives ("Tough Talk" 34). Campaigns like Dole's and, more important, thoughtful responses to them explode the myth of popular culture as apolitical entertainment, and make it imperative that oppositional voices enter the debate.

NOTES

1. Veterans' groups and certain members of Congress deemed the exhibit too sympathetic to the Japanese because it placed too much emphasis on the catastrophic effects of the bombs; conversely, the Japanese government and other critics complained that the postage stamp image and its caption appeared to justify the bombing.

2. *Time*'s "The Best Cinema of 1994" also includes "The Worst": "*Female Trouble*. Remember when popular movies had *women* in them? In 1994's top films, the ladies were lucky if the guys let them even drive a bus. . . . Affirmative action is démodé these days, but Hollywood needs some spur to bring women into full partnership with the Toms and Arnolds and Simbas" (132).

3. Dole also named the 1993 *True Romance* as a "nightmare of depravity" and three other 1994 films, *The Lion King*, *The Santa Clause*, and *The Flintstones*, as "friendly to the family."

4. Cassells, citing Abrams, defines structural irony as "supplied by the author, who 'introduces a structural feature which serves to sustain a duplicity of meaning and evaluation throughout the work'" (80). He uses the example of Forrest's description of Jenny's father to illustrate the concept.

5. Buchanan, for his part, argued in August that "*Forrest Gump* celebrates the values of conservatism, of the old America, of fidelity and family, faith and goodness. And the way of life this film holds up to be squalid and ruinous is the way of Woodstock. In *Forrest Gump,* the white trash are in Berkeley and the peace movement; the best of black and white are to be found in little towns in the South and in the army of the United States" (qtd. in Wang 114). And in the week before the election, Gingrich used the film to remind audiences that "in every scene of the movie in which the counterculture occurs, they're either dirty, nasty, abusive, vindictive, beating a woman, or doing something grotesque," and that "it is important to remember that in the period, Bill Clinton was on the side of the counterculture" (qtd. in Wang 114–15).

6. The phrase is the title of Alan Nadel's book on the cultural politics of the Cold War.

7. Anthony Lane, for example, wondered why no one said to the director, "Uh, Jim, I love the stuff with the missiles, but I don't quite see how it fits with the dancing dame" (78).

8. See Travers "*True Lies*"; Arroyo. Travers is especially concerned with the contemporary context of what he sees as "abusive male behavior passed off as comic relief between explosions": "At a time when the O. J. Simpson case has presumably raised consciousness about domestic violence, there's something unnerving about being asked to giggle along with an action comedy in which a jealous husband plots revenge on his wife for allegedly screwing around."

9. Writing in the late nineties, Mark Gallagher argued of this spectacular sequence that "viewers may take pleasure in computer-enhanced images of Harry piloting an Air Force jet and machine-gunning terrorists in a downtown office building without troubling over the scene's consequences. By foregrounding spectacular action, the sequence displaces concerns about the disproportionate use of force, property destruction, and loss of life. The scene also plays on the fantasy of demolishing the corporate infrastructure, appealing to viewers disenchanted with multinational capitalism" (219). Terrorist attacks by plane on the World Trade Center in 2001 have probably forever altered such a reading of the sequence, but, at any rate, as Gallagher argues, "at its conclusion, when Harry rescues his kidnapped daughter and subdues the terrorists, the film conflates protection of the family and service to the nation" (218).

10. Such criticisms eventually led to changes in the way in which documentary films are selected and nominated.

11. Such explanations were used to justify harsh social Darwinian economic policies and responses to crime. See especially Courtwright 199–200; Natoli 149–61; Simpson 125–29; and Sweeney.

12. *Natural Born Killers* spawned a series of lawsuits over copycat acts of murder and mayhem throughout the 1990s. See, for example, Douglas.

13. For a discussion of the conservative assault on public funding of the arts in the United States in the late 1980s and 1990s, see Zimmermann.

14. In interviews Rosenblatt has confirmed that this is the case. Uncannily, Richard J. Silberg, the actor whom he employed as his narrator for the film, also participated in this incident (Athitakis).

15. The phrase is Donna Britt's, but she actually defends the senator's position against those who "ignore that his most passionate attackers make fortunes off the depravity they're protecting" ("Tough Talk" 33). On the other hand, Katha Pollitt says she would "like to hear how Dole squares his anti-violence stand with his ardent support for the N.R.A. and the overturning of the assault weapons ban" ("Tough Talk" 34).

1995

Movies, Teens, Tots, and Tech

TIMOTHY SHARY

The middle year of the decade was marked by a visible concern for youth within the nation's media. The most disturbing evidence of this came in the aftermath of the bombing of Oklahoma City's Alfred P. Murrah Federal Building on 19 April. Many news sources initially assumed the attack had been perpetrated by foreigners, but within days authorities revealed that it had been the work of a few homegrown terrorists (Timothy McVeigh, Terry Nichols, and Michael Fortier). In this swirl of confusion, the majority of news media made an interesting symbolic choice, launching an emotional campaign featuring images of the children murdered and wounded in the blast to exemplify the tragedy, rather than exploring the complex political issues behind domestic terrorism. Of course, the children in the building's daycare center were not disproportionately represented among the victims; far more adults were killed. But the senseless victimization of young kids touched so many Americans that the adult casualties were accorded less coverage. The dead children became the icons of national outrage, allowing the public to focus its shock and sorrow on individual victims and families and displacing more probing examinations of the ideological state of the country.

Racism, too, remained a prominent topic, as witnessed by the coverage accorded the biggest news event of the year, the O. J. Simpson trial. The trial started on 24 January, and for over eight months the nation was riveted as it watched the unfolding courtroom drama of the former football star accused of killing his ex-wife Nicole and her friend Ron Goldman. O.J.'s defense attorneys strategically directed the trial as a debate on racism. Did white cops frame this famous black man, and would white America believe his innocence? On 3 October, the jury found Simpson innocent of all charges, and many in the media soon saw a clear divide between Blacks who agreed with the verdict and whites who remained suspicious. Race was a central issue, too, in the Million Man March held in Washington, D.C., just thirteen days after the Simpson trial ended. Organized by controversial Nation of Islam leader Louis Farrakhan, the event brought attention to continuing racial problems in the country, although some critics questioned its masculine emphasis.

Gender issues were germane to the Simpson case as well: O.J. had a record of beating Nicole, a fact that was essentially dismissed during arguments in and around the trial. Certainly, issues of spousal abuse and men's violence against women were elided by the strategy of the (all-male) defense. Macho culture exposed its fears of women even more in the ongoing Whitewater investigation, with Republican senators accusing First Lady Hillary Clinton of illegally removing important documents from the White House, a charge that was dismissed the following year. The effort appeared clearly directed at discrediting the Democratic president's (overly) ambitious wife who had previously been vilified for trying to overhaul the national health care system. Nevertheless, there was one prominent casualty for mistreatment of women: Bob Packwood (a five-term Republican senator from Oregon) resigned in October after a Senate panel concluded he was guilty of sexual misconduct.

Curious differences in gender status were evident in other cultural activities. In sports, Baltimore Orioles' baseball star Cal Ripken Jr. was a logical choice for the Associated Press Male Athlete of the Year (since he broke Lou Gehrig's fifty-six-year-old record for most consecutive games played), although the AP had few professionals to consider for Female Athlete of the Year, and thus gave the honor to college basketball player Rebecca Lobo. The music world was rocked when twenty-one-year-old Alanis Morissette released her massively popular debut album, *Jagged Little Pill,* which contained surprisingly aggressive songs about female resilience and sexual prowess. And other media challenged gender norms as well: television premiered the quasi-lesbian "Xena: Warrior Princess," comic books introduced a female detective with supernatural powers in *Witchblade,* and *The Orion Conspiracy* became the first video game to actually label a character as homosexual.

Global communities confronted many crises. African nations continued efforts to accommodate over two million refugees from the Rwandan genocide. The raging civil war in Bosnia-Herzegovina that had left at least 100,000 people dead was, oddly enough, settled in Dayton, Ohio, with a peace agreement signed in November. Russia reached a truce with its renegade republic of Chechnya in July, after a year of massive civil unrest. Domestic terrorism struck Japan even before the United States: on 20 March, the Aum Shinrikyo cult released a deadly nerve gas on the Tokyo subway system, killing twenty and sickening thousands. At the end of July, Islamic militants in Ethiopia attempted to assassinate Egypt's president

Hosni Mubarak, and in early November, a lone Jewish religious extremist assassinated Israeli prime minister Yitzhak Rabin.

A continuing wave of mergers and acquisitions in the media industry resulted in more productions being made by fewer, but richer, corporations. In July, the Walt Disney Company took over Capital Cities and its television network, ABC; the Westinghouse Electric Corporation took over another network, CBS, soon thereafter. The peak of this movement was reached on 22 September, when TimeWarner merged with the Turner Broadcasting System to become the world's largest media company. Now more than ever, decisions behind films were being made by business executives schooled in demographics and finance as opposed to any art, and the vertical integration of the studios that the government had worked so diligently to break apart fifty years earlier returned in a new form.

The accelerating integration of information and entertainment media meant that movies and television shows had become news themselves. Monday morning TV and radio broadcasts increasingly reported on weekend box office returns; financial shows employed film critics to discuss the quality of movies as well as their impact on corporate earnings. Disney became a Wall Street darling by releasing five of the top twelve highest-grossing films of the year: *Toy Story, Pocahontas, Crimson Tide, Dangerous Minds,* and *While You Were Sleeping.* Warner Bros., now part of the Time-Warner-Turner empire, was strong as well, with the year's number one film, *Batman Forever,* and three others in the top twenty. Universal had three films in the top ten—*Apollo 13, Casper,* and *Waterworld*—yet apparently concentrated their efforts on their biggest releases, since they placed only three other films in the top fifty. Paramount's alternative strategy, funding films with modest budgets, paid off with many lucrative hits, among them *Congo, Braveheart, Clueless,* and *The Brady Bunch Movie.* To illustrate the concentration of Hollywood products and profits, these four companies together released thirty-one of the top fifty highest-grossing films, and sixty-two of the top one hundred.

Computer-generated imagery (CGI) was more and more important. In preceding years, the virtually seamless integration of digital images (created on computers) and in-camera shots (captured on celluloid) had allowed numerous films to create spectacular visuals and even build entire characters. Now, the technology was used in more subtle ways as well, expanding the vastness of the sea in *Waterworld* or dramatizing the otherwise familiar rocket liftoff in *Apollo 13.* Technology was not only changing the visual frame but other cinematic processes as well, such as the rise of nonlinear digital editing (the Avid system, for example, was employed in the otherwise low-tech *The Bridges of Madison County*) and digital sound effects design. One of the more unusual instances of technology changing filmed "reality" is evidenced in *Die Hard with a Vengeance*. Bruce Willis was needed to walk through Harlem wearing a sandwich board bearing a racist epithet; the crew shot the scene on location with a blank board and digitally added the words later, so as not to offend the community.

Big-budget action spectacles demonstrated continuing appeal. Patient fans welcomed Pierce Brosnan as James Bond when the super-spy returned in *Goldeneye*, but the deterioration of Detective John McClane in the third *Die Hard* film seemed to suggest that even the charismatic Willis was struggling to keep that franchise alive. The more cerebral and foreboding stories of *Crimson Tide*, *Se7en*, and *Outbreak*—each of which featured a battle of wills between white and black characters in their respective conflicts with submarines, serial killers, and plagues—were well received alongside more escapist and unrealistic fables, such as the urban cop comedy *Bad Boys* and the tired terrorists-on-a-train tale *Under Siege 2: Dark Territory*, although the latter somehow managed to keep Steven Seagal on the Hollywood radar.

All these films, and numerous others as well, showcased male stars in men's stories. In fact, among the top ten highest-grossing films that year, the only story about a woman was in an animated feature, *Pocahontas*. Other popular films about women did not vary much from cliché roles. Witness the longing wallflower Sandra Bullock perfected in *While You Were Sleeping*, the unfulfilled housewife embodied by Meryl Streep in *The Bridges of Madison County*, and the catty friends and neighbors led by Julia Roberts in *Something to Talk About*. The few notable films about stronger women tended to disqualify their authority, showing Michelle Pfeiffer's physically powerful schoolteacher in *Dangerous Minds* being intimidated by her students and portraying Annette Benning's activist in *The American President* as putty in the hands of the chief executive. The two most lucrative films actually directed by women—*Clueless* (Amy Heckerling) and *The Brady Bunch Movie* (Betty Thomas)—revolved around impressionable teenage girls whose lives were still ruled by adult authority.

Several "indies"—some featuring men, others women, even girls—were also hits, if on a smaller scale. *The Usual Suspects* quickly developed a cult following with its mystery built around perhaps the most notorious villain of the year, Keyser Soze (Kevin Spacey). After winning big at Sundance in February, the low-budget *Brothers McMullen*, about three romantically challenged siblings, drew much attention, although it featured no name stars and a novice director. The unconventional stories and styles of *Welcome to the Dollhouse* (featuring an awkward middle schooler in a tormented love triangle), *Party Girl* (featuring a slacker who discovers her inner librarian), and *Living in Oblivion* (featuring the bizarre chaos of independent movie-making) all managed to find eager audiences. And Miramax managed to retain its edgy credibility with the chatty *Smoke*, the revisionist western *Dead Man*, the portmanteau oddity *Four Rooms*, and the singing sisters drama *Georgia*.

Supposedly light fare directed at older audiences was often tinged with disruptive pathos. Consider the medical and familial tensions of *While You Were Sleeping*, wherein a woman becomes accidentally engaged to a man in a coma only to have his brother fall in love with her, or the politics of *Nine Months*, which explores unwanted pregnancy, marriage phobia, and trial separation. Even one of the more unorthodox comedies of the year, the cross-dressing road movie To Wong Foo, *Thanks for Everything, Julie Newmar*, contained its share of moral lessons about prejudice and gender roles. *Waiting to Exhale*, which offered a rare portrait of the middle-class African American female population, also presented its laughs through the frustrations and sadness that its characters endured. *Get Shorty*, one of the most acclaimed comedies of the year, built its humor around a world of criminals and graft. Comedy without tragedy, it seemed, could only be found among the ranks of overgrown boys who still giggled at fart jokes, as with *Tommy Boy* and *Billy Madison*, two films that were not among the top fifty earners of the year.

Most noteworthy, perhaps, was Hollywood's return to youth audiences, according to Thomas Doherty the film industry's most vital population for income since the fifties (*Teenagers* 1–2). Once again, kids were kings at the box office. Three movies directed at children were among the top six highest-grossing films of the year: *Toy Story*, *Pocahontas*, and *Casper*. Films that appealed to teens were even more plentiful and profitable. Count among these *Batman Forever*, *Ace Ventura: When Nature Calls*, and *Mortal Kombat* (the first blockbuster film ever adapted from video games), while controversial independents, foremost among them *Kids*, were also relatively successful, if critically questioned. Five films taken together reveal how—and how much—films' texts, audiences, and critics invested in images of—and often for—children and teens.

Teens

By the mid-1990s, movies about, not just for, teenagers had fallen on hard times. African American crime dramas with teen protagonists raised issues of race and class, but also inflamed white fears, and teenage sex was no longer a matter for comedy with the specters of AIDS and teen pregnancy looming. Released unrated, Larry Clark's *Kids* taps into fears of AIDS, if not of teen pregnancy. Unlike the African American crime dramas, it focuses primarily on urban white teens. The subject matter and approach were so controversial that Disney forced its subsidiary Miramax to release the film under the name of a sham company, Shining Excalibur. (The corporation nevertheless probably enjoyed the film's earnings of $7.5 million domestically and $20 million worldwide; it cost only $1.5 million.) A polar opposite in story and style, Paramount's PG-13 *Clueless* proved even more profitable. Made for $20 million, it grossed nearly $50 million domestically and $77 million worldwide. The picture emphasizes a nostalgia for conspicuous consumption while continuing a celebration of economic security and sexual naiveté. *Clueless* also offers an optimistic (if shallow) perspective on teen life that had not been seen for a decade and, along with the other youth-oriented hits of the year, showed Hollywood once again how safe it could be to bank on films for young audiences.

Kids is gleefully graphic in its depiction of the dangerous lifestyles of a group of teens whose sexual escapades and drug use are killing them. The teens and preteens who populate this film exist in a world not only removed from structures such as high school and family (we are led to believe that the story takes place during summer vacation; only one parent is featured), but also without any need to work. Their days revolve around the quest for sex, drugs, and alcohol. Each image is composed to express the teens' familiarity with their supposedly natural territory while the slightly distorting wide-angle shots aim at disorienting the viewer. In praising Clark's teen portrait, Amy Taubin commented that it "suggests that adolescent socialization is less determined by culture than biology": the implication is that these teens were simply born with a base instinct for sexual and chemical abuse, an elitist perspective that the film celebrates ("Chilling" 17).

The depiction of Manhattan as a primal jungle results in an amoral world where teens make adult decisions with no idea of their consequences, and the absence of adults to guide them means there is no check on their choices. While their sexual actions can be a matter of life (pregnancy) or death (disease), *Kids* speaks aloofly and ironically about the potentially grave outcomes of unprotected sex. This tactic may appeal to the young audiences who were supposedly prevented from seeing the film— unrated films are not marketed to teens—but it fails to provide any information about the dangers (or, for that matter, the joys) of sex. As Tom Doherty put it: "If Heckerling [the director of *Clueless*] is an indulgent mother having fun with her kids, Clark [the director of *Kids*] is the absent

Larry Clark portrays the teens in *Kids* (Shining Excalibur) stalking Manhattan neighborhoods with an inflamed sense of menace. Collection Timothy Shary.

father, looking on detachedly, counting on the spectator to invest the narrative with moral meaning" ("Clueless Kids" 16). *Kids* thus purports to be a radically honest or even liberal depiction of contemporary urban youth, but becomes conservative, if not reactionary, in its message. We are shown that sex among teens is taboo (and lusciously prurient) despite how much young people claim to enjoy it, and the complexities of their pleasures and pain are left largely unexplored. This lack of complexity and nuance is mirrored in the film's faux-vérité approach in which the wobbly camera ogles its subjects with voyeuristic intoxication. The audio amplifies every slap of skin, every slurpy kiss, and every suck off a beer bottle. Such techniques only render the youth of the story more pathetic, avoiding any honest exploration of adolescent thoughts and feelings.

The feral hunt for pleasure that permeates *Kids* draws on a distinctly male mythology. As bell hooks charged, "What is being exploited is precisely and solely a spectacle of teenage sexuality that has been shaped and informed by patriarchal attitudes" (10). The film revolves around two teenage boys, Telly (Leo Fitzpatrick) and Casper (Justin Pierce). Telly wants to deflower as many pubescent girls as he can, while Casper seems interested in little more than constant beer consumption. The few girl characters are even less developed, but an early scene that means to shock us with their revelry in "hardcore pound fucking" implicates them in being just as sexually excitable as the boys who pursue them. The one conspicuous exception is Jennie, played by Chloë Sevigny in a lachrymose manner that betrays her confusion about sex. When she later learns that she is HIV positive due to her one and only sexual experience—with Telly—an unemotional picaresque journey follows, since Jennie seems to have little idea of how this disease could affect her and she is racing against time to find Telly before he infects another girl by the end of the day.

Even with Jennie's presence in the story, Harmony Korine's script is preoccupied with the objectification of young women. He may have been attempting some statement on the difficulties girls face in dealing with boys, for he appears himself as a friendly nerd who meets Jennie at a rave and persuades her to take a drug he insists will make her feel better. By the end of the film, however, Jennie is so stoned that she cannot even protest when Casper rapes her. Jennie's rape is made all the more brutal by Clark's sustained filming of it for two and a half minutes and by the fact that Jennie has found Telly, too late to stop him from having sex with yet another virgin. Therefore, this film offers a false sense of empowerment to its female characters: initially confident in their knowledge and pursuit of sex, ultimately they are victimized by it.

But Kids is not merely sexist or patriarchal, since its portrait of youthful sexuality is degrading for both genders. The main, if only, consequence of sexual contact in Kids is the potential spread of HIV, a serious issue to be sure, yet Telly's habitual practice of deflowering virgins is left unquestioned. When Casper tells Telly, "How you gonna fuck two virgins in one day? It's gotta be against the law," Telly merely takes pride in his prowess. The dangerous lesson of Kids—that sex and drugs can be deadly—is thus never realized onscreen. The film concludes with Telly infecting another girl with HIV. In voiceover, he says, "When you're young, not much matters . . . That's just it—fucking is what I love. Take that away from me and I really got nothing." If this is meant as ironic commentary on the fact that Telly is likely to die from his sexual escapades, he is relieved from any confrontation with that fact. As Owen Gliberman said in his review, "We never get to see if the little son of a bitch has a soul after all" (47). The film is so detached, so resolutely amoral, that it can easily seem voyeuristic, salacious, even pandering.

Clueless manages to provide a more nuanced view of teenage sexuality. Its virginal main character, ironically named Cher (Alicia Silverstone), negotiates a wider range of social roles, not all of which are related to sexual acts or sexual identity. Cher narrates her story in a voiceover indebted to the film's source, Jane Austen's *Emma*. She begins by noting that high school boys are unacceptably immature for her taste. For the first half of the film, she is uninterested in pursuing romantic or sexual involvements. Instead, she devotes her time to the "project" of matchmaking between two of her teachers, clearly for the purpose of improving her grades. Then Cher employs her supposedly sophisticated fashion sense to transform new student Tai (Brittany Murphy) from a frumpy outcast to a costumed cutie, thereby allowing this outsider to become part of the small but popular crowd in which Cher travels. Only after Cher has achieved romantic and sexual changes in others does she turn to herself.

Her self-reinvention begins after her virginity has been clearly established. In a candid exchange between girlfriends, Dionne (Stacey Dash) points out that Cher is "hymenally challenged," to which Cher rejoins, "You see how picky I am about my shoes, and they only go on my feet." Cher's implication that she has been careful and patient in waiting to have sex (at the age of fifteen) is thus equated with her taste in fashion. As Amanda Lipman says, Cher's "strong sense of morality is purely pragmatic" (46), so sex for her must be rational and purposeful. The initially resistant Dionne, on the other hand, gives up her virginity to her boyfriend after the "emotional" experience of surviving a drive on the Los Angeles freeway, suggesting the superficial stakes of sexual experience for these teens.

Cher develops a crush on a cool new guy at school (Justin Walker) who is clearly interested in her but will not take any romantic initiative despite her best efforts. She is shocked to discover he is gay when another friend tells her the boy is "a disco-dancing, Oscar Wilde–reading, Streisand ticket-holding friend of Dorothy." Ever resourceful, Cher is nevertheless able to capitalize on the situation: her ex-crush becomes a great shopping companion. More inexplicably, and as if her romantic/sexual momentum were now unstoppable, she next finds herself attracted to her college-age stepbrother, Josh (Paul Rudd). Heckerling allows this relationship to develop through shots that do not deny its incestuous implications: Josh begins ruefully ogling Cher, and his gaze only increases the tension of his longing for a stepsister many years younger (and underage). Cher is not coy, encouraging Josh to stay around for spring break, and reminding him that he's not

In *Clueless* (Amy Heckerling, Paramount), Cher (center, Alicia Silverstone) surrounds herself with teenage friends but ultimately desires her college-age stepbrother (far right, Paul Rudd), who doesn't quite fit in with this crowd. Jerry Ohlinger's Movie Materials Store.

really her brother. Such an attraction between stepsiblings may be possible, but any potential problems are ignored. When the film ends with Cher and Josh kissing at the wedding of her teachers, complete with Cher catching the bouquet, one might wonder, has sexuality become so difficult for teens to navigate that it may be safer to stay "close to home"?

Despite the wide appeal of *Clueless* and the art-house interest guaranteed fashion photographer Larry Clark's first film, *Kids,* both movies demonstrate studio unease with depictions of teens. In the case of *Clueless,* we have a seemingly innocuous comedy that elides serious issues surrounding sexual acts in a rather conservative fashion. In the case of *Kids,* we have teens depicted with such sexual excess that their lives are reduced to debauchery. Hollywood may have simply been seizing on a renewed interest in teenagers' stories, but both these examples pose serious moral and ethical dilemmas.

Tots

After the rise of the "kid vid" phenomenon in the 1980s (when parents began using selected VHS titles as an alternative to random television viewing for their children), Hollywood studios began catering big-budget films to family audiences and then spinning off lower-budget sequels straight to video. As time went on, the studios became adept at cross-promoting music and other movie merchandise to kids, creating secondary markets that were quite profitable. Initially, the $30 million Disney-Pixar collaboration *Toy Story* generated much of its attention for being the first fully digital feature film, but upon closer inspection, the film was clearly designed to engage youngsters in buying toys. When Universal rolled out the $55 million *Casper,* featuring a boy ghost who had debuted fifty years earlier, they added the contemporary quandaries of a young adolescent girl (Christina Ricci) and built a merchandising line around the spooky concept. Both films would be praised for their special effects and positive messages; both would make money at the box office (with domestic grosses of $192 million and $100 million, and worldwide grosses of $354 million and $282 million, respectively); and both would become fantastic vehicles for franchises that kids could buy, buy, buy over the following years.

Directed by Pixar co-founder John Lasseter, *Toy Story* is in fact just that, the story of the toys that populate a boy's room and come to life when people are not looking, a fantasy of literal animation that children—and adults—have enjoyed for generations. *Toy Story*'s toys have lives and identities of their own. They have grown attached to their owner, Andy (voiced by John Morris), as well as to each other, and they actively fear their replacement by other toys. In this way, the film likens toys to living pets or even (step-)siblings, which is not only relevant for the era's concerns about broken families but also endows the inanimate commodities that corporations like Disney mass produce with human attributes.

Andy lives in an apparently fatherless household, and his fixation on his two favorite toys—a marionette cowboy named Woody (voiced by Tom Hanks) and a new "space ranger" doll named Buzz Lightyear (voiced by Tim Allen)—calls attention to his longing for masculine direction and companionship. Dressed in drab, brownish garb, Woody fears his place as Andy's favorite toy is threatened by the arrival of the shiny new Buzz. This sets up a conflict in which the representative values of the cowboy (tradition, chivalry, loyalty) are explicitly challenged by those embodied by the space ranger (innovation, power, and escape). The plot hinges on this clash, an implicit allusion, furthermore, to questions posed by the film's preference for digital animation over the traditional hand-drawn cel animation. This high-tech look, as Peter Stack notes, gives the film a "slightly antiseptic, plastic quality," even though such a quality is "smartly suited to the subject, since most of the toys are plastic" (C1).

Unlike Woody and Buzz, the other toys in Andy's bedroom community are primarily products from actual toy companies, such as Hasbro's Tinker-toys, Etch A Sketch (from Ohio Art), Slinky Dog, and Milton Bradley's game Operation. The brand names are often visible, and we are further reminded of this branding when Mr. Potato Head (voiced by Don Rickles) asks Buzz where he's from. The spud proudly boasts that he's "from" Play-skool, identifying himself with his corporate parent and furthermore pro-viding a commercial recognition of that company. When Buzz says that he's come from an alien planet, the generic answer is less satisfying to everyone. More tellingly, a dinosaur doll with no brand name says that he's from Mat-tel, only to then confess that he's "actually from a smaller company that was purchased in a leveraged buy-out." This explains why he does not have a brand identity, and also rationalizes the insecurity and anxiety that mark him throughout the story. These "children" of companies are validated beyond this narrative through their real existence as retail items in stores. Curiously, Woody and Buzz were not extant toys before the film, but became so after its release (put out by Mattel, no less), so that they could further fill the coffers of Disney affiliates—and provide an enduring identity for the film's inevitable sequel. Clearly, a glaring irony is at work, as Bill Brown underlines: "What makes the film feel so anachronistic and nostal-gic is that, for pre-adolescent boys in the 1990s, video games and computer games (for instance, Disney Interactive's own *Toy Story* CD-ROM game) threaten to render the toys depicted all but obsolete" (962). Indeed, the film presents a veritably utopian vision of less expensive, longer-lasting, pre-electronic toys.

The contest between Woody and Buzz begins with the cowboy trying to invalidate the space ranger's supposed powers. When Buzz tries to zap Woody with his arm-mounted laser, to no avail, Woody laughs and accu-rately calls the device "a little light bulb that blinks." Thereafter, Woody continually reminds Buzz that he is not the "real" Buzz Lightyear, as if such a figure exists in the toy world or the human world beyond them. This sets up the existential crisis that permeates the story, since Buzz eventually discovers—through seeing a doll like himself on a TV commercial—that he is only a toy. In many ways, Woody's crisis is more emotional and childish, since he fears that Andy will no longer love him as his favorite toy and Buzz will take over. Buzz's metaphysical dilemma is more perplexing and mature. He wrestles with the question of his identity and authority. He doesn't seem to care about Andy's love and attention, but instead about loftier goals such as saving civilizations and planets with skills and tools that are beyond the reach of any old cowboy.

Another aspect of the protagonists' differing levels of maturity, as of the growing maturity of Andy as a boy, is realized in a sequence set to the tune "Strange Things (Are Happening to Me)." The song superficially comments on the unusual circumstances in which Woody and Buzz find themselves but is more an anthem to Andy's coming-of-age, when toys will play a less important role and new problems will arise. The fact that Andy's mother is planning to move the family out of town seems foreshadowed as well. Finally, the lyrics suggest that Woody realizes that technologically advanced toys like Buzz are causing strange things to happen to him, since he is being replaced by toys with complicated, even adult, attributes.

While Woody and Buzz have their own showdown, the true villain of the film emerges in the form of a neighbor boy named Sid (voiced by Erik van Detten). Sid tortures and destroys toys for fun, expressing his "creativity" by reassembling his toys into mutant creatures. This pathology is never explained, although there are subtle indications of why Sid is violent. His house and yard are cluttered and dingy, unlike Andy's clean and orderly house: probably his family is poorer. Although they live a few feet away, Sid and Andy never play together, even when Andy has a birthday party that many other boys attend. Clearly, Sid is a bad toy owner, and by extension a bad father. Woody, on the other hand, quickly regrets abusing his leadership position (he has convinced the other toys to evict Buzz from Andy's house) and tries to rescue Buzz. Alas, he lands them both in Sid's clutches, setting up a new conflict from which the two must escape, now together. In the process, Woody takes on a parental role, trying to convince the dejected Buzz that he is worthy as a toy, and enlisting the mutant toys of Sid's cellar to help him rescue Buzz from imminent destruction.

The climax of *Toy Story* is quite rousing. Sid, who has strapped a fireworks rocket to Buzz, is astonished when Woody breaks the toys' code of silence and admonishes him for hurting them, whereupon the mutant toys—who never talk, presumably due to their trauma—advance on Sid and chase him off, crying. Meanwhile, Andy and his mother are just about to move away when Woody and Buzz give chase. In a rapidly edited

Buzz and Woody use all their powers in *Toy Story* (John Lasseter, Buena Vista) to reunite themselves with their owner and return to the toy world in which they belong. Collection Timothy Shary.

sequence, the other toys help them, to no avail. Finally, Woody uses the focused light from Buzz's helmet to light the fuse on the rocket, sending them high into the sky until they finally, slowly, cruise down into Andy's car on Buzz's extendable wings. Andy is happy to see his two favorite toys, which he feared he had lost in the moving process, and order is restored to the toys and the boy.

The film nevertheless ends on a premonitory note, since the old toys remain concerned about what new toys Andy will be given. To their shock, his newest "toy" is one none of them can compete with, a live puppy. Once again, the issue of living identity is called forth, as well as the issue of Andy's growth into adolescence. Now he will have the responsibility of caring for another living creature. In this way, the film returns to human interests after concentrating on the lives of inanimate toys. Yet after leaving the theater or turning off the TV, millions of children were sold millions of toys directly connected to the film by companies that had little interest in connecting children to live pets or real people. Ed Guerrero commented on this in broader terms: "However innocent their makers allege animation to be, its ideological effects are pervasive. Cartoons and animated features most deeply influence the habits and perceptions of Hollywood's youngest and therefore longest-term consumers: children" ("Circus" 335).

Brad Silberling's *Casper* does not focus on toys, but its latent concern with consumption and possession makes Guerrero's remarks even more trenchant. Despite its reliance on computer-generated effects, the film is primarily live action. Like *Toy Story*, it seems geared toward a preteen audience, but it too deals with issues apropos to adolescence and the negotiation of adult authority. Here the animated characters are ghosts, and they have discovered a supposedly safe home in the form of Whipstaff, a decaying mansion that has been left to the greedy Ms. Crittenden (Cathy Moriarty) by her father. The film also raises fundamental metaphysical questions: Do human spirits live on after death, and if so, why?

Crittenden shows no interest in the spirit of her father, but she believes he has buried a treasure in the house and sets off with her lawyer to find it. When the two discover the poltergeists within, they turn to Dr. Harvey (Bill Pullman), a psychologist who believes he can counsel ghosts; he claims they are simply spirits wanting to "cross over" but who have "unfinished business" to complete before they can do so. The emphasis on business and corruption throughout the film speaks to contemporary worries about financial ethics, yet this is in many ways a sideline. What the film explores most centrally is how an adolescent ghost finds a girlfriend in a teenage girl recovering from the death of her mother.

The ghost is, of course, Casper (voiced by Malachi Pearson). Casper began as a "friendly ghost" boy character in theatrical cartoons and comic books starting in the 1940s, then achieved greater notoriety among children when the cartoons began running on television in the 1960s, and as the comic books ran into the 1980s. The girl in the picture is Kat (Ricci), Dr. Harvey's daughter, who has stood by him in his apparently fruitless quest to contact the spirit of his deceased wife and her mother. Such an endeavor is intended to reveal the doctor's delirium even as it celebrates Kat's dedication. It also comments on contemporary interests in mysticism, the occult, and therapy of all kinds. Casper is thrilled when Kat and her father move into Whipstaff. With three mischievous uncles (also ghosts) who bully and treat him like a servant, he wants a friend and hopes that Kat will not be afraid of him as is everyone else. He quickly develops a crush on her, revealed by such gestures as his thrilled fist-pumping when he sees "a girl on my bed!" Kat and her father are initially shocked at seeing Casper and his uncles, and there's a humorous series of battles between the uncles and Kat's father (with a bizarre family feud for authority over their nephew and daughter). Then the ghosts reluctantly begin their counseling with Kat's father, and she goes off to yet another new school.

The romantic tension builds after Kat becomes attracted to her classmate Vick (Garette Ratliff Henson). Casper grows jealous and suspicious of Vick, who has reluctantly agreed together with his girlfriend to sabotage a

Halloween party at Kat's house. Alarmed, the young ghost tries to convince Kat to take him to the party. The scenes that ensue are among the most bizarre of the film. First Kat tries to explain to Casper that she needs a human boyfriend—who can apparently do things a ghost cannot—and then Casper flies her out over the ocean to a lighthouse where he tells her he has no memory of his childhood. Kat needs a human touch because she is becoming a woman; Casper cannot "cross over" beyond the human realm because he is mired in an absent childhood state. Both conditions—the onset of romantic and sexual desire and the need to grow beyond childhood—are central to adolescence. Further, they illustrate these characters' similar needs to confront life after death (Casper is already dead; Kat is trying to move on after the death of her mother) and to engage in "real" romance (they each want a human partner). But how the film fulfills these goals is strange indeed.

After their conversation at the lighthouse, Casper lies with Kat in her bed, kissing her on the cheek and curling up at her feet after she falls asleep. This quasi-necrophilic moment leads to further bonding between the two when Kat discovers Casper's old toys in the attic and helps him recall his death as a child. As it turns out, Casper's inventor father had spent the end of his life trying to revive his son with his "Lazarus Machine." Before Casper and Kat have time to test the machine, however, Crittenden and her lawyer steal its secret elixir, and in an even more contrived episode, Kat's father accidentally dies after getting drunk with Casper's uncles and falling into a ditch. Meanwhile, Crittenden falls from a cliff and returns as a ghost herself, still determined to find Whipstaff's treasure and then use the Lazarus machine to come back to life. Kat cleverly tricks her when she does find the treasure: Crittenden declares that all of her work is done and therefore has no "unfinished business," which means she must "cross over" to the netherworld. Kat is so distressed when her father also returns as a ghost that Casper sacrifices the last remaining elixir to bring him back to life.

The backdrop for all these mystical machinations is the Halloween party that is simultaneously under way in the Whipstaff main hall. After Vick and his girlfriend attempt to scare the partygoers, they meet Casper's uncles and are themselves scared into running away. In more human (but still animated) form, Kat's mother arrives and grants Casper his wish to be a boy for the next few hours, which leads to the film's eerie resolution. Now human, Casper dances with Kat, then they float off the floor together. Their parting kiss is an ideal consummation for two young "adolescents": both are more interested in the validation a lover represents than in actually having a lover. Having experienced the human world again as well as the feeling of a girl's body, Casper can return to the ghost world to finish the business of reclaiming his childhood. Kat is fulfilled, both because she has kissed a boy and because her mother has briefly returned, providing her father with the closure he needed to move on in life. When the mother reminds the father, "Our daughter is . . . a teenager," the label identifies Kat as a new person, one who can now find healthy relationships with real boys and with a healed father. Nick James describes the film's marketing gambit as "a transformation that crosses the line between two potential audiences—children and adolescents—(both of which the film wants to appeal to) and demonstrates the identity crisis besetting so many films that might or might not be for either audience" (44).

Casper produced a line of toys and memorabilia, making the boy ghost one of the most conspicuous children's commodities for the rest of the decade. While both *Casper* and *Toy Story* sustain their legacy through marketing products to children, each can nonetheless also be appreciated because its preternatural characters seek authority in human terms, much as children and adolescents seek identity in adult terms. The films' successes certainly had much to do with their retail potential, yet they also spoke quite directly to young peoples' concerns about missing parents, broken families, and needs for friends, love, and respect. Through their conclusions, both films' stories remind young viewers that even after enduring childhood troubles and adolescent adjustments, there will be more challenges ahead as life brings further changes—new homes, new schools, and new relationships. Although neither film overtly confronts issues like crime, drugs, or sex, both give youngsters encouragement and empowerment via unreal stories and commercial contexts.

Tech

Casper's success stems importantly from changes in how Hollywood made movies for younger children at this time. While animated features had always been popular with young people, *Casper* and other children's films (e.g., *Jumanji* and *The Indian in the Cupboard*) now relied heavily on digital visual effects that allowed young actors to interact with various creatures. As box office receipts testify, children—who can easily suspend their disbelief and join in fantasies about ghosts, talking animals, and miniature Sioux natives—loved what the CGI effects brought to stories.

Of course, technology also played a major role in *Toy Story*, which could have easily (and less expensively) been filmed in a traditional cel animation format. Yet part of what gave this film its allure is the use of computer visuals. These had become remarkably versatile in rendering perspective, depth, and shadow. In fact, with the exception of the more traditionally designed *Pocahontas,* all of the most popular films geared toward children rely heavily on CGI effects (*Batman Forever, Babe,* and *Mighty Morphin' Power Rangers* are examples). Children's films that relied less or not at all on CGI, such as *A Goofy Movie, Free Willy 2, Major Payne, The Jungle Book, Operation Dumbo Drop, The Big Green,* and *Heavyweights,* made considerably less money, even though most were also produced by Disney. The correlation between high tech and high profits in children's films is thus exceptionally evident; not surprisingly, therefore, the studios would increasingly use CGI in films made for younger audiences in years to come.

One of the year's most unexpected hits, New Line/Threshold Entertainment's *Mortal Kombat,* illustrates the vital role that CGI and video game visuals had come to play in films aimed at younger audiences. The film's PG-13 rating and graphic (if often cartoonish) violence may have drawn somewhat older viewers than *Casper,* yet it also has a built-in audience based on the popularity of the arcade game on which the film is based. Its ultimate domestic earnings of $70 million have little to do with its cast (it features no big-name stars), director (the obscure Paul W. S. Anderson), or generic marketing hook (all previous movies based on video games had been box office duds). What sold *Mortal Kombat* was its deft integration of CGI within a simplistic plot built on multiple fight scenes. CGI allowed this film to overcome the liabilities of all films based on games, their lack of interactive participation and absence of multiple outcomes.

The story is based on both of the Mortal Kombat games that had been developed at that time. In these games, a player chooses an identity and encounters a series of increasingly difficult fights with characters possessing various special powers: flame throwing, sword chucking, magic karate moves, and so on. In the film, an alien sorcerer named Shang Tsung (Cary-Hiroyuki Tagawa) has sponsored victorious fighters for nine consecutive generations of the Mortal Kombat tournament. His goal is to win ten contests in a row, which will essentially cast Earth under the evil spell of his emperor. Rising to defend Earth is Rayden (Christopher Lambert), who must recruit three fighters to take on Tsung's minions and save civilization. Rayden—and presumably the film's producers—target global markets by choosing a diversity of Earthlings for the battle—a Chinese man (Robin Shou), a white man (Linden Ashby), and a Nordic woman (Bridgette Wilson)—*and* they are further aided by an Asian princess (Talisa Soto). The tournament takes place on an unspecified Asian island, following the stereotyped requirements of martial arts films.

Exceptionally, however, here the contestants' national affiliations are not mentioned.

If there is a message to youth in the film, it is to trust yourself and your own inner strength, then use that strength to fight adversity. This is carried out through each of the three Earth warriors. All overcome liabilities such as anger or fear. As with similar films, the villains are in many ways more intriguing than the supposed heroes, since as nonhumans they have fighting abilities the humans do not. These special abilities are what primarily motivate and necessitate the use of CGI throughout the film, and are among its most exciting aspects.

The first two fighters the Earth trio encounter are Sub-Zero (François Petit) and Scorpion (Chris Casamassa). Sub-Zero can freeze objects from a distance. Scorpion can project an enormous snake-like device from his hand. Both effects are accomplished with CGI, rendering somewhat bland the human fight moves with which the trio responds. Another character, Goro (Kevin Michael Richardson), is predominantly a CGI creation of an eight-foot-tall being with two pairs of arms, made much more menacing by his digital imaging than his human costuming. CGI is also used in more subtle ways, for digitally removing safety wires attached to the fighters, for example, or for producing or enhancing the sets and backgrounds of the towers and castles where the numerous fights take place.

Of course, the raison d'être of the film is the fights, which constitute the last two-thirds of the story, making it play even more like a video game. Augmenting the game aspect is the throbbing rock music that plays over almost every fight. To its credit, the film takes advantage of the three-dimensional aspects of the sets that the game could not show, and the stunt choreography of the fights is intricate. Yet the core thrills arise from the CGI effects, as when Scorpion blows fire at a fighter and then explodes or when another fighter throws a bucket of water at Sub-Zero, which forms a giant icicle and impales him. The climactic fight between Tsung and an Earth fighter is even more indebted to CGI, since the sorcerer conjures up the souls of fighters he has previously killed and morphs into the dead brother of the fighter he is confronting. These tricks, alas, do not save Tsung, who is thrown to his death by the Earthling and rapidly decays into a corpse through vivid CGI effects. Last and not least: the film concludes with yet another CGI moment. The emperor himself bursts out of a temple to fight the surviving warriors. Our heroes strike a fighting pose and the frame freezes—clearly setting up a sequel.

Mortal Kombat does not merely employ computer and digital effects; it exists because of them. The villains and their powers would not have been convincing or even possible without CGI. Because the CGI is so effective, however, *Mortal Kombat* can showcase the fighting with minimal character development, just as the video games do. *Mortal Kombat* is also impressive (for its time) because no fewer than fifteen different companies created the effects, animation, and opticals, all for a budget of $20 million. By no means is *Mortal Kombat* the first film to focus on fighting contests, nor the first to use so much CGI. But by successfully expanding upon a video game and reaching a wide audience, it again shows the appeal of integrating digital effects with live action and indicates ways Hollywood can tap into youth culture without portraying teens themselves.

Kids as Movie Minions

This year once again brought to light—on multiple levels— just how important youth audiences, and representations of children and teenagers, too, are to the American film industry. As the success of subsequent films based on video games, children's television shows, and comic books attests, young people remain an indispensable force at the box office. Nonetheless, the media industry's interest in youth is not innocent, which the strategic images from the Oklahoma City bombing made clear. Media products constantly and knowingly exploit children and teens, giving them behavior paradigms to follow, perhaps the most pervasive of which is excessive consumption. Films like *Casper* and *Clueless* did offer positive messages about family unity, perseverance, ethics, and other virtues, yet these and other popular youth films offered their messages while also pushing commercial products. Even a fringe indie film like *Kids* is stuffed with scenes where its characters drink generic alcohol and take illegal drugs, celebrating the dangers of noncommercial consumption. The technological developments in CGI and digital effects brought further creative liberation to films, but also further ways to lure youth audiences into theaters for additional product promotion, as *Toy Story* and *Mortal Kombat* did so well. Hollywood's appeal to and representation of young people thus became both more obvious and more suspect this year, as aesthetic and technological developments were more tightly tied to marketing and franchising. Hollywood had insights about how interested in—and vulnerable to—film entertainment youthful audiences were, and could expand on these insights, carrying entertainment about and for youth audiences to new highs—and lows—in theaters, on video, through toys, video games, and other product tie-ins, at home and, increasingly, around the world as well.

1996

Movies and Homeland Insecurity

DEBRA WHITE-STANLEY AND CARYL FLINN

At first glance, this seems like a rather stable year for the United States. President Bill Clinton was reelected, the first Democrat to achieve this feat since Franklin Roosevelt. Although partisanship was intense, his relationship to moderate Republicans was not unduly strained, despite Special Prosecutor Kenneth Starr's continuing investigation into alleged misconduct of the Clintons in the Whitewater case. The country's economy was sound. The nation was not at war, and Clinton was promising to bring home the few troops he had committed to Bosnia the previous year. Superficially at least, things seemed fine at home.

Many Americans simply wanted to be left alone to go about their own affairs without the interference of foreign interests or the federal government. Many, especially on the right, viewed these two forces with growing suspicion. Savvy to that perception, Clinton steered the country through a relatively isolationist course, recalling Dorothy's sighing at the end of *The Wizard of Oz* (1939), "If you can't find something in your own back yard, you've never really lost it to begin with." By the mid-1990s, however, "home" was at once problem, solution, freedom, and fear. Cracks in the image of home as a safe place were even tarnishing the first family's image. Since the demise of Hillary Clinton's proposal for a national health care bill in 1994, her public activities had become a source of unfavorable media attention. She was still trying to live down her infamous assertions from 1992 that she was not "some little woman standing by my man like Tammy Wynette" and that "I suppose I could have stayed home and baked cookies and had teas, but what I decided to do was fulfill my profession."

Much as her husband was trying to make things right at "home," events conspired to turn the federal government into a bit of a public relations joke. As the year began, Congress deadlocked over the budget, effectively shutting down the government for three weeks. Nothing could have better demonstrated Washington's fecklessness. Things that the federal government once controlled were being parceled out to corporate or state control. Clinton dissolved the Interstate Commerce Commission, handing authority over to the states, and he signed a welfare reform bill that shifted federal expenditures to states and curtailed benefits and eligibility. As if in response to the negative publicity surrounding his own marriage, he also signed the Defense of Marriage Act, halted his campaign for universal health care, and stopped advocating for the rights of lesbians and gays to serve in the military.

Signs of instability were overshadowing the American homeland. During the Olympics in Atlanta, a bomb went off that killed one and wounded over a hundred others. The "Unabomber," in the person of Theodore Kaczynski, was arrested for mailing explosive packages in protest of what he viewed as an overly industrialized society. Along with the suspicious explosion of a transatlantic TWA flight in July in which 230 people died, two months after a Valujet airliner crashed in the Florida Everglades, killing 110 people, these events helped set in motion an emergent besieged mentality in the country.

Some Americans blamed foreigners for the problems at home. Debates over the rights of immigrants continued to rage, and racism and xenophobia fueled a small explosion of homegrown militia groups, whose membership that year was estimated at a hundred thousand. Heavily armed, these survivalists, neo-Nazis, and self-proclaimed patriots readied themselves to take on all threats, even the FBI and the rest of the U.S. government. Global developments also fanned the flames of domestic anxieties: China became the fastest growing economy in the world (and the United States' greatest debtor nation), and fourteen Caribbean and Latin American nations formed an economic union with the eventual hope of becoming party to the North American Free Trade Agreement (NAFTA).

It was a year of exponential growth in the arts, the business world, and science. The Federal Trade Commission approved the massive $6.5 billion merger of TimeWarner and Turner Broadcasting. Family groups were pleased that the TV industry was proposing a ratings system. Book consumers snatched up CBS veteran's Walter Cronkite's memoirs, A Reporter's Life: it became the year's best-selling nonfiction hardback. Overseas demand for American movies was rising and Hollywood, for its part, benefited from Congress's push for bankruptcy overhaul, which protected the major studies from financial turmoil. In the world of computer technology, Google was developed this year, even as Apple stock sunk to a ten-year low of less than $18.00 per share. The number of new AIDS cases diagnosed in the United States declined for the first time in the history of the epidemic, though the disease remained the leading cause of death for African Americans ages twenty-five to forty-four. In October, the Dow Jones Industrial Average closed over 6,000 points for the first time in history. In December, the Mars *Pathfinder* lifted off and sped toward Mars on a 310-million-mile odyssey to explore the planet's surface.

Beneath the apparent progress being made, social conflict was a constant presence. Amid both controversy and approval, the Citadel, the all-male military college in South Carolina, voted in June to admit women, ending a 153-year tradition. Race rioting occurred in October and November in St. Petersburg, Florida, in response to the alleged beating of an eighteen-year-old black man by police officers.

Meanwhile, U.S. movies expressed growing anxieties concerning foreigners, domestic terrorism, and big government. Vulnerability and fear underpinned the year's biggest-budget pictures. Storm chasers in the disaster pic *Twister* ($241.7 million domestic gross) track monster tornadoes that decimate the American heartland. Terrorist acts threaten to end life as we know it in *Executive Decision, 12 Monkeys,* and *Escape from L.A.* In *Mission: Impossible,* which grossed over $180 million, Tom Cruise prevents the destruction of the Central Intelligence Agency. In *Eraser* ($101 million domestic gross), Arnold Schwarzenegger prevents enemies from obtaining a gun that can shoot through walls at the speed of light. In the action film *The Rock* ($134 million domestic gross), a high-ranking Marine Corps officer threatens the city of San Francisco with a nuclear bomb.

A wide variety of genres rehearses this oscillation between threats to the home and threatening elements within the home itself. John Travolta's characters in the melodramas *Phenomenon* (where he acquires supernatural powers after seeing a bright light) and *Michael* (where he is a chain-smoking archangel) show that home is anything but an ordinary place. In children's films such as *101 Dalmatians, Muppet Treasure Island,* and *Fly Away Home,* one can escape the problems of home with the help of new kinds of friends and special powers. A South Pacific island is home to miscreant half-animal, half-human beings in the remake of *The Island of Dr. Moreau.* In the horror film *Mary Reilly,* a housemaid (Julia Roberts) falls in love with the owner of the house, a perverse being who is half Dr. Jekyll and half Mr. Hyde. An investigation into a mutiny reveals the sexist values of military culture in the war film *Courage under Fire.* Even the comedian Jim Carrey turns pathological in *The Cable Guy,* as an apparently friendly cable repairman who stalks a customer (Matthew Broderick).

Smaller-budget films such as Spike Lee's *Get on the Bus* exposed deep-seated prejudices at home about race and political dissent. Independent pictures like the Coen brothers' *Fargo* and John Sayles's *Lone Star* explored the corruption and dangers of small-town America, a place most Americans would characterize as safe and unthreatening. In *The War at Home,* small-town parents struggle to help their son, a veteran of the Vietnam War who suffers from post-traumatic stress disorder.

Thus, the films of this year showcased threats that were perceived as coming not only from foreign lands but from within, in the government, in the country's towns, homes, even in the American Dream itself. Authorities are unable to help citizens cope with looming threats from terrorists, invading aliens, kidnappers, abusive step-parents, and masked serial killers. Individual characters are left to fight themselves, their families, and most of all the children who are left in their care and cast into an odd brew of victimhood and heroism.

Protecting the Homeland: *Independence Day* and *Mars Attacks!*

In the science fiction features *Independence Day* and *Mars Attacks!* everyday citizens must defend the United States from outer-space invaders. Both films connect the sense of national defense with enhanced family bonds. Roland Emmerich's *Independence Day* earnestly girds family drama onto political crises involving big government, foreigners, terrorism, and military action. By contrast, Tim Burton's *Mars Attacks!* sends up the cinematic and social clichés that underpin these institutions. By involving the family and the American home to the extent that they do, these two films—like many others—signal the growing significance of the private sphere with regard to political action and citizenship. That shift fits with Lauren Berlant's assertion that domestic space has taken on new political significance in American society. She argues that citizens now define political action solely in relation to protecting that which is private and personal—homes, families, personal rights, and desires—and contrasts this personally motivated activism to older protest movements that fought for causes defined in relation to social justice (such as the civil rights movement, labor unionism, and the women's movement) (13). Protecting children within domestic space becomes a centerpiece of this new private conception of domestic citizenry. As Patricia Holland has noted, the idea of saving a child generates adult pleasure and power (143). Parents save the day in these films, and by doing so feed the fantasies that circulate around childrearing in our culture.

The political significance of the roles of parent and child can clearly be traced in Fox's *Independence Day,* the highest grossing U.S. movie of the year. In the film, heavily armed alien spaceships arrive from the "mother ship," position themselves over Earth, and commence destroying it, with images of televised news reports emphasizing the extent to which the attacks impact women and children worldwide. To defeat the aliens, President Whitmore (Bill Pullman) turns to computer nerd David Levinson (Jeff Goldblum) and marine pilot Capt. Steve Hiller (Will Smith), who implant a virus into the aliens' computer system. After the alien ships are vanquished in an attack led by Whitmore, the flyboys return to Earth, having been transformed from misfit adolescents into heroic father figures.

Before the aliens strike, America appears to be the land of lost potential, its men trapped in childlike states. Living on the "fringe," these male characters are disenfranchised, don't know what they want, and handle their responsibilities poorly. For instance, a drunken Russell Casse (Randy Quaid) crop-dusts the wrong field; Hiller won't commit to being a father and husband and can't realize his dream of working at NASA; the MIT-educated Levinson pines for his ex-wife, Connie (Margaret Colin), and is constantly berated by his Jewish father (Judd Hirsch) for being a failure. Moreover, for some of these characters, their "not quite men" status depends on wild ethnic clichés: Quaid plays a stupid, drunk, white-trash hick; Hirsh's character is a nagging, overbearing, Jewish father; Goldblum portrays the loser brainiac son—all limited representations of diversity.

Even the president appears feckless and weak. Reviewers complained about Bill Pullman's inability to bring a sense of masculine gravitas to the role. At the time he was, after all, best known for his recent role in a "woman's film," the romantic comedy *While You Were Sleeping* (1995). *Independence Day* seems to acknowledge this lack of credibility at the outset, when presidential aides report that his opponents are ridiculing him for appearing childish and inexperienced. Whitmore's own advisors scarcely listen to him, and it's clear that to rule the nation better, he's going to have to get his own masculinity in order. The first shot of him shows him sweet-talking the absent First Lady (played by Mary McDonnell) over the phone while cuddling in bed with their young daughter.

In the absence of a strong and competent government, these male characters are presented as losers so that they may later be heroicized, physically changing from boys into he-men. Whitmore, for instance, becomes a veritable action-figure pilot by film's end. Hiller, after rescuing his girlfriend, stripper Jasmine Dubrow (Vivica Fox), and her son, Dylan (Ross Bagley), emerges from the rescue helicopter, his muscular frame silhouetted by edge lighting—a use of backlight that accentuates the contours of an object. Hiller then marries Jasmine and assumes fatherly responsibility for Dylan. Although his is a less quirky male hero than the other male characters, Hiller is no less stereotyped. As played by Will Smith, he exudes an easy authority, due in large part to Smith's star persona. The actor had gained credibility as a rap artist and in TV's "The Fresh Prince of Bel Air," where he was the most racialized of the main characters. To Amy Taubin, Will Smith is "probably the only African American actor in Hollywood guaranteed to be nonthreatening to a white middle-class audience" ("Playing" 8). Once Smith made his break into films, he produced a sense of "African American-ness" at once tough and macho.

Clearly, *Independence Day* deploys very specific notions of masculinity, featuring improbable national heroes whose ability to "act" reinstates their full, adult heterosexuality. Femininity receives equally specific treatment in the film. Mise-en-scène, for instance, creates decisive parallels between women's bodies—specifically, maternal ones—and the aliens, telegraphing larger anxieties about female sexuality and autonomy (Hobby 51). A subtle gendering begins with the movie's opening shot, in which we see a U.S. flag in the center of a desolate lunar landscape. The camera cranes downward into a close-up of a 1969 plaque that reads: "Here men from the Planet Earth first set foot upon the moon. We came in peace for all mankind." When the camera tilts up to position the earth center frame, the aliens' "mother ship" emerges from offscreen space. Soon, the entire frame is filled by the ship's massive underbelly, whose protrusions conspicuously resemble mechanized breasts, aligning the earth-bound ship with a grotesque femininity that Barbara Creed has called the "monstrous-feminine," and making it an archaic mother who haunts that film's mise-en-scène (47).

The use of the graphic design of the spaceship to suggest the monstrous feminine continues during the alien attack (a large spaceship structure opens up a vaginal interior that sprays fire to demolish the city). Alien carcasses held in Area 51—the Nevada military base that has become a focus of modern UFO and conspiracy theories—insinuate further connections between the film's female characters and the evil alien ship. In accordance with nautical custom, the spacecraft held there is described in openly gendered terms: "She's a beaut, ain't she? As you can see from the repairs we've been trying to put her back together since the 1960s." As the spaceship is repaired in secret, so does the script "repair" the three main female characters—the First Lady, Connie, and Jasmine. Each character is rewritten to become less angry, independent, and career-minded by the end of the story, diffusing any threat to male authority. When the First Lady dies, for instance, she apologizes, "I'm so sorry that I didn't come home when you asked me to."[1] Computer geek Levinson is reunited with Connie, who, like the First Lady, renounces her professional decisions. Each of these three female leads is as trapped as the three dead aliens shown to us in a tour of

The triptych of aliens encased in glass, domesticated like the three female leads of *Independence Day* (Roland Emmerich, Centropolis Entertainment and Twentieth Century Fox Film Corporation). Digital frame enlargement.

the Area 51 facilities. In three tanks, the otherworldly creatures hang suspended in fluid, inspiring fear and danger in the male characters who cluster around them. While the specimens on the right and left sides of the triptych clearly have male sexual organs, the camera zooms in on the alien body in the center tank, a creature conspicuously coded as female.

President Whitmore is caught in the crossfire between two feminized forces, conveyed via crosscutting between the First Lady's telephone calls home to him and the intercepted alien radio signals. Whitmore must re-masculinize the situation, the country, and himself, and this he does when he makes a speech celebrating the final triumph over the aliens. Redeploying the gendered language of the 1969 lunar plaque, he announces: "Mankind: that word should have new meaning for all of us today. We can't be consumed by our petty differences anymore. We will be united in our common interests." After completing the mission, the surviving characters—led by heroes who are African American and Jewish—unite as a band of outsiders who create the illusion of an interclass, interethnic international community. Its global inclusiveness is as fake as the film's misogyny is real: President Whitmore tells the crowds in the grand finale that the defeat of the aliens on the fourth of July means that Americans can share "their" Independence Day with the rest of the world.

Unlike *Independence Day*, *Mars Attacks!* does not take refuge in the fantasy of the redemptive potential of heroism, the sanctity of the nuclear family, or the glory of national holidays. This film eschews the straitlaced intensity of *Independence Day*, reversing the pattern in which the three lead male characters learn how to become fathers by defending the homeland by parodying the entire alien invasion genre.[2] The male authority figures in this film all perish, leaving only women and young people behind. Budgeted at $70 million, *Mars Attacks!* grossed less than $38 million domestically for Warner Bros., although it became a cult hit on video and DVD thanks to its irreverence and innovative campiness.

A quick tracing of the fortunes of mixed-up families in this film shows that the roles of child victim and adult male vigilante are both lampooned. Burton sends up the idea of children as hapless victims in a scene in which a Martian craft lasers the Washington Monument at its base and guides it to fall on a troop of boy scouts. Instead of feeling horrified, the viewer is hard-pressed not to laugh at this slaughter of the lambs. Just as Burton parodies the melodramatic figure of the endangered child, he also ridicules the figure of the patriarch who fights to protect that child and his family. For instance, the head of the white-trash Norris family (Joe Don Baker) goes down fighting in a blaze of dysfunction, digging his heels in to protect the family's doublewide trailer. The Martians effortlessly dispatch his gung-ho military son Billy Glenn (Jack Black, in a deliriously over-the-top performance), depriving him of his redemptive moment. It is gangly teen heartthrob Richie (Lukas Haas) and his forgetful grandmother Florence (Sylvia Sidney) who save the planet by accidentally discovering that whenever Slim Whitman's "Indian Love Song" is played, the heads of the aliens explode. As surviving U.S. military patrols blare the tune over loudspeakers, viewers are treated to green guts exploding in the aliens' transparent helmets.

While the white Norris family is saved by the teen geek and his distracted grandmother, the African American Williams family is saved by the kids' truancy. Former boxing champion Byron Williams (former football star Jim Brown) works as a guard in a Vegas casino, where he is costumed in a silly pharaoh outfit like a big camp god. He and estranged wife Louise (blaxploitation diva Pam Grier) are geographically separated for most of the film. Their space-gun expert kids Neville (Brandon Hammond) and Cedric (Ray J) eventually kick alien ass, in a scenario in which visiting the arcade has more educational value than attending class.

Free to wreak havoc on the American population, the Martians prove to be peeping toms who lavish perverse attention on undefended female bodies. In one scene the leader of the Martians interrupts his casual perusal of a *Playboy* centerfold to quake with desire at the spectacle of an imprisoned Sarah Jessica Parker. The unusual qualities of his fantasy life are manifest when he has Martian surgeons attach her Chihuahua's head to her body. Even if such a transformation were possible, what hero could rescue so surreal and hybrid a figure, and which part of the canine/human sex object would he save? In another scene the Martians peer through the window of a trailer where the Norris's daughter (Christina Applegate) is having sex with a man. Little windshield wipers clear the Martian helmets of steam. The Martians adeptly translate their newly acquired knowledge of female sexuality into action: a Martian soldier disguises himself as a prostitute (Tina Marie) to infiltrate the White House, whose halls she wanders robotically, poured into a skin-tight hourglass dress. This scene is one of many in which stylized costumes help lampoon the excesses of these female characters.

Burton's visual design was modeled on how Martians were supposed to look in the 1950s and in comic books, hence the swollen green heads ensconced in big bubble helmets (Che) derived from *Earth vs. the Flying Saucers* (1956). Indeed, the film's mise-en-scène is rife with silliness and playful disrespect. Burton seems to embrace every campy cliché in the book. His parodic depiction of the invasion led one critic to argue that *Mars Attacks!* levies a more "sustained questioning of military efficiency, governmental complicity, and corporate capitalism" than *Independence Day* (Kakoudaki 123).

Both *Mars Attacks!* and *Independence Day* come out of a historical moment in which vigilantism was celebrated as a way for Americans to secure themselves. Vigilantism—when people undertake law enforcement in the absence of competent government—tends to erupt in historical moments in which conventional authority—police, military, the state—is perceived as corrupt or inept, and this idea was taking root in U.S. culture (as evidenced, most dramatically, in the Oklahoma City bombing of the previous year). *Mars Attacks!* and *Independence Day* are vigilante narratives in which the viewer is invited to sympathize with the "lone wolf" who challenges corrupt, vicious, or dehumanized authority.

In *Independence Day,* vigilante actions renew social stability through old, familiar tropes: heterosexual couples (one African American, one white, side by side), the family (loving fathers and daughters), a newly virile president (cheered by crowds), and world unity (with the United States as unquestioned leader). In contrast, the social misfits of *Mars Attacks!* do not redeem conventional governmental or military authority. Indeed, here

male figures who save planet Earth and become kinder, gentler military figures in the process are cartoon-like at best. *Mars Attacks!* mocks vigilantism
in many ways: by making children into unwittingly effective vigilantes, by
exposing America's inflated sense of military prowess, and by showing the
dysfunction of American families. Ultimately, in *Mars Attacks!* the United
States survives (to the extent that it does) not because it is inherently superior to the Martians, but because of sheer coincidence and dumb luck.

Both *Independence Day* and *Mars Attacks!* address the shifting notions of
model citizenship and responsibility. Good citizens concentrate on themselves, do not complain, and do not ask the government for help. In fact,
these films show us that it's the federal government that needs help, yet in
both movies all those who step up and act collectively out of social or political responsibility are treated as fringe, irregular citizens. *Independence Day*
concludes with reassurances. *Mars Attacks!* suggests that the country's anxiety over security might be well founded. We have aliens that hate us (and
they won't tell us why!). More potently, *Mars Attacks!* suggests that bigger
damage will occur if we entrust our safety to conventional systems of power
and figurehead leaders, although the film's overwrought mise-en-scène and
style deliver this point with tongue so firmly in cheek that its "message"
implodes. The more earnest *Independence Day* reveals an even more ironic
truth: big government tells Americans that big government is bad, and yet
Americans must celebrate all that big government stands for, strives for, and
works for.

Rescuing the Family: *Ransom* and *Sling Blade*

Ransom and *Sling Blade* depict American families coming
under attack just when domestic happiness seems immanent. With these
features, however, the foes of domestic bliss are not space aliens but fellow
citizens who, as vigilantes, desperately lash out to resolve simmering griev-
ances that seem to gravitate around people who are seen as unable to
defend themselves. The rise of what Lauren Berlant has dubbed "the intimate public sphere" allows us to wage national struggles on behalf of those
entities that we set about rescuing: fetuses, children, immigrants, and people of color (21).

Director Ron Howard is the iconoclast of the intimate public sphere in
the United States. Many grew up with him on television, first as little Opie
on "The Andy Griffith Show" and later as Richie Cunningham on "Happy
Days." Howard seems the perfect choice to direct a movie about rescuing an
imperiled family. In *Ransom,* a thriller made for Touchstone Pictures, Mel

Gibson plays Tom Mullen, the wealthy CEO of Endeavor Airlines. In a TV ad, Mullen claims, "The most important thing to me these days is family—mine, yours. That's the good thing about an airline: it actually brings families closer together." As if acting on that directive, the film's visual design brings two families closer together, the wealthy Mullens and the family-like group of the kidnappers who prey upon them. The beginning of the film crosscuts between the Mullen home and the kidnappers' apartment, establishing the disparities between the two family groups. New York was chosen as the location for the film because there, in Ron Howard's words, "The rich and poor rub elbows all the time—they're forced to coexist" (qtd. in Berman 44). Polish cinematographer Piotr Sobocinski (1958–2001), who had served as cinematographer for Krzysztof Kieslowski's art film masterpiece *Red* (Poland, 1994), worked on *Ransom* as his first and only American genre film. Howard used Sobocinski's talents and innovations in lighting, camera angles, and camera movement to create links between the separate worlds of the kidnappers and the millionaire family, and to distinguish what otherwise could have been an unremarkable film (Rudolf 47).

Like *Independence Day*, *Ransom* shows how established authority fails to protect the status quo; to restore order, individual family members must act independently of the law. Just as in *Independence Day*, in which children are targets of the alien attack, Mullen's son Sean (Brawley Nolte) is the chief target in *Ransom*, kidnapped from under Tom's nose in Central Park at a science fair. The kidnapping is conducted by police officer Jimmy Shaker (Gary Sinise), his girlfriend Maris Conner (Lili Taylor), two brothers, Clark and Cubby Barnes (Liev Schreiber and Donnie Wahlberg), and computer hacker Miles Roberts (Evan Handler). *Ransom* pits the vigilantes of the bad family against Tom Mullen, who resorts to vigilante-style action on his son's behalf. *Ransom* invites us to side with Mullen by validating his vigilantism through editing that demonstrates that his actions are necessary in order to save his son, conforming to Berlant's insights about the importance of children in current conceptions of political activism.

Mullen comes to believe that, even if he pays the ransom, the kidnappers will kill his son, but it is clear he can only reach this conclusion by adopting the point of view of the kidnappers. He is able to adopt their perspective because he is as corrupt as they are. The film indicates Tom's corruption by paralleling the illegal means he uses to regain his son and his equally illegal efforts to quash past labor unrest at Endeavor Airlines. In the process, *Ransom*, perhaps unintentionally, shows how children and corporations—both pivotal aspects of the American Dream—reveal the interdependence of family, capital, and corporate achievement as markers of normativity and success. Unlike her husband, Kate Mullen (Rene Russo) turns to the FBI for assistance. Later, cutaways reveal her guilt that she may have been too busy at the science fair to prevent her son from being kidnapped. Like the First Lady in *Independence Day* and other films of the year, Kate is effectively punished for not placing her family above professional obligations and, again as in *Independence Day*, it is the father who must save the day.

Sean's image compels our sympathy for Tom's vigilantism. On his way to hand over the ransom money, Mullen, stuck in traffic, gazes at a group of schoolchildren crossing the street in front of him and imagines seeing Sean's face in the crowd. As he glances to his left, his son's face is actually being broadcast as part of the news reports playing on televisions in a store-front window. Catalyzed by this image, Mullen goes to a local TV station, where to the camera/kidnappers he impulsively announces a "change of plan": to convert the two-million-dollar ransom payment into a bounty. Two million dollars are spread across a desk: "If you return my son, alive and uninjured, I'll withdraw the bounty." Here the image of the child stands in for all that needs protection: the country, fatherhood, virtue itself. Children become conceptualized as ideal citizens, and protecting them— even through vigilantism—becomes the patriotic act of choice. We see this in *Independence Day*, which bypasses the First Lady to intensify the pathos of a father/national leader protecting his child. *Ransom* bases its story on precisely the same point.

Tom Mullen's economic authority is not seen as evil, although it is certainly compromised by his earlier dealings as "a guy who buys his way out of trouble." However, the intensity of Tom's vigilante acts in the end seems unbalanced and too macho for a family action drama. That tension befits the star image of Mel Gibson, whose film career moved from gallant action hero to family-values man. Gibson's contradictory persona thus enhances our suspicion that the likeable Tom Mullen is also an obstinate bully. Tom's mean streak emerges in his dismissive treatment of FBI agent Lonnie Hawkins (Delroy Lindo), the film's only African American. (By choosing to represent the FBI via an African American, *Ransom* uses a racist, classist coding to portray the government as weak and incompetent.)

Superficially, Sinise's kidnapper/cop represents the bankrupt authority figure common to films of the year. Jimmy Shaker is motivated almost entirely by class resentment, elaborated through a spiteful litany against the amenities of Mullen's uptown world—the Whitney Museum, the Four Seasons restaurant, the Metropolitan Opera. In its conceptual mapping of Mullen's penthouse and Shaker's rude city streets below, the film is "con-

sistently associating its working-class characters with predators and criminals while portraying the powerful and the elite as their victims" (Gabbard,
"Someone" 12). Yet, like a film noir detective who belongs in some way to
the underworld he investigates, Tom Mullen uses many of the same tactics
as his less-elevated enemies do.

Although *Ransom* sometimes celebrates the opulence of the Mullen
lifestyle (in tracking shots of the Mullens' apartment), it also gestures
toward the dangers that such immoderate money and power can bring
(making the family vulnerable to corruption). The film does not overtly
bless the CEO's lone-wolf acts, but the official actions of the FBI fare much
worse. Mullen complains that the agency's tactics are slow and uncertain,
and he's right. When Agent Lindo says, "I've been doing [these kinds of
cases] for eighteen years," it rings hollow, and Americans see another
insider to distrust. Who is left to run the country or to defend the family?
Once again it is private citizens, even if their wealth makes them the virtual
bedmates of government rather than its angry, underground opponent.

Fully unconcerned with penthouse drama, Billy Bob Thornton's *Sling
Blade* tilts down to explore the lower stratum of the rural poor. Thornton
directed, starred in, and adapted this low-budget film, producing one of the
more haunting movies from trendy independent production company
Shooting Gallery. The company's countercultural cachet helped net talent
such as composer Daniel Langlois, country and western singer Dwight
Yoakum in a feature role, and director Jim Jarmusch in a cameo. Made for
$1 million and sold to Miramax for distribution for $10 million, *Sling Blade*
grossed nearly $25 million and received strong critical acclaim.

The story follows the release of Karl Childers (Thornton) from a state
mental institution in rural Arkansas where he has spent seventeen years.
The film opens with a long take in which criminally insane inmate Charles
Bushman (J. T. Walsh) describes how much he relished committing vicious
sex crimes against young women, one a newlywed who he strangled with a
nylon cord. Karl is an adult with mental disabilities, and we apprehend his
distaste for Bushman's shocking monologue through the deep focus and
deliberate framing of this long take. Even though Karl is also a murderer, his
crimes have very little in common with those of Charles Bushman, and the
visual design of the shot underlines that difference. In the DVD commentary,
Thornton described this cinematography as "editor-proof," a guerilla strategy to preserve the film's controversial scenes once the footage was turned
over to the studio. He argues that the long take renders life's complexity: "I
believe that people really want to see life play out. I don't really buy the
thing about movies needing to be shot like MTV videos" (Thornton). For

scholar David Bordwell, *Sling Blade*, with its long average shot length (23.3 seconds), eschews hallmarks of contemporary studio style such as the casual use of close-ups and mobile framing (Bordwell, "Continuity" 21).

The effectiveness of *Sling Blade*'s cinematography is clear even before Karl is released, when a young journalism student interviews him at the hospital. In a powerful, dramatic monologue Karl describes the neglect and ridicule he suffered at the hands of his family, indirectly leading him to murder his mother and her lover. As one critic notes, the dramatic monologue, "long considered anathema among screenwriters," is in this scene used to good purpose (Hendrickson 41). The student reporter's question, "Will you ever kill anybody again, Karl?" sets up the film's plot, which unfurls the circumstances that induce Karl to do just that.

Immediately upon Karl's release, he happens upon the situation that will trigger him into committing another murder. The kindly warden finds him a job in a gas station and soon Karl befriends a young neighborhood boy, Frank Wheatley (Lucas Black), whose single mother Linda Wheatley (Natalie Canerday) allows Karl to live in the garage behind their house. Frank and Karl exchange stories at a special spot they have near a lake, and it's there that we learn about Karl's abusive upbringing and the details leading to Karl's institutionalization. "When I was about your age, boy," Karl says, he unleashed a sling blade on a ne'er-do-well whom he caught having sex with his mom. When he discovered the sex was consensual, Karl killed his mother as well.

Another long take dramatizes Karl's dismay at finding that his adopted family group has an abusive father figure and that conditions in the Wheatley home are firmly reminiscent of his own childhood abuse. Upon first arriving there, Linda's violent boyfriend Doyle Hargraves (Yoakum) speaks abusively and disrespectfully to Linda, Frank, and Karl, threatening them all with violence. Tensions build until, in an explosive argument, Linda finally stands up to Doyle and kicks him out of the house. The blocking, dialogue, and gestures accentuate the diverging reactions each character has to Doyle's abuse. Linda tells Frank, "Let's just try and forget about this mess." Family friend Vaughan Cunningham (John Ritter), who had been about to put his arms around Linda, instead cups his mouth with his hands in shock. Because Doyle is on a first-name basis with the local sheriff, it would be difficult for Linda to obtain a restraining order or any legal protection against him. This, coupled with her low-wage job at the local dollar store, makes her into a trapped character. Like the women from *Independence Day* and *Ransom*, Linda does what she can but is unable to defend her family without a man to take charge.

Karl becomes a father figure for Frank and grows protective of the boy. Doyle's violence toward Frank triggers Karl to remember how his own parents aborted his baby brother and then ordered him to throw the still-alive fetus into the garbage. Three destroyed childhoods are condensed in this moment, Frank's, Karl's, and his unborn brother's. When Karl tells Frank, "I don't think nothin' bad ought to happen to children. I think all the old bad things ought to be saved up for the folks that done growed up," we see that all "the folks that done growed up" were themselves once abused children. In *Sling Blade,* the family offers no refuge from injustice, but instead becomes the place where social inequalities and oppressions cycle repeatedly. As if to emphasize that persistence of the past in the present, Karl visits his own abusive father (Robert Duvall), who once again disowns him.

When Doyle decides to move in to the Wheatley home, he puts Karl and Frank on notice: Karl needs to move out and Frank must bend to his authority. It is not long after this that Karl arranges for Vaughn to bring Linda and Frank to his home for the night and then enters Linda's house where he kills Doyle with a lawn mower blade. Then he calls the police, has some biscuits, and the film concludes with the same shot with which it opens, Karl in the institution, staring out of the same window.

Karl kills to correct families that are headquarters to abuse, neglect, and extraordinary violence. Although the first murder is done in the heat of the moment and the second with deliberation and forethought, both are vigilante acts through which Karl seeks justice. By protecting Frank, Karl saves a child, thereby taking an unlikely "patriotic" step by defending the ideals now located in childhood and the private sphere. As one critic puts it, "Karl is a Forrest Gump version of the Grim Reaper. However much an innocent, he wields his blade in an act of undeniable justice" (Yacowar). Wildly different in scope and ambition, the vigilante acts of Tom Mullen and Karl Childers are motivated by the desire to save a child from a sinister man who terrorizes the family.

Yet unlike *Independence Day* or *Ransom, Sling Blade* acknowledges the moral and legal complexities of Karl's acts by, among other things, placing them at the hands of a man without the mental faculties of most adults. Character facial expression, mannerisms, and costume that might have been ridiculed or made "fringy" in *Independence Day* are given genuine depth and humanity in *Sling Blade*. Yoakum's performance as Doyle is so amazing and the writing so expert that all he has to do is sit calmly in Linda's living room chair to exude arrogance and menace. His evil is worse than that of the aliens of *Independence Day* or the kidnappers in *Ransom,* for Doyle is so firmly entrenched within the home that he rarely leaves its furnishings.

Cinematography and mise-en-scène work together in *Sling Blade* (Billy Bob Thornton, Shooting Gallery) to emphasize the brutality of the dysfunctional family. Digital frame enlargement.

Karl learns that the closest thing to a safe, comfortable "home" for him is the state facility, which, he says, is not "too big," too complicated, or corrupt. There, he is fine. Only when he tries to find a home, a family, do insecurity and terror come to the fore.

Teen Vigilantes: *Scream* and *The Crucible*

As we have seen, the helplessness of children in *Independence Day* and *Ransom* invites the male protagonists to save the day. The children and adult children of *Mars Attacks!* and *Sling Blade* fight back against would-be alien invaders and malevolent stepfathers. The teenage characters of *Scream* and *The Crucible* also enact the dramas of vigilantism and the intimate public sphere traced in films of this year. As in *Sling Blade,* young people in *Scream* and *The Crucible* cope with parents who are either unavailable or dysfunctional. These young people misdirect their pain and desires without an adult to guide or even notice them. In *Scream* this takes the form of raping and killing women, while in *The Crucible,* this becomes adulterous desire and feigned demonic possession. Prioritizing personal desires over the commonweal, the teens of *Scream* and *The Crucible* are much like the selfish adults featured prominently in these films, people who covet personal sensory gratification despite adverse social consequences. This pattern again rehearses the demise of collective, socially motivated political action as a mechanism of hope, replacing it with vigilantism and chaos.

Scream was made for about $14 million through Dimension Films, a subsidiary of Miramax that specialized in low-budget, mass-appeal genre films (Wee 59). The film was phenomenally successful, grossing $10 million its first weekend and attracting so many repeat viewers that it was later re-released to huge profits (Robb 182). This cumulative growth of the viewing audience is the exact opposite of typical viewing patterns in which audiences taper off after the initial weekend of a film's release (Phillips 165), but it is more common with youth-directed movies. Critics attribute *Scream*'s success to its appeal to a generation that came of age using media technologies like video games, cable television, cell phones, and the Internet. In fact, media savvy marks all the *Scream* films, through their reflexive references to horror conventions and the casting of stars from television programs familiar to a younger generation. As Valerie Wee explains, the makers of the *Scream* trilogy "recognize that the over-wrought, intense nature of the horror genre can no longer be experienced 'straight' by an American teen audience which has become overly familiar with and increasingly derisive of the genre's conventions" (49).

Scream's diegetic world is filled with broken marriages, absent parents, young men who are sexually aggressive and violent, and young women who do not feel safe. Clearly the affluent suburb depicted here, like the more modest homes seen in other films of this year, is unsafe. Young women must protect themselves, and they cannot rely on the police or their parents for help.[3] In the finale, *Scream*'s teen protagonist Sidney Prescott (Neve Campbell) despairs of finding a lawful solution to the violence and herself kills the murderers.

From its first scene, *Scream* uses offscreen space and film sound to foreground the vulnerability of the American home to an unseen assailant/vigilante who appears and disappears without warning. His terrifying Halloween mask resembles Edvard Munch's painting *The Scream* and turns him into a frightening marker of anxieties surrounding domestic space and the vulnerability of young women who are within that space. The first female victim, Casey Becker (Drew Barrymore), is drawn into the male killer's web when she answers the telephone. His disembodied, oddly mechanical, but intimate voice penetrates her home, filling it with menace. (Roger Jackson, who plays the unseen "voice," was also heard as the "translator device" in *Mars Attacks!* His voice here recalls the altered phone voice of Jimmy Shaker in *Ransom*.)

During Casey's conversations with the killer, our awareness of his presence in the unseen space around her home is enhanced by the increased volume of ambient noises outside (dogs barking, crickets chirping). During

Casey (Drew Barrymore) playfully fingering a knife in her parents' kitchen as she banters with her future killer in *Scream* (Wes Craven, Dimension Films and Woods Entertainment). Digital frame enlargement.

the attack, those seemingly innocuous acoustic details accompany the killer's violence and Casey's attempt to call to her parents, who have just arrived home. Although Casey is in her parents' range of vision as the assailant tries to strangle her, she cannot call out loudly enough for them to hear and they walk by her. They remain unaware that their daughter is being attacked until they enter the home, which is in complete disarray. When they try to call the police they hear—for Casey is still holding the phone—the killer stabbing Casey and dragging her away. Keeping its focus on the sound track, the scene concludes on Casey's mother's screams, in reaction to the vision of Casey hanging from a tree outside. A thunderclap resounds loudly.

Positioning the family home as a place inhabited by young people in the absence of their parents characterizes domestic space as dangerously unprotected. Sound motifs like the thunderclap and the wildlife surrounding the isolated suburban home invoke that lack of security. For instance, when Sidney is drawn to her bedroom window by strange sounds, she screams as a hand reaches up from the offscreen space of the night and grabs her. It is her boyfriend Billy Loomis (Skeet Ulrich) who climbs in through the window. Clearly, these nighttime spaces are gendered, with hostile masculine presences surrounding the home and sometimes even emerging from within it. When Sidney's father, Neil (Lawrence Hecht), comes by to remind her that he is about to depart on a business trip, his slightly suggestive smile raises the possibility that he may be the killer. The lack of safety in one's own home thus not only emanates from the *absence* of father figures, but ironically also from their *presence,* much as in *Sling Blade*. Mothers, by contrast, are rarely present to assist their daughters.

Sidney's mother, Maureen, was killed the year before, and her absence resonates powerfully for Sidney.

At one point when Sidney opens the front door to escape, she is startled by another man, Deputy Dewey (David Arquette).[4] Dewey is no experienced police investigator, but rather a representative of an incompetent local police force, another bumbling agent of the government populating this year's films. Dewey, in his early thirties, still lives in his parents' house and pleads with his sister to stop teasing him. As Sidney's sole male protector, Dewey is obviously no match for the sophisticated killer. In one scene, he hoists the American flag over the town, assuring Sidney that she will be safe. Such assurances are contradicted only moments later when Sidney arrives at school and is startled when a person runs by wearing the killer's costume. After an unsatisfactory conversation with Billy, Sidney retreats to the restroom and hears offscreen sounds of the killer breathing and whispering her name. The source of these sounds can't be located, by her or by us, until the killer steps down, becoming visible in the space underneath the stalls. In this way, the film renders the space of the high school no safer than the young women's upscale suburban homes.

In the culminating scene, Sidney—the iconic "Final Girl" theorized by Carol Clover as "the one who did not die" and who resourcefully fights back (35)—is able to mimic the killer's use of offscreen space and sound to reclaim the home. In doing so, like Mullen from *Ransom* or Karl from *Sling Blade,* she adapts the violent techniques of the vigilante in order to save a child—in this case, herself. This climatic scene is set at a party that is held, once again, in a parent-free home. As the teens assemble around the television to watch *Halloween* (whose influence informs countless aspects of *Scream*), the musical motives of that film match *Scream*'s plot details as they unfold here, such as Sidney's decision to have sex with Billy Loomis, the murder of Sidney's friend Tatum, and the stabbing of Dewey in the back. Ultimately, Billy and his friend Stu unmask themselves as the killers and admit having killed Sidney's mother in retaliation for her affair with Billy's father, Hank. As Billy explains, "Maternal abandonment causes serious deviant behavior," recalling the subtler forms of "blaming the mother" for the problems faced in *Independence Day*.

Sidney is able to reverse the terms of the killers' plan using the voice-distorting box to mislead them and donning the murderer's costume. She electrocutes Stu with the television set (which is still playing *Halloween*) and fatally shoots Billy before rescuing her father. The final musical theme plays over the closing credits: "We are, we are, we are, we're just children /

Fighting our way around indecision / We are, we are, we are rather help-
less / Stay kids forever / A whisper to a scream."

The screams of teenage girls are no less harrowing in Twentieth Century Fox's version of *The Crucible*, directed by Nicholas Hytner, another
movie that explores the iconic value of children in relation to the idea of
home and the incompetence of big government. Originally written in 1952,
Arthur Miller's play provided searing commentary to Senator Joseph
McCarthy's congressional hearings that scoured the entertainment world,
the military, and Congress itself for communists. Miller situated his Cold
War drama in the late-sixteenth-century Salem witch hunts, but the contemporary focus of his work was unusually transparent. Even in the fifties,
people were calling McCarthy's search for victims a "witch hunt." Hytner's
adaptation adds another layer of newer social and political anxieties. Wrote
Janet Maslin in the *New York Times*, "This agile film is so simply, abstractly
rooted in Salem's soil that it becomes free to suggest anything from the
impact of religious fundamentalism on politics to the hysterical excess of
tabloid television" ("Bewitching" C16). Peter Travers suggested in *Rolling
Stone* that the range of controversies connected to the film include political
correctness, accusations of child abuse at day-care centers, affirmative
action, abortion, and AIDS ("Devil" 89). Hytner's *The Crucible* also chronicles the demise of the image of home as a safe place, replacing it by the
same siege mentality we have seen dramatized by the other films analyzed
in this chapter. As Miller commented, "The enemy is within, and within
stays within, and we can't get out of within" (qtd. in Navasky H58).

As in *Scream*, *The Crucible* locates youthful transgression in the open
woods beyond family walls, here in voodoo rituals facilitated by the African
slave Tituba (Charlayne Woodard). Shot through blue filters, the long-
distance framing of this panorama captures the eagerness of the young
townswomen. As each woman utters the name of the man she hopes to
marry, she throws a bough into a cauldron. Only Abigail Williams (Winona
Ryder) wants something more, the death of Elizabeth Proctor (Joan Allen),
wife of John Proctor (Daniel Day-Lewis), with whom Abigail had had a
brief affair. This adulterous liaison threatens the family structure and
endangers the community, just as the adulterous affair between Maureen
Prescott and Hank Loomis would do in *Scream*. While Sidney remained
innocent of adulterous longings in *Scream*, Abigail's illicit desires here trigger social chaos.

During a frenzied moment of nude dancing, Abigail's uncle, the Rever-
ent Parris (Bruce Davidson), espies the young women; the next day, his suspicions that they may have been involved in witchcraft are confirmed when

several village children (including his daughter Betty) cannot wake up. Confronting Abigail, he reveals that a faction in Salem Village opposes him and "will destroy me now if my own house turns out to be the center of some obscene practice." To placate townspeople and clear the girls of the charge of witchcraft, he brings in the Reverend John Hale (Rob Campbell), a self-proclaimed authority on the occult.

Parris's attempt to navigate the contentious politics of Salem Village backfires when the girls, once confronted by Hale, band together in a collective lie, claiming that Tituba roused them with "those damned Barbados songs." Whipped into submission, Tituba confesses that the devil indeed has visited her. As the white girls follow Tituba's lead in naming names and recounting visits from evil spirits, they experience a degree of autonomy and independence usually denied to young Anglo women of the seventeenth century. For instance, Abigail almost wins back the affections of her former lover and soon finds it possible to intimidate property owners and other respected townspeople, including the judge in charge of the proceedings. A few elders of the Salem community exhibit reason and note the fallibility of the girls' testimony. But misplaced faith in the "innocence" of the children (coupled with their own self-interest) blinds most adults to the young women's gamesmanship. In his article on the film, Victor Navasky wrote that *The Crucible* most concerns "the fortitude it takes to protect the innocent and resist unjust authority" (H58).

In the frenzy of "unjust authority," court officials even disregard Hale—a sort of "expert witness." With their reputations hanging in the balance, provincial government members harangue the accused, "If you know not a witch how do you know you are not one?" Proctor attempts to expose Abigail's true motives for accusing his wife of witchcraft, protesting that "the little crazy children are jangling the keys to the kingdom" and recruiting his house servant, Mary Warren, to testify that the girls have actually been engaged in a prolonged fiction. When Reverend Danforth (Paul Scofield) queries, "This child [Abigail] would murder your wife?" Proctor replies, "That is not a child," admitting that his wife cast out Abigail because of their adulterous relationship. A close-up of Danforth reveals how difficult it is for him to consider Abigail as a young woman capable of intense sexual desires rather than as a child. Abigail is finally saved in court when Mary Warren recants her testimony and accuses Proctor himself of witchcraft, an act that also allows Danforth to save face by silencing the dissident. After this, John Proctor refuses Abigail's invitation to abscond with her to Barbados and accepts his fate. He is hanged, along with other innocent villagers who have refused to confess.

The audience could find *The Crucible* a story with resonance, even if the memory of the Blacklist had faded. The tale presents proto-governmental representatives as hypocrites acting on sanctimonious ideas and in their own self-interest. This government can be manipulated by those who wish to increase their land holdings, become authorities in matters they know nothing about, and realize private ambition. Still, although Miller's story captured the rising distrust of governmental authority, the film did not play well and grossed only $7 million. Of the films we have discussed, *The Crucible* goes furthest in dramatizing the pervasiveness of government corruption and the perils of resisting the weakening of due process. Unlike *Independence Day*, *The Crucible* dooms any possibility of resistance and rewards heroism with death. Whereas *Ransom* and *Sling Blade* restore the life of the family, even as the protagonist faces imprisonment, in *The Crucible* the social order has been irredeemably damaged: in a final scene, villagers dramatically stick a knife into Reverend Parris's door as a warning against any future "help." And far from granting its young people redemption, *The Crucible* leaves the fate of Abigail Williams uncertain. In contrast to *Scream*, which kills off its miscreant teens, *The Crucible* metes out no justice to sinners or to saints.

Conclusion: No Place Like the Homeland

However tranquil domestic life may have seemed this year, there was an ever-deepening sense of insecurity and anxiety tied to the ideas of nation and home. Government officials—and institutional authority in general—were held not merely in suspicion, as they had been during the 1960s, but were also regarded as weak, emasculated, corrupt, violent, and hypocritical. As government and citizenship were being redefined in terms of private business and individual action, the family was becoming an elevated player, with children functioning as the ideal citizens. To an extent, children and the family have always been at the symbolic and economic center of the American Dream, but defending them now seemed the means of justifying national self-defense, no matter what form that action might take. What's ironic is that this occurs even as films were positioning families as needing defense from a corrupt government.

Moreover, home, hearth, the girl left behind—all things that had been routinely feminized—were becoming gendered in more complex ways onscreen. Now, everyone could fight to defend the home front: women of all colors, rich male bankers, eco geeks, and ex-cons. Defense was becoming a fantasy of equal opportunity at the same time that its heroic dimensions were being wrested away from the hands of big government and put into the hands of screen vigilantes.

Where the films of the year differ from one another is in their responses to the idea that the home front was vulnerable to evildoing, or complicit with it. *Independence Day* and *Ransom* leave the wrongdoings of home, family, and state largely undeveloped. *Sling Blade* and *The Crucible* face these misconducts unflinchingly, showing that the emerging dangers come from, as one of the few sympathetic characters puts it, "ourselves, and *not* the Devil." What these films leave behind them is a paradox. For the image of the homeland to be secure, it must itself be insecure. Such an emptying-out process requires fear and vigilance, passivity and aggression, the lack of authority alongside its muscular reinvigoration. The films show just how well ensconced dread and anxiety about the homeland already were. We could certainly not chant "There's no place like home" with a sense of security and relief.

NOTES

1. Writes Dowell, "This First Lady also fulfills a great national fantasy, if polls are correct—she expires in midpicture" (40).

2. According to Roz Kaveney, although *Mars Attacks!* seems to parody *Independence Day,* the *Mars Attacks!* script predates that of *Independence Day* (44).

3. See Kathleen Rowe Carlyn's discussion of how *Scream* "narrativizes a girl's sense of boys as mysterious and unknowable entities."

4. This scene, a reference to a similar moment in *When a Stranger Calls* (1979), is one of *Scream*'s countless references to other films, including *Halloween* (1978), discussed by Wee.

1997

Movies and the Usable Past

JOSÉ B. CAPINO

The animus of this year is a peculiar mélange of death, commerce, and corpses. Princess Diana was killed in a car crash after being hounded by paparazzi through the streets of Paris. Five days later, Diana's friend, Mother Teresa, passed into immortality and quickly began her journey toward full-fledged sainthood. The Heaven's Gate cult took a less conventional route to the afterlife, staging the largest mass suicide in U.S. history. Believing they could rendezvous with a spaceship tailing the Hale-Bopp comet, Marshall Applewhite and thirty-eight of his followers (many of them professional web page designers, some of them neutered) took poison with their applesauce and left a collective suicide notice on their web site.

The death of Chinese leader Deng Xiaoping seemed equally poetic, having occurred just months before the expiration of the vestigial British Empire in Hong Kong and the territory's concomitant return to the mainland. Deng's contradictory legacy of economic liberalization and the Tiananmen Square massacre set the stage for a dance of attraction and repulsion between his country and the United States. Following Deng's demise, President Bill Clinton visited China, pushing a free-trade agenda while perfunctorily rehearsing criticism of China's human rights record. The financial crisis that hit the Asian region in the middle of the year made Clinton's proposition all the more appealing to China and the other countries of the Third World. A similar calculus of currency and corpses was seen in the high-profile trials of Timothy McVeigh and Terry Nichols. The process disinterred memories of the 168 souls who perished when the duo bombed the Oklahoma City federal building. Still more corpses were kept in circulation thanks to widely covered investigations into the previous year's killings: child beauty queen JonBenét Ramsey, an American infant at the hands of a British au pair, a woman during the Atlanta Olympic Park bombing, and 230 people in a Paris-bound TWA flight out of New York.

Major events in the domain of culture also revolved around narratives of life, death, and rebirth. The demise of the videocassette recorder was predicted anew with the American debut of the digital versatile disc (DVD). Beat luminaries Allen Ginsberg and William S. Burroughs went gently into the good night, while the Notorious B.I.G., the hip-hop superstar, was violently murdered when coming home from a party. The twentieth anniversary of Elvis Presley's death predictably inspired new rumors that he was still alive. On the Great White Way, old musicals such as *Annie* and *1776* were mounted in new revivals while Disney's animated film *The Lion King* and Robert Louis Stevenson's novel *The Strange Case of Dr. Jekyll and Mr.Hyde* each enjoyed a new afterlife onstage.

Hollywood made money on the dead by resurrecting them in pictures. Alan Parker's screen version of the musical *Evita* used Madonna to restore to life both Eva Peron's legacy and Andrew Lloyd Weber's 1970s rock musical. Another biopic, Gregory Nava's *Selena,* turned the Tejano singer's death into a star-making vehicle for Jennifer Lopez. Steven Spielberg successfully revived his dinosaur franchise with *The Lost World: Jurassic Park*. Cute extraterrestrials revivified the year's second highest grosser, *Men in Black,* and George Lucas hit pay dirt with a reissue of his *Star Wars* trilogy. Other figures exhumed from Hollywood's crypt via sequels and remakes included James Bond in *Tomorrow Never Dies,* the duo of Batman and Robin, blaxploitation star Pam Grier (through Quentin Tarantino's *Jackie Brown*), Ripley and her alien opponent in *Alien 3,* werewolves in the remake of *An American Werewolf in Paris,* the absent-minded professor in *Flubber,* the comic book Neanderthal in *George of the Jungle*, and the live-action but still myopic title character in *Mr. Magoo*. A man with no Hollywood past of his own, Austin Powers, successfully mooched off nostalgia for James Bond and sixties boy bands in *Austin Powers: International Man of Mystery.*

More sophisticated evocations of old times brought modest returns but better critical notices. With *Boogie Nights,* indie film maverick Paul Thomas Anderson boosted his commercial appeal by renewing interest in seventies pornography and the myth of John Holmes. Curtis Hanson's *L.A. Confidential* channeled American film noir and breathed life into the career of Kim Basinger. In *The Ice Storm,* Ang Lee returned to the scene of the sexual revolution in 1970s suburbia to show how the children of two swinging couples pay dearly for the sins of their parents. The film's death-by-electrocution climax, aided by the forces of nature, befitted Lee's disarmingly moralistic perspective on the heyday of sexual liberation.

Otherwise, and predictably, Hollywood lured moviegoers to multiplexes by churning out its perennial assortment of romance films (Julia Roberts's comeback *My Best Friend's Wedding* and the Jack Nicholson–Helen Hunt *As Good as It Gets*), science fiction flicks (*Contact, Starship Troopers, Event Horizon*), thrillers (*Air Force One, Con Air*), and comedies (*Liar, Liar*, Jim Carrey's collaboration with the transgressive Farrelly brothers). On the independent front, the critical acclaim and profits fetched by playwright Neil LaBute's *In the Company of Men* fed the dreams of the country's young directors. Films populated by African Americans and clearly aimed at that demographic performed well at the box office, among them *Kiss the Girls, Soul Food, Eve's Bayou, Booty Call, How to Be a Player*, and *Good Burger*. But their commercial success was not necessarily a good thing, according to Spike Lee, who publicly criticized some of the comedies for being "coonish" and "clownish" (Judell; Merida).

While this diverse corpus of films does not easily suggest a common theme or represent a specific development in Hollywood aesthetics and industry, a striking constellation of historical films commands attention, first and foremost for their authorial pedigree: Steven Spielberg's *Amistad*, Spike Lee's *4 Little Girls*, Martin Scorsese's *Kundun*, and James Cameron's *Titanic*. By linking these films to some of the year's most pressing issues and elucidating their discourses on the essential stuff of history—corpses, commerce, catastrophe, and the like—one can explore and answer questions of how and for what purpose they summon the usable past.

Amistad: Conversations and Reparations

Amistad and the year shared at least two significant things: dramatic trials involving Blacks and talk of doing good by those whose ancestors were slaves. Tony P. Hall, a white Democratic congressman from Ohio, introduced a one-sentence resolution asking the government to apologize "to African Americans whose ancestors suffered as slaves under the Constitution and laws of the United States until 1865" (U.S. Congress H3890). Hall's proposal coincided with a "great and unprecedented conversation about race" initiated by President Clinton to formulate policies he hoped would improve race relations in twenty-first-century America ("Remarks" 876). Clinton's project led to innumerable town and campus meetings, and mandated the establishment of a seven-member Race Initiative Advisory Board.

As these conversations proceeded across the states, Dreamworks SKG promoted and released a film about a key moment in the history of racial conflict in America. *Amistad*, like the inquiries of Clinton's race commission, centers on a public hearing about the plight of racialized bodies in America. While its putative subject is an 1839 court trial over the ownership of African slaves marooned in New England, *Amistad*'s politics are very much of the present, showing many of the problems that lurked behind Clinton's earnest yet misguided attempt to realize the fantasy of multiculturalism in late-twentieth-century America. One great difficulty of Clinton's project is the very idea of instituting a conversation—a sober discourse—in response to the spectacular conflagrations of racial conflict around the beating of Rodney King and trial of O. J. Simpson. Clinton imagined that town hall meetings and campus forums might work as a kind of talking cure. The therapeutic effect of articulating grievance, the enlarged understanding of race relations and conflicts that comes from dialogue, the citizenry's voicing of its difficulties and desires to its leaders—these practices of locution would somehow help in bridging the gaps within the nation, in realizing Clinton's dream of "one America in the twenty-first century" ("Remarks" 877).

Setting aside the improbability of such expectations of the power of talk, Clinton's dialogue expected articulate political subjects and, moreover, assumed that the problems of race were properly "speakable" in the first place. One finds in *Amistad* a symptom of this faith in the instantaneous legibility of race, the polity's locution, and an innate desire for dialogue. Spielberg places at the center of his narrative the interactions between upstart defense lawyer Roger Baldwin (Matthew McConaughey) and a black slave Cinque (Djimon Hounsou), nominal leader of the captives who earlier rose in mutiny aboard the schooner *La Amistad*. Spielberg imagines their relationship as one that transcends professional boundaries and is grounded in a primal sense of empathy and understanding. One particular episode functions as the film's main set piece. Crucially, before this scene, any effective communication between Baldwin and Cinque had been impossible—and the absence of subtitles for the Mende dialogue up to this point in the film echoes that deadlock. Yet in this scene, Baldwin and Cinque shatter the linguistic and cultural barriers between them through a decidedly symbolic and magical combination of primitive signs and psychic intuition. Baldwin asks Cinque, who understands only the Mende dialect, to help him prove to the court that he and the other captives did not originate in Cuba (where slave trading is allowed by the Spaniards) but rather came from West Africa (where slave trading is prohibited by the British).

The problem is instantly solved when the two figures rehearse a moment from another famous Spielberg film. Cinque reaches out to Baldwin, places his lawyer's hand over his heart, and speaks to him in Mende, indicating that he has come to understand the subtleties of Baldwin's case. In the ensuing exchange of hand gestures and sketches in the dirt, the two magically sustain a two-way conversation. "This is your home. You came all the way from here," Baldwin tells Cinque while pointing to a spot on the

An unlikely conversation. Roger Baldwin (Matthew McConaughey) and the African Cinque (Djimon Hounsou) break the language barrier with gestures, dirt sketches, and the magic of empathy in *Amistad* (Steven Spielberg, DreamWorks). Digital frame enlargement.

ground representing Africa. The latter walks a considerable distance away and says, in Mende (his dialogue suddenly accompanied by English subtitles): "This is how far I've come." His pacing translates Baldwin's words into a comprehensible physical distance and affirms the depth of their new-found understanding and empathy.

The successful connection between two creatures from disparate worlds recalls a signature Spielberg scene from *E.T. the Extra-Terrestrial* (1982). There the homesick alien puts together his first sentence in English and, his long fingers indicating his place of origin in the heavens, raspily says: "E.T., phone home." Spielberg's gesture of recycling this treasured moment has the unintended effect of underscoring the impossibility and sheer ridicu-lousness of his bourgeois fantasy of a smooth and easy racial dialogue in the midst of great social and political turbulence. Would that bridging the vast divide between *Amistad*'s African slave and Yankee lawyer—or, for that matter, between a white soccer mom and an African American mother with three jobs—were as easy as E.T. gesticulating with his limbs and typing his ideas through a Speak 'n' Spell toy!

The unchallenged assumption about the preconditions for the dialogue that Clinton envisioned was just as problematic as the implicit and, again, all too easy consensus-building behind his conversation on race. The implicit orientation of this bourgeois talk was, mistakenly, to tame the insurgent energies of racial outrage and grievance—the disarming rage that exploded in the L.A. riots and detonated the Oklahoma City federal building, among others—into pat, constructive lessons for a multicultural society. The fate of one minor character in *Amistad* is arguably symptomatic of the manner in which Clinton's multicultural state hoped to reform those insurgent, raced bodies that denounced and revolted against state-dispensed justice and the hidden hierarchies of race. Running parallel to the story of how some conscientious Americans won the freedom of the slaves, the film tracks the containment and uplifting of the captive Yamba (Razaaq Adoti) through a self-taught course in cross-cultural pedagogy. Early in the film, when the captives first enter the courtroom, Yamba grabs the Bible held by the bailiff. The captive is from this moment built up as the historical counterpart and, indeed, ancestor of the film's modern-day black audience. Throughout the film, his relationship to the Bible changes, paralleling the African captives' progress toward liberation. At first he is shown as not having any idea what a book is and for what it might be used. One day, he suddenly decodes the entire story of Christian salvation just by following the sequence of illustrations. His innate predilection toward Christianity serves as a relay between the West African subjects of the film and the more familiar figure of the pious, suffering, self-educated, and ultimately triumphant Blacks of the present. The latter is, of course, precisely the kind of spectator hailed by this ostensibly prestigious black heritage film. Yamba, ever committed to words rather than to violent deeds, is precisely the splendid vision of the black subject that might be generated from the transcriptions of Clinton's palliative racial caucus. Not so much a separate character from Cinque as his calmer, better-scrubbed, literate double, Yamba emerges at the end of the film as a true gentleman dressed in Western attire, calmed by religion and thoroughly transformed from his former incarnation as the rebellious Amistad captive.

There are other parallels between Spielberg and Clinton's projects, beyond their similar conjuring of images of harmonious and compliant racial subjects. Both are clearly invested in projecting multiculturalism's ideals of racial solidarity and a pluralist democracy. Spielberg pursues this goal from the very beginning of *Amistad,* devoting much attention to the formation of the racially diverse and politically plural coalition of the captives' mostly white defenders. The upstart defense lawyer Baldwin reaches out to black journalist Theodore Joadson (Morgan Freeman). They then approach ex-president, now congressman, John Quincy Adams (Anthony

Hopkins) to plead the case before the Supreme Court. Though recalcitrant, Adams eventually joins the fray and with great flourish in the halls of justice secures the freedom of the captives. It is telling that the film's purely fictitious character is the black journalist played by Freeman: this character's participation in the multicultural collective effectively retrofits the story to the racial solidarity politics of Clinton's millennial conversation.

Vinnette K. Pryce, a critic for the African American press, takes issue with Spielberg's multiculturalist pedagogy, particularly with the conciliatory portrait that he draws of this episode from the Middle Passage in order to broker a message of peace for the present. She describes *Amistad* as "the black folks' version of *Schindler's List*" (1993) and, in pointed reference to the director's adopted African American children, characterizes the bowdlerized telling of the Amistad captives' saga as Spielberg's "made-for-his-black-kids holocaust" (21). Pryce is correct in noting that the problem has much to do with Spielberg's insensitivity to his "speaking position" (Elsaesser 179) as a white director teaching black history to his "black children . . . and his white children" (Samuels and Giles 72). He perhaps too uncritically displaces his desire to consolidate his own multicultural (i.e., multiracial) family onto a national polity deeply divided by racial and other differences. Pryce points out that the ultimate effect of Spielberg's recycled salvation narrative is to posit "white folks' benevolence" as the historical lesson not only of the *Amistad* episode but of the larger saga of the Middle Passage. The minority that stood up for the slaves and the sovereign exception that prohibited a specific circumstance of slavery—these aberrations in the *Amistad* case could certainly give the wrong impression about history, Spielberg's good intentions notwithstanding. The questions that should be asked about Spielberg's film and Clinton's conversation are not "How then might one propose to retrieve an edifying lesson from the horrific experience of the Middle Passage?" or "How might one institute a conversation that might help America resolve its racial conflicts?" The questions are, rather, "At what cost should an edifying lesson be salvaged?" and "Why should we just talk about America's racial conflicts?"

The impossible stakes and expectations raised by both *Amistad* and Clinton's conversation cause both projects to collapse. While *Amistad* earned a modest share of positive notices from critics, the crucial box office "vote" pronounced the film a commercial failure, making back only $42 million of its reported $75 million budget (Willis and Monash 201; Bowman 36). The box office losses occurred despite the widespread promotion of the film as an educational supplement for students of American history, suggesting that *Amistad* failed not just as a motion picture but as a piece of multiculturalist pedagogy. Clinton's conversation, originally scheduled to last just one calendar year, was extended by several months through the "Presidential Initiative on Race." Nonetheless, the initiative achieved little more than putting race issues in the headlines and on the government's official agenda.

So what do we find among the ruins of both projects? If we probe *Amistad* for symptoms, the root of the failure may well be a shared, overdetermined will to nationhood that sanctioned what Homi Bhabha describes as a "strange forgetting" of "the violence involved in establishing a nation's writ" (160). The query posed to Clinton's project by *Time* correspondent Jack E. White traces a simple but stunningly instructive counter-logic to the terms of the conversation. "Okay, Mr. President, I'll accept your apology for slavery," writes White. "Now where's my forty acres and mule?" (35). This is the sort of insurgent question that cannot be properly addressed by the demands of either a polite conversation or a piece of multiculturalist pedagogy. What if Spielberg made a film about those who were not saved from slavery? What if, instead of instigating a national conversation about race and burdening the citizenry with the task of explanation, the Clintonian state made an attempt to answer its own demand for narrative about the spectacular conflagrations of racial strife and internal violence that erupt to everyone's great (or feigned) surprise within its borders?

4 Little Girls: **The Wounds of History**

It is through a similarly insurgent question that Spike Lee, America's foremost black director, intervenes in the conversation Clinton hoped to sustain. The manner and rhetoric of Lee's film enjoins a society that has forgotten to remember not just the forty acres and mule but also four precious black girls and the story of their violent demise. What has been done and what more could be done for those who have suffered the sentence of history? In posing this question, Lee evinces radically different concerns from Spielberg's interest in educating the present and future citizens of a multicultural America. The rhetorical means with which he asks this question stands in sharp contrast to the stylistic and budgetary excesses of Spielberg's black history film. Instead of using the grand canvas of a historical epic, Lee makes a feature-length documentary on a made-for-cable TV budget with a correspondingly limited stylistic palette. Expending just $1 million from the progressive documentary division of Home Box Office (HBO), *4 Little Girls* tackles a major flashpoint in the history of the civil rights movement using only talking-head interviews, stock footage, and pans across archival photos. Instead of a flashy Hollywood extravaganza commemorating black history for "generation multiplex," Lee produces an intimate and wildly affecting memorial to the four girls who died in the 1963 bombing of a church in Birmingham, Alabama.

The disarming simplicity of Lee's film contrasts not only with *Amistad*'s visual splendor but also with the visually complex screen historiography that prevailed during this decade, most notably in Oliver Stone's *JFK* (1991) and *Nixon* (1995). The economy of means with which Lee approaches his first documentary feature corresponds less to a simplistic take on the subject than to a clear-sighted—and strategically unequivocal—perspective on the events and their meaning. Lee deals with just two narratives: the progress of the civil rights movement in Birmingham and the brief lives and much-lamented deaths of the four girls, Addie Mae Collins, Denise McNair, Carole Robertson, and Cynthia Wesley. These parallel trajectories establish a direct relationship between the nation's history and the plight of its littlest, most vulnerable subjects. By carefully tracing both paths, the film mourns those who have fallen or those who have suffered the consequences of a historical amnesia enabled by the myth of interracial solidarity. This accounting and redress proceed in a predictable but scrupulous manner. In the first part of the film, each of the girls is introduced by relatives and friends, followed by a description of one stage in the progress of the civil rights movement. After these pairings of victims and events are exhausted, the film covers the details of the bombing, its political repercussions, and the subsequent trial. It then returns to the province of the domestic and the intimate, tackling how the families have learned to cope with the tragedy.

Contrary to conventional documentary predilections for objective distance, Lee courts proximity, aiming at an emotive telling of history that puts past and present on a continuum of mourning. The film's visual style repeatedly echoes this sense of intimacy and contiguity, which are already invoked by the endearing modifier "little" within the film's title. From the opening sequence, the film positions its work as that of a cinematic memorial. The camera pans down and sweeps across the ground to reveal the grave of each of the girls. The movement of the camera is not mechanically smooth but a bit shaky, as if mimicking the perspective of a person approaching the tombs. The shots linger lovingly on the headstones as the picture of each girl appears in an oval-shaped inset. After the visit to the four tombstones, the historical marker commemorating the death of the girls fills the screen and the four pictures seen earlier come directly from it. With Joan Baez's stirring rendition of "Birmingham Sunday"—a song about the bombing—functioning as a dirge, the opening sequence positions us to use this vision of history not only to remember what had been done to the girls but, equally important, to grieve the loss that is also profoundly ours.

Lee's images, beautifully shot by Ellen Kuras, enjoin us to embrace the grief of both the families and the society bereaved by the girls' death. The camera remains especially intimate with the deceased girls' loved ones and with the other Blacks who suffered along with them. We see this dynamic at work toward the film's beginning. As lively blues music plays in the background, the screen is filled with the comely faces of the interviewees, signaling intimacy with them. Carefully the camera observes moments when these faces light up in recollection of the four children. Various snapshots of the girls are presented in a spontaneous fashion, frequently tossed into the frame or manually held up, as if shown to us not by the filmmakers but by members of the girls' families.

In the most disturbing moments of grief, the constantly shifting but always proximate camera seems to console the film's subjects through a zooming motion, drawing us closer to the subjects in a gesture that works analogously as a cinematic embrace. In contrast, Lee frames the very few Caucasian interviewees in more distant, medium shots, shown amidst the clutter of their offices or in the center of an empty courtroom. Alabama governor George Wallace, one of the film's two villains, is shown either in menacing close-ups or in extreme close-ups that crop out significant portions of his face, or in off-kilter medium shots that emphasize his obsessive attachment to the symbolic icons of power in his office (an American flag, the state flag of Alabama, and a portrait of Wallace himself). In a fleeting but impressive shot, Lee shows us the ugliness of this white supremacist. An extreme close-up of the burning tip of the governor's cigar, with the governor's face in the background, presents us with the unflattering image of a raging bull, a grotesque beast full of uncontrollable anger. Just as we have seen how Lee cannot withhold sympathy from his other subjects, here he is patently unable to contain his anger toward Wallace—an emotion he clearly wants us to share. The recourse to caricature in this depiction foregoes objectivity in the service of taking a strong moral stand against the shameless historical figure.

The simple gestures performed by the camera during the interviews may seem elementary in comparison with the films of Spielberg or Stone, but within Lee's documentary, they are dynamic and effective. They stand out because they bear testimonies that restore the magnitude of history to the enumeration of names, dates, places, and events as well as to the stock footage, ephemera, and photographs culled from archives. Most important,

Subjective nonfiction: *4 Little Girls* (Spike Lee, Green Valley) depicts Governor George Wallace as a raging bull. Digital frame enlargement.

the testimonies enjoy full-color prominence and all the cinematographic dynamism the film chooses to afford because these acts of witnessing transparently accomplish the documentary's work of remembering and mourning the casualties of a violent history of racial conflict.

Only once in the film do we see the primacy of these testimonies undermined: when the filmmaker and the coroner serve us the mangled corpses of the deceased. A radical change in the film's visual design punctuates the images of an exploded head and scorched limbs. For about three-quarters of the documentary, right before the death of the children, the archival footage is tinted a melancholy blue. But when the autopsy photos are presented, the images appear "raw," in black and white, unequivocally asserting the incontrovertibility of the images and of the event. (The blue tint does not return for the rest of the film.) In black and white, the unadorned truth looks even more disturbing. It is at this wordless moment that history speaks most eloquently and manifests itself most expressively. This is when Lee, having concluded his survey of macro- and micro-histories, presents the corpses that, in order to stage the triumph of the civil rights movement, have been politely hidden from view. The fatal wounds on the girls' bodies not only register the violence of racism but more importantly bring to mind those gaping wounds in the nation's soul that cannot—

should not—be sutured but constantly felt and tended, to keep complacency at bay.

The contrast to Spielberg's black history film is most striking in Lee's resolution to *4 Little Girls*. Whereas *Amistad* offers the equivalent of a fairytale ending in which the captive's ungrammatical plea to "Give us free!" is honored by the white establishment, Lee's documentary ends pretty much as it began, with the unmistakable denial of justice and a surplus of grief. The suspected bomber's death in prison offers no cathartic resolution. The mourners' testimonies about coping seem less effective in consoling them (and the audience) than in reminding us all of a loss that cannot be grieved. So, while a new dirge about the slain girls concludes the film and completes the documentary's work of offering a "scriptural tomb" aimed at "calming the dead who still haunt the present" (De Certeau 2), *4 Little Girls* wisely avoids depleting the productive energies of outrage and melancholia that it unleashed.

A month after the film went on limited theatrical release, another explosive event in African American civil rights history affirmed the need to sing of the atrocities faced by black bodies. Several white cops from the NYPD were charged with police brutality and obstruction of justice in the case of Abner Louima, a Haitian immigrant who was beaten inside a patrol car and sodomized with a broomstick inside the bathroom of a police station in Brooklyn. The unnerving discussions about the effect of the assault on Louima's excretory system detailed the mangling of another black body and echoed the unflinching recollection of racial violence in *4 Little Girls*. Clearly Lee was right in instituting a different kind of conversation about race: one that lingered on the uncomfortable subject of how African Americans are still living the nightmare of black history rather than approaching the all-too-convenient white liberal fantasy of multiculturalism.

Kundun: Free Trade Dreams, Red Scare Visions

If *Amistad* and *4 Little Girls* deploy history to tackle domestic race issues and make direct references to the past in a vision of racial relations in the present, Martin Scorsese's *Kundun* returns to the past of the Tibetan-Chinese conflict as a way of dealing with the geopolitics of the Hong Kong handover, the worldwide fate of American-vetted free enterprise, and the ascendancy of Red China. Unlike the two black history films, *Kundun* traffics in allegory, projecting back onto the history of Tibet a paranoid vision of Hong Kong and global capitalism's future. Indeed, Hong Kong's transition from British colony to a special administrative region of China in

June registered on Hollywood screens as cause for considerable anxiety. Like *Kundun*, the Brad Pitt vehicle *Seven Years in Tibet* reached back into history to draw cautionary parallels between Chinese incursions into Tibet and the mainland's repossession of Hong Kong. Both biopics featuring the Dalai Lama circulated images of the Chinese military's past atrocities with an eye to provoking comparisons to television images of similarly attired forces descending upon the streets of Hong Kong.

Hollywood's fears of mainland China's irresistible rise, though shared by various concerned parties throughout the world, conform to what Richard Hofstadter calls "the paranoid style in American politics." The film's "heated exaggeration, suspiciousness and conspiratorial fantasy" (3) about the Chinese incursion into Tibet is a thinly veiled diatribe about the Middle Kingdom's threat to the superpower status of the United States and the mobility of its financial and capital interests (as represented in proxy by Hong Kong). While such fears, as represented in the films mentioned here, turned out to have had little predictive value in relation to Hong Kong's fate under the mainland, they do say a lot about both Hollywood's and the United States' relationship to China in the late 1990s.

Scorsese's film begins by establishing the divinity of China's soon-to-be-victim, the thirteenth Dalai Lama. The plot chronicles the search for his incarnation across Tibet. A two-year-old boy (Tenzin Yeshi Paichang) is identified as a candidate. His authenticity is confirmed by his uncanny ability to recognize the previous Dalai Lama's belongings. The story then moves swiftly into a lengthy treatment of the modern communist state's imperialist designs upon what is shown as a haplessly backward nation. This tale ends with the now fourteen-year-old religious leader's (Tenzin Thuthob Tsarong) daring escape and exile to India.

The adult Dalai Lama is presented not just as a holy teacher of the Buddhist faith or a symbol of Tibet's sovereignty but also, somewhat like Hong Kong this year, as a vulnerable figure to whom the defenders of the free world owe succor. This throwback to a binary, Cold War vision of weak and aggressive states incorporates a patently 1990s Hollywood montage of Orientalist tropes, ecological catastrophe, and (post–Cold War) "Red Scare" imagery. Tibetan artifacts and rituals, perpetually amber-lit and fog-shrouded to evoke their imponderable historicity, constitute concrete examples of the territory's fragile cultural heritage. Recurring images of the construction and destruction of an elaborate sand mandala underline this vulnerability to China. Tibet's decimation is staged through a slow-motion sequence in which thick clouds of red liquid overwhelm the pristine waters of a pond teeming with beautiful fishes. This ecological catastrophe signals, in the most literal terms, the peril of "Red" contagion. Similarly, when the adolescent Dalai Lama asks one of his tutors to "tell [him] . . . about China," the tutor replies, "Your Holiness, the Chinese are once again trying to convince the world that Tibet belongs to them. Now they are trying to rewrite history!" Manichean dichotomies of the evil, modern communist Chinese and the good, tradition-and-freedom-loving Tibetans abound in the first scene of Chinese incursion. In the middle of a cultural performance (signifying the endangered Tibetan culture), a messenger rushes in to declare that "the Chinese have invaded." This is followed by a militarized procession. Gigantic Chairman Mao banners loom large, red flags and streamers with communist slogans crowd the screen, a phalanx of stern-faced, robotic soldiers marches in perfect rhythm. As he goes to meet with Mao in Peking, the Dalai Lama's ornate garb stands in sharp contrast to the drab-colored, monstrously big vehicles, utilitarian structures, and drab gray attire of the stern-faced and stiff-postured chairman.

Nowhere are the excesses of Cold War hysteria displayed more blatantly than prior to the scene depicting another Chinese incursion. The scene opens with the Dalai Lama listening to radio propaganda from Mao Zedong (Robert Lin), during which a messenger arrives to announce that the Dalai Lama's father has died. Images of vultures circling an overcast sky soon fill the screen. As the father's corpse is chopped to bits and strewn over the plateau so that the hungry birds may devour it more easily, offscreen dialogue is delivered from four years in the future: "The Communists have taken control of China!" The shock of the father's death—a restatement of Cold War discourse about communism's inestimable threat to the universally valorized nuclear family—is thus paired with an Orientalist image of trauma as a way to particularize the Chinese communist menace.

Scorsese's rendition of Chinese violence owes something to the state of affairs in the pan-Chinese region not long before the film's release, when the People's Republic conducted missile tests and live-fire military exercises in the Taiwan Strait. Responding with the biggest show of naval force in the region since the war in Vietnam, the United States deployed two aircraft battle groups to protect the island nation from possible incursions by the communist mainland. But no armed confrontation between the free world and Red China took place and, by June (less than a month before the Hong Kong handover), President Clinton embarked on a visit to Beijing. Tibet's fate and China's dismal human rights record appeared on his agenda, but overall his visit sped up the post–Cold War thaw in East Asia rather than looked backward, as the film does, to a Free World/Iron Curtain dichotomy.

Within months after Clinton's visit, moreover, Chinese president Jiang Zemin journeyed to the United States, affirming his interest in a cooperative twenty-first-century relationship. This was the happy state of affairs by the time *Kundun* played in theaters. Yet here we need to remember economics and markets. *Kundun*'s unforgiving depiction of the Chinese incursion into Tibet seems particularly ironic when taken in the larger context of both late 1990s Hollywood and U.S. geopolitics. Although it was produced by Scorsese's ex-wife, Barbara De Fina, and made with the director's longtime artistic collaborators, *Kundun* was released by Touchstone Pictures, a subsidiary of the Walt Disney Company. Even as the film was peddling images of Chinese imperialism in Tibet, Disney was intensifying its own cultural and economic invasion of China. Michael Ovitz, during his brief term as president, negotiated aggressively to bring Disneyland to Shanghai and expand the company's cable and merchandising operations in China (Barnathan and Miller 51; Stein A17; Steyn 44–46). The *New York Times* reported that Disney even hired former secretary of state Henry Kissinger to advise its executives how to deal with China, following the government's much-publicized threats to freeze Disney's ventures in the Middle Kingdom because they objected to *Kundun* (Weinraub E7).

The economic promise of entering China, with a population of 260 million children younger than fifteen, proved too attractive for Disney to ignore. With Clinton's visit to China, the United States, while faintly echoing *Kundun*'s critical stance on Chinese human rights violations, signaled the inexorable turn of events that would in four short years bring China into the fold of the World Trade Organization. *Kundun*'s "allegorical intention," its invocation of correspondences between Chinese policy in Tibet and its future treatment of post-handover Hong Kong, could thus be counted as yet another case of the Hollywood culture industry concealing, and thus abetting, the work of U.S. economic imperialism. Following this line of reasoning, the film's invocation of the 1989 Tiananmen Square massacre through images of Tibetan carnage provides a smokescreen for the mercenary work of Disney's Magic Kingdom. The film's historical account of China's Red Scare and Yellow Peril—its political and racial threat— occludes the West's own record of imperialist violence and its longstanding complicity with the race and regime that it vilifies. There is no need, however, for *Kundun* to traffic in such hysteria or for an analysis of the film that adopts its dichotomies. In truth, the fate of China's political economy was in far greater alignment with that of the West than either the film or its white liberal makers would acknowledge. Deng Xiaoping had initiated in 1978 a program of economic liberalization that facilitated its "tumultuous entry and incorporation into the world market" (Harvey 120–21). From the mid-1990s and onward, American business interests took great interest in China as it opened up virtually the entire country to direct foreign investment of any type and gave access to its enormous internal market. Since Deng had already instituted several waves of neoliberal reforms during his long tenure, his successor Jiang's cooperative dance with Clinton was emblematic of further compromises with neoliberal rules of international trade rather than of a distinctly post–Cold War breakthrough.

One may also view Hollywood's and Washington's diverging views of China as a product of ideological differences within America's pluralist democracy. Indeed, if one were to give 1990s Hollywood some credit for its advocacy of human rights in Tibet and the cause of the Dalai Lama—including Richard Gere's highly publicized support of the religious leader, and Steven Seagal's ambivalently received posturing as the reincarnation of a Tibetan lama—then *Kundun*'s deployment of history would have to be considered as the brave, though unsuccessful, effort of an art-house aficionado to produce a patently uncommercial Dalai Lama biography (without a single star, except perhaps for its Philip Glass score) with a strong, cautionary message about liaising with the Chinese communist state. The tremendous risk of such an effort is affirmed by the film's very modest box office take: less than $5.7 million of its reported $28 million budget.

Both of these perspectives, and others that might be equally tenable, should not miss a final, ironic, historical development marked by the Dalai Lama biopics. Both *Kundun* and *Seven Years in Tibet*, with their worldwide publicity and multimillion-dollar budgets, register the incarnation of the Dalai Lama as a commodity on the American market. Spiritual leader, he's also a book author, video guru, inspirational speaker, New Age icon, and world peace mascot. Sadly, this peregrination into the world of products and platform politics may be the only sustainable form of rescue or refuge that Hollywood and neoliberalist America can (or chooses to) offer the Dalai Lama and the Tibetan people. Most disturbing, we find the Dalai Lama, China, and the United States harmonious in a common faith in a global exchange of affective objects (such as media) and capital. Here, perhaps, is where we find the absolute limit point of the *Kundun* allegory's analytic function, or what Angus Fletcher calls its "poetry of strict correspondences" (322). With his screen incarnation in *Kundun*, the Dalai Lama (and, by extension, Tibet) becomes *other than* an allegorical stand-in for Hong Kong after the handover. Instead, the "literal surface" of the Dalai Lama's image "becomes sufficient unto itself," seducing us "away from the allegorical message," moving us to contemplate him as a fetishized exotic object akin to the mass-produced, infinitely silk-screened likenesses of Bob Marley or the Guru Maharaji (317, 313).

Titanic: Class Critique, Millenarian Fantasy

If *Kundun*'s detour through the Tibetan past yields a hysterical cautionary tale about America's new partners in globalization, the spectacular antiquarianism of *Titanic* also tackles the intersection of money, politics, and epochal change but retrieves a very different message from history. The preferred reading of James Cameron's *Titanic* can be summed up quite succinctly: decadence sinks the ship. The film visualizes the history of the ill-fated vessel as a grand tragedy brought about by the upper crust's extravagance and their indifference toward the working class. Cameron himself acknowledged the film's "leftist" posturing, jocundly remarking that the film was "holding just short of Marxist dogma" (Maslin, "*Titanic*" E18).

If one were to take Cameron at his word, the twentieth century's highest grossing and most expensive film is also a critique of capitalist greed and its attendant social inequities. Following this logic, the film ostensibly proffers both a spectacular rendition of class history during the gilded age and a parable for the affluent West of the late twentieth century. Nevertheless, Laurie Ouellette contends that the film's ideological work falls radically short of Cameron's stated ambitions: *Titanic* ultimately "distorts and obscures the realities of class" by promoting "the idea that 'true love' exists independent of class relations, obscuring the ways money, social status, and education influence dating and marriage patterns" (185, 181). Instead of purveying "subversive" ideas as Cameron claims, the film, she says, traffics the "myth of American classlessness" and the idea that "class was a phenomenon of the past caused by cold-hearted, status-obsessed individuals," thus "promoting the illusion that the United States is now a classless society" (185, 171).

But her negation of Cameron's putative—and ironically expressed—authorial intent does not survive careful scrutiny, nor does it hold up against the scrupulous consistency of the film's discourse about class. A close analysis of *Titanic* shows that the film's explicit and implicit critiques of class antagonism are in fact encoded within many of the film's registers, from narrative to mise-en-scène. The possibility of the successful integration of these critiques into the economy of a $200 million prestige film must be entertained rather than dismissed. Cameron's extraordinary aptitude for mining the conjoined economies and logics of Hollywood pictures and capital allows him to resolve these contradictions. It is worth noting at the outset that the exposure of class antagonism is what distinguishes Cameron's *Titanic* picture from its predecessors (principally *An Affair to Remember* [1958]). Instead of blaming the innumerable deaths on a communication failure between the crews of the *Titanic* and the nearby *Carpathia*, Cameron's film explicitly indicts the ship's owners and builders for their complacency, greed, and hostility toward the lower classes. *Titanic* spotlights the insufficiency of the lifeboats, the refusal of the first-class passengers to rescue lower-class survivors, and the imposition of a class hierarchy in the evacuation procedures for the ship.

Moreover, the same critique is lodged within the film's narrative structure. The romantic line of action follows two lovers as they attempt to overcome the social constraints that hinder their coupling. Rose Bukater (Kate Winslet), an upper-class New Englander, falls in love with Jack Dawson (Leonardo DiCaprio), an American who has spent the last half-decade living as a bohemian in Europe. Their union is opposed by Rose's wealthy fiancé Cal Hockley (Billy Zane) and her widowed mother, Ruth (Frances Fisher). Rose's mother reminds her that the loss of the rich fiancé in favor of a charming amateur artist would result in humiliating penury for their debt-ridden-but-once-regal family. Cal dangles an expensive blue diamond and flaunts his wealth at every opportunity, trying to intimidate and bribe Rose into submission. The film's second line of action, typically assigned by Hollywood to conflicts of a social dimension, concerns the struggle of the steerage passengers to save their lives by symbolically and literally breaching the boundaries between the rigidly divided social worlds of the ship's various classes. This second plot trajectory dovetails with the first as Rose forfeits her place at the lifeboat to be with her lover and consequently shares the fate of the poorer characters.

The ubiquitous class critique also informs the film's depiction of its secondary characters, for everywhere the working class and their labor are conspicuously visible. Cameron surrounds his film's distinctly Hollywood-bred poor boy/rich girl couple with a cast of colorful émigrés, dedicated servants, and earthy working-class figures. The lower class labor that keeps the ship and high society secure and afloat is tracked relentlessly by both Cameron's narrative and his camera, reinforcing the film's over-arching, class-sensitive perspective. Waiters, stewards, and seamen move in and out of the story along with minor high society figures like Benjamin Guggenheim (Michael Ensign) and the Countess of Rothes (Rochelle Rose). When the ship scrapes the iceberg, the labor of saving the vessel, evacuating the passengers, and maintaining order falls squarely upon the workers. The risks they take are sympathetically catalogued. The passengers in steerage, valorized for their exuberance and humanity, bravely fight the willful and deliberate cruelty inflicted upon them. Prevented from ascending to the upper deck and thus denied all hope of evacuation, they band together and seek escape by locating the ship's possible outlets. Even in their acceptance of doom, these "expendable" working-class subjects act with great dignity: the musicians play until they drown and, in a stirring moment, a working-class mother (Jenette Goldstein) calmly tucks her children into bed for their eternal sleep. This sympathetic figuration of the working class and the ubiquitous presentation of their labor beg to be noted as an ethical gesture, one where Cameron remembers and praises the forgotten figures of the *Titanic* tragedy. (During one of several acceptance speeches at the Academy Awards, Cameron asked the audience to observe a few moments of silence for the victims of the *Titanic*.)

The preferred reading of *Titanic* is so thoroughly cogent that it resists quick assertions that "[the film] distorts and obscures the realities of class" or conceals "the ways money, social status, and education influence dating and marriage patterns" (Ouellette 185, 181). Indeed, rather than tarrying with the film's broadly sketched but compelling image of class history in the gilded age, I will scrutinize how the film salvages the (supposedly) broken dreams of the gilded age to idealize a future that belongs (once again) to the likes of Andrew Carnegie and Jack Dawson. *Titanic*'s pre-millennial re-staging of the collapse of the behemoth invokes the specter of another American century still to come. The untimely death of the fictitious Jack Dawson, a broke but ambitious, talented, and ethical American, creates prosthetic nostalgia for the "self-made" tycoons who rose from the ranks of penniless immigrants in the nineteenth century. The likes of Dawson who, the film implies, never got the chance to realize their ambitions, are designated as the heroes in this repurposing of the *Titanic*. The ship's failed journey is thus transformed into a proleptic one: through the technology of Hollywood special effects, the hubris of James Cameron, and the faith of the film's worldwide fans, the ship sails again, toward the "bold new world of the twenty-first century" heralded by the American president in his State of the Union address (Clinton, "1997" 290).

The millenarian fantasy of restarting the not-yet-concluded American century is conjured by *Titanic*'s conspicuous motif of instantaneous and spectacular renewal, of turning the debris of history into fascinating objects of vision and fantasy. The film stages the recovery of history by reflexively foregrounding the superior technology of seeing that brings us to the ship's largely inaccessible wreckage. We see a surplus of heavy machinery on the Russian research vessel above the site of the *Titanic*'s remnants. The blinking electronic instrumentation and techno-speak inside the submersible craft give credence even to the not-so-authentic images of the wreckage. The camera's lingering gaze on the mangled, coral-crusted steel represents and engenders obsessive attention to the historical artifact and to the history it represents. Cameron employs even the decrepit body of Gloria Stuart, the geriatric actor brought out of retirement to play the elder Rose, in both the film's visual discourse and its publicity campaign to evoke the aura of Hollywood's heritage and the presence of an authentic early-twentieth-century denizen.

The wreckage is magically transformed, to truly awe-inspiring effect, into Hollywood's ostensibly faithful reproduction of the ship. Traveling shots reverse the ravages of time in an instant as mangled barbs and sheets of steel metamorphose into the ship's elegant galleys and impeccably appointed cabins. In the wink of an eye, Old Rose and the ship's stern return to their pristine selves. Admiration of the sheer beauty of the replica and the accomplishment of its fabrication is intensified by our suspicion (or knowledge) of the fidelity of the ship's reconstruction, from the impressive, near life-size scale of the exterior set (just 10 percent smaller than the real thing) to the adherence to original plans and photographs from the ship's builders, to the hiring of the *Titanic*'s original suppliers to replicate its china and carpets.

The picaresque narrative that distributes events across the entire ship encourages profound nostalgia for these technologically generated images of the past, for the knock-off *Titanic* whose destruction we both dread and anticipate. The narrative's tour across the reproduced ship attaches the story of the ill-fated lovers to parts of the vessel that will soon age into artifacts of a lamented past. The lovers first meet at a very unglamorous part of the vessel, its unadorned, patently utilitarian stern. The film's iconic scene, which shows the lovers locked in an embrace as the ship cuts through wind and water, also happens here. So nondescript and unmemorable is this place that even Rose herself fails to remember its significance until she notices that she is hanging on to it in order to avoid being thrashed about as the vessel goes down. While she may not remember, the audience has been taught to see the stern as the equivalent of Juliet's window in Shakespeare's famous play about similarly star-crossed, class-separated lovers. Another one of the film's romantic and nostalgic spaces is the first-class dining room. While it is perhaps the most glamorized of all the spaces where the lovers romance each other, it is important to note that their happiest moments occur at a staircase: the liminal space where the classes meet, a place that signifies the promise of class mobility for Jack and freedom for Rose.

The rich in spirit costumed in material riches: Steerage passenger Jack Dawson (Leonardo DiCaprio) plays first-class escort to the cash-strapped socialite Rose Bukater (Kate Winslet) in a romantic moment from *Titanic* (James Cameron, Paramount). Digital frame enlargement.

The grand historical and emotional tour across these spaces is retraced during the purgative destruction that dominates more than a third of the film's three-and-a-quarter-hour running time. The effortless and instantaneous movement between states of destruction and reconstruction sustains the fantasy of a (re)usable past, an easily renewable history. The tragedy that sinks the ship and abbreviates the coupling of Jack and Rose thus also invokes the happy and prosperous future they could have lived together in the bold new world to come. More precisely, the film conjures the happy and prosperous future they could have lived together as the kind of future *to fantasize about*. In this anticipated future that is nothing but a distorted repetition of the past, the hometown boy strikes gold in the land of opportunity and becomes "the king of the world" once more.

The power of the film's anachronistic fantasy is intimated by audience attachment to the Heart of the Ocean, that oversized diamond that symbolizes both the love of the film's protagonists and the treasure-hunting mission that justifies the disturbance of the wreckage. Feeding a voracious nostalgia for an object that never existed, knock-offs of the fictitious treasure became the best-selling souvenir at traveling exhibits about the *Titanic,* their prefabricated aura outshining those of veritable artifacts from the wreckage. So successful is the film in supplanting history with fantasy that the gift shop at one of the exhibit's stops—the Museum of Science and Industry in Chicago—even felt ethically compelled to remind customers that the cherished emblem had no historical basis. As it turns out, the fictitious treasure produced by that titanic ship of dreams called Hollywood is perfectly emblematic of the collectively cherished illusion that keeps U.S. hegemony afloat even if the nation is sinking in debt, suffering the loss of its dominance in global production and the erosion of its power in global finance, losing its technological leadership role to other nations, and, perhaps most important, failing desperately to live up to its longtime ideal of social equality.

Conclusion

This discussion of four historical films—three fictional features and one documentary—illustrates some of the possibilities and pitfalls of using the past both to legitimize views of the present and propose ways of looking at the future. With *Amistad,* the major challenge for the historical film is in providing contemporary multicultural dreams with a legitimizing founding moment while also projecting an image of the past that does right by those who have suffered the sentence of history. Echoing Clinton's impossible dream of making "one America in the twenty-first century," Spielberg returns to the darkest era in black history to paint a picture of interracial solidarity for his black and white children and all America. Apart from its strained consensus building, his black history film ends up reinstating mythologies of white benevolence in his pursuit of an elusive multicultural American family/nation.

Lee's *4 Little Girls* discovers a more successful and ethical way of staging the past. The documentary restores the magnitude of history to the act of remembering and mourning, provoking in us unsettling feelings about an atrocious event and refusing to bowdlerize the past to win peace in the present. Its calculus of historical representation is remarkable both for its humbling modesty of means and its refusal to offer a palliative message. *Kundun's* hysterical vision of Chinese atrocities in Tibet draws parallels to the possible fate of Hong Kong upon its return to the Middle Kingdom. Ironically, the production of these demonizing images coincides precisely with the intensification of American maneuvers to penetrate and reform China's political economy.

Among the four films discussed here, *Titanic* is literally and figuratively the most successful in exploiting history. It resolves the paradox of being the most expensive film in history while also mounting a convincingly progressive critique of class antagonism. Moreover, it plays ambitious tricks with history and fact by turning the debris of history into spectacle, fabricating prosthetic nostalgia for both scrap metal and special effects, and purveying a fantasy of the "bold new world of the twenty-first century" built upon a rehabilitation of the gilded age spirit. The unprecedented success of the film throughout the world turned a new page in history, produced a global phenomenon, and indicated little resistance to the white American protagonist's unbounded optimism and proclamation that the world was *still* his for the taking.

1998

Movies, Dying Fathers, and a Few Survivors

KRIN GABBARD

Even the alignment of the stars predicted this would be a bad year for father figures. Early in the year, astrologers foresaw trouble for the powerful in the positions of Uranus and Pluto. In June, Chiron and shocking Uranus clashed, carrying the energy of Scorpio, the sign for secrets and sexuality. The conflict between Uranus and Chiron was massively magnified by a solar eclipse that soon followed, a classic warning to leaders. And all year long, Saturn, the traditional father figure, moved in and out of the sign of its debility. This particular weakening of Saturn occurs only once every twenty-nine years, and it too means that leaders are in for trouble (Beversdorf).

There's Something about Monica

Indeed, Bill Clinton, the leader of the free world, did not have a good year. He should have paid more attention to Scorpio. On 26 January, after months of rumors, Clinton declared, "I did not have sexual relations with that woman, Miss Lewinsky." He was responding to reports that Special Prosecutor Kenneth Starr was investigating his relationship with Monica Lewinsky, suddenly America's most notorious White House intern. Starr had found nothing illegal in the involvement of Bill and Hillary Clinton in the Whitewater land deal, the original impetus for his appointment as special prosecutor. But after Paula Jones claimed in a sexual harassment suit that Clinton had propositioned her and shown her his penis when she was an Arkansas state employee and he was governor, Starr switched gears and sought evidence that Clinton had perjured himself when he denied Jones's charges in court. In order to build his case, Starr turned to Lewinsky's claims that she had fellated the president and that he had inserted a cigar into her vagina. When Clinton testified before Starr's grand jury that Lewinsky's account of their relationship was largely true, after having denied it in a 1997 deposition, the special prosecutor recommended that articles of impeachment be filed. On 18 December, the Republican-controlled House of Representatives voted out two articles of impeachment against the president.

In spite of his troubles with Starr and the Republicans, Clinton consistently scored high in popularity polls. And no wonder. Most Americans saw the cries for impeachment as nothing more than the worst excesses of partisan politics, which they were. Meanwhile, the Clinton administration could claim an American budget surplus for the first time in almost thirty years. The Dow Jones Industrial Average was up 16 percent for the year, setting a record of four consecutive years of double-digit growth. As a large percentage of Americans watched their portfolios rapidly grow, very few regarded the stock market bonanza as a bubble about to burst.

Americans were inundated with details of Clinton's private life and public fortunes throughout the year, but other penises and other presidential affairs also made news. The pharmaceutical giant Pfizer experienced a windfall after the Federal Drug Administration approved Viagra, a pill that helped men gain and maintain erections. The drug sold briskly in spite of early reports that a few men died of heart attacks soon after taking it. The newly perfected use of DNA as evidence led researchers to conclude that Thomas Jefferson had indeed fathered a son by his slave Sally Hemings, as some historians had long surmised. The richest man in America, Microsoft's Bill Gates, who had made his Windows operating system an essential part of Americans' burgeoning dependence on computers, was at the center of an antitrust suit because Microsoft had rigged Windows so that only its own Internet browser could be loaded. In an unrelated confrontation, a man struck Gates in the face with a pie at an appearance in Belgium. Gates scarcely suffered from the antitrust suit. As for the pie, he mildly observed that it "just wasn't that good." He could not have foreseen the competition he would soon face from Google, which first appeared on computer screens this year.

In Texas, Karla Faye Tucker became the first woman to be executed in prison since 1863. Tucker had declared herself a born-again Christian, a claim many took to be sincere. Texas governor George W. Bush refused to stop the execution and publicly ridiculed the woman when asked about her pleas for clemency. In Amherst, New York, a sniper killed a doctor who performed abortions. The Supreme Court refused to hear Robin Shahar's case that she was denied a job because she wanted to marry a woman.

Although Americans might have foreseen the shape of the future in these events, they were more concerned with stories such as the home run derby among two sluggers in major league baseball. The ultimate winner was Mark McGwire, who notched seventy home runs and broke a record set by Roger Maris in 1961. With a hugely successful television series, Jerry Seinfeld was the highest paid entertainer in the country. Fleetwood Mac, Santana, Gene Vincent, and the Mamas and the Papas were inducted into the Rock and Roll Hall of Fame. Frank Sinatra, Sonny Bono, Phil Hartman, Eldridge Cleaver, and Roy Rogers passed away.

Beloved, a film based on the Pulitzer Prize–winning novel by Toni Morrison and starring the esteemed talk show host Oprah Winfrey, was perhaps the year's most celebrated flop. Still, it was a good year for black actors, many of whom landed great parts in high-profile films. More important, more blacks than ever were starring in films outside the hip-hop and "'hood" genres. Eddie Murphy and Will Smith, in particular, were instrumental in leading black actors out of the inner-city wilderness and into mainstream roles. In spite of his early success as a street-savvy homeboy, Murphy had appeared in a succession of flops set in conventional African American milieux. The tide turned after Murphy gave up on R-rated projects and began reaching out to larger audiences, including children. In 1996, he hit it big with a remake of *The Nutty Professor* (playing a part created by Jerry Lewis in 1963) and scored an even bigger hit with *Dr. Dolittle* (reprising a role originally taken by the English actor Rex Harrison in 1967).

Playing a successful labor lawyer in *Enemy of the State,* Will Smith continued a string of crossover hits that began with *Independence Day* (1996) and *Men in Black* (1997). Like Murphy at this stage in his career, Smith regularly played roles that could have gone to whites with virtually no changes in the scripts. Much the same was true for Denzel Washington in *Fallen,* Morgan Freeman in *Hard Rain,* Samuel L. Jackson in both *The Negotiator* and *Sphere,* and Danny Glover in *Lethal Weapon 4.* In *Deep Impact,* Freeman plays the president of the United States, anticipating his role as God in *Bruce Almighty* (2003). Freeman, Washington, Jackson, and Glover had all made their mark in American films in previous years, but never before had so many black actors taken prime roles in mainstream Hollywood films, and never before had so many played characters with limited connections to what most white Americans regarded as black culture.

But Hollywood was still shy about how African Americans should be represented. The role played by Cuba Gooding Jr. in *What Dreams May Come* epitomizes the marginalization of even the most respected black performers. Gooding, first seen welcoming Robin Williams to heaven, is revealed as the Williams character's son, who died as a child several years before his father and has simply chosen to appear to his father as a black man. By putting an enchanted African American at the service of a white hero, and by cutting him off from black culture, *What Dreams May Come* anticipated a rash of "black angel films" (Gabbard, "Black Angels" B15–16). Another solution to the problem of African American representation was to render them, in Ralph Ellison's essential metaphor, invisible. For many years, the music of unseen black musicians has enhanced the amorous interactions of white couples in Hollywood films. *Pleasantville* provided one of the most elaborate examples of the practice, using the music of Miles Davis, Lloyd Price, and Etta James to add a sense of mystery, romance, and the forbidden to the lives of the white residents of a 1950s TV sitcom. Although no African American actors appear on the screen, the music of Blacks dignifies and legitimizes what is essentially a civil rights movement for white people (Gabbard, *Black Magic* 90–104).

In a stunning reversal of this tradition, Spike Lee used several compositions by the white composer Aaron Copland to transform the story of the conflicts between a young African American basketball star (Ray Allen) and his mostly absent father (Denzel Washington) in *He Got Game*. Having been convicted of killing his wife, Washington's character is imprisoned at the beginning of the film, still another paternal figure under assault in the year's roster of films. In *He Got Game*'s most memorable juxtaposition of music and action, a group of black youths fast-break, trash-talk, and slam-dunk their way through a game of playground basketball, while the audience hears Copland's "Hoe-Down" from his ballet suite *Rodeo*. Such a dramatic connection between white music and black athleticism would have been unthinkable in films by most white directors and probably even in the films of black directors who lack the provocative imagination of Spike Lee.

In *Smoke Signals,* for one of the first times in history, Native Americans did not function simply as accoutrements to a white hero's ego. A charming and unpretentious oedipal fable in which Native Americans can be funny without being buffoons, *Smoke Signals* narrates a young man's picaresque journey to retrieve the ashes of a father who had abandoned his family years earlier. By centering on the family dramas of Native Americans and frequently ridiculing its white characters, the film broke away from a long Anglo-American tradition that ranges from James Fenimore Cooper's "Leatherstocking" tales to TV's "The Lone Ranger" and Kevin Costner's *Dances with Wolves* (1990). Many other independent films were equally thoughtful and challenging, especially π, *Happiness, Buffalo 66, Zero Effect, Apt Pupil, Henry Fool, Men with Guns, Next Stop Wonderland, A Simple Plan, The Last Days of Disco, Rushmore*, and *The Ice Storm*. A relatively small film if not an indie, Miramax's *Shakespeare in Love* was one of the year's leading award winners. Unlike the best of the independents, however, *Shakespeare in Love* steered clear of controversy, essentially heterosexualizing a story that might have paid more attention to the young men who played Shakespeare's heroines.

Although two of the most honored films in American history, *Gone with the Wind* (1939) and *The Wizard of Oz* (1939), were screened anew, the year's most important re-release was the restored print of Orson Welles's *Touch of Evil*. The film, first distributed in 1958, had been taken away from Welles and reedited. Most disastrously, the studio layered Henry Mancini's music over the elaborate sound design that Welles had given to the extraordinary shot that took up the first three minutes and twenty seconds of the film. The veteran editor Walter Murch worked with producer Rick Shmidlin to retrieve the footage that had been removed. Together, they reedited it, using as a guide a fifty-eight-page memo that Welles had sent to Universal International Pictures asking for changes after he had been fired. Many critics found the restored version more satisfying than the original release, noting the subtle ways in which the characters took on new depth.

The year also included a boomlet for gay characters and/or a queer sensibility in films such as *Love and Death on Long Island*, *High Art*, *Gods and Monsters*, and *Velvet Goldmine*. Although none of the gay and lesbian characters in these films was heroic, all were treated as complex individuals, worthy of respect and sympathy. In general, however, as has been the case for many years, American audiences were extremely cautious, preferring familiar plots and characters to more original material. Accordingly, the studios churned out thirteen sequels, fourteen remakes, and eight films based on TV programs. There were even hybrids within these groups: *The Mask of Zorro* was both a remake and the cinematization of a television series while *Star Trek: Insurrection* and *The Odd Couple II* were sequels and films based on TV shows.

Father figures were targets in the movies as well as in politics. In fact, it was a major year for oedipally driven films, even if Raymond Bellour is correct when he suggests that every plot is the Oedipus story (93). While astrological hermeneutics offers one way to explicate the films of the year, I am convinced that psychoanalytic theory provides the best way to understand the oedipal rage, masochism, and idealization of parental figures central to *There's Something about Mary*, *The Waterboy*, *Saving Private Ryan*, *Armageddon*, and *Deep Impact*. In addition, changes in racial and ethnic representation in two extremely popular films, *Blade* and *Rush Hour*, show the beginnings of a transformation of the American cinema.

Brothers and Mothers

The third biggest moneymaker of the year, after *Armageddon* and *Saving Private Ryan*, was the Farrelly brothers' *There's Something About Mary* for Twentieth Century Fox. With its worldwide returns of $317 million from a relatively modest $23 million in production costs, Jeffrey Spaulding argues that *There's Something About Mary* may have been the single most profitable film of the year in net profit (53). Although still very much a lowbrow film, *There's Something About Mary* marked a slight turning away from the Farrellys' in-your-face gross-out comedies. The huge success of the film rested on its careful combination of transgressive humor balanced with a highly conventional treatment of romantic love. As Ted Stroehmann, Ben Stiller continued his career of revising familiar notions of the romantic hero. It's difficult to imagine Hugh Grant or Tom Cruise catching "franks and beans"—his penis *and* his testicles—in the zipper of his trousers. Although he also has his romantic moments, the filmmakers inflict pratfalls and humiliations on Ted and everyone else in the film, including a pizza boy (Lee Evans) who masquerades as a cripple in order to get closer to Mary (Cameron Diaz). The only character in the film not savaged is the idealized Mary. Suffering no pratfalls, she is presented as generous, self-sacrificing, and socially conscious as well as beautiful and sexually appealing. Even the presence of several large drops of semen in her coiffure cannot disturb her equanimity. If audiences had not already fallen in love with Diaz in her earlier films, they were definitely lining up to see her maintain her charm and dignity while all around her were losing theirs.

A psychoanalytic reading of the Farrellys' delicate handling of Diaz's character might involve the unconscious pressures on artists who share a mother. When brothers speak to each other, they tend to slip into a more guarded mode when the subject of women is raised. They have, after all, shared the breasts and caresses of the same woman. When making movies together, brothers are likely to put aside conventional male attitudes about women and collaborate in the creation of an idealized woman. Once that woman is in place, they are free to fall back on more traditional male attitudes, as the Farrellys have done with all the other female characters in *There's Something About Mary*, especially the leather-skinned, saggy-breasted, dog-fetishizing Magda (Lin Shaye). *There's Something About Mary* is the most financially successful example of brothers delivering shared oedipal fantasies of an idealized woman to delighted audiences (Gabbard, *Black Magic* 138–41).

Not far behind *There's Something About Mary* in American box office receipts was Touchstone's *The Waterboy*, the first of several mega-hits for

No fishhooks on Mary (Cameron Diaz), with Ben Stiller in *There's Something About Mary* (Bobby Farrelly and Peter Farrelly, Twentieth Century Fox). Jerry Ohlinger's Movie Materials Store.

Adam Sandler. In fact, Sandler had two successful films this year. Although *The Wedding Singer*'s domestic returns of $123 million were no match for *The Waterboy*'s $161 million, it probably did more for Sandler's long-term career. Not only did it pave the way for his "serious" work in subsequent films; in 2006 Sandler transformed *The Wedding Singer* into a successful Broadway musical with songs. The show played at the Al Hirschfeld Theatre for nine months. But audiences for *The Waterboy* were much more interested in seeing Sandler as a character based on "Cajun Man," one of several figures he created for television's "Saturday Night Live." Unlike the vast majority of actors who graduated to Hollywood after an apprenticeship on that show, Sandler is neither an ironist nor an accomplished mimic. As Bobby Boucher, the innocent who supplies water for a college football team, he simply folds his lips over his teeth and speaks in a loose approximation of a Louisiana accent.

In interviews Sandler portrays himself as an uncomplicated fellow who simply wants to have a good time and help out his friends, including his college buddy Frank Coraci, who directed both *The Waterboy* and *The Wedding Singer*. But it is not merely Sandler's innocence that appeals to the young men in that crucial eighteen-to-twenty-five demographic. They take great pleasure in seeing a pronounced underdog succeed. Even more so, Sandler's fans enjoy watching him unleash enormous amounts of anger in many of his films. In *The Waterboy*, his Bobby is an emasculated mama's boy who was long ago abandoned by his father. Having won a pyrrhic victory in the oedipal battle, Bobby now has mother all to himself, even if that mother (Kathy Bates) is overtly phallic. At one point she even serves a roasted snake for dinner, complete with an apple in its mouth.

In fact, with his phallic mother and his untiring willingness to endure constant abuse from bullies, Bobby exhibits many of the classic features of clinical masochism. The film suggests that Bobby must repress a great deal of rage in order to retain his innocence and his child-man status. Only when he is promoted from waterboy to full-fledged player on a losing college football team does that anger take over and find a socially acceptable outlet. Bobby gives the team its first winning season with his astounding ability to demolish opposing players who have ridiculed or otherwise provoked him. On one occasion, Bobby's rage extends beyond the football field when he viciously tackles a college professor who has made light of his mother's wisdom. (What young man in Sandler's audience has not dreamed of wreaking violence on a teacher, regardless of whether or not his mother has been offended?) Although he wins the favors of the aggressively seductive Vicki Vallencourt (Fairuza Balk) at the end of the film, Bobby retains his essentially masochistic role in the shadow of his mother. Indeed, with Vicki he is likely to be dominated by two phallic women. But if he remains devoted to his mother, he continues to be semi-murderous to a range of father figures. When Bobby's natural father finally appears at the end of the film, however, he is tackled not by the son but by the mother. Bobby's rage has been safely contained, even if his mother's has not.

Hong Kong Comes to Hollywood

The rage of the Chinese people against the patriarchal British Empire was also safely contained. Although another type of oedipal conflict characterized this process, I am more interested in how the industry changed its patterns of racial and ethnic representation. When Hong Kong became part of the People's Republic of China in 1997, the city's thriving film industry continued to function efficiently, but many of its most important actors, directors, and technicians left for Hollywood. Chow Yun Fat, for example, the glamorous hero of innumerable Hong Kong films, was not able to make the transition to Hollywood stardom. After awkward attempts at playing English-speaking leading men in *The Replacement Killers* and a few other American films, Chow went back to China for a more successful star turn in *Crouching Tiger, Hidden Dragon* (2000). Jackie Chan, however, had substantially more success. As the single most eminent player in the Hong Kong cinema of the late twentieth century, Chan had already made unsuccessful passes as a star in Hollywood films, and a few of his Hong Kong films had been dubbed into English for American audiences, often with good box office. But it was in New Line Cinema's *Rush Hour*, one of the year's top ten moneymakers ($240 million worldwide), that Chan powerfully connected with audiences beyond Asia. Appropriately, an early scene in *Rush Hour* carries the title, "Hong Kong: Last Day of British Rule."

For all its silliness and familiar genre material, *Rush Hour* is a profoundly multicultural film. Chris Tucker, who stars alongside Jackie Chan and actually received the larger salary, joined the ranks of black actors who appeared in the year's most successful films. As Gina Marchetti points out, African Americans have long been a major part of the audience for kung fu and Hong Kong action films. When theaters closed in African American neighborhoods, Blacks bought or rented Asian action films on videocassette and even sought them out in Chinatown theaters ("Jackie Chan" 138). Indeed, by the early 1970s, Asian action flicks had effectively replaced blaxploitation as the favored genre of inner-city Blacks (Desser 38). Like Bruce Lee before him, Jackie Chan draws on African and African American culture, both for comic as well as for political purposes. If Chan takes a moment to moonwalk like Michael Jackson or engage in a bit of break dancing, he has also purposefully set his films in African and inner-city American locations. *Rush Hour* is typical of Chan's films in providing a prominent role for a Latina woman (Elizabeth Peña) as well as for African American men.

But in many ways *Rush Hour* marked a new direction for Chan. Most important, he was for the first time prominently starring in a film directed by an American and produced within the Hollywood system. Director Brett Ratner declared himself a major fan of Chan and Hong Kong action and permitted the actor to direct his own fight scenes, even allowing him to bring over the crew he had worked with in Hong Kong. A substantial list of Chinese names rolls across the screen during the end credits. Nevertheless, as the employee of New Line, Ratner was much more economical in his handling of *Rush Hour*'s fight scenes. Consequently, the editing of these segments is tighter than in Chan's previous films, and the battles never match the epic length typical of his Hong Kong films.[1]

Another significant difference between *Rush Hour* and its Hong Kong predecessors is the kind of outtakes that run with the credits. In Chan's

Jackie Chan prepares for battle in *Rush Hour* (Brett Ratner, New Line Cinema). Jerry Ohlinger's Movie Materials Store.

Hong Kong films, the outtakes at the end are an important part of the film. They frequently show Chan grimacing after he takes a painful fall or when some object that was supposed to miss by inches lands on top of him. But in *Rush Hour* Chan's sufferings are withheld, and the outtakes mostly show the actors flubbing their lines and laughing out of character. At least part of this switch is explained by Chris Holmlund in her essay on the aging of Jackie Chan ("Project AARP"). Born in 1954, Chan was in his mid-forties when he finally achieved success in American movies. Although he is still performing his own stunts in *Rush Hour*, and although his astoundingly agile body is still an essential attraction, the film was less about kung fu and acrobatics and more about the bonding rituals of the Asian and African American protagonists. At one point, Chan fights several opponents in a room full of large and ancient vases, identified in the exposition as honored icons of Chinese heritage. Chan must use both hands to prevent a vase from crashing to the floor even as his antagonists pound him with their fists. One wag in the popular press pointed out that the "elegantly crafted fight involving strategically placed antique vases plays on ideas of fragility that must have some pertinence" for the aging actor (Lawrenson 60).

What *Rush Hour* lacks in fight sequences it makes up in the inter-actions between Chan and the helium-voiced Tucker. Chan and Tucker seem to click in their collaboration, each making excellent use of the other as foil. Of course, the familiar fish-out-of-water plot mechanics were well established in Hollywood long before anyone had the idea of mixing a Chinese martial arts expert with a hyperactive African American. Like many other odd couples of the American action cinema, the two learn to respect each other as they cooperatively fight off villains, share their preferences in music, and discover that each has a respected father from the world of law enforcement. During the dialogue scenes, Chan even shows a talent for light comedy that was repressed in much of his Hong Kong career. At the climax of the bonding scenes, Chan and Tucker perform a perfectly synchronized medley of arm and hip movements as they saunter along the sidewalk to the tune of "War (What Is It Good For?)" The choice of an antiwar song, performed by an African American group whose grunts Chan knows by heart, is typical of Chan's identification with other diasporic peoples as well as the anticolonialist sentiment that runs through his films.

Still another aspect of *Rush Hour* that unites it with African American culture is its debt to the two Eddie Murphy vehicles, *48 Hrs.* (1982) and *Beverly Hills Cop* (1984). In both films a cocky African American impresses white partners after they initially resist his improvisatory approach to law enforcement. But Chris Tucker is no Eddie Murphy, if only because he lacks the studied cool that Murphy could turn on between his more manic episodes. Tucker, by contrast, is always manic. If anyone filled the Eddie Murphy role in *Rush Hour*, it was Jackie Chan. For example, in *Beverly Hills Cop*, Murphy comes from exotic Detroit to a California precinct house where he is completely unwelcome, just as the Chan of *Rush Hour* leaves exotic China to work with a police force intent on keeping him as far away from the action as possible. By the end, however, it is abundantly clear that the exotic outsider is the only one capable of bringing the criminals to justice. Much as audiences are supposed to sympathize with Murphy in his two films, Chan is meant to be the audience favorite in *Rush Hour*. If this was the year in which a large number of black actors were allowed to play dramatic roles that might otherwise have gone to white actors, it was also the year in which a black actor played the role usually assigned to a white actor in an interracial buddy film. Even more remarkably, the star of a hit movie in America was a Chinese actor with broken English and a long history of making films that criticized Western imperialism.

With the beginning of Chan's highly successful career in American films, and with the arrival of so many talented Hong Kong personnel, Hollywood became part of what David Bordwell has called "Planet Hong

Kong." *Rush Hour* was released in November, but a film arrived in the summer that is just as central to the early stages of the "Hong Konging" of Hollywood: *Blade,* based on characters from Marvel comic books, starred Wesley Snipes as a vampire who masters his blood lust and devotes considerable energy to destroying less domesticated vampires. Produced and distributed by New Line, this $45 million film makes abundant use of martial acrobatics unmistakably inspired by Hong Kong action, especially the practice of sending characters somersaulting impossibly high in order to kick their antagonists, who often fly dozens of feet through the air, usually at an upward angle. Given the history of black fascination with the Hong Kong cinema, it was appropriate that a black actor introduced the kind of action that characterizes *Blade* to a large American audience.

Indeed, as one of *Blade's* three producers, Wesley Snipes specifically requested that the film's action sequences include stunts previously unique to the Hong Kong cinema. The end credits do not include names such as Yuen Wo Ping and Cheung-Yan Yuen, fight choreographers who were soon to become essential to the American cinema. Nevertheless, as with *Rush Hour,* Hollywood found ways to domesticate Hong Kong–style fight choreography. For one thing, the vampires in *Blade* fly high in the air during the fight sequences, a tradition long associated in the American imaginary with supernatural physical powers. And unlike the Hong Kong cinema, *Blade* included many computer-generated effects. In the film's climactic battle, for example, Snipes uses his sword to slice completely through the midriff of the film's villain (Stephen Dorff). The top half of the body flies several feet above the bottom half but then floats back down and reattaches itself. For financial and/or aesthetic reasons, Hong Kong filmmakers never relied on computer imaging for this kind of effect. Hollywood, by contrast, was finding ways to enhance Hong Kong action with its industrialized light and magic, a process it would soon perfect in films such as *The Matrix* (1999).

In fact, as Blade, Snipes wears dark glasses and long, flowing, black leather outfits. Many of the scenes take place in low-tech, often dilapidated rooms filled with gadgets. In this sense, *Blade* anticipates the look and feel of *The Matrix.* But *The Matrix* made stunning use of the services of Hong Kong fight choreographer Yuen Wo Ping and his staff. Even without the Hong Kong personnel, however, *Blade's* world box office of $113 million paved the way for the extraordinary success of Hong Kong action in a number of American films. Indeed, few would have suspected this year that a science fiction fantasy such as *The Matrix,* a cinematized version of the old TV jiggly show *Charlie's Angels* (2000), and even Quentin Tarantino's lavish

Wesley Snipes flies through the air in *Blade* (Stephen Norrington, New Line Cinema). Jerry Ohlinger's Movie Materials Store.

genre hybrid *Kill Bill: Vol. 1* (2003) would borrow so extensively from the Hong Kong cinema.

War Profiteers

Both *Bulworth* and *Primary Colors* address the strange processes by which Americans elect a president. But neither of these films enters into the real-life discourse of presidential politics as thoroughly as did the $70 million *Saving Private Ryan*. The film clearly derives its power from a profound, oedipally driven ambivalence toward fathers who were dying of old age at the end of the twentieth century. Although no one involved with the project could have anticipated its role in the Republicans' attack on Bill Clinton, the film's conservative agenda made it ripe for the picking. In its horrific opening scenes of carnage at the D-Day landing on 6 June 1944, the film seems to promise a critique of the brutality and stupidity of warfare, even of "The Good War." Ultimately, however, the film falls back on old Hollywood myths about the bravery and selflessness of American soldiers under fire. Early on, General George Marshall (Harve Presnell) imports the moral authority of Abraham Lincoln into his decision to risk the lives of several soldiers and an officer in order to bring home Private James

Ryan (Matt Damon) after his three brothers have been killed in battle. Back-lit like a saint in a Baroque painting, Presnell is photographed in a highly idealized headquarters clearly inspired by Norman Rockwell. Although Captain Miller (Tom Hanks) cannot know how General Marshall arrived at his decision, the film suggests that he naturally supports the general's unassailable conviction that Private Ryan must be saved. Nonetheless, the uncritical adulation of father figures such as Marshall and Miller must be placed alongside the extreme violence directed at the men of the "The Greatest Generation" throughout the film. As has been the case throughout his career, Spielberg knew how to make his own oedipal ambivalence connect with audiences.

Unlike most of the infantrymen in World War II, the men in *Saving Private Ryan* admire and protect their captain. As Paul Fussell has written, more than one American officer was killed by his own troops during World War II, a practice that most Americans now associate exclusively with the Vietnam War (109). Spielberg's film suggests that Captain Miller is part of an organic chain of command stretching seamlessly upward to the saintly General Marshall. Back then, the film says, and unlike today, the film implies, there *was* moral clarity, and a large group of men acted upon that morality when they went to war.

Most Americans now believe that Germany and the Nazis embodied pure evil in World War II and that they had to be stopped. At the time, however, most white Americans despised the Japanese almost as much as they despised African Americans. Americans fought the Germans because they declared war on the United States after the Japanese attacked Pearl Harbor in 1941. Few Americans knew the extent to which Germans were committing genocide during the war years. The real horror of the camps was not widely known in the United States until several months after D-Day. Spielberg has surreptitiously relied upon the American memory of the Holocaust to support the morality of the American role in World War II as well as to justify the film's almost total dehumanization of its German characters.

More important for the events of the year, the film makes no apologies for the racism and sexism of American culture in the 1940s. The idealized white males who save the world in 1944 do so without affirmative action or quotas. The film does not even acknowledge the importance of British and Canadian troops, not to mention French freedom fighters, in the days after the Normandy invasion. Nor does the film acknowledge the extent to which the German army of 1944 was drastically depleted after years of intense battles with Russian forces. More revealingly, the film has little sympathy for women. When Private Ryan reminisces about the last time he and his three brothers were all together, he recalls their shared experience of a girl named Alice Jardine. Spielberg and his screenwriter Robert Rodat may or may not have known that Alice Jardine is the name of a scholar who was at that time teaching in the Department of Romance Languages and Literature at Harvard University and who was the author and editor of several important books of feminist criticism. But Private Ryan describes the Alice Jardine of *Saving Private Ryan* this way: "Picture a girl who just took a nose dive from the ugly tree and hit every branch coming down." He then tells the story of how he and two of his brothers surprised the fourth brother as he was undressing Alice in the barn behind the house. The older Ryan had pulled up the girl's shirt and was attempting to remove her bra. When the other brothers surprised her, Alice attempted to flee the barn, but with her shirt still over her head, she ran into a wall and knocked herself unconscious. Ryan/Damon laughs heartily and unselfconsciously as he tells the story.

Placing *Saving Private Ryan* within the oedipal dynamics of its day may help explain its reactionary politics. Many of the men who served in the Second World War were dead or dying by the late 1990s. Tom Brokaw's *The Greatest Generation* was high on the best-seller lists as were several books by Stephen Ambrose, the historian who chronicled the "Citizen Soldiers" who fought in World War II. In his books, Ambrose unquestioningly repeated anecdotes he picked up from aging veterans, including many stories about how they tinkered together spur-of-the-moment solutions to battlefield problems. When Captain Miller uses chewing gun to attach a mirror to a bayonet to get a better look at a sniper, or when he instructs his men on the construction of "sticky bombs," *Saving Private Ryan* is presenting Ambrose's war. Spielberg, Brokaw, and Ambrose allowed baby boomers to believe that their fathers and grandfathers made selfless sacrifices at the same time that they displayed tactical ingenuity during World War II. The year's second biggest moneymaker, *Saving Private Ryan* took in $216 million in domestic box office and $440 million worldwide.

Spielberg's own father had been a radio operator with a B-24 squadron in Burma during the war, and Spielberg himself has indicated that relations between father and son were often strained (Corliss, "I Dream" 62). Perhaps as a result, Spielberg has repeatedly returned to World War II in films such as *1941* (1979), *Empire of the Sun* (1987), *Schindler's List* (1993), and two of his Indiana Jones films. Victor Fleming's *A Guy Named Joe* (1943), which reassured American audiences that their fighting men were not really dying in World War II, was remade by Spielberg in 1989 as *Always*.

Saving Private Ryan marks a moment when Spielberg's obsession with World War II came together with a largely uncritical view of American life in the 1940s. Spielberg's feelings about his aging father may have contributed to his reverential treatment of American soldiers in World War II as well as to his turning away from the polemical style of the World War II films of previous decades. If *Saving Private Ryan* is without antiwar diatribes, it also has none of the giddy satire of Spielberg's own *1941*.

Richard Goldstein has argued that Spielberg may even have included an unflattering portrait of baby boomers among the characters in *Saving Private Ryan*. With his typewriter and his collegiate manner, Corporal Upham (Jeremy Davies) could be compared to the young men who sat out the Vietnam War with student deferments and refused to be tested in the crucible of battle (Goldstein 46). Although he freezes like a coward when he first experiences combat, Corporal Upham ultimately discovers that even the German soldier he had argued should be spared does in fact deserve death. Having learned the lessons of battle, the crypto-baby boomer takes up his rifle and kills the German. Regardless of how we wish to interpret Upham's character arc, the film resembles many other texts from the late 1990s that invite baby boomers to see themselves standing small in the shadows of their fathers.

Nowhere was this supposed disparity between generations more prominently foregrounded than in the trials of Bill Clinton. *Saving Private Ryan* and the attacks on Clinton's character reached celestial alignment when Tom Hanks, upon learning that Clinton had not told the truth about Monica Lewinsky, publicly regretted contributing to Clinton's defense fund earlier in the year. Republican congressmen Lindsay Graham and Henry Hyde were surely inspired by Spielberg's film as they invoked the men who fought in World War II in their attacks upon the best known of all the baby boomers who refused to participate in *his* war. The invocation of D-Day, however, opened the way for the president's attorney, Charles Ruff, to trump the Republicans by citing his own father's actual landing at Normandy. In his defense of the president, Ruff cited D-Day in arguing that Americans had fought and died for the sake of the Constitution and what it means for the country. But as Roland Barthes has pointed out, left-wing mythology is inconsequential (147). At least this year, *Saving Private Ryan* belonged to the Republicans.

At least one other film figured prominently in the case against Clinton. *Wag the Dog* (1997), still in release, was often cited by Clinton's critics after he ordered Tomahawk cruise missiles to be lobbed into Afghanistan and Sudan. Clinton gave the order on 20 August, the same day on which Monica Lewinsky first told a grand jury about her affair with the president. By a remarkable coincidence, in *Wag the Dog* a group of politicians and Hollywood producers create a phony war in order to distract the public's attention from a president's dalliance with an intern. Clinton, however, was attacking Afghanistan in order to kill Osama bin Laden two weeks after he had staged the bombing of U.S. embassies in Tanzania and Kenya. According to intelligence reports, the strike missed bin Laden by less than an hour.

Why the Fathers Had to Die

   Armageddon and *Deep Impact* arrived three years before Bin Laden went from a narrow escape in Afghanistan to engineer the destruction of the World Trade Center and a large swath of the Pentagon. But Americans were already thinking about malevolent forces in the sky bringing destruction to their cities. Both films revel in scenes of skyscrapers and national landmarks laid low. Intriguingly, both films attach fantasies of massive destruction to oedipally charged father-daughter narratives. In Touchstone's *Armegeddon* the threat from outer space is an asteroid, while in Dreamworks SKG's *Deep Impact* it is a comet. But this was only one of many significant differences between the two films.

   From the outset, *Armageddon* unspools at a frantic, testosterone-fueled pace. With a huge initial investment of $140 million, the film was the year's box office champion, earning more than $450 million worldwide by the end of the year. The film's manic tempo is extreme even for producer Jerry Bruckheimer and director Michael Bay. The crew of misfits employed by Harry Stamper (Bruce Willis) has only days to prepare for an elaborate drilling mission on the approaching asteroid, but this does not stop the film from including a succession of scenes in which the more flamboyantly obstreperous members of the crew narrowly escape earthly disasters. Before the two spaceships land on the asteroid, they must stop for refueling at a space station occupied only by a deranged Russian cosmonaut, played with eye-popping excess by Peter Stormare. Only minutes after arriving there, a leak in the station's fuel system leads to a series of spectacular explosions, eventually vaporizing the station milliseconds after the two spaceships take off for their rendezvous with destiny. Indeed, the last half of the film consists of one last-minute escape after another, always recalling the most familiar clichés of the suspense cinema.

   In one of the film's earlier climaxes, men on the asteroid lean over the interior of a ticking bomb with only seconds to decide whether to clip the red wire or the blue wire. (It's the blue wire, but the red one seems like the logical choice right up until the last second.) When Stamper is about to destroy the asteroid by detonating the warhead that his crew has buried inside the asteroid, a sudden eruption knocks the detonator out of his hand and lands him inside a deep crater. His hand rising out of the darkness in a close-up that recalls the beginnings of a *Frankenstein* sequel, Stamper manages to press the button on the detonator with absolutely no time left on the clock. If he had been even one second later, we are told, the asteroid would not have been properly blown off course and would have totally destroyed the human race once and for all.

In keeping with the film's macho hysteria, the politics of *Armageddon* are far to the right, even for a Hollywood blockbuster. When we first meet Harry Stamper, the world's most reliable drilling technician, he is perched on an oil rig driving golf balls at a shabby boat full of Greenpeace protestors. When we briefly see the president of the United States (Stanley Anderson), he is a gray, indecisive bureaucrat with no faith in the capabilities of Stamper and his rowdy crew. *Armageddon* is typical of what Peter Biskind calls right-wing films (48) and Robert Ray has called Right cycle films (296). At least since the 1950s, films from the right have expressed profound mistrust of governmental institutions, including the presidency and the military. Individual solutions by charismatic loner heroes are always the answer.

The most sympathetic character who is *not* Bruce Willis or a member of his crew is Dan Truman, the head man at the space center in Houston, played as a straight-talking good ol' boy by Billy Bob Thornton. When Truman addresses members of Stamper's crew as "cowboy," he means it as a compliment. Unbeknownst to Truman, the nonbelievers in the president's inner circle have given secret instructions to Sharp (William Fichtner), a pilot sent along with the drilling crew. If it appears that the roughnecks cannot drill deep enough into the asteroid before the deadline, Sharp is to detonate a nuclear warhead on the asteroid's surface as the next best solution to the earth's dilemma. When the president's men believe that Stamper has taken as much time as he deserves, military forces ominously march into the space center and take control while Sharp brings out a pistol and sets the timer on the nuclear device. Once again, with seemingly no time left, Stamper overpowers Sharp and convinces him that his crew can still get the job done, which of course they do, in spite of their constant hysterical shouts of "It's gonna blow." As in many of the Right cycle films, the hero's ability to know right from wrong with intuitive certainty is extremely effective when doubters need to be converted. Just in case doubt exists about the kind of men Stamper and his crew most resemble, the camera cuts from the crew to the famous statue of soldiers raising the flag at Iwo Jima. Photographed directly in front of the sun, the warriors of the Greatest Generation take on golden hues.

Women in *Armageddon* are relegated to the role of dutiful daughters, resentful ex-wives, and floozies. Except for the neutered female military technician who blasts off with the rest of the drilling crew, the women work as strippers or not at all. Liv Tyler, who plays Stamper's daughter Grace, anxiously twists her engagement ring while she watches the progress of the team from her seat in the NASA center. But in keeping with the film's constant hyperactivity, in one scene she pounces on Thornton/Truman, throwing him to the floor and demanding that he save her father. Otherwise, she has little to do except look concerned and pretty.

Deep Impact tells its story at a more relaxed pace. The comet is months rather than days away from Earth. Although there is some drilling on the surface of the comet, *Deep Impact*'s end-of-the-world scenario is *not* played out as the heroic efforts of space cowboys. In fact, *Deep Impact* is very much a "woman's film." Directed by Mimi Leder with a budget almost half of what was lavished on *Armageddon*, the film takes a much gentler view of its characters, even espousing a tepidly liberal set of politics. The president, played by Morgan Freeman at his most avuncular, is clearly well intentioned. He and his government have no evil schemes to prevent working-class heroes from getting the job done. Rather, the president and his staff keep the survival of the American spirit uppermost as they make the best of a desperate situation. The film's $320 million world box office, placing it eighth among the year's top grossers, was driven by its gentle but emotionally powerful melodrama. *Deep Impact* is centered primarily around the career of a television reporter, Jenny Lerner (Téa Leoni). Early on she suspects that a cabinet member has resigned to cover up his affair with a woman named Ellie. Jenny picks up this information while strolling through a picturesque Washington park with the cabinet member's wife. The problem is not Ellie, we soon learn, but the approaching comet and the Extinction Level Event that it will cause. The wife mistook the acronym E.L.E. for a mistress. Even the end of the world has been feminized.

At least half of *Deep Impact* consists of characters saying goodbye. Unlike the paranoid, incompetent president in *Armageddon*, Freeman's chief executive has made elaborate plans to place one million Americans along with plants and animals in an "ark" buried deep inside the mountains of Missouri. In several scenes, those who have been chosen to spend the next two years in the ark deliver heartfelt farewells to those who have not. Later, when the astronauts detonate the nuclear device they have buried inside the comet, the explosion succeeds only in breaking the comet into two pieces, a smaller one that will reach the Earth before a larger one. The smaller piece will wreak devastation on the Earth, especially the coastal regions around the Atlantic, but the planet will survive. The astronauts know that the larger piece, however, will put an end to all life. With little time remaining, the crew realizes that their only option is to drive their ship directly into the heart of the comet, giving their lives to save the world. In one of the film's few jokes, an astronaut says, "We'll have a lot of high schools named after us." Each member of the crew then has an extended tear-jerking encounter with loved ones back on Earth. Jenny, the Leoni character, jerks some tears of her own when she gives up her place in the ark to a colleague with a baby. For most of the film, Jenny is part of a network of working women who regularly support each other emotionally and professionally. This includes her mother as well as her co-workers and the wife of the cabinet officer. All that unites Jenny with the one and only significant female character in *Armageddon* is a highly strained relationship with her father.

Early in *Armageddon* A. J. Frost (Ben Affleck) is found sleeping with Grace, provoking the murderous rage of Harry Stamper. While the men on the oil rig are mostly amused, Stamper chases Frost with a shotgun, firing several shots perilously close to the young man who is also an essential member of his drilling crew. The infectious country music that plays in the background while Stamper blasts away tells us that it's all in good fun, but subsequent scenes reveal the extent to which Stamper deeply resents giving away his daughter. In *Deep Impact*, Jenny is estranged from her father, Jason (Maximilian Schell), because he has left Jenny's mother, Robin (Vanessa Redgrave), for a younger woman. In an early mother-daughter sequence, Robin tells Jenny that her father is about to marry a woman only two years older than his daughter. In other words, he has rejected Robin *and* Jenny, choosing a woman like his daughter rather than the daughter herself. In two subsequent scenes, Jenny stubbornly refuses all of Jason's gestures of reconciliation, including several that the film treats as entirely sincere.

As Slavoj Žižek has observed, an object in space with immense destructive power is discovered only after Jenny Lerner has heard the worst about her father and only after Harry Stamper sees his daughter sleeping with another man ("Thing" 1023). The comet and the asteroid embody the oedipal rage of the protagonists. Both films must therefore end with spectacular resolutions of their oedipal conflicts. In *Armageddon*, as world destruction is imminent, the men on the asteroid discover that the remote device on the warhead will not function and that one man must remain to detonate the warhead while the others blast off to safety. When they draw straws to determine who will give his life to save the others, Frost picks the short straw. As the younger man is about leave the spaceship, Stamper pushes him back in, ripping away his breathing device to ensure that he cannot proceed to the surface of the asteroid. In spite of Frost's protests, Stamper has decided that he will die instead of Frost. Stamper is also, of course, turning his beloved daughter over to his rival for her affections. The oedipalization of the suspense plot—as well as the constant infantilizing of Grace—is especially clear when Stamper gives his final orders to Frost: "You go take care of my little girl. That's your job now."

In *Deep Impact*, in the hours before the comet strikes, Jenny's mother dresses elegantly and applies her makeup before silently committing suicide. We also learn that the father has been abandoned by his young wife. The daughter then decides to reconcile with her father, now that he can no longer return to his first love. It becomes clear that Jenny has given up her place in the ark so that she can spend her final moments with her father. She drives to Jason's lavish house on the Atlantic shore just prior to the arrival of the smaller portion of the comet. After still another tearful scene in which Jenny and her father reminisce about the good times, the bad times, and the few "perfect days" they have shared, they hold each other tight as they see the comet approaching. They watch as the sea subsides and then as an enormous tidal wave comes crashing down on them. Jenny cries out, "Daddy!" For Žižek, the arrival of the comet has prevented father-daughter incest, just as the destruction of Harry Stamper along with the asteroid in *Armageddon* has prevented a similar scenario of a father moving too close to his daughter ("Thing" 1024).

The old metapsychology is still with us. The sexual dimension of parent/child dramas is only slightly repressed in our national entertainment, even if we know these dramas best from century-old Viennese narratives. Oedipal dynamics dominated the fantasy films *Armageddon* and *Deep Impact* as much as the historical drama *Saving Private Ryan*, with its desire to provide an authentic experience of warfare. (In the chorus of praise for *Saving Private Ryan*'s D-Day sequence, however, few critics remarked upon the oxymoron of an extremely elaborate collection of cinematic effects serving up "realism.") Regardless of their genre, these oedipally driven narratives had special poignancy at a time when the culture industry was taking special pains to elaborate the achievements of one particular generation of parents. But at the same time that the white sons and daughters were saying goodbye to parents from the "Greatest Generation," the sons and daughters of people from "nonwhite" cultures were actively transforming the American cinema.

NOTE

1. Chan's masterpiece, *Drunken Master II* (1994), edited, dubbed, and re-released in the United States in 2000 as *The Legend of the Drunken Master*, concludes with a seven-minute fight scene that took four months to shoot. Each day produced an average of three seconds of usable film ("Trivia").

1999

Movies and
Millennial Masculinity

CHRIS HOLMLUND

On 20 April, the 110th birthday of Adolf Hitler, Eric Harris and Dylan Klebold executed a plan they had hatched more than a year earlier. Storming Columbine High School near Littleton, Colorado, the two teens killed thirteen people and wounded more than thirty before committing suicide. Having named themselves the Trench Coat Mafia, the eighteen-year-old Harris and seventeen-year-old Klebold fired an estimated nine hundred rounds using two shotguns, a semiautomatic carbine, and a semiautomatic handgun. Terrified students with cell phones flooded 911 lines as more than eight hundred police massed outside. Mercifully, the thirty-plus pipe bombs the young killers had rigged around the school did not detonate. The media could not resist posing larger questions. Why would two white kids in a wealthy suburb close to Denver do such a thing? What was happening to our nation's youth? What shape was American masculinity taking on the verge of what was widely—and anxiously—regarded as the new millennium? How much were the media, violent video games, and the Internet to blame?

By the end of elementary school, it was reported, most children have seen eight thousand murders on various visual media (Cloud, "What?" 39). And from videos that Klebold and Harris had taken before their crime, released in December, it was clear that media violence *really* turned them on. "It's going to be like fucking 'Doom'!" said Harris, referring to one of his favorite video games. "Directors will be fighting over this story!" predicted Klebold. They speculated whether Spielberg or Tarantino would make a better film out of their story. With everyone—"niggers, spics, Jews, gays, fucking whites"—a potential target, the two promised they would "kick-start a revolution!"

Not surprisingly, in May, when President Bill Clinton implored cinema owners to require young people to show photo I.D.s before granting admission to R-rated movies, Americans were not mollified. Nor were they

225

satisfied in June when Clinton commissioned a study on possible links between violent films, video games, and child violence. The killings continued to haunt the American imaginary the rest of the year. Hate crimes by kids and adults—not to mention racially motivated killings by cops—occurred nearly every month. Also troubling, hate had logged on. Right-wing racist and fascist Internet sites had increased by 55 percent the previous year, and local cells boasting a philosophy of leaderless resistance were mushrooming (Cloud, "Trading" 30). Renewed cries for gun control went unheeded; the National Rifle Association even held its national meeting in Denver, despite charges of poor taste in site selection.

Chaos and violence were global themes. In the last days of November, more than 100,000 anti–free trade activists, labor supporters, and environmentalists rioted outside the annual World Trade Organization (WTO) meeting in what became known as the "Battle of Seattle." After months of air strikes, NATO peacekeepers entered the Serbian-dominated province of Kosovo in June only to discover that Serbs had massacred as many as 10,000 Albanians. Boris Yeltsin resigned suddenly as president of Russia on 31 December and designated Prime Minister Vladimir Putin to replace him. China cracked down on the Falun Gong spiritual sect, but continued human rights violations proved no obstacle to the country's membership in the WTO. The United Nations imposed sanctions on Afghanistan for refusing to hand over Osama bin Laden, while U.N. weapons inspectors prepared to resume their work in Saddam Hussein's Iraq. There were deadly mud slides in Venezuela, earthquakes in Turkey and Taiwan, and the West Nile virus arrived in New York. Nearly one-third of the world's population—which by this time had reached six billion—was infected by the TB bacterium, and more than fifty million were HIV positive. Climate change and disease threatened the world.

On the brighter side, the world economy was booming, led by the United States for the ninth year in a row. A less auspicious statistic was seldom reported, however: the income gap between rich and poor was widening rapidly. The Dow Jones average ended the year at nearly 11,500 for the first time, and the U.S. budget showed an unprecedented surplus of $236 billion. The euro was introduced as the currency of the European Union. There were positive political and scientific developments, too. Northern Ireland was granted home rule; Panama assumed control of the Canal Zone; and Doctors without Borders was awarded the Nobel Peace Prize. Human stem cells left over from frozen embryos were the focus of intense research, following the discovery that they could be cloned and perhaps used to treat a range of degenerative diseases.

Sick of more than a year's media coverage, most Americans breathed a sigh of relief when the Senate voted on 12 February not to remove President Clinton from office for lying about his sexual peccadilloes with White House intern Monica Lewinsky. Congress let the independent counsel statute expire. Long before any caucuses or primaries were held the following year, Vice President Al Gore was battling a surprisingly spirited challenge for the Democratic presidential nomination from former New Jersey senator Bill Bradley; meanwhile, the Republican machine was raising a record $67 million for Texas governor George W. Bush's campaign.

The decade closed with global celebrations amid fears (largely unwarranted, it turned out) that "Y2K" would bring massive computer failures with the millennial date change. Handheld devices, desktop and laptop computers, cell phones, video games, scanners, and digital cameras all surged in popularity, although there was a marked digital divide between rich and poor even in the United States. Led by Ricky Martin, Latin Pop exploded. Cancer survivor Lance Armstrong won the Tour de France; the U.S. women's soccer team won the Women's World Cup. Thanks to advance Internet sales, three volumes about the brave young wizard Harry Potter and his friends topped the best-seller list simultaneously. The long-running comic strip *Peanuts* came to an end in December; its creator, Charles M. Schulz, died the day before the last strip was published. Jordan's King Hussein died after forty-six years in power. Actors George C. Scott, Dirk Bogarde, Madeline Kahn, and Victor Mature also passed away, as did director Stanley Kubrick and critic Gene Siskel. The death of John F. Kennedy Jr. in a plane crash on 16 July made the whole world weep.

Media mergers set records and technology continued to change the industry. In a move to become the nation's largest cable provider, telecommunications giant AT&T announced an offer of $54 billion to cable TV's MediaOne Group. With holdings already including cable TV channels and Paramount Studios, Viacom announced plans to acquire CBS for $36 billion. Digital TV began appearing in stores, and NBC's "Tonight Show" became the first to broadcast in the HDTV format. Intel announced that its Pentium III chip would facilitate full-screen, full-motion video on personal computers. Several films were shot wholly or in part on digital video. As with previous generations of technological innovations, experts predicted the doom of movies shown in theaters, in this case speculating that celluloid would soon be dumped in favor of films downloaded from the Internet.

Meanwhile, Hollywood still dominated world screens. The visually dazzling prequel *Star Wars: Episode I—The Phantom Menace* netted $430.5 million and topped box office charts. The major studios released most of the top 250 films, but stand-alone independent Artisan struck gold with *The Blair Witch Project*, a $60,000 horror picture shot on 16 mm film stock and video, presented as if assembled from found footage left by three film students who had disappeared while trying to film the site of a Maryland witch legend. Heavily promoted on the Internet and via word of mouth, *Blair Witch* grossed $140.5 million.

As usual, the majority of the year's films were helmed by white men and centered on male characters. Working with top male stars, several old masters had critical hits. Martin Scorsese offered *Bringing out the Dead*, with Nicolas Cage as a manic New York paramedic. Woody Allen proffered *Sweet and Lowdown*, with Sean Penn as a 1930s jazz guitarist. In an oblique study of his own aging, Clint Eastwood directed and starred in the detective thriller *True Crime*. One of the year's most touted releases, Kubrick's *Eyes Wide Shut*, featuring then husband-and-wife team Tom Cruise and Nicole Kidman, offered a compelling psychosexual observation of a "happily married" couple. German Wim Wenders turned to energetic unknowns, showcasing four elderly Cuban musicians in one of the year's most popular documentaries, *The Buena Vista Social Club*, and surrealist aficionado David Lynch shifted gears with *The Straight Story*, a sweet film about an old man (Richard Farnsworth) driving his riding mower from Iowa to Wisconsin to see his estranged, dying brother. A new generation of formerly independent directors—among them Alexander Payne (*Election*) and Kevin Smith (*Dogma*)—made their first studio films. According to Payne, not since 1939 had "Hollywood brought so many narrative innovations screaming into the mainstream" (Gordinier 39). Finally, it seemed, Hollywood had "injected itself with some of independent film's DNA" (Kliot and Vicente 53).

Actors were inspired by novel scripts offering edgy male roles. Kevin Spacey and Denzel Washington provided riveting performances in *American Beauty* and *Hurricane*, respectively. Bruce Willis let his gentler side shine through opposite a boy (Haley Joel Osment) who sees dead people in *The Sixth Sense*, while Eddie Murphy and Steve Martin spoofed low-budget independent filmmaking in *Bowfinger*. Matt Damon and Jude Law brought overt homoeroticism to *The Talented Mr. Ripley*, Anthony Minghella's lush retelling of Patricia Highsmith's novel and René Clément's 1960 *Plein soleil* (Purple Noon).

The real shape of millennial masculinity, however, may have been captured most elegantly in seven intriguing films made by young Turk "Generation-X" directors. Whether produced as blockbusters or small independents, all were released by major studios. All reference events, issues, and people in nineties news. All, in fact, belong to a set of late nineties films that Jeffrey Sconce labels "smart cinema," positioning themselves in opposition to mainstream cinema by using irony, experimenting with tone, and concentrating on dysfunction and identity in white, usually middle-class culture. Two new books, Susan Faludi's *Stiffed* and Susan Bordo's *The Male Body*, are pertinent here as popularizing takes on millennial masculinity. Faludi argued that the "hard bodies" of the Reagan eighties were being replaced by cheated men from the middle and working classes; Bordo maintained that cosmetic surgery and androgynous fashion were turning masculinity into a fluid, problematic category. Additionally, the largely university-educated directors and screenwriters who authored these seven films respond to vulgarized versions of the high theory practiced by Gilles Deleuze, Félix Guattari, Judith Butler, and Jean Baudrillard.[1]

Men on the Verge of a Nervous Breakdown

A number of the year's films showcase macho men in crisis. With substantial cult followings and domestic box office takes of $37 million and $171.5 million, *Fight Club* and *The Matrix* are two of the most controversial. Somewhat less successful at $22 million, *Magnolia* nonetheless netted an Oscar nomination for star Tom Cruise. Directed by David Fincher from Chuck Palahniuk's novel and even more violent screenplay, Twentieth Century Fox's $68 million *Fight Club* is a drama/black comedy that pairs a nerdy automobile recall insurance coordinator known solely as the Narrator (Edward Norton) with butch idol Tyler Durden (Brad Pitt). An operatic epic of nine interwoven Southern Californian lives, written and directed by Paul Thomas Anderson, New Line's $38 million *Magnolia* showcases Cruise as men's group guru Frank T. J. Mackey. *The Matrix*, which began as a comic book years earlier by the Wachowski brothers, became a $63 million science fiction/martial arts extravaganza from Warner Bros. The film capitalizes on Keanu Reeves's blankly kinetic portrayal of a superhero named Neo. All three movies are ambivalent about life in fin de siècle America, critiquing and promoting consumerism, fascinated by and yet fearful of digital potentialities. All are haunted by apocalyptic visions of millennial masculinity, proffering buff male bodies while recasting the robust masculinity they tender as, at heart, mere performance.

From the first tracking shots through the Narrator's brain out to his sweaty face as he swallows a gun held by another man, *Fight Club* centers on the Narrator's torment. In deadpan voiceover Norton says, "And suddenly I realize that all of this . . . has got something to do with a girl named Marla Singer." As Singer, Fincher cleverly casts Helena Bonham Carter against her recognizable uppercrust British character type, instead depicting her as a slovenly slacker. Norton's next sentence deflects attention onto the man who is, arguably, the true object of the Narrator's affections: "People are always asking me if I know Tyler Durden." A shock cut; a flashback. Buried between the "bitch tits" of former bodybuilder and testicular cancer survivor Big Bob (Meat Loaf Aday), the Narrator sobs affirmation to Bob's statement: "We're still men." "Yes, we're men. Men is what we are." Emasculated by his lifestyle, the Narrator cannot sleep. Like the penguin he visualizes as his totem animal at a support group, he is confined by drab suits and skinny ties; he needs, he believes, to learn to "slide." Through his constant traveling, space and time blur: "You wake up at O'Hare. You wake up at LaGuardia. . . . You wake up, and have to ask where you are. . . . You wake up, and you're nowhere."

He gets a new lease on life when he meets Tyler on a trip. Clad in pimp's clothes, Tyler is everything the Narrator is not: toned, honed, and tough. Back home, the Narrator witnesses his apartment explode; on a whim, he calls Tyler. After beers, the two pummel each other. Other men watch. The pain of blows and taste of blood provide the Narrator with the "reality" he craves. Wanting more, he moves into Tyler's dark, dank, dilapidated house. Soon fight clubs are popping up around the country, consisting primarily of working- and middle-class white men, but with a smattering of Blacks, Latinos, and Asians. Hardly a cross-section of the oppressed in America, these men nevertheless channel the rage they feel at their "victimization" into tests of stamina and (temporary) victories. Earlier nineties films also registered male frustration, but *Fight Club* turns to terrorism. At first Tyler is perversely comic: as a waiter, he pees into the soup; as a projectionist, he splices "big cocks" into family films; as an entrepreneur, he raids liposuction clinics for fat from wealthy women to make soap to sell back to them. But then he launches "Project Mayhem" with the help of black-clad fighters who have become blindly obedient, nameless "space monkeys": "In Tyler we trusted."

As the terse tag line, "Mischief. Mayhem. Soap" suggests, *Fight Club*'s narrative is elliptical and illogical. Rapid edits and chiaroscuro lighting confound what we see, hence what we think we know. Increasingly there are clues that, as in *The Sixth Sense*, the Narrator/narrator is unreliable. He jealously believes Marla is having an affair with Tyler. Bewildered, she insists she is involved only with him. Midway through the film, he beats himself up in his boss's office: "For some reason, I thought of my first fight with Tyler." In the finale, following a chase where only the Narrator is visible on closed-circuit TV monitors, the two buddies confront each other in the office where the story began. To kill the man he now realizes is his *doppel-gänger*, the Narrator shoots off part of his own head. Amazingly, he survives.[2]

Fight Club's emphasis on homoerotic fantasy and corresponding insistence on spectacle undercut its critiques of consumerism. Tyler comments caustically of Gucci underwear models, tersely claiming that "self-improvement is masturbation"; Pitt's cut body is everywhere on display. Tyler's diatribes are cliché; Pitt delivers them compellingly. "Advertising has us chasing cars and clothes, working jobs we hate so we can buy shit we don't need." But the film depends on product placement and advertising. Early on, the Narrator describes himself as "slave to the IKEA nesting instinct." Magically, his apartment is redecorated with items from the IKEA catalogue. Starbucks is ubiquitous. A naturalist aesthetics of low-key cinematography and "heavily desaturated colors in . . . costuming, makeup, and art direction" (Probst 43) shapes production design. Having learned his trade at Industrial Light and Magic before moving on to music video and advertising, Fincher revels in extensive computerized effects, though the work was divided among several digital companies. The end of the movie, different from the novel's, is particularly riveting. Rocked by explosions, five skyscrapers collapse as Marla and the injured Narrator look on, hand in hand. "Unmanned," the Narrator wears only a T-shirt and boxer shorts; Marla's outfit matches Tyler's. Suddenly an erect cock is spliced between the two. Is Tyler still at work? All in all, hardly a happy heterosexual ending!

Fight Club intimates that traditional masculinity is under attack by capitalism. The Narrator's lines also recall Judith Butler's claim that all is performance, a copy without an original. "With insomnia nothing is real, everything is far away, a copy of a copy of a copy," he laments. When he moves in with Tyler and the two begin new roles as "Ozzie and Harriet" he mutters, "I'd like to thank the Academy." Moreover, although a wanna-be macho, the Narrator is not simply split, to quote Marla, into "Dr. Jekyll and Mr. Jackass." He is divorced from his body, lacking a singular sex, a being reminiscent of Deleuze and Guattari's "body without organs": "I am Jack's medulla oblongata. I am Jill's nipple. . . . I am Jack's broken heart. . . ."[3]

Released in October, *Fight Club* with its random destruction seems not only to prefigure the next month's "Battle of Seattle," today its ending evokes 9/11 and the Twin Towers' collapse. In Washington, Oregon, and Utah, fight clubs inspired by the movie sprang up, with girls as well as boys participating. Were these groups rhizome-like manifestations of a new politics that, per Deleuze and Guattari, would prove progressive or regressive depending on context? Either way, young fans watched the video repeatedly.[4] Some film critics were vocal in opposing the violence, charging the movie with promoting fascism. *Variety*'s Eugene Levy was among those who preferred *Magnolia* (36). Yet *Magnolia* also makes a misogynist chest-thumper its (anti-)hero. Showcasing his talent as a writer, Anderson's first studio venture was inspired by the Beatles' "A Day in the Life," designed to *"build build build*—fall off a cliff and then start building back up again" (Anderson, qtd. in Gordinier). The ensemble cast includes a number of Anderson veterans, but it is Cruise who steals the show, sending up his star image in a part written expressly for him.

A fifteen-minute prologue of three short vignettes ponders the meaning of fate, then a magnolia blossom unfolds and the braided main narrative begins.[5] Subdivided by three titles describing the weather, the movie is organized around parallel crises, shots of television screens, Aimee Mann's music, and startling sound bridges. Corrupt patriarchs are blamed for dysfunctional families. The relationship between the dying Earl Partridge (Jason Robards, reprising his own recent illness) and his son Jack, who is so angry with his father that he has changed his name to Frank Mackey, is primary. Their troubled bond is doubled by that of Jimmy Gator (Philip Baker Hall) and the cocaine-addicted daughter (Melora Waters) he once molested. It is also echoed by an abusive relationship between a failed actor (Michael Bowen) and his whiz-kid son (Jeremy Blackman). Finally, there's a forlorn, middle-age, gay, former whiz kid (William H. Macy), too.

If all the actors seem to be "playing at something, the magnitude of which we can only suspect" (Harmon 116), Cruise gives the most pyrotechnic performance, shifting from manic pride to nervous fidgets to uncontrollable grief. Profoundly troubled, his character recalls TV evangelists and Faludi's born-again Promise Keepers (*Stiffed* 224–88). Cruise based his guru character on a 1993 videotape entitled "Speed Seduction" featuring skinny self-help sage Ross Jeffries (Stevens). Frank hosts a program called "Seduce and Destroy," gyrating his pelvis as he teaches an enthusiastic all-male audience "How to Turn that 'Friend' into Your Sperm Receptacle." "WE ARE MEN! . . . Come August we like to celebrate, suck my big fat fucking sausage!" As prelude to an interview with an attractive African American journalist (April Grace), Frank strips off his shirt and does a back flip. We glimpse a mammoth bulge in his pants. Intrigued, *Village Voice*'s Michael Musto investigated. "Everyone . . .—from the producer to Cruise's costar in that scene—insists the garden hose is one hundred percent real meat. . . . *My* on the set source says it's an utter fake" ("La Dolce"). Blustering "I'm a fucking action hero," Frank is intimidated by the journalist's probing of his past. Back onstage he recovers: "You see what society does to little boys. We

As macho motivational speaker Frank Mackey (aka Jack Partridge), Tom Cruise incarnates late decade white male anger and resentment in *Magnolia* (Paul Thomas Anderson, New Line). Digital frame enlargement.

are taught to apologize. . . . I will not apologize for who I am! . . . for what I need! . . . for what I want!"

Yet when called to his father's deathbed by a devoted hospice nurse (Philip Seymour Hoffman), Frank falls apart, sobbing, "Don't go away you fucking asshole!" Frank's "farewell" is combined with a deluge of frogs in an elaborate digital, creature, and practical effects final sequence that took Industrial Light and Magic nine months to craft. All the major characters appear, as do two pudgy white saviors (John C. Reilly and Hoffman) and the young black street kid (Emmanuel Johnson) who rescues Earl's trophy wife (Julianne Moore) from suicide. Earl and Jimmy die, paving the way for the next generation's redemption. An anonymous male voice insists that "we may be through with the past, . . . [but] the past ain't through with us," and the final frames hint at a reconciliation between Frank and his stepmother. *Magnolia* thus ends quasi-optimistically.

In stark contrast, *The Matrix* worries about the future *and* the present. Tag lines intimate the tension: "Be afraid of the future" and "Reality is a thing of the past." Like William Gibson's 1986 cyber punk classic, *Neuroromancer, The Matrix* is concerned with virtual reality. Simultaneously paranoiac and nostalgic, the Wachowskis' second studio film moves between parallel narratives. The "Matrix"—the present workaday world—is only a computer simulation. "Reality"—the twenty-first century—is a wasteland where humans are raised as crops by artificial intelligence machines that harvest their energy. Those "slaves" who have escaped, among them Morpheus (Laurence Fishburne) and his spaceship crew, search for "the One" who will save humankind. Yet like most blockbusters, *The Matrix* has a happy heterosexual ending. Action starts as Trinity (Carrie-Anne Moss) rescues "the One," computer-drone-by-day/sleepless-rebel-hacker-by-night Thomas Anderson (Reeves) from Agent Smith (Hugo Weaving) and the Matrix's evil police. Anderson becomes "Neo" with the help of computer programs that load skills directly into his brain. By film's end, Trinity and Neo fight side by side, using mind-boggling martial arts moves, innumerable guns, and more. Together they deliver Morpheus from bondage and torture; single-handedly, Neo defeats Smith. Free at last? In the world of the spaceship, Trinity kisses Neo. In the world of the Matrix, Neo zooms into the sky.

Many thought the idea that machines would harvest humans for energy was absurd. Fishburne instead emphasized the film's pessimism: "The idea that machines are using us for batteries is pretty fucking severe" (Clover, *Matrix* 41). Fishburne is entrusted with the exposition; Reeves handles much of the action. "Focused, trim, and haggard" (Newman 9), he exhibits moves that are minimalist but fluid. More indebted to silent film stars than to Method acting edicts, his impassivity and bursts of energy are carefully calibrated. At maximal moments, his jaw clenches, brow furrows, neck veins pop. Yet he often seems bewildered, mouth half open, eyes fathomless pools. His tenor, slightly breathy delivery of lines like "Whoa!" "Holy shit!" and "No way!" suggests his naiveté. He moves gracefully; crucially, he wears clothes well. The cookie-baking Oracle (Gloria Foster) whom Neo consults finds him appealing but "stupid": "You're cuter than I thought. . . . Not too bright, though." Even more than the Narrator or Frank Mackey, Neo's masculinity is in flux, the "lack of fixity" figured in the film's "emphasis on movement" (Rutsky 185). Costuming, makeup, framing, and editing combine to portray him as Trinity's queer double, and the fact that Reeves has a substantial gay following further fuels the film's sublimated homoeroticism (DeAngelis). Trinity herself sometimes seems queerly "male." When the two meet she says, "My name's Trinity." "THE Trinity? Who cracked the IRS d-base? . . . I just thought . . . you were a guy," answers Neo. "Most guys do," she acknowledges.

Inside the Matrix, Nokia cell phones, designer sunglasses, and couturier outfits are de rigueur. Visuals are as important as plot. One hundred ten visual artists and forty photographic artists worked to ensure that the film would be "monumental, groundbreaking, with a new visual style that will be remembered" (Gaeta and Staenberg). Production design contrasts the murky future with a glistening, neo-noir present. Reflections—in a door knob, glasses, mirrors—are omnipresent. Three spectacular special effects sequences introduce "bullet time" (slow-motion events shot at 12,000 frames per second) and "flow-mo" (almost unlimited control of the speed and movement of onscreen elements). Helped by his Hong Kong stunt team, famed fight choreographer Yuen Wo Ping wedded wire work to martial arts, giving each main character a signature fighting move (Clover, *Matrix* 64). Unlike Hong Kong films, however, where the fight choreographer would be the second unit director or even the co-director, here the Wachowskis ruled (Hunt 279). As might be expected of filmmakers with a college background, the brothers' script revels in allusions to the Bible, Greek mythology, Plato, Japanese animé, *Alice in Wonderland,* classic films, and so on. There's an "almost parodically literal Lacanian mirror scene" (Kilbourn 48) where a mirror melts to merge with and become Neo. With virtuality so important, Baudrillard is key, jokingly referenced when Thomas Anderson opens a copy of *Simulacra and Simulation* (it proves to be a shell containing computer disks), and cited again when Morpheus intones the line, "Welcome to the desert of the real!" (see Constable).

The Matrix was released in the United States three weeks before the Columbine shootings, and audiences who saw the film after the massacre gasped at the resemblances. Worried about criticism from lawmakers, Warner Bros. chose to release the movie on DVD rather than video: with the DVD market still in its infancy, the company felt it less likely that teens and preteens would purchase copies. But the film proved a colossal DVD success, topping the year-end charts (Clover, *Matrix* 49), the first ever for the new medium. A game version from Atari grossed over $1 million in a week, while Reeves's mixed (Hawaiian, Chinese, English) background helped the movie cross national boundaries: it earned $258 million overseas, 50 percent more than it cleared in North America. Small wonder: with Brad Pitt and Tom Cruise, Keanu Reeves makes tormented, hysterical, macho millennial masculinity look sexy, in no small part because they make nonwhite masculinity their own, adopting black styles and attitudes while black characters recede into the background or look on from the sidelines. The same cannot be said of the lead "male" characters in two overtly queer films: *Being John Malkovich* and *Boys Don't Cry.*

We're Here, We're Queer: "Can't We All Just Get Along?"

As low-budget, independently produced films (costing $13 million and $2 million, from Gramercy Pictures/Propaganda Films/Single Cell Pictures and Killer Films, respectively), *Being John Malkovich* and *Boys Don't Cry* move beyond the sublimated homoeroticism of *Fight Club, Magnolia,* and *The Matrix*. Both offer intriguing roles for actresses as well as actors and showcase lesbian, transgendered, and/or intersexed characters as lead characters. Polar opposites with respect to "reality," each tells a decidedly nonmainstream story. The contrast is elegantly encapsulated in the tag lines: "Ever wanted to be someone else? Now you can!"/"A true story about the courage to find yourself." *Malkovich* is a giddy comedy premised on the idea that digital is everywhere, gay is more than OK, and life in New York is manic but good. Set in a bleak Nebraska town, *Boys* transforms the 1993 hate-crime killing of Brandon Teena, born Teena Brandon, into a romantic melodrama. Although both films did well at the domestic box office (*Malkovich* took in $20 million, *Boys* $11.5 million), neither inspired copycats. Significantly, however, a post-studio era Hollywood that had never been as welcoming of independent film or as interested in positive portrayals of queer sexuality acclaimed both films.

Full of "jumpy, manic camerawork" (Rooney 21) and benefiting from director Spike Jonze's background in music video, *Being John Malkovich* is nevertheless classically edited. The provocative narrative (penned by Charlie Kaufman) portrays puppeteer and quintessential loser Craig Schwartz (John Cusack) as the victim of a "wintry economic climate" who lives in a Manhattan basement apartment with his frumpy wife, Lotte (Cameron Diaz). To pay the bills, he takes a filing job on the 7½ floor of the Mertin Flemmer Building. Here space saving literally means "low overhead": managers, workers, and visitors all must stoop. One day Craig discovers a mysterious portal behind a filing cabinet. He crawls in and is swept down a tunnel into John Malkovich's head. After twenty minutes "as" Malkovich (indeed, as the real-life actor), he's dumped on the side of the New Jersey Turnpike. Intrigued by the business possibilities the "ride" offers, Craig's co-worker Maxine (Catherine Keener) convinces him to sell tickets at $200 a pop. Life looks up, but then Lotte begs for a ride. Showering and toweling off as Malkovich, she feels so "right" as a man she contemplates sexual reassignment surgery. Going back into Malkovich is easier. As "Malkovich," Lotte falls in love with Maxine and vice versa. Malkovich, too, finds Maxine appealing. Desperate to recover control of his wife and also in love with Maxine, Craig locks Lotte into a cage with her pet chimp and hijacks Malkovich's body. For once, there's a thoroughly unhappy heterosexual ending: trapped inside a new portal in Maxine and Lotte's little girl, Craig is condemned to witness her parents' bliss: while in Malkovich, Lotte has gotten Maxine pregnant, and now the two are happily raising their child together.

Cast in the kind of shaggy-dog outsider role he does best, Cusack endows a thoroughly masochistic character with comedic pathos. His face is

Nebbishy puppeteer Craig (John Cusack) tries to seduce Maxine (Catherine Keener) while at work on the 7½ floor of the Martin Flemmer Building in *Being John Malkovich* (Spike Jonze, USA Films). Digital frame enlargement.

barely visible under a dark beard and stringy hair as he grovels to Maxine. Sadistically chic, Keener vamps it up. And Diaz, virtually unrecognizable in bad perm and baggy sweats, is a mistress of comic timing. In a role obviously written for him, John Malkovich camps wildly, unleashing as never before the creepy narcissism of his "polymorphous star" persona (Baron 19). At one point his character (called John *Horatio* Malkovich to distinguish him slightly from the actor, whose middle name is Gavin) goes up his own portal. Suddenly he finds himself in a restaurant where everyone is John Malkovich: the female lounge singer, the waiters, the maître d,' the pianist, a female dinner date, two gay male diners, and so on. The only words anyone says or sings are also "Malkovich, Malkovich." There's a running joke that no one can think of a Malkovich film except the one in which he played a jewel thief. A good sport about all the ribbing, Malkovich encouraged Jonze and his fellow actors to skewer him: "The meaner, the better" (Lim 49). Balding and paunchy, he caricatures the rakes he played in films like *Dangerous Liaisons* (1988). He also does impressions of Diaz and Cusack. In his extraordinary enactment of "Craig's Dance of Despair and Disillusionment" he cavorts around his bedroom, arms and legs flapping as if a puppet, and even executes a perfect flip. Persistently, the film makes irreverent fun of celebrities and our desire for them. Top nineties stars Sean Penn and Brad Pitt appear in cameos. As Malkovich's confidant, Charlie Sheen mocks his real-life, girl-magnet persona, advising his friend not to let go of those "hot lesbian witches!" Of course, the film depends on our "buying John Malkovich" (Baron): we want, as he does, to know what it's like to luxuriate in fine restaurants, live in a penthouse, take on smart, sexy lovers.

But upending identity is more important to *Being John Malkovich* than criticizing consumerism and stardom. In its zaniness, the film surpasses Bordo's postulate that the codes defining "masculine," "feminine," "gay," and "straight" have become "less reliable" (41). With "all the characters appear[ing] to be inhabited—like those Russian dolls within dolls" (Rainer 63), *Malkovich* adopts Lacan and Butler's postulate that identity is an empty signifier. Craig sums up the conundrum: "Am I me? Is Malkovich Malkovich?" He views Malkovich's body as "a really expensive suit that I enjoy wearing." Lotte finds it "sexy that Malkovich has a portal. It's like he has a vagina. Like a penis and a vagina." When she gets Maxine pregnant, she becomes, as she puts it, "the father, the other mother, whatever." As for Malkovich, his unconscious is a model of Freudian child development: inside his portal, a young Malkovich watches his parents copulate, another suffers public humiliation after wetting his pants, and so forth (Dragunoui). Even Lotte's chimp suffers from feelings of inadequacy due to repressed childhood trauma. Yet a residue of "true identity" grounded in "experience" and "self" remains: Lotte is, after all, sure that she's a man.

A similar experiential certitude undergirds *Boys Don't Cry*. From early on Brandon (Hilary Swank) knows that he is a man who has been raised as a woman. But how to be sure of "reality" when language is so inadequate? How to describe someone, as Brandon puts it, "with both girl and boy parts?" What of the changes in any "identity"? We age. We have different backgrounds and experiences, hopes and dreams. No single identity category can adequately describe who we are, let alone encompass how we are seen. What can we say of "transsexuals who are in transition, where identity is in the process of being achieved, but is not yet there?" or of "transsexuals who understand transition to be a permanent process?" (Butler, *Undoing Gender* 142).

First-time director Kimberly Peirce's goal in making *Boys* was to encourage audience acceptance of queer lives and love and to "show the mechanics of hate" (qtd. in Musto "Indie"). She spent years researching the murder of Brandon by his ex-con "friends" John Lotter (Peter Sarsgaard) and Tom Nissen (Brendan Sexton II), plowing through court transcripts, attending the murder trial, visiting the farmhouse where Brandon was killed. To cast Brandon, she interviewed every butch lesbian and transgender actor she could find, insisting the base person be a biological woman "because that's what Brandon was" (qtd. in Musto "Indie"). Selecting Swank, Peirce had the actress live as a boy for several months, then shot the film in thirty days. When she ran out of money while editing, legendary indie producer Christine Vachon made an unprecedented sale to Fox Searchlight from just a trailer. To obtain an R rating, Peirce cut and recut, sacrificing documentary truth for dramatic power: she knew that NC-17 would mean no mall release, sharply limiting those who could see her picture (Peirce 46).

The finished film is more tragic love story than biopic. Cinematographer Jim Denault makes rural Nebraska a magical world of "disappearing roads and illuminated refineries" full of "rich, saturated colors" (Hoberman, "Use" 201). Back, top, and side lighting bring out the best of Brandon and his girlfriend Lana (Chloë Sevigny). A classic three-acter, the film first shows Brandon's rites of passage. The second act centers on the love relationship. The third, extremely painful to watch, is told in "four frame flashes viscerally knocking into you, a memory knocking on consciousness" (Leitch, "Wonder" 20) and depicts Brandon's rape by John, then Tom, at times making it seem a crucifixion. That the redneck sheriff cruelly interrogates Brandon, not the rapists, adds an extra layer of horror, especially since his interrogation is intercut with the rape. Brandon and Lana decide to run away. Lana changes her mind. John and Tom find Brandon hiding at Candace's (Alicia Goranson) house and gun down Brandon and Candace in front of Lana and Candace's baby. Peirce emphasizes Brandon's transformations and Lana's collusion. Surely she sees Brandon steal tampons at the local convenience store! Their sex life is largely left to the imagination. One scene suggests, via a close-up on Lana's face, that Brandon orally stimulates her. In the next, she starts to tell Candace and Kate (Alison Folland) "what happened," but stops. "I can't talk about it! It's too intense!" A subjective flashback shows Brandon pleasure her, perhaps with a dildo; Lana looks up to see a bit of cleavage peep out from his shirt. Her girlfriends persist: "Well, did you do it?" Coyly, Lana replies, "What do you think?"

Boys is intensely concerned with performance. There's Lana's karaoke. Brandon and Lana posture and primp before mirrors, trying to get "masculinity" and "femininity" down. John and Tom have less need to rehearse; actors Sarsgaard and Sexton make it easy to believe that their characters are men, simultaneously scared and scary. Tom mutilates himself to prove he's in charge; John oscillates between being abusive, needy, and patronizingly kind. Does the film show Brandon as a woman? A lesbian? A passing man? As transgendered? Critical debates hinge on these questions. Judith Butler, Rachel Swan, and Judith Halberstam agree that when Lana and Brandon make love in a barn after the rape and Brandon interacts "as if he were a woman" (Halberstam, "Transgender" 297), *Boys* returns him to status of "woman," inscribing the relationship here as lesbian. For Halberstam, *Boys* is nonetheless primarily a "transgender film" that foregrounds an "authentic masculinity" rather than a masquerade. In contrast, Michele Aaron finds *Boys* a cross-dressing, transvestite film: for her, those moments where Brandon's biology disrupts his passing are key. Patricia White claims Brandon fixes *her* gaze on Lana and her girlfriends. As White sees it, *Boys* presents a "convergence of queer, feminist, and what I would like to call . . . girl-viewer optics" ("Girls" 218). For me, *Boys* is an independent film with a message to disseminate and can thus afford to have it all ways. Many, however, were troubled by the appearance of a slinky, beautiful Swank with loving husband at the 2000 Academy Awards. B. Ruby Rich summed up queer reaction: "The good news? That was all acting. The bad news? The same" ("Queer and Present Danger" 22). For Rich, who coined the term "new queer cinema" in 1992, queer was now just another niche market.

Of course, that the year's queer audiences were sometimes courted is not a bad thing. Far more troubling is the fact that the third murder victim, a disabled black man named Phillip De Vine, was written out of the script.[6] This means that in the final analysis the film's plea for tolerance not only silences African Americans, it disappears them. *Being John Malkovich*, too, employs Blacks only as extras. Both films might be said to echo and adapt beating victim Rodney King's appeal from the 1992 L.A. riots, "Can't we all just get along?" But because nonwhite subjects are of little importance, millennial masculinity at its most queer sadly equals *white* masculinity.

Charge of the Lite Brigade

Not surprisingly, black characters—and Arabs, too—are most visible when smart cinema leaves home for foreign shores. Witness the acerbic appraisals offered by two studio comedies: *Three Kings* and *South Park: Bigger Longer & Uncut*. *Three Kings* and *South Park* lambaste U.S. domestic and foreign policy, flogging corporate greed, military muscle, and media ineptitude. Given Hollywood's openness to new voices this year, the miracle is not that these films got made but that they were awarded substantial budgets: *Three Kings* received $45 to $50 million from Warner Bros., *South Park* nearly $60 million from Paramount. *South Park* turns Iraqi dictator Saddam Hussein into the devil's gay lover and pokes fun at actors (Winona Ryder, the Baldwin brothers, Brooke Shields), media celebrities (Conan

O'Brien), and even President Clinton. A warped musical from irrepressible cable TV cartoonists Trey Parker and Matt Stone, *South Park* tells its tall tales using a "handmade," 2D cut-out aesthetic unseen in film animation for decades.

Three Kings exposes American support of Hussein, before and after the 1991 Gulf War, and accuses President George H. W. Bush of abandoning Iraqi rebels. The film's lead character was based on a real person, Sergeant Major Jim Parker, one of three military advisors on the film, and was originally a high-concept action story written for a black lead. In indie darling David O. Russell's hands, the original action story morphed into a caper film cum combat thriller cum conversion melodrama, shot through with disturbing special effects. The movie opens with a bloody bang. The war has ended, but the news hasn't reached all the troops. "Are we shooting people or what?" yells Sergeant Troy Barlow (Mark Wahlberg). From a distant mound in the sun-bleached desert, he watches an Iraqi soldier wave a gun and a white rag. Taking no chances, he shoots the man in the neck; blood spurts up in long shot; a reverse shot registers Barlow's dismay. Compare American news coverage at the time, when the Gulf War was shown as little more than a video game devoid of dead or dying bodies. Writing in the French newspaper *Libération,* Baudrillard charged, "We never experience the bare material event but only the informational coating which renders it 'sticky and unintelligible' like the oil-soaked sea bird" (*Gulf* 32).[7] In contrast, *Three Kings* forces its viewers to contemplate what happens to people—and a cow—when bullets fly and bombs explode. Thanks to special effects, we twice see green bile swell around internal organs after a bullet's impact. One shoot-out is rendered as a slow-motion homage to *The Wild Bunch* (1969), but violence is never glorified. Given such material, the marketing department must have been worried: the tag line emphasizes normalcy, not controversy: "They're deserters, rebels, and thieves, but in the nicest way."

Built around tonal shifts, *Three Kings*'s first two acts are hard-hitting; the third turns saccharine. Smooth-talking Major Archie Gates (George Clooney) leads a mixed race, cross-rank band of men—Barlow, Chief Elgin (Ice Cube), and Private Conrad Vig (Spike Jonze)—on an unauthorized search to "recover" Kuwaiti gold stolen by Iraqi troops. Basing his script on lists of things he found fascinating during eighteen months of research, Russell's goal was to overturn American self-satisfaction at having won a "moral victory" in Operation Desert Storm (Edelstein 18). As the quartet sets off, Gates stops to teach his pals what death looks like: the charred and decomposing bodies he shows his troops recall the "Highway of Death," where U.S. bombs killed over 100,000 Iraqis as they retreated. Before film's end, the four encounter poison gas, land mines, cluster bombs, and torture, too (see McCrisken and Pepper; Patton "Introduction").

Three Kings's second act ferociously indicts late-nineties consumerism: in Russell's view, love of expensive "stuff" transcends national boundaries. In a hidden Iraqi bunker, Gates and Co. stumble on pillaged exercise equipment, Rolex watches, brand-name blue jeans, Cuisinarts, mini-stereos, televisions, jewelry, as well as the gold. U.S. culture is pervasive: Saddam's soldiers watch an Eddie Murphy movie and Rodney King on TV; in a back-room Captain Said (Said Taghmaoui) goads a rebel in English while administering electric shocks. By the end of the act Barlow is captured and in turn tortured using techniques learned, Said confides, from American Special Forces. "What about Michael Jackson, my main man?" asks Said between jolts. "Pop king of sick fucking country. . . . Make the black man hate himself." To illustrate why the United States is in Kuwait, he pours a ladle of crude down Barlow's throat. "You . . . destabilize the region. . . . This is your fucking stability, my main man." Acting tough, the Arab purveyor of American culture speaks black ghetto slang. But Said is both victim and agent. "Collateral damage" becomes personal as he shares his story. His street was bombed by the United States, his wife lost her legs ("crushed by big fucking block of concrete"), his one-year-old son was killed in bed ("sleeping with his doll when the bomb come"). We witness the tragedies. Said asks Barlow to imagine how he would feel if his own wife and baby were killed. Suddenly Barlow's wife appears, their baby in her arms, screaming as her kitchen explodes in flames. Sobbing, Barlow admits their loss would hurt "worse than death."[8]

Taghmaoui and Wahlberg's performances are so persuasive that when Gates rescues Barlow it makes perfect sense that, convinced of Said's essential humanity, Barlow doesn't kill him, only shoots him in the leg. Clooney, too, plays his part with panache. Cinematographer Newton Thomas Sigel captures the surrealism of war with different film stocks as well as "bleach bypass" development, a process that leaves a layer of silver on the film negative. As the treasure hunters leave base camp, for example, Ektachrome provides flashes of unnatural color: a Bart Simpson doll blazes yellow from the hood of a jeep; pink and green footballs packed with explosives fly above the desert. Jump cuts, freeze frames, whip pans, canted angles, rapid editing, and handheld footage convey frenzy and disturbance. In the third act, when only three "kings" are left alive (Vig has been shot by Saddam's men), Sigel chooses a warmer stock to translate their redemption. The story ends with Gates, Elgin, and a severely injured Barlow giving the Iraqi

Three Kings (David O. Russell, Warner Bros.) offers a chilling look at the first Gulf War and the U.S. government's collusion with Saddam Hussein. The film teams Major Archie Gates (George Clooney) with Chief Elgin (Ice Cube) and Iraqi freedom fighters (Maori actor Cliff Curtis, far right; Iraqi actor Fadil Al-Badra, far left). Jerry Ohlinger's Movie Materials Store.

rebels some of the gold, escorting them to safety in Iran, and surrendering the rest of the bullion to the U.S. Army. A coda shows their subsequent life as civilians.

With Iraqi advisors on set to check dialects, hand gestures, religious motifs, and cultural icons, and with Iraqi Americans and exiles in the cast, *Three Kings* offers even-handed portraits of its Arab characters (Divine 58; Steinman; *Three Kings* press book). Distressed by orders not to intervene when Iraqi insurgents rose up at Bush Sr.'s urging only to be slaughtered by Hussein's men, Gulf War veterans were enthusiastic about the film (Edelstein 18). Intrigued, President Clinton requested a private screening, afterward commenting, "Apart from being a fabulous movie, this is an important movie because people need to know how this war really ended" (Divine 55).

South Park's fans were younger and thirsty for transgression in the "rancid atmosphere of . . . anxiety and hysteria" that followed Columbine (Felperin 56). Adults, too, appreciated Parker and Stone's cheek. A tale of four mischievous tots who save the world while swearing like marines, Parker and Stone's feature tackles sanctimonious concerns about language, violence, and the shape of *youthful* masculinity head on. They gleefully characterize their picture as "like *Spartacus,* only with more farting" (*South*

Park press book 13).[9] This Swiftian extravaganza gets off to a rollicking start by nailing the self-absorbed smugness of the peaceful "little mountain town" where third-graders Kenny McCormick, Stan Marsh, Eric Cartman, and Kyle Broflovski live. As they walk along snowy streets, the quartet sings insouciantly: "You can see your breath hanging in the air. You can see homeless people but you just don't care." Looking for adventure, they sneak into *Asses of Fire,* an R-rated movie starring their heroes, Canadian "fartistes" Terrance and Phillip. The kids' rhapsodic mimicry of the Canadians' cursing and flatulence seduces other children, too, reaching a highpoint in "Uncle Fucka," where the "f-word" is repeated at bewildering pace innumerable times.

Concerned parents flock to a PTA meeting. There they approvingly witness Dr. Gouache (voiced by George Clooney) implant an electronic chip in Cartman: he gets a shock every time he says a dirty word. Kenny tries to light one of his farts on fire and dies, catapulting to hell where he encounters Hitler, Gandhi, George Burns, Saddam, and Satan. Cultural figures are roasted throughout the film. News media in particular take it on the chin via a special report delivered by a midget in a bikini. Thanks to the kids' mothers' anti-Canada campaign ("Blame Canada!"), censorship leads to war and African American troops are sent to the front as "Operation Human Shield" (slogan: "Get behind the darky"). With their friends, Cartman, Stan, and Kyle risk their lives to foil Saddam's plot to rule the world. In the netherworld, Kenny becomes Satan's confidant, giving him the courage to leave a bad relationship.

The animation is flat if colorful. Most movement is horizontal. Satan's lament, "Up There," delivers "a spot-on parody of many a lyrical montage of Disney protagonist suffering" (Felperin 56). Canadian characters are distinguished from Americans by their jointed heads and "silly" pronunciation ("aboot" instead of "about"); Saddam alone has a photographic face. The voicing is virtuoso: Parker and Stone play all the main kid characters and several adults; Mary Kay Bergman does the mothers and other female characters; Isaac Hayes *is* "Chef," elementary school cook, all-round cool guy, and ultimate macho stud.

Tellingly, *South Park*'s primary couples are gay. The closest thing to a happy heterosexual relationship is Stan's successful courtship of Wendy—after throwing up on her. Satan and Saddam's partnership replicates unhappy heterosexual pairings. In one scene, Satan lounges on a bed reading *Saddam Is from Mars, Satan Is from Venus.* He tries to talk with his partner but Saddam just gets turned on. Sobbing, Satan complains to Kenny: "Saddam doesn't nurture my emotions. He just wants sex, and can't learn to communicate." A bit later Saddam demonstrates what a cad he is, ordering Satan to "relax, bitch, you're better seen, not heard." In contrast, the inseparable Terrance and Phillip are ideally matched, as their "rhythmical, reciprocal farting and dancing proves" (Gardiner 54). Ending with a rainbow, symbol of happiness and gay pride, replete with other gay characters, too (entertainer Big Gay Al and his chorus line; teacher Mr. Garrison), *South Park* enjoyed extended runs in gay neighborhoods. Predictably, the Christian group ChildCare Action Project Ministry found the film "INCREDIBLY dangerous," warning: "The most foul of the foul words is clearly spoken *by the children* at least 131 times and many other times in a muffled or garbled way. Four-letter words were used at least 119 times. God's name was taken in vain eleven times without the four-letter expletive and seventy-six times with it. . . . Satan was glorified" (ChildCare Action Project).

Although the ChildCare Action Project didn't get it, almost everyone in the film is satirized. Stone downplays the film's left-wing politics: "If there is an over-riding message . . . it's just to question authority" (cited in Wild 86). What's perturbing is the fact that, like *Three Kings*'s Chief Elgin, Chef is a buddy at best, a "sexual soulster, alternately exhorting the children to stay out of trouble and serenading them about 'making sweet love all night long'" (Chaney 172). And where *Three Kings* continues stereotypes of dumb southerners when Private Vig blasts stuffed animals from the roof of his pickup truck, *South Park* has clichéd characters in outlandishly "native" costumes perform "Kyle's Mom's a Bitch." Misogyny is rife. As Judith Kegan Gardiner says, "The one woman central to the movie's action is its chief villain" (60). Most of *Three Kings*'s female characters also look like idiots. In this sense, then, both films rehearse contradictions subtending late-nineties life. Straight, white, male dominance and queer liberation coexist. Free speech is hailed but media hegemony is taken for granted. Last and not least, there's either room for white women *or* for nonwhite men, but never room for both.

■ "Party Like It's 1999"

So how "smart" is smart cinema? What shapes does millennial movie masculinity assume? What attitudes does it empower? Parallel lines of aesthetic engagement readily emerge among these seven films. Though presenting a range of narratives—from intricately interwoven stories to conventional three-acters—all alter and expand classic American myths via genre mixes, the better to appeal to newly recognized publics. Visual anomaly, dark comedy, and irony are as common as moving cameras.

Most films condemn mainstream media and consumerism while simultaneously employing dazzling effects. *The Matrix* and *Fight Club* embraced the burgeoning DVD market as a way to broadcast their stories and evade censorship. In all, MTV and advertising influenced editing, prompting a kind of "intensified continuity" where "traditional continuity [is] amped up, raised to a higher pitch of emphasis" (Bordwell, "Intensified" 16).

Together, these seven films present a picture of millennial masculinity in crisis, simultaneously fluid *and* fixed: Bordo and Faludi both got it right. What Alexandra Juhasz says of *Fight Club* and *South Park* holds for all: "A fully masculine figure can register only in the imagination" (221). Nostalgia for "real" "he-"men pervades every film *because* all are about "worlds of men fully peopled by un-males, quasi-males, uncertain-males, males-in-waiting" (212). White men (*pace* Keanu) are always the stars, and they effortlessly eclipse any male characters of color at the same time as they steal black looks for their own. Women characters are trivialized, even demonized, except in the two independents about "lesser" white men.[10] The most expensive, *Fight Club* is the most ferociously—and tellingly—misogynist: though Tyler's fashion sense resembles Marla's, he wears yellow latex gloves while making violent love to her; imaginary "he"-men" may don female dress, but they can't bear to touch female flesh.

As in the year's news coverage, hate and fear often outweigh tolerance, in large part because six of these films are preoccupied with visions of violence. (*Being John Malkovich* is the lone exception.) Although every story presents dysfunctional whites, African American characters are sidelined or suppressed. Given their disproportionately strong numbers in audiences and increasing importance as voters, an absolutely stunning lack of Latinos exists. Save for *Three Kings* and *South Park,* all these films (indeed "smart cinema" in general) are single-mindedly, insularly preoccupied by the hopes and dreams of white America. One might even argue, per Baudrillard, that even *Three Kings* portrays its "others" as more of "the same": "through a kind of egocentric generosity or stupidity, [Americans] can only imagine and combat an enemy in their own image" (Gulf 37).

With liberal humanism so perversely linked to U.S. imperialism, can the solution lie, at least in part, in performance (à la Butler) or in rhizome-like actions undertaken by bodies without organs or formal organizations (per Deleuze and Guattari)? These films provide no real answers, at least in part because they handle exposition and character development "in much the ways they would have been before 1960" (Bordwell, "Intensified" 16). All of them foreground individualism and back away from overt political engagement. In every film but *Magnolia,* we meet a maximum of four protagonists. Blocking persistently neglects the ensemble in favor of close-ups (Bordwell 25). All films accordingly fail to imagine a "collectivity" that might be able to address economic imbalance and include real cultural diversity.

Writing in 1991, Baudrillard signaled dangers to come: "The more the hegemony of the global consensus is reinforced, the greater the risk, or the chances, of its collapse" (*Gulf* 87). Writing earlier, in 1982, musician/poet Prince recognized the thrill and threat posed by millennial apocalypse *and* the delusory safety net that hedonism, through entertainment, can offer:

> When I woke up this mornin,' coulda sworn it was judgment day.
> . . . You know I didn't even care.
> 'Cuz they say two thousand zero zero party over, oops, out of time.
> So tonight I'm gonna party like it's 1999.

NOTES

1. P. T. Anderson briefly studied film at New York University. Later he received financial and development help from the Sundance Lab for an early film. Larry Wachowski studied for two years at Bard College; Andy Wachowski for two years at Emerson College. Screenwriter Charlie Kaufman studied film at both Boston University and NYU. Kimberly Peirce was a Columbia film graduate and Sundance Directors' Lab participant. David O. Russell earned a B.A. in English and Political Science from Amherst College. Trey Parker and Matt Stone met as undergraduates at UC-Boulder, where they both spent two years.

2. Their connection has already been signaled in subliminal single-frame cuts, engineered for DVD viewers alone (Martin, "World" 121).

3. Numerous critical assessments of *Fight Club* invoke high theory. See, for example, Diken and Laustsen; Giroux and Szeman; Grønstad; Juhasz; Palladino and Young; Petersen; Windrum; and Žižek "Ethical."

4. By December 2000 *Fight Club* was the seventy-fifth most popular video of the one thousand tracked by trade association Vid Trac (Thompson, "Punk" 61).

5. Magnolia Avenue is the main road through the San Fernando Valley. Production design emphasizes the magnolia flower's greens, whites, and browns. The film is based on stories by one of Theodore Dreiser's favorite writers, Charles Fort (Gaydos). The first episode is shot with a hand-cranked Pathé camera (Turan, "Random" F10). For critical assessments, see especially Goss; Sippi.

6. Compare Susan Muska and Greta Olafsdottir's documentary, *The Brandon Teena Story* (1998). See also Brody; Halberstam.

7. With the Gulf War we all became "information hostages on the world media stage . . . confined to the simulacrum of war as though confined to quarters" (Baudrillard, *Gulf* 24–25). Yet the United States dropped more high explosives in one month than did the entire Allied air offensive during World War II (Patton, "Introduction" 1–2).

8. By inscribing nonwhite agency, this scene offers a welcome alternative to most contemporary Hollywood screenwriting (Dancyger and Rush 248–49).

9. The first time Parker and Stone submitted the film to the MPAA it was called *South Park: All Hell Breaks Loose*. They were told titles must be G-rated and were given a list of things to change to obtain an R (Lewis, "Those" 29). They so resented the censorship that they "made things ten times worse and five times longer." A week after the final title was

approved, the MPAA called back: "Wait, we just got it. You can't use that title." Parker and Stone responded: "No, you approved it. (Expletive) you" (Levitan K16).

10. My analyses of gender and race in these films have profited from discussions with Krin Gabbard and Diane Waldman.

1990 – 1999

Select Academy Awards

1990

Best Picture: *Dances With Wolves,* Orion

Best Actor: Jeremy Irons in *Reversal of Fortune,* Warner Bros.

Best Actress: Kathy Bates in *Misery,* Columbia

Best Supporting Actor: Joe Pesci in *Goodfellas,* Warner Bros.

Best Supporting Actress: Whoopi Goldberg in *Ghost,* Paramount

Direction: Kevin Costner, *Dances With Wolves,* Orion

Writing (screenplay based on material from another medium): Michael Blake, *Dances With Wolves,* Orion

Writing (screenplay written directly for the screen): Bruce Joel Rubin, *Ghost,* Paramount

Cinematography: Dean Semler, *Dances With Wolves,* Orion

Film Editing: Neil Travis, *Dances With Wolves,* Orion

Music (original score): John Barry, *Dances With Wolves,* Orion

Music (song): Stephen Sondheim (music and lyrics), "Sooner or Later (I Always Get My Man)," from *Dick Tracy,* Buena Vista

1991

Best Picture: *The Silence of the Lambs,* Orion

Best Actor: Anthony Hopkins in *The Silence of the Lambs,* Orion

Best Actress: Jodie Foster in *The Silence of the Lambs,* Orion

Best Supporting Actor: Jack Palance in *City Slickers,* Columbia

Best Supporting Actress: Mercedes Ruehl in *The Fisher King,* TriStar

Direction: Jonathan Demme, *The Silence of the Lambs,* Orion

Writing (screenplay based on material previously produced or published): Ted Tally, *The Silence of the Lambs,* Orion

Writing (screenplay written directly for the screen): Callie Khouri, *Thelma & Louise,* Metro-Goldwyn-Mayer

Cinematography: Robert Richardson, *JFK,* Warner Bros.

Film Editing: Joe Hutshing, Pietro Scalia, *JFK,* Warner Bros.

Music (original score): Alan Menken, *Beauty and the Beast,* Buena Vista

Music (song): Howard Ashman (lyrics), Alan Menken (music), "Beauty and the Beast," from *Beauty and the Beast*, Buena Vista

▬▬▬▬▬▬▬ 1992

Best Picture: *Unforgiven*, Warner Bros.

Best Actor: Al Pacino in *Scent of a Woman*, Universal

Best Actress: Emma Thompson in *Howards End*, Sony Pictures Classics

Best Supporting Actor: Gene Hackman in *Unforgiven*, Warner Bros.

Best Supporting Actress: Marisa Tomei in *My Cousin Vinny*, Twentieth Century Fox

Direction: Clint Eastwood, *Unforgiven*, Warner Bros.

Writing (screenplay based on material previously produced or published): Ruth Prawer Jhabvala, *Howards End*, Sony Pictures Classics

Writing (screenplay written directly for the screen): Neil Jordan, *The Crying Game*, Miramax

Cinematography: Philippe Rousselot, *A River Runs Through It*, Columbia

Film Editing: Joel Cox, *Unforgiven*, Warner Bros.

Music (original score): Alan Menken, *Aladdin*, Buena Vista

Music (song): Tim Rice (lyrics) Alan Menken (music), "A Whole New World," from *Aladdin*, Buena Vista

▬▬▬▬▬▬▬ 1993

Best Picture: *Schindler's List*, Universal

Best Actor: Tom Hanks in *Philadelphia*, TriStar

Best Actress: Holly Hunter in *The Piano*, Miramax

Best Supporting Actor: Tommy Lee Jones in *The Fugitive*, Warner Bros.

Best Supporting Actress: Anna Paquin in *The Piano*, Miramax

Direction: Steven Spielberg, *Schindler's List*, Universal

Writing (screenplay based on material previously produced or published): Steven Zaillian, *Schindler's List*, Universal

Writing (screenplay written directly for the screen): Jane Campion, *The Piano*, Miramax

Cinematography: Janusz Kaminski, *Schindler's List*, Universal

Film Editing: Michael Kahn, *Schindler's List*, Universal

Music (original score): John Williams, *Schindler's List*, Universal

Music (song): Bruce Springsteen (lyrics and music), "Streets of Philadelphia," from *Philadelphia*, TriStar

1994

Best Picture: *Forrest Gump,* Paramount

Best Actor: Tom Hanks in *Forrest Gump,* Paramount

Best Actress: Jessica Lange in *Blue Sky,* Orion

Best Supporting Actor: Martin Landau in *Ed Wood,* Buena Vista

Best Supporting Actress: Dianne Wiest in *Bullets over Broadway,* Sony/TriStar

Direction: Robert Zemeckis, *Forrest Gump,* Paramount

Writing (screenplay based on material previously produced or published): Eric Roth, *Forrest Gump,* Paramount

Writing (screenplay written directly for the screen): Quentin Tarantino, *Pulp Fiction,* Miramax

Cinematography: John Toll, *Legends of the Fall,* Sony/TriStar

Film Editing: Arthur Schmidt, *Forrest Gump,* Paramount

Music (original score): Hans Zimmer, *The Lion King,* Buena Vista

Music (song): Tim Rice (lyrics), Elton John (music), "Can You Feel the Love Tonight," from *The Lion King,* Buena Vista

1995

Best Picture: *Braveheart,* Paramount

Best Actor: Nicolas Cage in *Leaving Las Vegas,* United Artists

Best Actress: Susan Sarandon in *Dead Man Walking,* Gramercy

Best Supporting Actor: Kevin Spacey in *The Usual Suspects,* Gramercy

Best Supporting Actress: Mira Sorvino in *Mighty Aphrodite,* Miramax

Direction: Mel Gibson, *Braveheart,* Paramount

Writing (screenplay based on material previously produced or published): Emma Thompson, *Sense and Sensibility,* Sony

Writing (screenplay written directly for the screen): Christopher McQuarrie, *The Usual Suspects,* Gramercy

Cinematography: John Toll, *Braveheart,* Paramount

Film Editing: Mike Hill, Dan Hanley, *Apollo 13,* Universal

Music (original dramatic score): Luis Enrique Bacalov, *The Postman (Il Postino),* Miramax/Alliance

Music (original musical or comedy score): Stephen Schwartz (lyrics), Alan Menken (music), Alan Menken (orchestral score), *Pocahontas,* Buena Vista

Music (original song): Stephen Schwartz (lyrics), Alan Menken (music), "Colors of the Wind," from *Pocahontas,* Buena Vista

▮ 1996

Best Picture: *The English Patient,* Miramax

Best Actor: Geoffrey Rush in *Shine,* Fine Line Features

Best Actress: Frances McDormand in *Fargo,* Gramercy

Best Supporting Actor: Cuba Gooding Jr. in *Jerry Maguire,* Sony/TriStar

Best Supporting Actress: Juliette Binoche in *The English Patient,* Miramax

Direction: Anthony Minghella, *The English Patient,* Miramax

Writing (screenplay based on material previously produced or published): Billy Bob Thornton, *Sling Blade,* Miramax

Writing (screenplay written directly for the screen): Ethan Coen, Joel Coen, *Fargo,* Gramercy

Cinematography: John Seale, *The English Patient,* Miramax

Film Editing: Walter Murch, *The English Patient,* Miramax

Music (original dramatic score): Gabriel Yared, *The English Patient,* Miramax

Music (original musical or comedy score): Rachel Portman, *Emma,* Miramax

Music (original song): Tim Rice (lyrics), Andrew Lloyd Webber (music), "You Must Love Me," from *Evita,* Buena Vista

▮ 1997

Best Picture: *Titanic,* Paramount

Best Actor: Jack Nicholson in *As Good As It Gets,* Sony

Best Actress: Helen Hunt in *As Good As It Gets,* Sony

Best Supporting Actor: Robin Williams in *Good Will Hunting,* Miramax

Best Supporting Actress: Kim Basinger in *L.A. Confidential,* Warner Bros.

Direction: James Cameron, *Titanic,* Paramount

Writing (screenplay based on material previously produced or published): Brian Helgeland, Curtis Hanson, *L.A. Confidential,* Warner Bros.

Writing (screenplay written directly for the screen): Ben Affleck, Matt Damon, *Good Will Hunting,* Miramax

Cinematography: Russell Carpenter, *Titanic,* Paramount

Film Editing: Conrad Buff, James Cameron, Richard A. Harris, *Titanic,* Paramount

Music (original dramatic score): James Horner, *Titanic,* Paramount

Music (original musical or comedy score): Anne Dudley, *The Full Monty,* Fox Searchlight

Music (song): Will Jennings (lyrics), James Horner (music), "My Heart Will Go On," from *Titanic,* Paramount

1998

Best Picture: *Shakespeare in Love*, Miramax

Best Actor: Roberto Benigni in *Life Is Beautiful*, Miramax

Best Actress: Gwyneth Paltrow in *Shakespeare in Love*, Miramax

Best Supporting Actor: James Coburn in *Affliction*, Cinema Service

Best Supporting Actress: Judi Dench in *Shakespeare in Love*, Miramax

Direction: Steven Spielberg, *Saving Private Ryan*, DreamWorks

Writing (screenplay based on material previously produced or published): Bill Condon, *Gods and Monsters*, Lions Gate

Writing (screenplay written directly for the screen): Marc Norman, Tom Stoppard, *Shakespeare in Love*, Miramax

Cinematography: Janusz Kaminski, *Saving Private Ryan*, DreamWorks

Film Editing: Michael Kahn, *Saving Private Ryan*, DreamWorks

Music (original dramatic score): Nicola Piovani, *Life Is Beautiful*, Miramax

Music (original musical or comedy score): Stephen Warbeck, *Shakespeare in Love*, Miramax

Music (song): Stephen Schwartz (lyrics and music), "When You Believe," from *The Prince of Egypt*, DreamWorks

1999

Best Picture: *American Beauty*, DreamWorks

Best Actor: Kevin Spacey in *American Beauty*, DreamWorks

Best Actress: Hilary Swank in *Boys Don't Cry*, Fox Searchlight

Best Supporting Actor: Michael Caine in *The Cider House Rules*, Miramax

Best Supporting Actress: Angelina Jolie in *Girl, Interrupted*, Columbia

Direction: Sam Mendes, *American Beauty*, DreamWorks

Writing (screenplay based on material previously produced or published): John Irving, *The Cider House Rules*, Miramax

Writing (screenplay written directly for the screen): Alan Ball, *American Beauty*, DreamWorks

Cinematography: Conrad L. Hall, *American Beauty*, DreamWorks

Film Editing: Zach Staenberg, *The Matrix*, Warner Bros./Village Roadshow

Music (original score): John Corigliano, *The Red Violin*, Lions Gate/Odeon

Music (song): Phil Collins (lyrics and music), "You'll Be in My Heart," from *Tarzan*, Buena Vista

WORKS CITED
AND CONSULTED

Aaron, Michele. "Pass/Fail." *Screen* 42.1 (Spring 2001): 92–96.

Abrams, M. H. *A Glossary of Literary Terms.* 5th ed. Fort Worth: Holt, Rinehart, and Winston, 1988.

Acland, Charles R. *Screen Traffic: Movies, Multiplexes, and Global Culture.* Durham, N.C.: Duke UP, 2003.

Ahmed, Shantanu Dutta. "'I Thought You Knew!': Performing the Penis, the Phallus, and Otherness in Neil Jordan's *The Crying Game.*" *Film Criticism* 23.1 (Fall 1998): 61–73.

Alcalay, Ron. "Morphing Out of Identity Politics: Black or White and *Terminator 2.*" *Bad Subjects: Political Education for Everyday Life.* Ed. Michael Bérubé and Janet Lyo. New York: New York UP, 1998. 136–42.

Allen, Michael. *Contemporary U.S. Cinema.* New York: Pearson Education, 2003.

Allis, Sam. "What Do Men Really Want?" *Time* (Special Issue, Fall 1990): 80–82.

Ambrose, Stephen. *Citizen Soldiers: The U.S. Army from the Normandy Beaches to the Bulge to the Surrender of Germany, June 7, 1944–May 7, 1945.* New York: Simon & Schuster, 1997.

"American Cultural History—Decade 1991–1998." http://kclibrary.nhmccd.edu/decade90. html. Accessed 27 June 2006.

Andrews, David. *Soft in the Middle: The Contemporary Softcore Feature (Between Art and Porn).* Columbus: Ohio UP, 2006.

"Arab-Americans Protest *True Lies.*" *New York Times* 16 July 1994: 1:11.

Arroyo, José. "Cameron and the Comic." *Sight and Sound* (Sept. 1994): 26–28.

Arthur, Paul. "The Four Last Things: History, Technology, Hollywood, Apocalypse." *The End of Cinema as We Know It: American Film in the Nineties.* Ed. Jon Lewis. New York: New York UP, 2001. 342–55.

Arthur, Paul, and Janet Cutler. "On the Rebound: *Hoop Dreams* and Its Discontents." *Cineaste* 21.3 (July 1995): 22–25.

Athitakis, Mark. "The 10-Minute Masterpiece." *San Francisco Weekly* 13–19 Dec. 2000: n.p.

Baker, Aaron. "Hoop Dreams in Black and White: Race and Basketball Movies." *Basketball Jones: America Above the Rim.* Ed. Todd Boyd and Kenneth L. Shropshire. New York: New York UP, 2000. 215–39.

Baker, Houston. "Scene . . . Not Heard." *Reading Rodney King, Reading Urban Uprising.* Ed. Robert Gooding-Wilson. New York: Routledge, 1993. 38–48.

Baker, James N. "The Future of Gay America." *Newsweek* 12 March 1990: 20–24.

Baker, Laura. "Screening Race; Responses to Theater Violence at *New Jack City* and *Boyz n the Hood.*" *Velvet Light Trap* 44 (1999): 4–19.

Balides, Constance. "Jurassic Post-Fordism: Tall Tales of Economics in the Theme Park." *Screen* 41.2 (2000): 139–60.

Balio, Tino. "'A Major Presence in All the World's Important Markets': The Globalization of Hollywood in the 1990s." *The Film Cultures Reader.* Ed. Graeme Turner. New York: Routledge, 2002. 206–17.

Barnathan, Joyce, and Matt Miller. "Has Disney Become the Forbidden Studio?" *Business Week* 4 Aug. 1997: 51.

Baron, Cynthia. "Buying John Malkovich: Queering and Consuming Millennial Masculinity." *Velvet Light Trap* 49 (Spring 2002): 18–38.

Barthes, Roland. *Mythologies*. Trans. Annette Lavers. New York: Hill and Wang, 1972.

Bates, Karen Grigsby. "'They've Gotta Have Us': Hollywood's Black Directors." *New York Times Magazine* 14 July 1991: 15–19, 38–44.

Baudrillard, Jean. *The Gulf War Did Not Take Place*. Trans. Paul Patton. Bloomington: Indiana UP, 1995.

———. *Simulations*. New York: Semiotext(e): 1983.

Beebe, Roger Warren. "After Arnold: Narratives of the Posthuman Cinema." *Meta-Morphing: Visual Transformation and the Culture of Quick-Change*. Ed. Vivian Sobchack. Minneapolis: U of Minnesota P, 2000. 159–79.

Beene, Geoffrey, and Tom Kalin, Grace Mirabella, Matthew Yokobosky. "Fashion and Film: A Symposium." *PAJ: A Journal of Performance and Art* 20.3 (1998): 12–21.

Bellour, Raymond. "Alternation, Segmentation, Hypnosis: Interview with Janet Bergstrom." *Camera Obscura* 3–4 (1979): 91–104.

Benjamin, Walter. "Theses on the Philosophy of History." *Illuminations*. Ed. Hannah Arendt. Trans. Harry Zohn. New York: Schocken, 1969. 253–64.

Berglund, Jeff. "'The Secret's in the Sauce': Dismembering Normativity in *Fried Green Tomatoes*." *Camera Obscura* 42 (1999): 125–59.

Berlant, Lauren. *The Queen of America Goes to Washington City: Essays on Sex and Citizenship*. Durham, N.C.: Duke UP, 1997.

Berman, Avis. "On the Set of Ron Howard's *Ransom*." *Architectural Digest* 53 (April 1996): 36, 40, 44, 48.

Berry, Chris. "*Wedding Banquet*: A Family (Melodrama) Affair." *Chinese Films in Focus: 25 New Takes*. Ed. Chris Berry. London: BFI, 2003. 183–90.

Bertellini, Giorgio. "Black Hands and White Hearts: Southern Italian Immigrants, Crime, and Race in Early American Cinema." *Mob Culture: Hidden Histories of the American Gangster Film*. Ed. Lee Grieveson et al. New Brunswick: Rutgers UP, 2005. 207–37.

"The Best Cinema of 1994." *Time* 26 Dec. 1994–2 Jan. 1995: 132.

Beversdorf, Anne. Conversation with Krin Gabbard. 7 June 2005.

Bhabha, Homi. *The Location of Culture*. New York: Routledge, 1994.

Biskind, Peter. *Down and Dirty Pictures: Miramax, Sundance, and the Rise of Independent Film*. New York: Simon & Schuster, 2004.

———. *Seeing Is Believing: How Hollywood Taught Us to Stop Worrying and Love the Fifties*. New York: Pantheon, 1983.

Bordo, Susan. *The Male Body: A New Look at Men in Public and in Private*. New York: Farrar, Straus, and Giroux, 1999.

Bordwell, David. "Intensified Continuity: Visual Style in Contemporary American Film." *Film Quarterly* 55: 3 (Spring 2002): 16–28.

———. *Planet Hong Kong: Popular Cinema and the Art of Entertainment*. Cambridge, Mass.: Harvard UP, 2000.

———. *The Way Hollywood Tells It: Story and Style in Modern Movies*. Berkeley: U of California P, 2006.

Bordwell, David, and Kristin Thompson. *Film History: An Introduction*. 2nd ed. New York: McGraw-Hill, 2003.

Borger, Gloria. "Middle-Class Warfare." *U.S. News & World Report* 25 June 1990: 51.

Bourdieu, Pierre. "The Essence of Neoliberalism." Available at http://www.analitica.com/bitblioteca/bourdieu/default.asp. Accessed 1 June 2006.

Bowman, James. "Sinking Ships." *National Review* 26 Jan. 1998: 36.

Brigham, Ann. "Consuming Pleasures of Re/Production: Going Behind the Scenes in Spielberg's *Jurassic Park* and at Universal Studios Theme Park." *Genders* 36 (2002). Available
at http://www.genders.org/g36/g36_brigam.html. Accessed 1 Jan. 2006.

Brody, Jennifer Devere. "Boyz Do Cry: Screening History's White Lies." *Screen* 43.1 (Spring
2002): 91–96.

Brokaw, Tom. *The Greatest Generation.* New York: Random House, 1998.

Brown, Bill. "How to Do Things with Things (*A Toy Story*)." *Critical Inquiry* 24.4 (1998):
935–64.

Browne, Nick, ed. *Francis Ford Coppola's Godfather Trilogy.* Cambridge: Cambridge UP, 2000.

Buckland, Warren. *Directed by Steven Spielberg: Poetics of the Contemporary Hollywood Blockbuster.*
New York: Continuum, 2006.

Buhler, Stephen. "*The Lion King* and the Disneyfication of Hamlet." *The Emperor's Old Groove:
Decolonizing Disney's Magic Kingdom.* Ed. Brenda Ayres. New York: Peter Lang, 2003.
117–29.

Burgoyne, Robert. *Film Nation: Hollywood Looks at U.S. History.* Minneapolis: U of Minnesota
P, 1997.

Butler, Judith. *Bodies That Matter: On the Discursive Limits of "Sex."* New York: Routledge, 1993.

———. *Gender Trouble: Feminism and the Subversion of Identity.* New York: Routledge, 1990.

———. *Undoing Gender.* New York: Routledge, 2004.

Byers, Thomas. "History Re-Membered: *Forrest Gump*, Postfeminist Masculinity, and the Bur-
ial of the Counterculture." *Modern Fiction Studies* 42.2 (1996): 419–44.

Caputi, Jane. "Small Ceremonies: Ritual in *Forrest Gump, Natural Born Killers, Seven,* and *Follow Me Home.*" *Mythologies of Violence in Postmodern Media.* Ed. Christopher Sharrett.
Detroit: Wayne State UP, 1999. 147–74.

Carlson, Margaret. "Is This What Feminism Is All About?" *Time* 24 June 1991: 57–59.

Cassells, Clayton. "Gump Across America: Politics, Melodrama and the Postmodern Un-
ironic." M.A. thesis, University of Denver. Nov. 2001.

Certeau, Michel de. *The Writing of History.* Trans. Tom Conley. New York: Columbia UP, 1988.

Chaney, Michael A. "Representations of Race and Place in *Static Shock, King of the Hill,* and
South Park." *Journal of Popular Film & Television* 31.4 (1 Jan. 2004): 167–75.

Che, Cathay. "Design for Living." *Advocate* 24 Dec. 1996. Available at http://search.ebsco-
host.com.proxy.ulib.iUPui.edu/login.aspx?direct=true&db=afh&AN=9612272468&site
=ehost-live. Accessed 19 Sept. 2006.

ChildCare Action Project. "*South Park: Bigger Longer & Uncut.*" *http://www.capalert.com/
capreports/southpark.htm.* Accessed 8 March 2006.

Chong, Sylvia. "From 'Blood Auteurism' to the Violence of Pornography: Sam Peckinpah
and Oliver Stone." *New Hollywood Violence.* Ed. Steven Jay Schneider. Manchester: Manchester UP, 2004. 249–68.

Clinton, Bill. "1997 State of the Union Address: The Bold New World of the Twenty-First
Century." *Vital Speeches of the Day* 63.10 (1 March 1997): 290–96.

———. "Remarks at the University of California San Diego Commencement Ceremony in
La Jolla, California; June 14, 1997." *Weekly Compendium of Presidential Documents* 33.25
(23 June 1997): 876–82.

Cloud, John. "Trading White Sheets for Pinstripes." *Time* 8 March 1999: 30–31.

———. "What Can the Schools Do?" *Time* 3 May 1999: 38–40.

Clover, Carol. *Men, Women, and Chainsaws.* Princeton: Princeton UP, 1992.

Clover, Joshua. *The Matrix*. London: BFI, 2004.

Cohan, Steven. "Censorship and Narrative Indeterminacy in *Basic Instinct*." *Contemporary Hollywood Cinema*. Ed. Steve Neale and Murray Smith. London: Routledge, 1998. 263–79.

Cole, C. L., and Samantha King. "The New Politics of Urban Consumption: *Hoop Dreams, Clockers,* and 'America.'" *Sporting Dystopias: The Making and Meaning of Urban Sport Cultures*. Ed. Ralph C. Wilcox, David L. Andres, Robert Pitter, and Richard L. Irwin. Albany: State U of New York P, 2003. 221–46.

Colley, Iain. *Goodfellas: Director, Martin Scorsese*. Longman: York, 2001.

Constable, Catherine. "Baudrillard Reloaded: Interrelating Philosophy and Film via *The Matrix Trilogy*." *Screen* 47.2 (Summer 2006): 233–49.

"A Conversation with William Bennett." *Newsweek* 26 Dec. 1994–2 Jan. 1995: 112.

Corliss, Richard. "I Dream for a Living: Steven Spielberg, the Prince of Hollywood, Is Still a Boy at Heart." *Time* 15 July 1985: 61–64.

———. "Married to the Mob." *Time* 24 Sept. 1990: 83.

———. "There's Gold in That There Schlock." *Time* 26 Aug. 1996: 55–56.

Corrigan, Timothy, and Patricia White. *The Film Experience: An Introduction*. Boston and New York: Bedford/St. Martin's, 2004.

Courtwright, David T. "Way Cooler Than Manson: *Natural Born Killers*." *Oliver Stone's USA: Film, History, and Controversy*. Ed. Robert Brent Toplin. Lawrence: UP of Kansas, 2000. 188–201.

Creed, Barbara. "Horror and the Monstrous-Feminine: An Imaginary Abjection." *The Dread of Difference: Gender and the Horror Film*. Ed. Barry Keith Grant. Austin: U of Texas P, 1996. 35–65.

Dancyger, Dan, and Jeff Rush. *Alternative Scriptwriting: Successfully Breaking the Rules*. 4th ed. Boston: Focal Press, 2006.

Darnton, Nina. "An Old Look is New Again." *Newsweek* 16 Oct. 1989: 78.

DeAngelis, Michael. *Gay Fandom and Crossover Stardom*. Durham, N.C.: Duke UP, 2001. 179–234.

Deleuze, Gilles and Félix Guattari. *A Thousand Plateaus: Capitalism and Schizophrenia II*. Minneapolis: U of Minnesota P, 1987.

Denby, David. "Skin Deep." *New York* 17 June 1991: 75–77.

Desser, David. "The Kung Fu Craze: Hong Kong Cinema's First American Reception." *The Cinema of Hong Kong: History, Arts, Identity*. Ed. Poshek Fu and David Desser. New York: Cambridge UP, 2000. 37–58.

De Vany, Arthur. *Hollywood Economics: How Extreme Uncertainty Shapes the Film Industry*. London: Routledge, 2004.

Dika, Vera. "The Representation of Ethnicity in *The Godfather*." *Francis Ford Coppola's Godfather Trilogy*. Ed. Nick Browne. Cambridge: Cambridge UP, 2000. 76–108.

Diken, Bülent, and Carsten Bagge Laustsen. "Enjoy Your Fight!—*Fight Club* as a Symptom of the Network Society." *Cultural Values* 6.4 (2002): 349–67.

Divine, Christian. "Flirting with Hollywood: An Interview with David O. Russell." *Creative Screenwriting* 7.1 (Jan. 2000): 55–59.

Doherty, Thomas. "Clueless Kids." *Cineaste* 21.4 (1995): 15–16.

———. "Quiz Show." *Cineaste* 21.1/2 (Feb. 1995): 85.

———. *Teenagers and Teenpics: The Juvenilization of American Movies in the 1950s*. Rev. and expanded ed. Philadelphia: Temple UP, 2002.

Douglas, Susan J. "The Devil Made Me Do It: Is *Natural Born Killers* the Ford Pinto of Movies?" *Nation* 5 April 1999: 50.

Dowell, Pat. "*Independence Day*." *Cineaste* 22.3 (Dec. 1996): 39–42.

Dragunoui. "Psychoanalysis, Film Theory, and the Case of *Being John Malkovich*." *Film Criticism* 26.2 (Winter 2001–02): 1–18.

Dyson, Michael Eric. "Between Apocalypse and Redemption: John Singleton's *Boyz n the Hood*." *Cultural Critique* 21 (1992): 121–41.

Eberwein, Robert. "The IFC and Sundance: Channeling Independence." *Contemporary American Independent Film*. Ed. Chris Holmlund and Justin Wyatt. New York: Routledge, 2005. 265–82.

Edelstein, David. "One Film, Two Wars: *Three Kings*." *New York Times* 6 April 2003: 1, 18.

Elliott, Michael. "Forward to the Past." *Newsweek* 26 Dec. 1994–2 Jan. 1995: 130–33.

Ellison, Ralph. "What America Would Be without Blacks." *Black on White: Black Writers on What It Means to Be White*. Ed. David R. Roediger. New York: Schocken, 1998. 160–71.

Elsaesser, Thomas. "Subject Positions, Speaking Positions: From Holocaust, *Our Hitler* and *Heimat* to *Shoah* and *Schindler's List*." *The Persistence of History: Cinema, Television, and the Modern Event*. Ed. Vivian Sobchack. New York: Routledge, 1996. 145–79.

Epstein, Edward Jay. *The Big Picture: Money and Power in Hollywood*. New York: Random House, 2006.

Faludi, Susan. *Backlash: The Undeclared War against American Women*. New York: Anchor Books, 1992.

———. *Stiffed: The Betrayal of the American Man*. New York: William Morrow, 1999.

Farred, Grant. "*Menace II Society*: No Way Out for the Boys in the Hood." *Michigan Quarterly Review* 35.3 (1996): 475–92.

Felperin, Leslie. Rev. of *South Park: Bigger Longer & Uncut*. *Sight and Sound* (Sept. 1999): 55–56.

"Film History of the 1990s." *Http://www.filmsite.org/90sintro.html*. Accessed 14 July 2006.

Fletcher, Angus. *Allegory: The Theory of a Symbolic Mode*. Ithaca: Cornell UP, 1964.

Foner, Eric. "Hollywood Invades the Classroom." *New York Times* 20 Dec. 1997: A13.

Freeland, Cynthia. "Penetrating Keanu: New Holes, But the Same Old Shit." *The Matrix and Philosophy: Welcome to the Desert of the Real*. Ed. William Erwin. Chicago and La Salle, Ill: Open Court, 2002. 216–24.

Friedman, Lester D. *Citizen Spielberg*. Urbana: U of Illinois P, 2006.

Fussell, Paul. *Wartime: Understanding and Behavior in the Second World War*. Oxford: Oxford UP, 1989.

Gabbard, Krin. "Black Angels." *Chronicle of Higher Education* 49.39 (6 June 2003): B15–16.

———. *Black Magic: White Hollywood and African American Culture*. New Brunswick: Rutgers UP, 2004.

———. "'Someone Is Going to Pay': Resurgent White Masculinity in *Ransom*." *Masculinity: Bodies, Movies, Culture*. Ed. Peter Lehman. New York: Routledge, 2001. 7–23.

Gaeta, John, and Zach Staenberg. Commentary on *The Matrix*. Dir. Andy Wachowski and Larry Wachowski. Produced by Warner Bros. in association with Village Roadshow Pictures and Groucho II Film Partnership. DVD Warner Home Video, 1999.

Gallagher, Mark. "I Married Rambo: Spectacle and Melodrama in the Hollywood Action Film." *Mythologies of Violence in Postmodern Media*. Ed. Christopher Sharrett. Detroit: Wayne State UP, 1999. 199–225.

Gardiner, Judith Kegan. "Why Saddam Is Gay: Masculinity Politics in *South Park—Bigger Longer & Uncut*." *Quarterly Review of Film and Video* 22.1 (2005): 51–62.

Gaydos, Steven. "*Magnolia*'s Enigmatic Roots in an Old Fort." *Variety* 378 (28 Feb.–5 March 2000): 6.

Geller, Theresa L. "Queering Hollywood's Tough Chick." *Frontiers* 25.3 (2004): 8–34.

Giddens, Gary. "Performance." *Village Voice* 25 Sept. 1990: 60, 62.

Gilroy, Paul. "It's a Family Affair." *Black Popular Culture*. Ed. Gina Dent. Seattle: Bay Press, 1993. 303–16.

Giroux, Henry A., and Imre Szeman. "Ikea Boy Fights Back: *Fight Club*, Consumerism, and the Political Limits of Nineties Cinema." *The End of Cinema as We Know It: American Film in the Nineties*. Ed. Jon Lewis. New York: New York UP, 2001. 95–104.

Gliberman, Owen. "Bold Before Their Time." *Entertainment Weekly* July 1995: 47.

Goldstein, Richard. "World War II Chic." *Village Voice* 19 Jan. 1999: 46.

Gomery, Douglas. "Economic and Institutional Analysis: Hollywood as Monopoly Capitalism." *Understanding Film: Marxist Perspectives*. Ed. Mike Wayne. London: Pluto Press, 2005. 168–81.

———. "The Hollywood Blockbuster: Industrial Analysis and Practice." *Movie Blockbusters*. Ed. Julian Stringer. London: Routledge, 2003. 72–83.

———. "The Hollywood Film Industry: Theatrical Exhibition, Pay TV, and Home Video." *Who Owns the Media?: Competition and Concentration in the Mass Media Industry*. 3rd ed. Ed. Benjamin M. Compaine and Douglas Gomery. Mahwah, N.J.: Lawrence Erlbaum Associates, 2000. 359–436.

Gordinier, Jeff. "1999: The Year That Changed Movies." *Entertainment Weekly* 514 (26 Nov. 1999): 39–40, 42.

Goss, Brian Michael. "'Things Like This Don't Just Happen': Ideology and Paul Thomas Anderson's *Hard Eight*, *Boogie Nights*, and *Magnolia*." *Journal of Communication Inquiry* 26.2 (April 2002): 171–92.

Gould, Stephen Jay. "Dinomania." *New York Review of Books* 40.14 (1993). Available at http://www.nybooks.com/articles/2483. Accessed 1 Jan. 2006.

Greene, Naomi. "Family Ceremonies: or, Opera in *The Godfather Trilogy*." *Francis Ford Coppola's Godfather Trilogy*. Ed. Nick Browne. Cambridge: Cambridge UP, 2000. 133–55.

Grieveson, Lee, et al. "Introduction." *Mob Culture: Hidden Histories of the American Gangster Film*. Ed. Lee Grieveson et al. New Brunswick: Rutgers UP, 2005. 1–10.

Griggers, Cathy. "*Thelma and Louise* and the Cultural Generation of the New Butch-Femme." *Film Theory Goes to the Movies*. Ed. Jim Collins, Hilary Radner, and Ava Preacher Collins. New York: Routledge, 1993. 129–41.

Grønstad, Asbjørn. "One-Dimensional Men: *Fight Club* and the Poetics of the Body." *Film Criticism* 28.1 (Fall 2003): 1–23.

Grundmann, Roy. "The Fantasies We Live By: Bad Boys in *Swoon* and *The Living End*." *Cinéaste* 19.4 (1993): 25–29.

Guerrero, Ed. "A Circus of Dreams and Lies: The Black Film Wave at Middle Age." *The New American Cinema*. Ed. Jon Lewis. Durham, N.C.: Duke UP, 1998. 329–52.

———. "Spike Lee and the Fever in the Racial Jungle." *Film Theory Goes to the Movies*. Ed. Jim Collins, Hilary Radner, and Ava Preacher Collins. New York: Routledge, 1993. 170–81.

Guglielmo, Jennifer. "White Lies, Dark Truths." *Are Italians White? How Race Is Made in America*. Ed. Jennifer Guglielmo and Salvatore Salerno. New York: Routledge, 2003. 1–14.

Halberstam, Judith. "Skin-Flick: Posthuman Gender Identity in Jonathan Demme's *Silence of the Lambs*." *Camera Obscura* 27 (1992): 37–53.

———. "The Transgender Gaze in *Boys Don't Cry*." *Screen* 42.3 (Autumn 2001): 294–98.

Hansen, Miriam Bratu. "*Schindler's List* Is Not *Shoah*: The Second Commandment, Popular Modernism and Public Memory." *The Historical Film: History and Memory in Media.* Ed. Marcia Landy. New Brunswick: Rutgers UP, 2001. 201–17.

Harmon, A. G. "Ordered Chaos: Three Films by Paul Thomas Anderson." *Image* 27 (2000): 107–16.

Hart, Lynda. "'Til Death Do Us Part': Impossible Spaces in *Thelma and Louise*." *Journal of the History of Sexuality* 4.3 (1999): 430–46.

Harvey, David. *A Brief History of Neoliberalism.* Oxford: Oxford UP, 2005.

Hayes, Dade, and Jonathan Bing. *Open Wide: How Hollywood Box Office Became a National Obsession.* New York: Hyperion, 2004.

Hendrickson, Nancy. "We Like the Way He Talks: The Dialogue of Billy Bob Thornton." *Creative Screenwriting* 5.1 (1998): 40–43.

Hess, John. "*Godfather II*: A Deal Coppola Couldn't Refuse." *Movies and Methods.* Ed. Bill Nichols. Berkeley: U of California P, 1976. 81–90.

Hobby, Teresa Santerre. "*Independence Day*: Reinforcing Patriarchal Myths about Gender and Power." *Journal of Popular Culture* 34.2 (Fall 2000): 39–55.

Hoberman, J. "Like Godfather . . ." *Village Voice* 25 Dec. 1990: 73, 76.

———. "Use Your Illusion." *Village Voice* 5 Oct. 1999: 201.

Hofstadter, Richard. *"The Paranoid Style in American Politics" and Other Essays.* New York: Alfred A. Knopf, 1966.

Holland, Patricia. *Picturing Childhood: the Myth of the Child in Popular Imagery.* New York: I. B. Taurus, 2004.

Holmlund, Chris. "Cruisin' for a Bruisin': Hollywood's Deadly (Lesbian) Dolls." *Cinema Journal* 34.1 (1994): 31–51.

———. "Introduction: From the Margins to the Mainstream." *Contemporary American Independent Film.* Ed. Chris Holmlund and Justin Wyatt. New York: Routledge, 2005. 1–20.

———. "Project AARP: Jackie Chan, Aging Asian in Transnational Action." Paper delivered at the Society for Cinema and Media Studies conference. London, March 2005.

hooks, bell. "Dreams of Conquest." *Sight and Sound* (April 1995): 22–23.

———. "White Light." *Sight and Sound* (May 1996): 8–11.

Hull, Stephanie, and Maurizio Viano. "The Image of Blacks in the Work of Coppola, De Palma, and Scorsese." *Beyond the Margin: Readings in Italian Americana.* Ed. Paolo A. Giordano and Anthony Julian Tamburri. Madison and London: Associated University Presses, 1998. 169–97.

Hunt, Leon. "The Hong Kong/Hollywood Connection: Stardom and Spectacle in Transnational Action Cinema." *Action and Adventure Cinema.* Ed. Yvonne Tasker. New York: Routledge, 2004. 269–83.

Jacobson, Matthew Frye. *Whiteness of a Different Color: European Immigrants and the Alchemy of Race.* Cambridge, Mass.: Harvard UP, 1998.

James, Nick. Rev. of *Casper. Sight and Sound* (Aug. 1995): 43–44.

Jeffords, Susan. *Hard Bodies: Hollywood Masculinity in the Reagan Era.* New Brunswick.: Rutgers UP, 1994.

Jones, Jacquie. "The Accusatory Space." *Black Popular Culture.* Ed. Gina Dent. Seattle: Bay Press, 1993. 95–98.

Jones, Lisa. "The Defiant Ones: A Talk with Film Historian Donald Bogle." *Village Voice* 4 June 1991: 69, 88.

Judell, Brandon. "An Interview with Spike Lee, Director of *4 Little Girls*." *Indiewire*. http://www.indiewire.com/people/int_Lee_Spike_971212.html. Accessed 24 June 2005.

Juffer, Jane. *At Home with Pornography: Women, Sex, and Everyday Life*. New York: New York UP, 1998.

Juhasz, Alexandra. "The Phallus UnFetished: The End of Masculinity as We Know It in Late-1990s 'Feminist' Cinema." *The End of Cinema As We Know It: American Film in the Nineties*. Ed. Jon Lewis. New York: New York UP, 2001. 210–21.

Kael, Pauline. "New Age Daydreams." *New Yorker* 17 Dec. 1990: 115–21.

Kakoudaki, Despina. "Spectacles of History: Race Relations, Melodrama, and the Science Fiction/Disaster Film." *Camera Obscura* 17.2 (2002): 109–53.

Karlyn, Kathleen Rowe. "*Scream*, Popular Culture, and Feminism's Third Wave: 'I'm Not My Mother.'" *Genders* 38 (2003). Available at http://www.genders.org/g38/g38_rowe_karlyn.html. Accessed 18 Sept. 2006.

Kaveney, Roz. *From Alien to The Matrix: Reading Science Fiction Film*. New York: I. B. Taurus, 2005.

Kilbourn, Russel J. A. "Re-writing 'Reality': Reading *The Matrix*." *Revue canadienne d'études cinématographiques* 2 (2000): 43–54.

Kimball, A. Samuel. "Conceptions and Contraceptions of the Future: *Terminator 2, The Matrix,* and *Alien Resurrection.*" *Camera Obscura* 17.2 (2002): 69–107.

King, C. Richard, and David J. Leonard. "Is Neo White? Reading Race, Watching the Trilogy." *Jacking in to the Matrix Franchise: Cultural Reception and Interpretation*. Ed. Matthew Kapell and William G. Doty. New York: Continuum, 2004. 32–47.

King, Geoff. "Stardom in the Millennium." *Contemporary Hollywood Stardom*. Ed. Thomas Austin and Martin Barker. London: Arnold, 2003. 62–73.

King, John. "Attacking Hollywood, Dole Laments 'Mainstreaming of Deviancy.'" Associated Press 31 May 1995. http://0-web.lexis-nexis.com.bianca.pen . . . b&_md5= ec73fa4e73be3b7120b9963e9e3f4e6c. Accessed 25 March 2004.

Klawans, Stuart. "Films." *Nation* 5 Nov. 1990: 537–40.

———. Rev. of *Ed Wood*. *Nation* 17 Oct. 1994: 433–34.

———. Rev. of *Forrest Gump, True Lies. Nation* 5–12 Sept. 1994: 249–51.

Kleinhans, Chuck. "Independent Features: Hopes and Dreams." *New American Cinema*. Ed. Jon Lewis. Durham, N.C.: Duke UP, 1998. 307–27.

———. "Siempre Selena!" *Jump Cut* 42 (1998): 28–31, 121.

Klinger, Barbara. *Beyond the Multiplex: Cinema, New Technologies, and the Home*. Berkeley: U California P, 2006.

Kliot, Jason, and J. Vicente. "Past Is Prologue." *Filmmaker* (Fall 2002): 53–54.

Knapp, John. "Ideology, Rhetoric, and Blood-Ties: From *The Oresteia* to *The Godfather.*" *Mosaic* 32.1 (1999): 1–16.

Kolker, Robert. *A Cinema of Loneliness: Penn, Stone, Kubrick, Scorsese, Spielberg, Altman*. 3rd ed. New York: Oxford UP, 2000.

Körte, Peter, and Georg Seeslen. *Joel & Ethan Coen*. Trans. Rory Mulholland. New York: Limelight, 2001.

Kroll, Jack. "The Corleones Return." *Newsweek* 24 Dec. 1990: 58–61.

Lacayo, Richard. "Violent Reaction." *Time* 12 June 1995: 24–30.

Landy, Marcia. "The International Cast of Irish Cinema: The Case of *Michael Collins.*" *boundary 2* 27.2 (2000): 21–44.

Lane, Anthony. "The Current Cinema: The Spy Who Loved Me." *New Yorker* 25 July 1994: 77–79.

Lang, Robert. "Oedipus in Africa." *Masculine Interests: Homoerotics in Hollywood Film*. New York: Columbia UP, 2002. 14–51.

Lawrenson, Edward. "*Shanghai Knights*." *Sight and Sound* (May 2003): 60.

Leitch, Danny. "Wonder Boy." *Sight and Sound* (March 2000): 18–20.

Leitch, Thomas M. "Know-Nothing Entertainment: What to Say to Your Friends on the Right, and Why It Won't Do Any Good." *Literature Film Quarterly* 25.1 (1997): 7–17.

Lesage, Julia, and Linda Kintz, eds. *Media, Culture, and the Religious Right*. Minneapolis: U of Minnesota P, 1998.

Levine, Josh. *The Coen Brothers: The Story of Two American Filmmakers*. Toronto: ECW, 2000.

Levitan, Corey. "Wild Wild South." *RAVE!* 2 July 1999: K4, 16.

Levy, Emanuel. Rev. of *Boys Don't Cry*. *Variety* 2 Sept. 1999: 4, 7.

———. Rev.of *Magnolia*. *Variety* 10 Dec. 1999: 6, 36.

Levy, Steven. "Shot by Shot." *Premiere* (March 1990): 64–68.

Lewis, Jon, ed. *The End of Cinema As We Know It*. New York: New York UP, 2001.

———. "Following the Money in America's Sunniest Company Town: Some Notes on the Political Economy of the Hollywood Blockbuster." *Movie Blockbusters*. Ed. Julian Stringer. London: Routledge, 2003. 61–71.

———. "Those Who Disagree Can Kiss Jack Valenti's Ass." *The End of Cinema as We Know It: American Film in the Nineties*. Ed. Jon Lewis. New York: New York UP, 2001. 23–32.

———. *Whom God Wishes to Destroy: Francis Coppola and the New Hollywood*. Durham, N.C.: Duke UP, 1995.

Lighting, Robert K. "What's Love Got to Do with It?: The Resilience of the Woman's Film." *CineAction* 40 (1997): 18–31.

Lim, Dennis. "Brain Humor." *Village Voice* 26 Oct. 1999: 45–46, 49.

Lipman, Amanda. "*Clueless*" [review]. *Sight and Sound* (Oct. 1995): 46.

Lipp, Martina. "Welcome to the Sexual Spectacle: The Female Heroes in the Franchise." *Jacking in to the Matrix Franchise: Cultural Reception and Interpretation*. Ed. Matthew Kapell and William G. Doty. New York: Continuum, 2004. 14–31.

Lippe, Richard. "For *Philadelphia*." *CineAction* 35 (1994): 25–28.

Lipsitz, George. *The Possessive Investment in Whiteness: How White People Profit from Identity Politics*. Philadelphia: Temple UP, 1998.

Marchetti, Gina. "Jackie Chan and the Black Connection." *Keyframes: Popular Cinema and Cultural Studies*. Ed. Matthew Tinkcom and Amy Villarejo. New York: Routledge, 2001. 137–58.

———. "*The Wedding Banquet*: Global Chinese Cinema and the Asian American Experience." *Countervisions: Asian American Film Criticism*. Ed. Darrell Y. Hamamoto and Sandra Liu. Philadelphia: Temple UP, 2000. 274–97.

Martin, Kevin. "A World of Hurt." *Cinefex* 60 (Jan. 2000): 114–31.

Martin, Nina K. *Encountering Soft-Core Thrills: Gender, Genre and Feminism in the Erotic Thriller Film*. Urbana: U of Illinois P, 2007.

Maslin, Janet. "The Bewitching Power of Lies." *New York Times* 27 Nov. 1996: C9, C16.

———. "*Titanic*: A Spectacle as Sweeping as the Sea." *New York Times* 19 Dec. 1997: E1, E18.

Mason, Fran. *American Gangster Cinema From Little Caesar to Pulp Fiction*. New York: Palgrave Macmillan, 2002.

Massood, Paula. "Mapping the Hood: The Genealogy of City Space in *Boyz n the Hood* and *Menace II Society*." *Cinema Journal* 35.2 (1996): 87–97.

May, Elaine Tyler. *Homeward Bound: American Families in the Cold War Era.* New York: Basic Books, 1988.

Mayne, Judith. *Cinema and Spectatorship.* New York: Routledge, 1993.

McCrisken, Trevor B., and Andrew Pepper. *American History and Contemporary Hollywood Film.* Edinburgh: Edinburgh UP, 2005. 187–210.

McDermott, John. "And the Poor Get Poorer." *Nation* 14 Nov. 1994: 576–78.

McKim, Richard. "Review of *Miller's Crossing.*" *Cineaste* 18.2 (1991): 45–47.

"Media History Timeline: 1990s." *Http://www.mediahistoryumn.edu/time/1990s.html.* Accessed 9 July 2006.

Menand, Louis. "Gross Points: Is the Blockbuster the End of Cinema?" *New Yorker* 7 Feb. 2005: 82–87.

Mercer, Kobena. *Welcome to the Jungle: New Positions in Black Cultural Studies.* New York: Routledge, 1994.

Merck, Mandy. "The Medium of Exchange." *In Your Face: 9 Sexual Studies.* New York: New York UP, 2000. 21–37.

Merida, Kevin. "Spike Lee, Holding Court." *Washington Post.* http://www.washingtonpost.com/wp-srv/style/features/lee.htm. Accessed 24 June 2005.

Miller, Toby, et al. *Global Hollywood 2.* London: BFI, 2005.

Mills, Katie. "Revitalizing the Road Genre: *The Living End* as an AIDS Road Film." *The Road Movie Book.* Ed. Steven Cohan and Ina Rae Hark. New York: Routledge, 1997. 307–29.

"The Monster That Ate Hollywood." *Frontline.* 2000. Available at http://www.pbs.org/wgbh/pages/frontline/shows/hollywood/. Accessed 1 Dec. 2006.

Monush, Barry, ed. *Motion Picture Almanac 1994.* New York: Quigley, 1994.

———. *Motion Picture Almanac 1995.* New York: Quigley, 1995.

Morrison, Toni, ed. *Race-ing Justice, En-gendering Power: Essays on Anita Hill, Clarence Thomas, and the Construction of Social Reality.* New York: Pantheon, 1992.

Mottram, James. *The Coen Brothers: The Life of the Mind.* Dulles, Va.: Brassey's, 2000.

———. *The Sundance Kids: How the Mavericks Took Back Hollywood.* London: Faber and Faber, 2006.

Munby, Jonathan. *Public Enemies, Public Heroes: Screening the Gangsters from Little Caesar to Touch of Evil.* Chicago: U of Chicago P, 1999.

Musto, Michael. "Indie First-Timer Kimberly Peirce: Fast, Cheap and in Control." *Village Voice* 44 (5 Oct. 1999): 212.

———. "La Dolce Musto." *Village Voice* 8 Feb. 2000: 12.

Nadel, Alan. *Containment Culture: American Narratives, Postmodernism, and the Atomic Age.* Durham, N.C.: Duke UP, 1995.

Naficy, Hamid. "King Rodney: The Rodney King Video and Textual Analysis." *The End of Cinema As We Know It: American Film in the Nineties.* Ed. Jon Lewis. New York: New York UP, 2001. 300–304.

Natoli, Joseph. *Speeding to the Millennium: Film and Culture 1993–1995.* Albany: State U of New York P, 1998.

Navasky, Victor. "The Demons of Salem, With Us Still." *New York Times* 8 Sept. 1996: H37, H58.

Negra, Diane. *Off White Hollywood: American Culture and Ethnic Female Stardom.* New York: Routledge, 2001.

———. "'Queen of the Indies': Parker Posey's Niche Stardom and the Taste Cultures of Independent Film." *Contemporary American Independent Film.* Ed. Chris Holmlund and Justin Wyatt. New York: Routledge, 2005. 71–88.

Newman, Kim. "Rubber Reality." *Sight and Sound* (June 1999): 8–9.

Nichols, Bill. *Introduction to Documentary*. Bloomington: Indiana UP, 2001.

Nicholls, Mark. S*corsese's Men: Melancholia and the Mob*. Victoria, Australia: Pluto, 2004.

"1994 Perspectives." *Newsweek* Dec. 26, 1994-Jan. 2, 1995: 49–105.

Nyce, Ben. *Scorsese Up Close: A Study of the Films*. Lanham, Md.: Scarecrow, 2004.

Ouellette, Laurie. "Ship of Dreams: Cross-Class Romance and the Cultural Fantasy of *Titanic*." *Titanic: Anatomy of a Blockbuster*. Ed. Kevin Sandler and Gaylyn Studlar. New Brunswick: Rutgers UP, 1999. 169–88.

Oxoby, Marc. *The 1990s*. Westport, Conn.: Greenwood Press, 2003.

Palladino, P., and T. Young. "*Fight Club* and the World Trade Center: On Metaphor, Scale, and the Spatio-temporal (Dis)location of Violence." *Journal for Cultural Research* 7.2 (2003): 195–218.

Palmer, R. Barton. *Joel and Ethan Coen*. Urbana: U of Illinois P, 2004.

Patton, Cindy. *Inventing AIDS*. New York: Routledge, 1990.

Patton, Paul. "Introduction." In Jean Baudrillard, *The Gulf War Did Not Take Place*. Bloomington: Indiana UP, 1995. 1–22.

Paulin, Diana. "De-Essentializing Interracial Representation: Black and White Border Crossing in Spike Lee's *Jungle Fever* and Octavia Butler's *Kindred*." *Cultural Critique* 36 (1997): 165–93.

Pearl, Monica. "AIDS and New Queer Cinema." *New Queer Cinema: A Critical Reader*. Ed. Michele Aaron. New Brunswick: Rutgers UP, 2004. 23–35.

Peirce, Kimberly. "Brandon Goes to Hollywood." *Advocate* 28 March 2000: 44, 46.

Perez, Gilberto. "Films in Review." *Yale Review* 84.3 (1996): 186–95.

Perren, Alisa. "Sex, Lies and Marketing: Miramax and the Development of the Quality Indie Blockbuster." *Film Quarterly* 55.2 (2001): 30–39.

Petersen, Per Serritslev. "9/11 and the 'Problem of Imagination': *Fight Club* and *Glamorama* as Terrorist Pretexts." *Orbis Litterarum* 60 (2005): 133–44.

Pfeil, Fred. *White Guys: Studies in Postmodern Domination and Difference*. New York: Verso, 1995.

Phillips, Kendall R. *Projected Fears: Horror Films and American Culture*. Westport, Conn.: Praeger, 2005.

Pizzello, Steven. "*Natural Born Killers* Blasts Big Screen with Both Barrels." *Oliver Stone Interviews*. Ed. Charles L. P. Silet. Jackson: UP of Mississippi, 2001. 137–57. Reprinted from *American Cinematographer* 55 (Nov. 1994): 36–46, 48, 50, 52–54.

Prince, Stephen. "A Disputed Legacy." *Savage Cinema: Sam Peckinpah and the Rise of Ultra Violent Movies*. Austin: U of Texas P, 1998. 213–53.

Probst, Christopher. "Anarchy in the U.S.A." *American Cinematographer* (Nov. 1999): 42–44, 46, 48–53.

Pryce, Vinnette K. "*Amistad*'s Spiel on History." *New York Amsterdam News* 18 Dec. 1997: 21.

Rafferty, Terrence. "The Current Cinema: Helter Skelter." *New Yorker* 5 Sept. 1994: 106–07.

———. "Skin Deep." *New Yorker* 17 June 1991: 99–101.

Rainer, Peter. "Get Outta My Face." *New York* 8 Nov. 1999: 63–64.

Ray, Robert B. *A Certain Tendency of the Hollywood Cinema, 1930–1980*. Princeton: Princeton UP, 1985.

Reid, Mark A. *Black Lenses, Black Voices: African American Film Now*. Lanham, Md.: Rowman & Littlefield, 2005.

Rich, B. Ruby. "New Queer Cinema." *New Queer Cinema: A Critical Reader*. Ed. Michele Aaron. New Brunswick: Rutgers UP, 2004. 15–22.

———. "The New Queer Wave." *Sight and Sound* (Sept. 1992): 30–34.

———. "Queer and Present Danger." *Sight and Sound* (March 2000): 22–25.

Richardson, John H. "The Joel & Ethan Story." *Premiere* 4 Oct. 1990: 94–101.

Robb, Brian J. *Screams and Nightmares: The Films of Wes Craven.* Woodstock, N.Y.: Overlook Press, 1998.

Robbins, Bruce. "Murder and Mentorship: Advancement in *The Silence of the Lambs.*" *boundary 2* 23.1 (1999): 71–90.

Robson, Eddie. *Coen Brothers.* London: Virgin, 2003.

Rodriguez, Robert. *Rebel without a Crew: Or How a 23-Year-Old Filmmaker With $7,000 Became a Hollywood Player.* New York: Dutton, 1995.

Rogin, Michael. *Blackface, White Noise: Jewish Immigrants in the Hollywood Melting Pot.* Berkeley: U of California P, 1998.

———. "Spielberg's List." *New Left Review* 230 (July/Aug. 1998): 153–60.

Rohter, Larry. "Coppola: It Was an Offer He Couldn't Refuse." *New York Times* 23 Dec. 1990: 2:1.

Romano, S. "DLP: A Report from the Trenches." *Boxoffice* 138.2 (Feb.): 36–37.

Rooney, David. Rev. of *Being John Malkovich. Variety* 3 Sept. 1999: 2, 21.

Roth, Matt. "*The Lion King*: A Short History of Disney-Fascism." *Jump Cut* 40 (Mar. 1996): 15–20.

Ruberto, Laura E. "Where Did the Goodfellas Learn to Cook? Gender, Labor, and the Italian American Experience." *Italian Americana* 21.2 (2003): 164–76.

Rudolf, Eric. "*Ransom* Presses the Ante: Director Ron Howard and Cinematographer Piotr Sobocinski Use Intriguing Methods to Tell a Tale of Kidnapping and Retribution." *American Cinematographer* 77.11 (Nov. 1996): 46–48, 50, 52, 54.

Rutsky, R. L. "Being Keanu." *The End of Cinema As We Know It: American Film in the Nineties.* Ed. Jon Lewis. New York: New York UP, 2001. 185–94.

Samuels, Allison, and Jeff Giles. "Unchained Melody." *Newsweek* 7 Apr. 1997: 70–72.

Samuelson, Robert J. "Debt." *Newsweek* 31 Dec. 1990: 22–23.

Sanders, William B. *Gangbangs and Drive-Bys: Grounded Culture and Juvenile Gang Violence.* New York: Aldine de Gruyter, 1994.

Sanjek, David. "Home Alone: The Phenomenon of Direct-to-Video." *Cineaste* 21.1–3 (1995): 98–100.

Schatz, Thomas. "The New Hollywood." *Film Cultures Reader.* Ed. Graeme Turner. New York: Routledge, 2002. 184–205.

Schauer, Bradley, and David Bordwell. "A Hollywood Timeline, 1960–2004." In David Bordwell, *The Way Hollywood Tells It: Story and Style in Modern Movies.* Berkeley: U of California P, 2006. 191–242.

Schickel, Richard. "Gender Bender." *Time* 24 July 1991: 52–56.

Schneider, Karen. "With Violence If Necessary: Rearticulating the Family in the Contemporary Action-Thriller." *Journal of Popular Film and Television* 27.1 (1999): 2–11.

Sconce, Jeffrey. "Irony, Nihilism and the New American 'Smart' Film." *Screen.* 43.4 (Winter 2002): 349–69.

Sedgwick, Eve Kosofsky. *Between Men: English Literature and Male Homosocial Desire.* New York: Columbia UP, 1985.

Sharrett, Christopher. "Genocidal Spectacles and the Ideology of Death." *BAD: Infamy, Darkness, Evil, and Slime on Screen.* Ed. Murray Pomerance. Albany: State U of New York P, 2004. 65–77.

Simon, John. "Difficult Crossings." *National Review* 3 Dec. 1990: 54–56.

———. "The Mob and the Family." *National Review* 28 Jan. 1991: 63–65.

Simpson, Philip L. "The Politics of Apocalypse in the Cinema of Serial Murder." *Mythologies of Violence in Postmodern Media*. Ed. Christopher Sharrett. Detroit: Wayne State UP, 1999. 119–44.

Sippi, Diane. "Tomorrow Is My Birthday: Placing Apocalypse in Millennial Cinema." *Cine-Action* 53 (2000): 3–21.

Smith, Gavin. "Interview with Martin Scorsese." *Film Comment* Sept./Oct. 1990: 27–30, 69.

Smith, Valerie. "The Documentary Impulse in Contemporary African American Film." *Black Popular Culture*. Ed. Gina Dent. Seattle: Bay Press, 1993. 56–64.

Smith-Shomade, Beretta E. "'Rock-A-Bye, Baby!': Black Women Disrupting Gangs and Constructing Hip-Hop Gangsta Films." *Cinema Journal* 42.2 (2003): 25–40.

Sobchack, Vivian. "Introduction: History Happens." *The Persistence of History: Cinema, Television, and the Modern Event*. Ed. Vivian Sobchack. New York: Routledge, 1996. 1–14.

Sonnet, Esther, and Peter Stanfield. "'Good Evening Gentlemen, Can I Check Your Hats Please?': Dressing Masculinity and the Retro Gangster Cycles of the 1990s." *Mob Culture: Hidden Histories of the American Gangster Film*. Ed. Lee Grieveson et al. New Brunswick: Rutgers UP, 2005. 163–84.

South Park: Bigger Longer & Uncut pressbook. Margaret Herrick Library, Academy of Motion Picture Arts and Sciences, Beverly Hills, Calif.

Spaulding, Jeffrey. "The 24th Annual Grosses Gloss: Asteroid Shower." *Film Comment* 35.2 (March/April 1999): 52–55.

Stack, Peter. "Computers 'Toy' with Us." *San Francisco Chronicle* 22 Nov. 1995: C1.

Stein, Peter. "Hong Kong Shuns Two Films on Tibet, Hinting at Change in Political Tolerance." *Wall Street Journal* 21 Oct. 1997, eastern ed.: A17.

Steinman, Louise. "War with Iraq; *Kings*: Iraq War Primer?" *Los Angeles Times* 11 April 2003: E20.

Stevens, Joe. "Outrageous Example." *Long Beach Press-Telegram* 20 March 2000: C1, C3.

Steyn, Mark. "The Michael Mouse Club." *American Spectator* 30.2 (Feb. 1997): 44–46.

Studlar, Gaylyn. "A Gunsel Is Being Beaten: Gangster Masculinity and the Homoerotics of the Crime Films, 1941–42." *Mob Culture: Hidden Histories of the American Gangster Film*. Ed. Lee Grieveson et al. New Brunswick: Rutgers UP, 2005. 120–45.

Sturken, Marita. *Thelma and Louise*. London: BFI, 2000.

Sullivan, John P., and Martin E. Silverstein. "The Disaster within Us: Urban Conflict and Street Gang Violence in Los Angeles." *Journal of Gang Research* 2.4 (Summer 1995): 11–30.

Swan, Rachel. "*Boys Don't Cry*." *Film Quarterly* 54.3 (2001): 47–52.

Sweeney, Gael. "The Trashing of White Trash: *Natural Born Killers* and the Appropriation of the White Trash Aesthetic." *Quarterly Review of Film and Video* 18.2 (2001): 143–55.

Tasker, Yvonne. "The Family in Action." *Action and Adventure Cinema*. Ed. Yvonne Tasker. New York: Routledge, 2004. 252–66.

———. *Working Girls: Gender and Sexuality in Popular Cinema*. New York: Routledge, 1998.

Taubin, Amy. "Branches." *Village Voice* 13 July 1993: 45.

———. "Chilling and Very Hot." *Sight and Sound* (Nov. 1995): 17–18.

———. "Playing it Straight: R.E.M. Meets a Post–Rodney King World in *Independence Day*." *Sight and Sound* (August 1996): 6–8.

Taylor, Carl S. "Gang Imperialism." *Gangs in America*. Ed. C. Ronald Huff. Newbury Park, Calif.: Sage, 1990. 103–15.

Thompson, Kristin. *Storytelling in the New Hollywood: Understanding Classical Narrative Technique*. Cambridge, Mass.: Harvard UP, 1999.

Thompson, Stacy. "Punk Cinema." *Cinema Journal* 43.2 (Winter 2004): 47–66.

Thornton, Billy Bob. Commentary. *Sling Blade*. Dir. Billy Bob Thornton. Produced by David Bushell, Larry Meistrich, and Brandon Rosser. Perf. Billy Bob Thornton, Dwight Yoakam, and John Ritter. 1996. DVD. Mirimax Home Entertainment, 2005.

Three Kings pressbook. Margaret Herrick Library, Academy of Motion Picture Arts and Sciences, Beverly Hills, Calif.

Tomasky, Michael. "False Truths." *Village Voice* 13 June 1995: 21.

Torres, Sasha. *Black, White, and In Color: Television and Black Civil Rights*. Princeton: Princeton UP, 2003. 97–103.

"Tough Talk on Entertainment." *Time* 12 June 1995: 32–35.

Travers, Peter. "The Devil Made Them Do It." *Rolling Stone* 12 Dec. 1996: 89.

———. "*True Lies* and Sexual Violence." *Rolling Stone* 25 Aug. 1994: 96.

"Trivia for *Jui kuen II*." Internet Movie Database. http://www.imdb.com/title/tt0111512/trivia. Accessed 7 June 2005.

Turan, Kenneth. "Random Lives, Bound by Chance." *Los Angeles Times* 17 Dec. 1999: F1, F10.

———. *Sundance to Sarajevo: Film Festivals and the World They Made*. Berkeley: U of California P, 2002.

Tyler, Parker. *A Pictorial History of Sex in Films*. Secaucus: Citadel Press, 1974.

U.S. Congress. House. "Apologizing for Those Who Suffered As Slaves Under the Constitution and Laws of the United States Until 1865." 105th Cong., 1st sess, H. Con. Res. 96. *Congressional Record* 18 June 1997: H3890-H3891.

Vachon, Christine, and David Edelman. *Shooting to Kill*. New York: Avon Books, 1998.

Wang, Jennifer Hyland. "'A Struggle of Contending Stories': Race, Gender, and Political Memory in *Forrest Gump*." *Cinema Journal* 39.3 (Spring 2000): 92–115.

Warshow, Robert. "The Gangster as Tragic Hero." 1948. *The Immediate Experience: Movies, Comics, Theatre & Other Aspects of Popular Culture*. New York: Atheneum, 1975. 127–33.

Wasko, Janet. *Hollywood in the Information Age*. Austin: U of Texas P, 1994.

Watson, Roland. "U.S. Killers Blame *The Matrix* after Random Shootings." *The Times (London)* 19 May 2003: 15.

Wee, Valerie. "The *Scream* Trilogy, 'Hyperpostmodernism,' and the Late-Nineties Slasher Film." *Journal of Film and Video* 57.3 (Fall 2005): 44–61.

Weinraub, Bernard. "Disney Hires Kissinger." *New York Times* 10 Oct. 1997: E7.

White, Jack E. "Sorry Isn't Good Enough." *Time* 30 June 1997: 35.

"White Male Paranoia: Are They the Newest Victims—or Just Bad Sports?" *Newsweek* 13 March 1993: 1.

White, Patricia. "Girls Still Cry." *Screen* 42.2 (Summer 2001): 217–21.

Wideman, John Edgar. "Serious Game." *Hoop Dreams '94*. Booklet accompanying Criterion Collection DVD.

Wild, David. "*South Park* Under Attack." *Rolling Stone* 8–22 July 1999: 85–86.

Williams, Linda. *Playing the Race Card: Melodramas of Black and White from Uncle Tom to O. J. Simpson*. Princeton: Princeton UP, 2001.

Williams, Linda Ruth. *The Erotic Thriller in Contemporary Cinema*. Edinburgh: Edinburgh UP, 2005.

Willis, John, and Barry Monash. *Screen World 1998 Film Annual*. New York: Applause Books, 1998.

Willis, Sharon. *High Contrast: Race and Gender in Contemporary Hollywood Film*. Durham, N.C.: Duke UP, 1997.

Windrum, Ken. "*Fight Club* and the Political (Im)potence of Consumer Era Revolt." *New Hollywood Violence*. Ed. Steven Jay Schneider. Manchester: Manchester UP, 2004. 304–17.

Winokur, Mark. "Eating Children Is Wrong." *Sight and Sound* (Nov. 1991): 10–13.

Wollen, Peter. "Theme Park and Variations." *Sight and Sound* (July 1993): 6–9.

Wood, Robert. "Somebody Has to Die: *Basic Instinct* as White Noir." *Post Script* 12.3 (1993): 44–51.

Wood, Robin. "Finale: The Doom Generation." *Sexual Politics and Narrative Film: Hollywood and Beyond*. New York: Columbia UP, 1998. 336–43.

Wyatt, Justin. "The Formation of the 'Major Independent': Miramax, New Line and the New Hollywood." *Contemporary Hollywood Cinema*. Ed. Steve Neale and Murray Smith. London: Routledge, 1998. 74–90.

———. *High Concept: Movies and Marketing in Hollywood*. Austin: U of Texas P, 1994.

———. "Marketing Marginalized Cultures: *The Wedding Banquet*, Cultural Identities, and Independent Cinema of the 1990s." *The End of Cinema As We Know It: American Film in the Nineties*. Ed. Jon Lewis. New York: New York UP, 2001. 61–71.

Yacowar, Maurice. "Love vs. Honour: *Donnie Brasco* and *Sling Blade*." *Queen's Quarterly* 104.1 (Spring 1997): 56–70.

Young, Elizabeth. "*The Silence of the Lambs* and the Flaying of Feminist Theory." *Camera Obscura* 27 (1992): 5–36.

Zimmermann, Patricia R. *States of Emergency: Documentaries, Wars, Democracies*. Minneapolis: U of Minnesota P, 2000.

Žižek, Slavoj. "An Ethical Plea for Lies and Masochism." *Lacan and Contemporary Film*. Ed. Todd McGowan and Sheila Kunkle. New York: Other Press, 2004. 173–86.

———. "*The Matrix*: Or, The Two Sides of Perversion." *The Matrix and Philosophy: Welcome to the Desert of the Real*. Ed. William Irwin. Chicago and La Salle, Ill: Open Court, 2002. 240–66.

———. "The Thing From Inner Space: *Titanic* and *Deep Impact*." *International Journal of Psychoanalysis* 80.5 (1999): 1021–24.

CONTRIBUTORS

JOSÉ B. CAPINO is an assistant professor of English, Cinema Studies, and Gender and Women's Studies at the University of Illinois, Urbana-Champaign. His study of documentary film and U.S. empire won the 2003 dissertation award of the Society for Cinema and Media Studies.

CARYL FLINN is a professor of Women's Studies at the University of Arizona. Her publications include *Brass Diva: The Life and Legends of Ethel Merman* (2007), *The New German Cinema: Music, History, and the Matter of Style* (2004), *Strains of Utopia: Gender, Nostalgia, and Hollywood Film Music* (1992), and *Music and Cinema* (co-editor, 2000).

KRIN GABBARD teaches cinema studies, comparative literature, and cultural studies at the State University of New York at Stony Brook. His most recent books are *Hotter Than That: The Trumpet and American Culture* (2008) and *Black Magic: White Hollywood and African American Culture* (2004).

CHRIS HOLMLUND is a professor of Cinema Studies, Women's Studies, and French at the University of Tennessee–Knoxville and chair of the Cinema Studies Program. She is the author of *Impossible Bodies* (2002), co-editor (with Justin Wyatt) of *Contemporary American Independent Film: From the Margins to the Mainstream* (2005) and (with Cynthia Fuchs) of *Between the Sheets, In the Streets: Queer, Lesbian, Gay Documentary* (1997). She is currently working on a book on *Stars in Action*.

CHUCK KLEINHANS is co-editor of *Jump Cut: A Review of Contemporary Media*. He teaches in the Radio/TV/Film Department at Northwestern University. His current research continues his previous publications on sexual images in mass culture, experimental film and video, and ideological analysis of Hollywood.

LINDA MIZEJEWSKI is a professor of Women's Studies at Ohio State University. Her most recent book is *Hardboiled and High Heeled: The Woman Detective in Popular Culture* (2004), and she is currently working on a book about *It Happened One Night*.

TIMOTHY SHARY is the director of the Film and Video Studies Program at the University of Oklahoma. His publications include *Generation Multiplex: The Image of Youth in Contemporary American Cinema* (2002), *Teen Movies: American*

Youth on Screen (2005), and *Youth Culture in Global Cinema* (2007), co-edited with Alexandra Seibel. He is the featured expert on teen films in the IFC Series "Indie Sex," which aired in 2007. His further research on film has appeared in over a dozen other books, journals, and encyclopedias. His current projects include editing an anthology on masculinity in American movies and writing *The Silver Screen*, a study of the elderly in American cinema.

AMY VILLAREJO has a joint appointment in Film Studies and in the Feminist, Gender, and Sexuality Studies Program at Cornell University. She is author of *Lesbian Rule: Cultural Criticism and the Value of Desire* (2003; winner of the Katherine Singer Kovacs Award from the Society for Cinema and Media Studies) and, recently, *Film Studies: The Basics* (2006). She is also co-editor of the forthcoming anthology *Capital Q: Marxism after Queer Theory*. Her articles on documentary cinema, queer TV, thrift shopping, and other topics have appeared in journals such as *GLQ, Social Text,* and *New German Critique*.

DIANE WALDMAN teaches in the Mass Communications department at the University of Denver. She is the co-editor (with Janet Walker) of *Feminism and Documentary* (1999) and the author of various essays on feminism and film history, film and social history, and popular culture and the law.

DEBRA WHITE-STANLEY is an assistant professor of Film Studies at Indiana University/Purdue University Indianapolis. Her research interests include film sound and gender, and the war film. Forthcoming essays include "Sound Sacrifices: Representing the Pain of War on the Cinema Soundtrack" in *Lowering the Boom: New Essays on the History, Theory and Practice of Film Sound* (2008) and "Lavishing the Body Politic in *The Manchurian Candidate*" in *War Isn't Hell, It's Entertainment*. She is currently writing a book on the representation of medical workers in the war film.

SHARON WILLIS is a professor of Art History and Visual and Cultural Studies at the University of Rochester. A co-editor of *Camera Obscura*, she is author of *Marguerite Duras: Writing on the Body* (1987) and *High Contrast: Race and Gender in Contemporary Hollywood Film* (1997). She is also completing a book project on the civil rights movement and popular cinema.

INDEX